AFRICAN AMERICANS IN THE NINETEENTH CENTURY

Selected titles in ABC-CLIO's Perspectives in American Social History series

African Americans in the Nineteenth Century: People and Perspectives

American Revolution: People and Perspectives

Baby Boom: People and Perspectives

British Colonial America: People and Perspectives

Civil Rights Movement: People and Perspectives

Civil War: People and Perspectives

Cold War and McCarthy Era: People and Perspectives

Colonial America: People and Perspectives

Early Republic: People and Perspectives

Industrial Revolution: People and Perspectives

Jacksonian and Antebellum Age: People and Perspectives

Jazz Age: People and Perspectives

Making of the American West: People and Perspectives

Reconstruction: People and Perspectives

Vietnam War Era: People and Perspectives

Westward Expansion: People and Perspectives

Women's Rights: People and Perspectives

PERSPECTIVES IN
AMERICAN SOCIAL HISTORY

African Americans in the Nineteenth Century

People and Perspectives

Dixie Ray Haggard, Editor
Peter C. Mancall, Series Editor

ABC-CLIO

Santa Barbara, California • Denver, Colorado • Oxford, England

Library of Congress Cataloging-in-Publication Data
African Americans in the nineteenth century : people and perspectives / Dixie Ray Haggard, editor.
 p. cm. — (Perspectives in American social history)
 Includes bibliographical references and index.
 ISBN 978-1-59884-123-7 (hard copy : alk. paper) — ISBN 978-1-59884-124-4 (ebook)
 1. African Americans—History—19th century. 2. African Americans—Social conditions—19th
century. 3. United States—Race relations—History—19th century. I. Haggard, Dixie Ray.
 E185.18.A375 2010
 973'.0496073—dc22   2009049683

ISBN: 978-1-59884-123-7
EISBN: 978-1-59884-124-4

14 13 12 11 10   1 2 3 4 5

This book is also available on the World Wide Web as an eBook.
Visit www.abc-clio.com for details.

ABC-CLIO, LLC
130 Cremona Drive, P.O. Box 1911
Santa Barbara, California 93116-1911

This book is printed on acid-free paper ∞

Manufactured in the United States of America

Contents

Series Introduction

S ocial history is, simply put, the study of past societies. More specifically, social historians attempt to describe societies in their totality, and hence often eschew analysis of politics and ideas. Though many social historians argue that it is impossible to understand how societies functioned without some consideration of the ways that politics works on a daily basis or what ideas could be found circulating at any given time, they tend to pay little attention to the formal arenas of electoral politics or intellectual currents. In the United States, social historians have been engaged in describing components of the population that had earlier often escaped formal analysis, notably women, members of ethnic or cultural minorities, or those who had fewer economic opportunities than the elite.

Social history became a vibrant discipline in the United States after it had already gained enormous influence in Western Europe. In France, social history in its modern form emerged with the rising prominence of a group of scholars associated with the journal *Annales Economie, Societé, Civilisation* (or *Annales ESC* as it is known). In its pages and in a series of books from historians affiliated with the École des Hautes Études en Sciences Sociale in Paris, brilliant historians such as Marc Bloch, Jacques Le Goff, and Emanuel LeRoy Ladurie described seemingly every aspect of French society. Among the masterpieces of this historical reconstruction was Fernand Braudel's monumental study, *The Mediterranean and the Mediterranean World in the Age of Philip II*, published first in Paris in 1946 and in a revised edition in English in 1972. In this work Braudel argued that the only way to understand a place in its totality was to describe its environment, its social and economic structures, and its political systems. In Britain the emphasis of social historians has been less on questions of environment, per se, than on a description of human communities in all their complexities. For example, social historians there have taken advantage of that nation's remarkable local archives to reconstruct the history of the family and details of its rural past. Works such as Peter Laslett's *The World We Have Lost*, first printed in 1966, and the multiauthored *Agrarian History of England and Wales*, which began to appear in print in 1967, revealed that painstaking work could reveal the lives and habits of individuals who never previously attracted the interest of biographers, demographers, or most historians.

Social history in the United States gained a large following in the second half of the 20th century, especially during the 1960s and 1970s. Its development sprang from political, technical, and intellectual impulses deeply embedded in the culture of the modern university. The politics of civil rights and social reform fueled the passions of historians who strove to tell the stories of the underclass. They benefited from the adoption by historians of statistical analysis, which allowed scholars to trace where individuals lived, how often they moved, what kinds of jobs they took, and whether their economic status declined, stagnated, or improved over time. As history departments expanded, many who emerged from graduate schools focused their attention on groups previously ignored or marginalized. Women's history became a central concern among American historians, as did the history of African Americans, Native Americans, Latinos, and others. These historians pushed historical study in the United States farther away from the study of formal politics and intellectual trends. Though few Americanists could achieve the technical brilliance of some social historians in Europe, collectively they have been engaged in a vast act of description, with the goal of describing seemingly every facet of life from 1492 to the present.

The sixteen volumes in this series together represent the continuing efforts of historians to describe American society. Most of the volumes focus on chronological areas, from the broad sweep of the colonial era to the more narrowly defined collections of essays on the eras of the Cold War, the baby boom, and America in the age of the Vietnam War. The series also includes entire volumes on the epochs that defined the nation, the American Revolution and the Civil War, as well as volumes dedicated to the process of westward expansion, women's rights, and African American history.

This social history series derives its strength from the talented editors of individual volumes. Each editor is an expert in his or her own field who selected and organized the contents of his or her volume. Editors solicited other experienced historians to write individual essays. Every volume contains first-rate analysis complemented by lively anecdotes designed to reveal the complex contours of specific historical moments. The many illustrations to be found in these volumes testify too to the recognition that any society can be understood not only by the texts that its participants produce but also by the images that they craft. Primary source documents in each volume will allow interested readers to pursue some specific topics in greater depth, and each volume contains a chronology to provide guidance to the flow of events over time. These tools—anecdotes, images, texts, and timelines—allow readers to gauge the inner workings of America in particular periods and yet also to glimpse connections between eras.

The articles in these volumes testify to the abundant strengths of historical scholarship in the United States in the early years of the twenty-first century. Despite the occasional academic contest that flares into public notice, or the self-serving cant of politicians who want to manipulate the nation's past for partisan ends—for example, in debates over the Second Amendment to the U.S. Constitution and what it means about potential limits to the rights of gun ownership—the articles here all reveal the vast increase in knowledge of the American past that has taken place over the previous half century. Social historians do not dominate history faculties in American colleges and universities, but no one could deny them a seat at the intellectual table. Without their efforts, intellectual, cultural, and political historians would be hard pressed to understand why certain ideas circulated when they did, why some religious movements prospered or foundered, how developments in fields such as medicine and engineering reflected larger concerns, and what shaped the world we inhabit.

Fernand Braudel and his colleagues envisioned entire laboratories of historians in which scholars working together would be able to produce *histoire totale*: total history. Historians today seek more humble goals for our collective enterprise. But as the richly textured essays in these volumes reveal, scholarly collaboration has in fact brought us much closer to that dream. These volumes do not and cannot include every aspect of American history. However, every page reveals something interesting or valuable about how American society functioned. Together, these books suggest the crucial necessity of stepping back to view the grand complexities of the past rather than pursuing narrower prospects and lesser goals.

Peter C. Mancall

Series Editor

Introduction

History is the key to understanding our present and the light that illuminates the path to our future. In 2008, the United States celebrated a landmark event in its history, the election of an African American to the presidency of the United States. Many scholars trace the origins of this event to the efforts of Martin Luther King, Jr., in the 20th century or Abraham Lincoln's issuance of the Emancipation Proclamation in the 19th century, and in part, they are justified in their argument. These scholars, however, miss the proverbial forest by looking at a couple of large trees. Since 1800, millions of African Americans made sacrifices that blazed a trail that led directly to the election of Barack Obama to the presidency of the United States. Specifically, in the 19th century, people like Gabriel Prosser, Charles Deslondes, Paul Cuffe, Levi Coffin, Richard Allen, Denmark Vesey, Edward Jones, David Walker, Nat Turner, Harriet Tubman, Sojourner Truth, Dred Scott, Edward Alexander Bouchet, Henry O. Flipper, Booker T. Washington, George Washington Williams, Ida B. Wells, Homer Plessy, W. E. B. Du Bois, and the communities they represent literally sacrificed everything including their lives to lay down a foundation for the eventual freedom of all African Americans. These individuals paved a path to a future in which an African American could be elected president of the United States. Probably no one person did more for the betterment of the African American community in the 19th century and the achievement of their hopes in a later century than did Frederick Douglass.

Frederick Douglass is the perfect, singular example of the African American experience in the 19th century. He experienced life in a slave community in the South and in free African American communities in the North before the Civil War. In 1818, Douglass was born a slave in Maryland, and while a slave, he became all too familiar with the brutality, inhumanity, and inherent evil of the slavery institution.

While still a child and a slave, Douglass learned how to read even though it was forbidden by law. Eventually, he was forced to labor for his owner as he reached maturity. In 1838, Douglass managed to escape to the North and freedom, and by the early 1840s, he became an outspoken and public advocate of abolition, despite the risk to his freedom due to his status as a runaway slave. In 1845, Douglass published his autobiography to further the cause of abolition, again at great risk to his freedom. After publication of his autobiography, Douglass left for a lecture tour of Great Britain. While there, British friends of Douglass raised funds to purchase his freedom.

During the Civil War, Douglass worked tirelessly to ensure the war would guarantee an end to slavery and for African Americans to be allowed to serve in the Union Army. After the Civil War, Douglass campaigned vigorously to achieve civil, economic, and social rights for African Americans, and he lectured constantly, albeit in vain, to have the Civil War remembered primarily as a war for the emancipation of slaves. Douglass was politically active in the Republican Party and held several government appointments, including the marshal for the District of Columbia and minister and consul general to Haiti. Douglass passed away on February 20, 1895.

Frederick Douglass's life story vividly reveals the basic contradictions of a democratic republic that espoused the concept of equality for all, at the same time it allowed the enslavement of some of its population. Few if any American writers have so clearly and succinctly revealed and attacked the moral and economic nature of slavery, and few have argued so eloquently for the potential of civil, economic, and social equality in the natural rights tradition.

The purpose of this volume is to introduce the reader to the social world that Douglass and other African Americans experienced during the 19th century and help the reader explore and understand that world. This was a world that few 21st-century Americans fully appreciate. It was a world of struggle and fulfillment, justice and injustice, civility and brutality, and acceptance and racism.

More specifically, this monograph seeks to describe the social life of African Americans in the 19th century. Much has been published about the cultural, economic, environmental, military, and political accomplishments of African Americans in that century, but little has been written about the day-to-day affairs and the face-to-face interactions of African Americans with each other and others in American society. Although social history is the focus here, the cultural, economic, environmental, military, and political activity of these people will be used as methods of historical exploration to provide gateways into the social life of African Americans.

Frederick Douglass's birth came at a transition point in African American social history. Slave communities in the South were quickly becoming African American in their makeup rather than African because of the ban on the importation of slaves into the United States beginning in 1808. Before this ban, slaves born in Africa exceeded the number of those born in America. This had been the case since the first Africans were brought to North America in 1619. The history of Africans and African Americans in the Colonial and Revolutionary eras led up to and shaped this transition period, and this transition period is important to understanding African American history during the rest of the 19th century, because it created a division among African American leaders as to whether or not African Americans should seek inclusion in American society.

The first Africans to arrive in America probably ended up as indentured servants rather than slaves, but as the 16th century progressed, American colonists developed African chattel slavery as a replacement for indentured servitude. Chapter 1 describes how African chattel slavery, and the racism that accompanied it, provided the framework within which African and African American, free and enslaved communities developed socially and culturally in the 18th and early 19th centuries. Although this framework existed throughout America during this time, the nature and structure of African and African American society differed from time to time and place to place.

In the colonial period, the social structure and the culture produced by slave communities was influenced heavily by which African ethnicities lived within them and by when these ethnicities arrived. The different ethnicities from varying parts of Africa arrived at different times in different combinations to different places. The varying ways whites employed slaves in the different regions of North America combined with the white-to-black ratio to produce altering social settings for African slaves. This fact prevented enslaved and free blacks from developing any concept of racial unity during the colonial period.

The rhetoric of freedom and liberty that accompanied the revolutionary era caused black societies to reorganize at the end of the 18th and beginning of the 19th centuries. This trend combined with the reduction of African-born slaves and resulted in the development of a nascent, racial consciousness throughout black America. The rise of economically successful, black elites during this same period, the Revolutionary era to the 1820s, formed a classism that hindered and restrained the growth of an African American racial consciousness.

These two differing visions of the black future in America solidified after the 1820s. One vision looked toward inclusion in America, hoping that eventually the promise of liberty would be extended to them due to the influence of Christianity and the rhetoric of freedom. Frederick Douglass can be counted among those who adhered to this view. The second vision recognized that American racism would not accept anyone of African descent as equal. Therefore, those that followed this last view continued to develop their own African-influenced institutions and organizations and attempted to preserve their communities and their African heritage apart from white society. This division among African Americans continued to affect black society throughout the rest of the 19th century and into the 20th century. It manifested itself at the turn of the 20th century as some chose to follow the leadership of Booker T. Washington, and his focus on developing black economic independence first and the acquisition of civil rights later, and others chose to follow Frederick Douglass and W. E. B. Du Bois and their pursuit of immediate civil and social equality.

When Frederick Douglass made his escape and gained his freedom in 1838 he found, as Shelby Callaway writes in Chapter 2, that "the American practice of associating slavery with race made the existence of free black people a thorny issue" in the North as well as in the South for white Americans. Free blacks disrupted a system based on blackness equaling slavery, and this fact affected the legal, economic, and social makeup of antebellum America. During the early 19th century, free blacks established their position in American society and began to create a distinctly African American culture and society. Separate and distinct from the slave culture of the South and heavily influenced by their African heritage, "African American culture and society grew out of the free black communities and institutions of the 1800s." Black Christian churches and their leaders served as the focal points of these communities. The church "produced most of the social and political leaders, founded schools, started mutual aid societies, and contributed to a more distinct and unified African American consciousness and culture."

Most of the members of the free black communities during the early 19th century were the descendants of freed slaves or were freed slaves themselves. Many of these gained their freedom during the Revolutionary era as some white Americans and many black Americans took the concepts of liberty and equality literally. Those that were freed at this time and their descendants merged African culture and revolutionary American ideals into a distinctly African American society. Antebellum free blacks did not try to escape their African roots and never lost solidarity with Africans in bondage despite divided opinions about whether or not to seek inclusion with whites in American society. Frederick Douglass and others like him campaigned for the rights of all black people, free and slave. Churches, schools, and social organizations, the abolition societies and the Underground Railroad all spawned from the free black society.

In his autobiography, Frederick Douglass exposed the abuses and the harshness of slavery as it existed in the South during the 19th century. In several sections, Douglass clearly and poignantly illustrated the affect that slavery had on female slaves. Because of the nature of slavery, as Crystal L. Johnson demonstrates in Chapter 3, female slaves occupied four basic roles: an oppressed object, the resistant foe, the center of the slave family, and a survivor.

Overseers and owners viewed black female slaves as objects or as pieces of property. As a result of these white attitudes, slave women often faced abuse and cruelty. White owners and overseers stripped these women of their sense of femininity and replaced it with the deplorable notion of the black female slave as a breeder and a commodity to sell, buy, or trade at will. Commonly, sexual exploitation proved to be the method used to objectify black female slaves. It was not uncommon for white men to rape female slaves.

The female slave as a resistant foe was also a role black women fulfilled under the oppression of slavery. Black female slaves exhibited the wits and desire to resist the immoral atrocities of slavery. From the boarding of the slave vessels to the point of settling into slave quarters, black women participated and assisted in slave insurrections and work slowdowns, broke tools, set fires, and even in some case, poisoned their owners.

Johnson notes that "while the role of resistor empowered the female slave, the one significant role that has passed from generation to generation is that of the black female being the center of the family." Because male slaves often were sold away from their families or kept away from their families, female slaves were forced to take care of their families alone or with the help of other female slaves. In so doing, they demonstrated self-sufficiency, independence, and female solidarity that helped the slave family survive the institution of slavery.

Johnson emphasizes that female slaves also had to take on the role of survivor to perpetuate their lineages. "The psychological, sexual, and mental anguish suffered by the black female slave created a woman with thick skin." The female slave embraced the different roles thrust on her and survived. "It took phenomenal women to endure the pains, tribulations, and the daily injustices of the institution of slavery. These women had the will to survive a barbaric institution."

Frederick Douglass, through his writings and his talks on the lecture circuit, often discussed the nature of social life in slave communities. His discussions used these communities to demonstrate the humanity and ingenuity of enslaved African Americans to enlighten a primarily racist, white public in the North as well as the South. He illustrated the willingness of slaves to band together to help each other and their ability to maintain connections with friends and family beyond the immediate confines of their own plantations.

Before the Civil War, the majority of African Americans lived in slave communities in the United States. To survive the harsh realities of the institution of slavery, they established bonds inside and outside their home communities, as Karen Wilson demonstrates in Chapter 4. If friends and family members were sold to nearby plantations, slaves managed to maintain ties with these same friends and family members by visiting at night. Members of slave communities built a network of support that extended beyond the home plantation by sustaining family and friendship connections.

These networks kept individuals informed as to what was going on in the outside world despite the fact that slaveholders wanted to keep their slaves ignorant. This network helped slaves connect with the Underground Railroad when they wanted to escape, and with the coming of the Civil War, it helped many slaves track the advancement of Union armies to time the abandonment of plantations *en masse*. This last activity put pressure on Abraham Lincoln to issue the Proclamation of Emancipation, specifically because the U.S. government needed a policy established to guide the military's response to thousands of ex-slaves flooding into Union camps.

Within the institution of slavery, whites expected slaves to act childish, subhuman, and dull. Knowing this, slaves presented this expected image to the world outside of their slave communities. This façade hid a society that flourished. On plantations, the young were trained to avoid the dangers of slavery and survive. Slaves used stories, songs, dance, and other creative forms of expression to train the young. The most famous of these stories include the Brer Rabbit stories. Specifically, children were taught to act as whites expected and hide their true nature. Additionally, they were taught to keep the activities of their communities secret from all whites.

At the same time children were taught how to survive, the elders also taught them about Africa. Many of the African traditions that survived in slave communities centered on religion and religious ceremony. Elements of African culture that slave communities preserved include but are not limited to the ring shout, voodoo, hoodoo, and various forms of dancing. In a way, slave communities were the archives for slaves to store and maintain African traditions. Just as Douglass revealed the nature of slave communities in his writings and in his talks, he also exposed the true state of interactions between slaveholders and the slaves to expose the false claims of paternalism on plantations and uncover the stark inhumanity of these relationships.

Slavery was a coercive, brutal institution, but according to Jennifer Hildebrand in Chapter 5 slaves survived the horrors of the peculiar institution because of their psychic and spiritual strength. Despite the unequal power relationship that existed between master and slave, the relationship between the two was not one-sided. Slaveholders wanted to believe that slaves were childlike and simple. To preserve this belief, they created a system in which slaves were dependent on them for most of their needs. For example, many slaveholders forbid their slaves from growing their own gardens so that their slaves depended on the owner for food. The helplessness forced upon the slaves reinforced the owner's belief that he had a paternalistic relationship with his childlike slaves. When they were beyond the owner's view, most slaves supplemented their diets by growing secret gardens, hunting, gathering, and fishing. Despite what the owner believed he knew about his slaves and his relationship with them, however, the reality was far different from those perceptions. Just as they hid the ways they supplemented their diets, slaves quickly learned to keep the owner in the dark about the inner workings of their society, and they used his desire to be seen as paternalistic as a means to ease their circumstances within the institution of slavery.

Slaves expressed their desire for freedom and their frustration with the institution of slavery through their singing. The songs they sang revealed their feelings in a veiled form often hiding their true meaning with Biblical themes. Their folktales allowed them to protest their condition in a veiled fashion.

Despite the slaves' abilities to keep their owner in the dark about much of their activities and improve their situation, some things the slaves could not prevent. They could not escape beatings. Depending on the temperament of their specific owner, some slaves were exposed on a regular basis to violence. In some cases, no appeal to paternalism could spare the helpless victim of the slaveholder's wrath, and a slave could suffer a beating for doing little more than being too slow. Thankfully, the Civil War brought an end to this evil institution.

During the Civil War, Frederick Douglass fought to make emancipation the primary goal of the war, and he constantly urged the government to allow African Americans to serve in the military. Once African Americans were allowed to serve, Douglass worked tirelessly to recruit African Americans to enlist. Importantly, as David Williams and Teresa Crisp Williams argue in Chapter 6, the activities of blacks (free blacks like

Douglass and slaves) during the Civil War and not the efforts of the Lincoln administration led to the emancipation of the slaves. Basically, enslaved blacks took freedom for themselves by heading for Union lines as soon as possible. The farther south the Union Army went, the more slaves stopped working and set off for freedom. This forced Lincoln to grudgingly recognize what slaves had already forced on his administration and what free blacks in the North had been demanding all along.

From the beginning of the Civil War, Douglass had advocated the enlistment of African Americans in the Union Army. However, the Lincoln administration and the military leadership resisted with many in the military questioning the capacity of blacks to perform on the battlefield. Yet despite these racist fears, the casualty rate Union troops faced forced their hand. Eventually, 200,000 blacks served in the Union armed forces with 80 percent coming from southern states. Another 200,000 worked in auxiliary support services for the military helping in logistics and other capacities. By the war's end, African Americans had played a major and important role in the defeat of the Confederacy and the final abolition of slavery in North America.

Happily experiencing the abolition of slavery after the Civil War, it appeared to Frederick Douglass, albeit briefly, that his dream of black equality and inclusion in American society might be achieved, but he quickly learned that the promise of Reconstruction in the South would be short-lived. As Dawn J. Herd-Clark points out in Chapter 7, for African Americans living in the former southern states Reconstruction brought substantial changes. Reconstruction began with the implementation of President Abraham Lincoln's Ten Percent Plan for reconstructing the South in 1863, and it continued through Congressional Radical Reconstruction until the last of the federal troops were removed from the former Confederate States in 1877.

During Reconstruction, former African American slaves experienced freedom for the first time. As a result, African Americans could receive an education, own land, vote, and hold political office for the first time. Unfortunately, by the end of the 19th century after Reconstruction ended, racism and discrimination by southern whites and northern white apathy stripped many of these civil liberties from freedmen living in the South. The rights African Americans fought to achieve during Reconstruction were lost until the modern civil rights movement of the 1950s and 1960s.

Douglass experienced the implementation of segregation in the North in the years preceding the Civil War, and the rise of Jim Crow in the South in the years after the termination of Reconstruction. According to Mary Block in Chapter 8, "The Jim Crow system entailed not only the customary and legal racial segregation and political disenfranchisement of African Americans, but also the violent and brutal tactics that whites employed to gain and maintain dominance over blacks. The function of Jim Crow was to maintain white supremacy through the denigration and humiliation of African Americans. Although Jim Crow is associated with the South . . . it also existed in the North and the West."

"Laws mandating racial segregation and black disenfranchisement originated in the North, where states had abolished slavery by the 1820s," Block writes. "A majority of northern whites shared the belief with their southern counterparts that white folks constituted a superior race of people and justified segregation and disenfranchisement on the grounds that blacks were innately inferior and therefore could not meet the vital responsibilities of citizenship. . . . southern legislatures modeled their respective post–Civil War Jim Crow statutes on the North's antebellum discrimination laws. Most northern states had barred free blacks from voting, office-holding, and jury service, and mandated the separation of the races in public schools and public accommodations. Blacks were discriminated against in employment. These discriminations were not uniform in all northern states, and they were not enforced consistently from jurisdiction to jurisdiction." This was not the case in the South after the end of Reconstruction. By the end of the 19th century, Jim Crow evolved in the South into a rigid and reasonably uniform code of laws and customs that prohibited African American civil, economic, and social equality with whites and attempted to guarantee the complete and perpetual "denigration and humiliation of African Americans." As a result of the development of Jim Crow, African Americans in the South had to make choices as to what they should do to survive and persevere.

In the late 19th century, Booker T. Washington began to advocate the pursuit of economic self-sufficiency by African Americans in the South rather than civil and social equality with whites. Frederick Douglass opposed this position feeling that African Americans needed to demand equality in all aspects of life. W. E. B. Du Bois carried Douglass's campaign forward after Douglass's death in 1895. The divide between Washington and Douglass/Du Bois continued the divisions in African American society that started early in the 19th century. Douglass and Du Bois looked toward inclusion in America, hoping that eventually the promise of liberty would be extended to them. Washington and his followers believed that American racism, especially in the South, prevented African Americans from being seen as equals, and therefore, African Americans should keep to themselves and seek to provide their own economic security separate from white society.

Washington's belief, argues Mark D. Hersey in Chapter 9, was based on the fact that most African Americans remained in the South after the Civil War, and most were "caught in an economic system that more or less trapped them in a position of debt peonage. The various sorts of farm tenancy that marked the South from Reconstruction through World War II emerged out of two principal factors: the economic devastation attended the South in the aftermath of the Civil War and the prevailing social mores of the region. . . . Ultimately, the tenant system that emerged in the years following the Civil War remained in place through World War II, and for its duration, black tenant farmers carried on in much the same way. Indeed, the lives of black tenants in the late 1920s differed but little from those of the 1880s. Though the prospect of financial independence was comparatively bleak for most black farmers in the South, they continued to hope for better things, contribute to their communities, and follow the seasonal rhythms of their vocation." While some African Americans chose to stay in the South and cope with Jim Crow and growing white hostility as best they could, others chose to abandon the South.

After the termination of Reconstruction, many freedmen feared for their future in the South because of the increase of black debt peonage created by share-cropping and tenant farming, the rise in lynching, and the expansion of Jim Crow laws. Therefore, many turned to the West as a land of opportunity, despite the protests of leaders like Frederick Douglass who believed African Americans should remain in the East and aggressively pursue civil and social equality there. Those who ventured West during the late 19th century found other African Americans there with roots deeply embedded.

African Americans moved into the West throughout the 19th century. Sometimes they worked in what James N. Leiker in Chapter 10 calls "stereotypical 'western' jobs such as ranching and soldiering, but more often engaged in mundane but important tasks such as building schools, establishing towns, and creating black communities that would champion the civil rights causes of the 20th century." Most of the blacks who went west did so, however, after the conclusion of Reconstruction.

As southern leaders began to reassert "the primacy of local rule after the end of Reconstruction, African Americans saw their hopes for civil, economic, and social equality vanish." In response to this loss of hope, many African Americans turned to the West as a place of refuge where their dreams might be fulfilled. Racism followed them into the West, but opportunity was also found in the region.

Few people are aware that Frederick Douglass had some Native American ancestry, which, in essence, made him a Black Indian. Chapter 11 relates how the tragic conquest of Native America and the horrific enslavement of Africans created Black Indians as the circumstances of history brought the two oppressed people together in North America. Black Indians managed to persevere and survive despite America's historic problem with accepting racial and cultural diversity; however, because of the denial of racial and cultural plurality in the United States, Black Indians continually had to negotiate their identity in the face of white, and sometimes Native and African American, denial of their dual heritage.

From the first arrival of Africans to North America in 1619 until the end of the 19th century, European colonists, and later white Americans, worked continually to prevent blacks and Native Americans from uniting against whites by playing the two groups against each other through the exploitation of racial differences and ethnic rivalries. White Americans used Natives as slave hunters and eventually turned some in the southern tribes into slaveholders. They transformed Africans and African Americans into Indian fighters to further antagonize potential relationships between these two groups. Thus, by creating real and fictional animosity between the two groups, white Americans successfully hid the cultural similarities between them. This allowed both groups to be exploited by white society well into the 20th century. Yet despite the efforts of Europeans and Anglo Americans, Africans and Native Americans intermingled from the beginning, survived the 19th century into the present, and added to the social and cultural milieu that is the United States.

During his lifetime, Frederick Douglass published his memoirs several times and remained a constant figure on the lecture circuit until his death in 1895. For most of the 19th century, Douglass was the most prominent leader of the black community in the United States. However, he did not lead alone. As Paige Haggard points out in Chapter 12, other African Americans provided key leadership at important times, and many of those left written records of their efforts as well.

Some African American leaders resisted slavery outright in the form of leading slave rebellions. Many were slaves, such as the blacksmith Gabriel Prosser and Charles Deslondes, and others were free blacks in the South, such as Denmark Vesey, who hoped to help their enslaved brethren. Rebellious slaves and free blacks alike demonstrated that they accepted neither the institution of slavery nor their place in southern society.

In the North, African American leaders, prior to the Civil War focused on the abolition of slavery and the acceptance of blacks as civil, economic, and social equals in northern society. Often, these leaders came out of African American churches and were pastors in these churches, such as Reverend Daniel Cook and Reverend H. Easton. Other African Americans, including Frederick Douglass, David Walker, and Sojourner Truth, used the lecture circuit and publications to argue for the inclusion of blacks in American society and the abolition of slavery. Others such as Harriet Tubman and Lewis and Harriet Hayden attacked slavery more directly by participating in the Underground Railroad and helping enslaved blacks escape to northern states and Canada.

During the Civil War, African American leaders worked to ensure a Union victory. Harriett Tubman worked as a spy for the Union Army. Many African American leaders followed Frederick Douglass's lead and called for the use of African American soldiers from the outset of hostilities. After the Union Army began to recruit African Americans to serve, leaders like Douglass strove to guarantee that African Americans answered that call and to ensure that emancipation of the slaves was a war aim.

After the war, many African American leaders began to hold political office in the South. Others set about the task of establishing schools and churches for blacks. Still others began to engage in business activity for the first time. During Reconstruction, most of the efforts of African American leaders were successful, but over time, white resentment grew. After Reconstruction ended, whites began to establish Jim Crow laws to separate the races legally and socially. At the same time, white supremacy groups rose up and began to terrorize African Americans in the South. African American leaders like Homer Plessy and Ida B. Wells led campaigns to stop the legalization of segregation and lynching, but they ultimately failed during the 19th century.

By the time he passed away on February 20, 1895, Frederick Douglass had witnessed the end of slavery, the granting of citizenship to African Americans, and the election of many former slaves, including himself, to political office. Unfortunately, he also saw the rise of debt peonage among southern African Americans, the African American loss of civil rights nationwide, the legalization of segregation in the South, and the steady rise of lynching in the South during the late 19th century. Despite the downward turn he saw in the fortunes of African Americans during the late 19th century, Douglass continued to strive to improve the conditions for African Americans in the United States until his last breath. Douglass continued to struggle because he knew how bright the future could be for African Americans, and all Americans, if good people continued the good fight.

The efforts of African Americans, enslaved and free, during the 19th century changed their daily lives and the future of African Americans and the United States. They helped end the peculiar institution of slavery, ensured the freedom of blacks, worked to bring justice to an oppressed population, and fought diligently to end racism in America. Their work not only changed their lives during the 1800s, but also sowed the seeds of the civil rights movement that blossomed in the following century, thereby changing generations of African American lives and paving a path to a future in which an African American could become president of the United States.

About the Editor and Contributors

Dixie Ray Haggard is associate professor of Native American history at Valdosta State University. He teaches graduate and undergraduate courses in Native American history, colonial North America and Atlantic world history, the Revolutionary era in American history, and U.S. history. He received his bachelor's and master's degrees from Georgia Southern University and his doctorate from the University of Kansas. His publications include a forthcoming book entitled *Indian Country, 1866 to 1933*, articles with *Indigenous Nations Studies Journal* and *History Compass*, and numerous essays in *The Social History of Colonial America*, *Encyclopedia of U. S. Indian Policy and Law*, *Encyclopedia of American Indian Wars: A Social, Political and Military History*, *Encyclopedia of North American Colonial Conflict to 1775: A Political, Social, and Military History*, *The Encyclopedia of Native American Religious Traditions*, *The Encyclopedia of Native Americans and Sport*, and *Three Worlds Meet*.

Mary Block earned her doctorate in history from the University of Kentucky. She is an assistant professor of history at Valdosta State University where she teaches courses in American constitutional and legal history, early national America, the American West, colonial and modern Latin America, and historical methods. Her research area is law and sexual violence in 19th-century America. Besides a number of book reviews, Block has published articles in *The Register of the Kentucky Historical Society* and *History Compass*, and has multiple entries in *The Encyclopedia of Rape* as well as in several volumes of *The Greenwood Encyclopedia of Love, Courtship, and Sexuality through History*.

Shelby Callaway is a student in the doctoral program at the University of Kansas. He received his bachelor's and master's degrees from Valdosta State University.

Paige Haggard received her bachelor's degree with magna cum laude honors from Georgia Southern University and her master's in fine art in English from the University of South Carolina. She taught composition and literature for six years at the University of South Carolina with an emphasis on rhetoric and political theory, especially in race and gender theories. Haggard participated in the South Carolina Civil Rights Oral History Project, which collected narratives for *The Civil and Human Rights Anthology*. She has sixteen years journalism experience; her work has appeared in *The Southern Reflector, The George-Anne, The Gamecock, The Garnet and Black, INsite, Break, Free Times,* and *The Ministry of Whimsy* among others. Paige's publishing credits also include "The Feature from the Black Lagoon" in McGraw-Hill's *How to Do Everything with iLife '04* as well as providing research for Alice M. Klement and Carolyn B. Matalene's *Telling Stories, Taking Risks: Journalism Writing at the Century's Edge*. She is an independent scholar in addition to being a freelancing editor, copywriter, and graphic designer.

Dawn J. Herd-Clark holds a bachelor's degree from Ball State University and master's and doctoral degrees from Florida State University. In addition to published essays and encyclopedia entries, she is preparing for publication "Dorchester Academy: The American Missionary Association in Liberty County, Georgia, 1867–1950." She is assistant professor of history at Fort Valley State University where she teaches African American history, the modern civil rights movement, and recent U.S. history.

Mark D. Hersey is an assistant professor of history at Mississippi State University. His research focuses on the environmental, agricultural, and rural components of the southern experience, particularly as they relate to African Americans. He earned a bachelor's degree from the University of Alabama and a doctorate from the University of Kansas, where he also served as the project director for *This Week in KU History* and *Kansas History Online*. He has published articles in *Environmental History* and *The Historian*, along with entries in *The Encyclopedia of American Environmental History, Modern American Environmentalists: A Biographical Encyclopedia*, and BlackPast.org, an online reference guide to African American history. He is working on a manuscript about the environmental thought of George Washington Carver.

Jennifer Hildebrand is an assistant professor of African American history at the State University of New York, Fredonia. She received her doctorate from the University of California, Riverside. She enjoys researching African American culture, and she teaches survey courses in African American history, African American studies, and the civil rights movement, as well as seminars dealing with slave culture and the New Negro Movement.

Crystal L. Johnson is a faculty history instructor of U.S. history at Metropolitan Community College–Maple Woods in Kansas City, Missouri. She teaches undergraduate courses in American history, African American history, and western civilization history. She received her bachelor's degree from the University of Wisconsin–Madison and her master's degree from the University of Kansas. She is currently a doctoral candidate in history at the University of Kansas.

James N. Leiker is associate professor of history at Johnson County Community College in Overland Park, Kansas, where he teaches courses in

U.S. history, western civilization, African American studies, and history of the Middle East. His publications include *Racial Borders: Black Soldiers along the Rio Grande*, as well as numerous articles in *Great Plains Quarterly, Encyclopedia of the Harlem Renaissance*, and *Western Historical Quarterly*.

David Williams is the author of nearly fifty articles and seven books, including *Bitterly Divided: The South's Inner Civil War, A People's History of the Civil War: Struggles for the Meaning of Freedom, Plain Folk in a Rich Man's War: Class and Dissent in Confederate Georgia* (with Teresa Crisp Williams and David Carlson), *Johnny Reb's War: Battlefield and Homefront*, and *Rich Man's War: Class, Caste, and Confederate Defeat in the Lower Chattahoochee Valley*. A native of Miller County, Georgia, Williams holds a doctorate in history from Auburn University. He is a professor of history at Valdosta State University, where he served a three-year term as chair of the History Department and has for the past twenty years taught survey courses in U.S. history as well as upper division and graduate courses in Georgia history, the Old South, and the Civil War era.

Teresa Crisp Williams is co-author of *Plain Folk in a Rich Man's War: Class and Dissent in Confederate Georgia* (with David Williams and David Carlson), and is author of numerous articles that have appeared in such publications as *The Georgia Historical Quarterly, Contiguities: An Interdisciplinary Journal of Women's Studies*, and *The Encyclopedia of the American Civil War: A Political, Social, and Military History*. A native of Columbus, Georgia, she holds a master's degree in history and a master of public administration degree from Valdosta State University. She has served at Valdosta State University in various capacities since 1992. For the past ten years, she has been the administrative coordinator of the graduate school and has taught survey courses in U.S. history.

Karen Wilson is assistant director of the Gluck Fellows Program at the University of California–Riverside. She received her PhD in history from the University of California–Riverside and is a well-known singer-storyteller and teaching artist of the African diaspora. Her research and writing focuses on the African intellectual and cultural presence in the United States and the Caribbean as well as African American women and the Blues.

Chronology

1619 The first Africans were brought to North America at Jamestown, Virginia, in a Dutch ship.

1739 Stono Revolt took place in South Carolina. Armed slaves trying to flee to Florida killed dozens of whites before the rebels were defeated in an open battle.

1746 Lucy Terry (c. 1730–1821) wrote "Bars Fight" which is the earliest known work of literature by an African American, Josiah Holland first published it in his *History of Western Massachusetts* in 1855.

1760 Jupiter Hammon (1711–ca. 1806) published the poem, "An Evening Thought: Salvation by Christ, with Penitential Cries," which was the first published work by an African American in the United States.

Briton Hammon published *The Narrative of the Uncommon Sufferings and Surprizing Deliverance of Briton Hammon, a Negro Man*, which was the first in a long line of autobiographical slave narratives.

1773 Phyllis Wheatley (ca. 1753–1784) published *Poems on Various Subjects, Religious and Moral*.

1789 Olaudah Equiano (1745–1797) published *The Interesting Narrative of the Life of Olaudah Equiano, Written by Himself*, which set the form for the slave narrative genre.

1793 Eli Whitney (1765–1825) invented the cotton gin. He received a patent for his invention on March 14, 1794.

February 12 Congress passed the Federal Fugitive Slave Law, which provided for the return of escaped slaves who had crossed state lines.

1800 A group of African Americans who left the John Street Methodist Church in 1796 formed their first church called Zion. It later organized as the Black

Methodist church in the United States in 1821 and became known as the African Methodist Episcopal Zion Church in 1848.

In the Census of 1800, the U.S. population was 5,308,483 and the African American population was 1,002.037, making up 18.9 percent of the total population, including 108,435 free African Americans.

The U.S. Congress rejected an antislavery petition delivered by free Philadelphia African Americans by a vote of 85–1.

August 30 Gabriel Prosser (1775–1800), an enslaved African American blacksmith, conspired to lead a slave revolt in Virginia with the intent of marching to Richmond, Virginia. After the conspiracy was uncovered, Prosser and several other rebels were hanged, and in response to the incident, Virginia tightened its slave laws.

1802 The Ohio Constitution outlaws slavery, and at the same time, it prohibits free African Americans from voting. The Ohio Legislature also passed the first Black Laws that placed additional restrictions on free African Americans in the state.

The Richmond Recorder published James Callender's (1758–1803) accusation that Thomas Jefferson (1743–1826) "for many years past kept, as his concubine, one of his own slaves," Sally Hemings (1773–1835). The Federalist press quickly printed this story throughout the country.

1807 **March 2** Congress passed the law that ended the importation of slaves into the United States from Africa and other places outside the country.

1808 **January 1** The constitutional ban on the importation of slaves into the United States became official, but the ban was consistently broken. The illegal importation of slaves into the United States brought about 250,000 people into the country between 1808 and 1865. The domestic slave trade within the United States continued until the end of the Civil War.

1810 In the U.S. Census of 1810, the U.S. population was 7,239,881 and the African American population was 1,377,808, making up 19 percent of the total population, including 186,446 free African Americans.

The U.S. Congress prohibited African Americans from working for the U.S. Postal Service.

1811 **January 8–11** Charles Deslondes (ca. 1780–1811) led Andry's Rebellion on the Manuel Andry plantation in Louisiana.

1812 Boston absorbed the previously independent African American schools into its public school system.

In New York, two African American regiments were formed to fight in the War of 1812, which continued a tradition of African Americans serving in the military that started in the War for American Independence.

1814   Six hundred African American troops served with Andrew Jackson's army of 3,000 at the Battle of New Orleans.

1815   Paul Cuffe (1759–1817), an African American businessman, financed the settlement of thirty-eight African Americans in Sierra Leone, Africa.

Abolitionist Levi Coffin (1798–1877) created the Underground Railroad to help slaves in the South escape into northern free states and Canada.

1816   Richard Allen (1760–1831) organized the African Methodist Episcopal Church in Philadelphia. It was the first African American church denomination in the United States. In 1787, a group of African Americans left the St. George's Methodist Episcopal Church in Philadelphia because they faced discrimination. Bishop Francis Asbury (1745–1816) of the Methodist Episcopal Church ordained Richard Allen as the minster of this new congregation in 1799, and in 1816, Asbury consecrated him bishop of the African American Methodist Church. This denomination grew quickly in the North, and after the Civil War, it became popular in the South.

Robert Finley (1772–1817), a Presbyterian minister and later president of the University of Georgia, founded The American Colonization Society and established the colony of Monrovia (which later became the country of Liberia) in western Africa. Approximately 12,000 former slaves voluntarily relocated there.

1817–1818   Runaway slaves from Georgia, South Carolina, and Alabama joined the Florida Seminoles in their resistance to the United States.

1818   The state of Connecticut disenfranchised black voters.

1819   The Canadian government began its policy of refusing to return fugitive slaves living in Canada to the United States.

1820   In the U.S. Census of 1820, the U.S. population was 9,638,452 and the African American population 1,771,656, making up 18.4 percent of the total population, including 233,504 free African Americans.

Daniel Coker (1780–1846) of Baltimore led eighty-six African Americans to permanently settle in Liberia.

March 3   The Missouri Compromise banned slavery in the Louisiana Purchase above thirty-sixth parallel, and allowed Missouri to enter the Union as a slave state and Maine to enter as a free state.

1821   The African Company, the first African American theater company in the United States, was founded in New York City.

1822   Rhode Island disenfranchised African American voters.

May 30 George Wilson, a slave, informed his master about an insurrection of free and enslaved African Americans in the Charleston area being planned for July. The leader of the plan was Denmark Vesey (1767–1822), a carpenter.

June 23 Denmark Vesey was hanged for planning a slave revolt in South Carolina. Militia and federal troops mobilized to quell potential protest by African American supporters of Vesey.

1824   New York abolished property qualification requirements for white voters but maintained the same qualifications for African American voters.

Missouri disenfranchised free African American voters.

1826   **August 23** Edward Jones graduated from Amherst College in Massachusetts to be the first African American to graduate from college in the United States.

1827   New York abolished slavery.

March 16 *Freedom's Journal* became the first African American newspaper published in the United States. It was a weekly published in New York until 1829.

1829   **September** David Walker (1796–1830), an African American activist, published the pamphlet "Appeal to the Colored Citizens of the World," which called for a national slave rebellion.

White mob violence forced more than half of Cincinnati's African American residents to leave the city. These riots marked the beginning of white violence against northern black urban communities that lasted more than a century.

1830   In the U.S. Census of 1830, the U.S. population was 12,866,020 and the African American population was 2,328,842, making up 18.1 percent of the total population, which included 319,599 free African Americans.

The first in a series of National Negro Conventions held by African American delegates from New York, Pennsylvania, Maryland, Delaware, and Virginia met in Philadelphia to develop methods to challenge racial discrimination in the North and the existence of slavery in the South.

1831   The *Liberator*, a weekly abolitionist newspaper, was first published by William Lloyd Garrison (1838–1909) to advocate the immediate end of slavery.

North Carolina banned the teaching of reading and writing to slaves.

Alabama banned African Americans, slave or free, from preaching.

November 11 Nat Turner (1800–1831), an African American preacher was hanged for leading a slave uprising in Southampton, Virginia, on August 21–22 that killed at least fifty-seven whites. As a result of this revolt, the state legislature in Virginia almost abolished slavery, but instead it chose, in a close vote, to retain slavery and to implement a repressive policy against both slave and free African Americans.

1831–1861 During the thirty years of its existence, the Underground Railroad freed nearly 75,000 slaves using a system in which free African American and white abolitionists guided and sheltered the escapees in their flight to the North and Canada.

1832 Oberlin College was founded in Ohio to provide a college education to African American men and women and white women.

The African American women's abolitionist society, the Female Anti-Slavery Society, was founded in Salem, Massachusetts.

1833 The American Anti-Slavery Society was established in Philadelphia, Pennsylvania.

The British Parliament abolished slavery throughout the British Empire.

1834 New York absorbed the African Free Schools into its public school system.

South Carolina banned the education of African Americans, enslaved or free, within its borders.

October 14 In receiving his patent for a cotton-planting machine, Henry Blair (1807–1860) became the first African American to receive a patent.

1835 Texas declared its independence from Mexico, and the new nation ratified a constitution that legalized slavery and passed laws intended to drive free African Americans out of the Lone Star Republic.

1836–1844 Congress passed the "Gag Rule" that prohibited it from considering petitions regarding slavery for almost twenty years.

1837 The Institute for Colored Youth (later Cheyney University) was founded in Southeastern Pennsylvania.

Dr. James McCune Smith (1813–1865) became the first African American to hold a medical degree when he graduated from the Medical School of the University of Glasgow, Scotland.

1838 Pennsylvania disenfranchised African American voters.

1839 **August 29** *The Amistad*, a Spanish ship that had been seized by fifty-three slaves on board, arrived in New London, Connecticut.

1840 In the U.S. Census of 1840, the U.S. population was 17,069,453 and the African American population was 2,873,648, making up 16.1 percent of the total population, which included 386,293 free African Americans.

1841 **March 9** In the *United States v The Amistad*, the slaves of the Spanish ship Amistad received their freedom and were returned to Africa.

1842   Frederick Douglass (1817–1895) led a successful campaign resisting Rhode Island's proposed Dorr Constitution that would have continued the ban on African American voting rights.

1843   At the National Negro Convention meeting in Buffalo, New York, the Reverend Henry Highland Garnet (1815–1882) delivered his controversial "Address to the Slaves," which called for a slave rebellion.

William Wells Brown (1814–1884) and Sojourner Truth (ca. 1797–1883) initiated their resistance against the institution of slavery.

Martin R. Delany (1812–1865) published *The Mystery*, an antislavery narrative.

1844   **June 25**   The Territory of Oregon passed the first in a series of African American exclusion laws.

1845   Former slave and abolitionist leader Frederick Douglass published his *Narrative of the Life of Frederick Douglass*.

March 1   Texas annexed into the United States.

1846   The Wilmot Proviso passed the House of Representatives, but failed to pass the Senate. The proviso banned slavery in the Mexican Cession gained at the end of the Mexican-American War.

1847   William Wells Brown published *Narrative of William W. Brown, A Fugitive Slave*. A former slave and abolitionist leader, Brown went on to write and publish the first novel, the first play, and the first travel book by an African American.

Frederick Douglass first published *The North Star* in Rochester, New York.

Missouri passed a prohibition on the education of free African Americans.

1848   **February 2**   In the Treaty of Guadalupe Hidalgo, Mexico ceded California, Arizona, New Mexico, Nevada, and Utah and gave up its claim to Texas at the conclusion of the Mexican-American War in exchange for $15 million. Controversy over whether to allow slavery in the Mexican Cession divided the country politically until the Compromise of 1850.

July 19–20   A Women's Rights Convention met at Seneca Falls, New York, and Frederick Douglass was among the handful of men that attended.

1849   Harriet Tubman (1820–1913) escaped from slavery and became a leader in the Underground Railroad. She made numerous trips back into the South to help free other slaves.

Henry Bibb (1815–1854) published *Narrative of the Life and Adventures of Henry Bibb, an American Slave*.

In *Roberts v. City of Boston*, the Massachusetts Supreme Court ruled that racially segregated schools in Boston did not violate the guarantee of equality under the law established by the Massachusetts constitution.

The California gold rush began, and eventually 4,000 African Americans migrated to California during this period.

William Augustus Hodges published his autobiography.

1850   Compromise of 1850 ended the debate over whether slavery could exist in the Mexican Cession. The compromise allowed California to be admitted into the Union as a free state, created the Territories of Utah and New Mexico and left them to decide the issue of slavery in their territories by popular sovereignty. The slave trade was prohibited in the District of Columbia, a stricter fugitive slave law was passed and the boundary between New Mexico and Texas was given its modern proportions.

Sojourner Truth (ca. 1797–1883) published *Narrative of Sojourner Truth*.

In the U.S. Census of 1850, the United States population was 23,191,876 and the African American population was 3,638,808, making up 15.7 percent of the total population, which included 433,807 free African Americans.

August 27   Lucy Stanton of Cleveland graduated from Oberlin Collegiate Institute (now Oberlin College) to become the first African American woman to receive a degree from an American college or university.

1851   **May 29**   Sojourner Truth spoke to the Women's Rights Convention, Akron, Ohio, and delivered her "Aren't I a Woman" speech.

1852   Harriet Beecher Stowe (1811–1896) published *Uncle Tom's Cabin*, which heavily influenced the abolition movement.

Martin R. Delany (1812–1825) published *The Condition, Elevation, Emigration and Destiny of the Colored People of the United States*.

The first medical facility solely for the care of African American patients, Jackson Street Hospital was established in Augusta, Georgia.

1853   Solomon Northup (1808–?) published *Twelve Years a Slave: Narrative of Solomon Northup*.

1854   The Republican Party formed as a party to promote wage labor and American business as well as an opposition to the extension of slavery in the western territories.

James A. Healy (1830–1900) was ordained in France as the first African American Jesuit priest. In 1875, he became the Bishop of Portland, and held that post for twenty-five years.

May 24   Under the provisions of the Fugitive Slave Act, Anthony Burns (1834–1862), a Virginia fugitive slave, was captured in Boston and returned to slavery. Fifty thousand Boston residents watched him hauled through the streets in shackles. Afterward, a Boston church raised $1,500 and purchased his freedom, and in 1855, Burns returned to the city as a free man.

May 30 The Kansas-Nebraska Act which established the territories of Kansas and Nebraska, opened these territories up to popular sovereignty, and repealed the Missouri Compromise was passed by Congress. Soon thereafter, violence broke out in "Bleeding Kansas" as armed groups of pro- and antislavery factions fought over control. The violence did not end until 1858.

October 13 John Miller Dickey and his wife Sarah Emlen Cresson founded Ashmun Institute (renamed Lincoln University in 1866) as the first institution of higher learning specifically for young black men.

1855   John Mercer Langston (1829–1897) became the first elected African American official in the nation when he was elected town clerk of Brownhelm Township, Ohio.

The Massachusetts Legislature prohibited racially segregated schools.

William C. Nell (1816–1874) published *The Colored Patriots of the American Revolution*, which was the first history of African Americans.

1856   Founded by the African Methodist Episcopal Church, Wilberforce University became the first school of higher learning owned and operated by African Americans. Bishop Daniel A. Payne (1811–1893) served as its first president.

1857   The U.S. Supreme Court issued its decision in the Dred Scott case, which denied citizenship to all African Americans whether they were free or not.

Austin Steward (1793–1860) published *Twenty-two Years a Slave and Forty Years a Freeman*.

1858   Arkansas enslaved free blacks who refused to leave the state.

1859   Martin L. Delaney published *Blake, or the Huts of America*.

Harriet E. Wilson (1825–1900) published *Our Nig, or Sketches from the Life of a Free Black*, which became the first novel to be published in the United States by an African American woman.

October 16 With twenty-one followers, John Brown (1800–1859) attacked the federal arsenal at Harpers Ferry, Virginia, in an attempt to acquire the arms to supply a slave revolt in the South.

1860   In the U.S. Census of 1860, the U.S. population was 31,443,321 and the African American population was 4,441,830, making up 14.1 percent of the overall population, which included 488,070 that were free African Americans.

November 6 Abraham Lincoln was elected president.

December 20 South Carolina seceded from the Union.

1861   Congress passed the First Confiscation Act to prevent Confederate slaveholders from re-enslaving runaways.

Harriet A. Jacobs (1813–1897) published *Incidents in the Life of a Slave Girl. Written by Herself*, an important slave narrative that vividly described slave society and culture in the antebellum era.

April 12 Confederate forces fired on Fort Sumter in the harbor at Charleston, South Carolina, and thus ignited the Civil War.

1861–1865 In the Civil War, approximately 200,000 African Americans (most former slaves) served in Union armed forces and more than 20,000 were killed in combat.

1862 Mary Jane Patterson (1840–1894) received a bachelor's degree from Oberlin College.

The U.S. Congress recognized Haiti and Liberia marking the first time diplomatic relations were established with these predominately black nations.

March The Port Royal (South Carolina) Reconstruction Experiment began.

April 16 Congress abolished slavery in the District of Columbia.

May Robert Smalls (1839–1915), an African American coastal pilot, escaped Charleston, South Carolina, in a captured Confederate vessel, *The Planter*, with sixteen slaves.

July 17 Congress permitted the enlistment of African American soldiers in the U.S. military.

1863 **January 1** Abraham Lincoln's Emancipation Proclamation, issued after the Battle of Antietam, took effect freeing all slaves living within the states associated with the Confederacy still in rebellion as of January 1, 1863. It did not include slaves in the Border States and Territories that did not join the Confederacy.

The Port Royal Commission created the first school for freed slaves in the South on St. Helena Island, South Carolina.

May 21–July 9 Eight African American infantry regiments fought in the Battle of Port Hudson, attacking bravely despite heavy losses under scathing Confederate fire.

July 13 At least 100 of New York City's residents were killed during draft riots that erupted and that continued for four days.

July 18 The first African American regular army regiment, the Fifty-fourth Massachusetts, assaulted Fort Wagner in Charleston, South Carolina, losing half its men, and for his efforts in this battle, Sergeant William H. Carney (1840–1908) became the first African American to receive the Congressional Medal of Honor for bravery under fire.

1864 **April 12** Confederates on orders from Nathan Bedford Forrest, a future Grand Imperial Wizard of the Ku Klux Klan, massacred African American Union troops in cold blood after taking the Union-held Fort Pillow in Tennessee.

June   The first African American woman to earn a medical degree, Dr. Rebecca Lee Crumpler (1831–1891), graduated from the New England Female Medical College in Boston.

June 15   Congress authorized equal pay, equipment, arms, and health care for African American Union troops.

October 4   The first daily newspaper produced by African Americans, *The New Orleans Tribune*, began publication.

1865   Atlanta University is founded in Georgia.

January 16   Union General William T. Sherman (1820–1891) issued a field order setting aside forty-acre plots of land in Georgia, South Carolina, and Florida for African Americans to settle.

February 1   Abraham Lincoln (1809–1865) signed the Thirteenth Amendment prohibiting slavery.

March 3   Congress created the Bureau of Refugees, Freedmen, and Abandoned Lands (Freedmen's Bureau) to provide health care, education, and technical assistance to former slaves.

Congress chartered the Freedman's Bank to develop savings and thrifty habits among the former slaves.

April 9   Robert E. Lee (1807–1870) surrendered to Ulysses S. Grant (1822–1885) at Appomattox Court House, Virginia, ending the Civil War.

April 14   John Wilkes Booth (1838–1865) shot President Lincoln in Washington, D.C.

April 15   President Abraham Lincoln died from a gunshot wound and Andrew Johnson (1808–1875) became president.

May 29   Presidential Reconstruction began.

June 19   In Texas, enslaved African Americans finally received news of their emancipation and later commemorate that day as "Juneteenth."

November 24   Mississippi limited the rights of African Americans by passing the first black code.

December   The states ratified the Thirteenth Amendment ending slavery in the United States.

Among the 32,000 U.S. soldiers sent to the Rio Grande as a show of force against Emperor Maximilian's French troops occupying Mexico and to enforce the Monroe Doctrine were 20,000 African American troops.

The Ku Klux Klan is formed in Tennessee in Pulaski, Tennessee.

1865–1866   Black codes and other types of discriminating legislation were passed by southern states.

1866   The Equal Rights Association was founded with Elizabeth Cady Stanton (1815–1902) as president, Frederick Douglass as vice president, and Susan B. Anthony (1820–1906) as secretary. This organization was created to promote the civil rights of women and African Americans.

Congress authorized the creation of four all-black regiments: two cavalry regiments, the Ninth and Tenth, and two infantry regiments, the Twenty-fourth and Twenty-fifth, in the U.S. Army. They were the only units in which black soldiers could serve until the Spanish American War.

January 9 Fisk University was founded in Nashville, Tennessee.

April 9 The 1866 Civil Rights Act granted certain rights to African Americans and implied citizenship for them.

May 1–3 During the Memphis Massacre, white civilians and police killed forty-six African Americans and injured many more, and burned ninety houses, twelve schools, and four churches in Memphis, Tennessee.

June 16 Congress passed the Fourteenth Amendment, which guaranteed citizenship for African Americans and granted them due process and equal protection under the law as citizens.

July 30 In their support of the Democratic mayor, the New Orleans police attacked a Republican meeting of blacks and whites, killing thirty-four black and three white Republicans.

1867   **January 8** Congress gave African American citizens the right to vote in the District of Columbia.

January 10 Congress passed the Territorial Suffrage Act, which allowed African Americans in the territories to vote.

February 14 Morehouse College was founded in Atlanta.

March 2 Congress overrode President Johnson's veto of the first Reconstruction Act, which divided the South into military zones and made ratification of the Fourteenth Amendment a requirement for readmitting a state into the Union. Congress reorganized postwar southern governments, disenfranchised former high-ranking Confederates and enfranchised former slaves in the South, and divided ten of the eleven ex-Confederate states into military districts.

Named after General Oliver O. Howard (1830–1909) who headed the Freedman's Bureau, Howard University, the predominantly black university, was founded in Washington, D.C.

1868   **February 22** Congress began impeachment proceedings against President Andrew Johnson.

March 16 Johnson's removal from office failed by one vote.

July 21 The Fourteenth Amendment to the Constitution was ratified and defined citizenship as any person born or naturalized in the United States. It overturned the 1857 Dred Scott Decision.

September 28 The Opelousas Massacre occurred in Louisiana with an estimated 200 to 300 African Americans killed by whites opposed to Reconstruction and African American voting.

November 3 Civil War general Ulysses S. Grant was elected president.

John Willis Menard (1838–1893), from Louisiana's Second Congressional District, became the first African American elected to Congress, but a disputed election resulted in neither he nor his opponent being seated in Congress.

November 9 Howard University Medical School opened.

1869   Howard University's law school becomes the country's first African American law school.

Frances E. W. Harper (1825–1911) published *Minnie's Sacrifice*.

Isaac Myers organized the Colored National Labor Union in Baltimore.

February 27 Congress proposed the Fifteenth Amendment making it unconstitutional to deny the right to vote to an individual on the basis of race, color, or previous condition of servitude.

April 6 Ebenezer Don Carlos Bassett became the first black American diplomat and presidential appointee when he was appointed minister to Haiti.

1870   In the U.S. Census of 1870, the U.S. population was 39,818,449 and the African American population was 4,880,009, which made up 12.7 percent of the overall population.

June The states ratified the Fifteenth Amendment to the Constitution.

The first African American, Richard T. Greener, graduated from Harvard University.

November Hiram R. Revels of Mississippi was elected as the first African American U.S. senator and Joseph H. Rainey (1832–1887) of South Carolina was elected the first African American member of the U.S. House of Representatives. Sixteen African Americans served in Congress and approximately 600 served in state legislatures during Reconstruction.

1871   **February** Congress passed the Civil Rights Act of 1871.

October 6 Fisk University's Jubilee Singers began their first national tour.

1872   Charlotte E. Ray (1850–1911) received a law degree from Howard University and became the first African American woman admitted to the bar in Washington, D.C.

November 4 Ulysses S. Grant was reelected president.

December Lieutenant Governor Pinckney Benton Stewart Pinchback (1837–1921) of Louisiana began serving as governor until January 1873. He was the first African American to hold that position.

1873   Colfax Massacre occurred in Colfax, Louisiana, in which approximately 300 African Americans were killed.

The Forty-third Congress had seven black members.

The first African American to preside over a predominately white university, Bishop Patrick Healy (1834–1910) became President of Georgetown University and served to 1881.

April 14 The Supreme Court restricted the scope of the Thirteenth and Fourteenth Amendments with its ruling in the *Slaughter-House Cases*.

1874   Costing African American depositors and investors more than $1 million, the Freedman's Bank failed and caused African Americans to not trust white-run institutions.

1875   The Forty-fourth Congress had eight black members.

January Sent to protect African Americans as they attempted to vote, federal troops were deployed to Vicksburg, Mississippi.

February 23 The first southern Jim Crow laws were enacted in Tennessee and resembled similar statutes that had existed in the North before the Civil War.

March 1 Congress passed a more expansive civil rights bill that guaranteed equal rights to black Americans in public accommodations and jury duty.

March 3 When he took his seat in the U.S. Senate, Blanche Kelso Bruce (1841–1898) of Mississippi became the first African American to serve a full six-year term as senator.

1876   Whites rioted and used other forms of terrorism against African American voters in South Carolina, and as a result, President Grant sent in federal troops to stop the violence.

May Edward Alexander Bouchet (1852–1918) became the first African American to receive a doctorate from an American university when he graduated from Yale University.

October 13 The Freedman's Aid Society of the Methodist Church founded Meharry Medical College.

November Featuring Samuel Tilden (1814–1886), a Democrat, against Rutherford B. Hayes (1822–1893), a Republican, the presidential election of 1876 resulted in a contested election over disputed voting in the Electoral College.

1877   **January** As part of the Compromise of 1877, Republicans promised to end Reconstruction if southern Democrats agreed to support the Republican candidate Rutherford Hayes's efforts to obtain the disputed electoral votes of Florida, Louisiana, and South Carolina despite the fact that Democratic presidential candidate Samuel Tilden won the popular vote. Ending

Reconstruction meant the U.S. government withdrew federal troops from the South and terminated federal efforts to protect African Americans and preserve their civil rights.

March 5   Rutherford B. Hayes was inaugurated.

April 24   Reconstruction officially ended in the South.

The Forty-fifth Congress had three black members.

June 15   Henry O. Flipper (1856–1940) became the first African American to graduate from West Point.

July 30   African American settlers from Kentucky established the town of Nicodemus in western Kansas, the first of hundreds of all or mostly African American towns founded during this period in the West.

Frederick Douglass was appointed U.S. Marshal for the District of Columbia.

1878   When she presented a musical program to President Rutherford B. Hayes and his guests, Marie Selika Williams (1849–1937) became the first African American entertainer to perform at the White House.

1879   The African American exodus to Kansas occurred as approximately 6,000 African Americans left Louisiana and Mississippi and followed a former slave, Benjamin "Pap" Singleton (1809–1892) in the "Exodus of '79."

Mary Eliza Mahoney (1845–1926) graduated from the New England Hospital for Women and Children in Boston and became the first African American professional nurse.

1880   The Foreign Mission Baptist Convention (an African American Baptist organization) of the United States was founded in 1880.

Joel Chandler Harris (1848–1908) first published *Uncle Remus: His Songs and Sayings*.

In the U.S. Census of 1880, the U.S. population was 50,155,783 and the African American population was 6,580,793, which made up 13.1 percent of the overall population.

May 14   Commanding a detachment of African American soldiers, Sergeant George Jordan (1847–1904) of the Ninth Cavalry, successfully defended Tularosa, New Mexico Territory, against an attack by Apache Indians.

1881   Josiah Henson (1789–1883) published *An Autobiography of The Reverend Josiah Henson ("Uncle Tom")*.

January   The Tennessee State Legislature segregated railroad passenger cars, and the rest of the South imitated Tennessee in the following order: Florida (1887), Mississippi (1888), Texas (1889), Louisiana (1890), Alabama, Kentucky, Arkansas, and Georgia (1891), South Carolina (1898), North Carolina (1899), Virginia (1900), Maryland (1904), and Oklahoma (1907).

April 11   Sophia B. Packard (1824–1891) and Harriet E. Giles founded the Atlanta Baptist Female Seminary (later Spelman College), the first college for just black women in the United States.

July 4   Booker T. Washington (1856–1915) founded Tuskegee Normal and Industrial Institute in Alabama. The institute stressed the practical application of knowledge.

1882   George Washington Williams (1849–1891), an African American historian, published the first comprehensive history of African Americans, *History of the Negro Race in America from 1619 to 1880*.

1883   **October 15**   The Supreme Court ruled in the *Civil Rights Cases* that the 1875 Civil Rights Act was unconstitutional because the U.S. government could not bar corporations or individuals from discriminating on the basis of race.

November 3   White conservatives in Danville, Virginia, killed four African Americans in an attempt to seize control of the local, racially integrated, and popularly elected government.

1884   Ida B. Wells (1862–1931) won her discrimination suit against the Chesapeake, Ohio, and Southwestern Railroad, but the case was later overturned by the Tennessee Supreme Court. Wells published her first article in *Living Way* about the lawsuit.

1885   **June 25**   The Episcopal Church ordained African American Samuel David Ferguson (1842–1916) as a bishop.

1886   The Knights of Labor reached its peak membership of 700,000, which included about 75,000 African American members.

An African American organization, the American National Baptist Convention, was founded.

December 8   The American Federation of Labor organized, and excluded African American workers from joining.

1887   Major league baseball banned African American players with a "gentlemen's agreement" between the owners.

In Houston County, Texas, The National Colored Farmers' Alliance formed.

1888   The Savings Bank of the Grand Fountain United Order of the Reformers, in Richmond, Virginia, and Capital Savings Bank of Washington, D.C., two of the earliest African American–owned banks, opened.

April 11   Edward Park Duplex was elected mayor of Wheatland, California, and became the first African American mayor of a predominantly white town in the United States.

1889   Florida became the first state to use the poll tax to disenfranchise African American voters.

Frederick Douglass was appointed Minister to Haiti.

Henry O. Flipper (1856–1940) published *The Colored Cadet at West Point*.

1890   Louisiana passed a Jim Crow law that made equal but separate accommodations on first-class railroad cars legal.

The National Woman Suffrage Association and the American Woman Suffrage Association united to form the National American Woman Suffrage Association.

Mississippi passed a high poll tax to keep African Americans from voting.

Mrs. A. E. Johnson published *Clarence and Corinne; or, God's Way*.

In the U.S. Census of 1890, the U.S. population was 62,947,714 and the African American population was 7,488,676, which made up 11.9 percent of the overall population.

January 25   Timothy Thomas Fortune (1856–1928) founded the National Afro-American League in Chicago, the forerunner of the National Association for the Advancement of Colored People (NAACP).

November 1   The new Mississippi Constitution disenfranchised African American voters.

1891   Ida B. Wells wrote an editorial criticizing the all-white Memphis Board of Education and loses her teaching position as a result. She then became a full-time journalist.

Dr. Daniel Hale Williams (1856–1931) founded the first African American-owned hospital, Provident Hospital in Chicago.

September 1   African Americans in New Orleans organized to make a judicial challenge to the state's separate railroad car law.

1892   Ida B. Wells published *Southern Horrors: Lynch Law in All Its Phases*. This book launched Wells' crusade to investigate the lynchings of African Americans.

Anna Julia Cooper (1858–1964) published an essay collection entitled *A Voice from the South*, which appealed for the civil rights of African American women.

This year became the first peak in mob violence and lynching against African Americans. A record 230 people were lynched in the United States—161 were black and 69 white. A second peak was reached in 1919, and a third peak occurred in 1930.

African American physicians formed the National Medical Association in Atlanta because they were barred from the American Medical Association.

February 24   In Louisiana, Daniel F. Desdunes was arrested for riding in a white railroad car on an interstate trip.

May 21   Ida B. Wells published her editorial entitled "Eight Men Lynched" in *Free Speech*. Threats on her life forced her to leave the South, and she became a reporter for the *New York Age*.

June 7 In Louisiana, Homer Plessy was arrested for riding in a white car on an interstate trip.

June 15 Operatic soprano Sissieretta Jones became the first African American to perform at Carnegie Hall.

July 9 Justice John Howard Ferguson of Louisiana declared that states' separate railroad car law constitutional on interstate travel in the Desdunes case.

October 5 Ida B. Wells began her public speaking career in front of 250 African American women in New York City.

November 18 Justice Ferguson upheld charges against Plessy.

1893 The Louisiana Supreme Court upheld the Ferguson decision in *Ex Parte Plessy*.

Ida B. Wells first toured Great Britain.

Frederick Douglass, Ferdinand L. Barnett (1864–1932), I. Garland Penn (1867–1930), and Ida B. Wells published a pamphlet entitled *The Reason Why the Colored American is Not in the World's Columbian Exposition*.

African American physician Daniel Hale Williams (1856–1931) performed the world's first successful open-heart surgery with the patient surviving and living another twenty years.

Henry Ossawa Tanner (1859–1837) paints "The Banjo Lesson," which is eventually hailed as one of the major works of art of the late 19th century.

An African American organization, the Baptist National Educational Convention, was founded.

1894 Ida B. Wells made her second tour of Great Britain. The *Inter Ocean* in Chicago published articles written by Wells on this trip called "Ida B. Wells Abroad."

Mrs. A. E. Johnson published *The Hazeley Family*.

1895 Ida B. Wells published her second pamphlet, *A Red Record*.

At Friendship Baptist Church in Atlanta, the Foreign Mission Baptist Convention of the United States, the American National Baptist Convention, and the Baptist National Educational Convention combined to form the National Baptist Convention of America, Inc., resulting in the largest black religious denomination in the United States.

South Carolina disenfranchised African American voters.

February 20 Frederick Douglass died.

March 11–12 White terrorists attacked African American workers in New Orleans, killing six.

June W. E. B. Du Bois (1868–1963) became the first African American to receive a doctorate from Harvard University.

September 18 Booker T. Washington gave his controversial "Atlanta Compromise" speech at the Cotton Exposition in Georgia in which he stated that

African Americans should focus on economic advancement rather than pursue civil rights to gain the trust of whites through accommodation.

1896   W. E. B. Du Bois published *The Suppression of the African Slave Trade.*

Paul Laurence Dunbar (1872–1906) published *Lyrics of Lowly Life.*

The National Association of Colored Women (NACW) was founded with Mary Church Terrell (1863–1954) as its first president.

May 18 The Supreme Court in *Plessy v. Ferguson* found racial segregation or Louisiana's equal-but-separate law for public facilities constitutional.

September World-famous agricultural researcher George Washington Carver (1864–1943) accepted an appointment at the Tuskegee Institute. His research in farming techniques helped to revolutionize farming in America especially peanut, sweet potato, and soybean farming.

1897   The first Phillis Wheatley Home was founded in Detroit. Established in most cities with large African American populations, these shelters provided temporary accommodations and social services for single African American women.

March 5 In Washington, D.C., the American Negro Academy was established to encourage African American participation in art, literature, and philosophy.

1898   The North Carolina Mutual and Provident Insurance Company of Durham, North Carolina, and the National Benefit Life Insurance Company of Washington, D.C., were created.

Robert "Bob" Cole (1868–1911) produced "A Trip to Coontown," the first full-length musical written, directed, performed, and produced by African Americans, on Broadway.

Louisiana disenfranchised African American voters with a "grandfather clause."

April 21 The Spanish-American War began and sixteen regiments of black volunteers were recruited with five African Americans winning Congressional Medals of Honor during the conflict and black officers commanding troops for the first time.

September 15 In Washington, D.C., the National Afro-American Council was founded, and it elected Bishop Alexander Walters as its first president.

November 10 As conservative Democrats drove from power African American and white Republican officeholders in the city, eight black Americans were killed during white rioting in Wilmington, North Carolina.

1899   Charles W. Chesnutt (1858–1932) published *The Conjure Woman and Other Tales.*

Scott Joplin (ca. 1867–1917), a pianist and composer, published "The Maple Leaf Rag," a major hit that popularized ragtime music.

The Afro-American Council designated June 4 as a national day of fasting to protest lynching and massacres.

1900 A significant West Indian (primarily of African descent) immigration to the United States began this year.

North Carolina disenfranchised African Americans.

Ida B. Wells published her third pamphlet, *Mob Rule in New Orleans*.

In the U.S. Census of 1900, the U.S. population was 75,994,575 and the African American population 8,833,994, which made up 11.6 percent of the overall population.

January James Weldon Johnson (1871–1938) wrote the lyrics and his brother John Rosamond Johnson (1873–1954) composed the music for *Lift Every Voice and Sing*, which was eventually adopted as the black national anthem, to celebrate the birthday of Abraham Lincoln.

April 14–November 10 The U.S. Pavilion at the Paris Exposition housed an exhibition on black Americans called the "Exposition des Negres d'Amerique."

July Organized by Trinidad attorney Henry Sylvester Williams, the first Pan African Conference met in London.

July 23 Also known as the Robert Charles Riot, the New Orleans Race Riot erupted and lasted four days, killing twelve African Americans and seven whites.

August 23 In Boston, Booker T. Washington founded the National Negro Business League to promote business enterprise.

September At its meeting in Richmond, Virginia, Nannie Helen Burroughs helped established the Women's Convention of the National Baptist Convention.

1901 Booker T. Washington published *Up From Slavery*.

Alabama and Virginia disenfranchised African Americans.

1902 Gertrude Bustill Mossell (1855–1948) published the collection of essays entitled *Afro-American Women and Work*.

1903 W. E. B. Du Bois published *The Souls of Black Folk*.

Sarah Breedlove MacWilliams (1865–1919) started an African American hair-care business in Denver and eventually became America's first self-made female millionaire.

Robert S. Abbott began publishing *The Chicago Defender*, Chicago's first African American newspaper.

1905 W. E. B. Du Bois founded the Niagara movement, a forerunner to the NAACP. The movement was formed in part as a protest to Booker T. Washington's policy of accommodation to white society with the Niagara movement calling for immediate equality in all areas of American life for African Americans.

Georgia disenfranchised African Americans.

1909   The NAACP was founded as an interracial organization dedicated to social and legal reform.

Black explorer Matthew Henson reached the North Pole along with Admiral Robert Perry. They are the first men known to have reached the North Pole.

Oklahoma disenfranchised African Americans.

1910–1920   The Great Migration of southern African Americans to northern industrial towns began.

The National Urban League was founded to help African Americans who had migrated to the cities find jobs and housing.

1912   James Weldon Johnson (1871–1938) published *The Autobiography of an Ex-Colored Man*.

The so-called Father of the Blues, W. C. Handy (1873–1958) published his hit song "Memphis Blues."

1914   Marcus Garvey (1887–1940) founded the Universal Negro Improvement Association, an influential African American nationalist organization dedicated to promoting pride and worldwide unity in the African race.

White resentment of African Americans working in wartime industry in East St. Louis, Illinois, resulted in race riots. Forty African Americans and eight whites were killed.

In New York City, thousands of African Americans participated in a march organized by the NAACP to protest racial violence and discrimination.

1919   Sparked by white resentment of African Americans working in industry and their large-scale migration from South to North, scores of race riots across the country left at least 100 people dead during the so-called Red Summer.

A pioneering director-producer of "race movies," Oscar Micheaux (1885–1951) produced his first film, *The Homesteader*, based on his novel.

1920   Mamie Smith (1883–1946) recorded the first blues record, "Crazy Blues," on the Okeh label.

The Harlem Renaissance flourished and fostered a new black cultural identity in the 1920s and 1930s.

Africans and African Americans to the 1820s | 1

Dixie Ray Haggard

From their first arrival in America, Africans and African Americans played a key role in the building and development of the United States. Specifically, slave and free Africans and African Americans provided the labor that drove the early American economy. Slaves lived and worked in all thirteen of the British North American colonies. They also labored in French Louisiana. They worked growing and harvesting indigo, rice, Sea Island cotton, and tobacco. Slaves also served as servants in large and small homes and worked as craftsmen and provided basic manual labor in urban areas. Everything that whites did to build the colonies, slaves could be found doing the same thing.

Furthermore, African social and cultural influences provided key elements in the distinctive and unique society and culture that evolved during the 18th and 19th centuries in North America. The first Africans to arrive in America probably ended up as indentured servants rather than slaves, but as the 16th century progressed, the American colonies developed African chattel slavery as a replacement for indentured servitude.

African chattel slavery and the racism that accompanied it provided the framework for African and African American social and cultural development in the 18th and early 19th centuries for both the free and the enslaved. Although this framework existed throughout America during this time period, the nature and structure of African and African American society differed from time period to time period and place to place.

In the colonial period, the social structure and the culture produced by slave communities were influenced heavily by the African ethnicities that lived within them and by the time when these ethnicities arrived. Basically, different ethnicities from varying parts of Africa arrived in different combinations to different places at different times. This set of circumstances combined with the alternate ways whites in various regions of North

TO BE SOLD on board the Ship *Bance-Island*, on tuesday the 6th of *May* next, at *Ashley-Ferry*; a choice cargo of about 250 fine healthy

NEGROES,

just arrived from the Windward & Rice Coaft. —The utmost care has already been taken, and shall be continued, to keep them free from the leaft danger of being infected with the SMALL-POX, no boat having been on board, and all other communication with people from *Charles-Town* prevented.

Aufin, Laurens, & Appleby.

N. B. Full one Half of the above Negroes have had the SMALL-POX in their own Country.

A notice from the 1780s advertising slaves for sale. Slavery in America began in the early 17th century and ended with the adoption of the Thirteenth Amendment in 1865. (Library of Congress)

America used slaves, with the total number Africans brought to each region, and with the ratio of blacks to whites to create different social settings for Africans and African Americans. The resulting patchwork quilt of African and African American societies worked against Africans and African Americans developing any concept of racial unity during the colonial period. However, the Revolutionary era with its accompanying rhetoric of freedom and liberty caused black societies to reorganize at the end of the 18th and beginning of the 19th centuries. By the 1820s, the U.S. ban on the importation of slaves in 1808 caused slave communities to gradually become more African American by birth than African. These simultaneous trends resulted in the development of a nascent, racial consciousness throughout black America. Alternately, the rise of economically successful, black elites developed during the period from the Revolutionary era to the 1820s to form classism that hindered and restrained the growth of an African American racial consciousness.

The different regions in which slaves initially were introduced during the colonial period included the North, which consisted of New England and the Mid-Atlantic colonies, the Chesapeake Bay colonies, the Low Country of Georgia and South Carolina, and French Louisiana. New England consisted of Connecticut, New Hampshire, Massachusetts, and Rhode Island. The Mid-Atlantic colonies contained New Jersey, New York, and Pennsylvania. French Louisiana covered territory that today is located in western Alabama, Arkansas, western Florida, Louisiana, Mississippi, western Tennessee, and eastern Texas. Over time, North Carolina (originally settled as one colony with South Carolina) became associated economically with the Chesapeake Bay colonies. The same was true of Delaware, which originally was part of the Mid-Atlantic colonies. The term Upper South is applied when referring to the combination of the Chesapeake Bay colonies, Delaware and North Carolina.

African Ethnicity in North America

A majority of the Africans brought to North America came primarily from the three regions on the West Coast of Africa known as the Bight of Biafra (located on the middle West Coast below the Bight of Benin), the Gold Coast (primarily encompassed by modern Ghana below Sierra Leone), and Senegambia (located on the upper West Coast) and from the interior of West Central Africa. Smaller numbers came from Sierra Leone (located below Senegambia on the West Coast) and the Bight of Benin (located below Senegambia and above the Bight of Biafra on the West Coast). More specifically, the Akan (Gold Coast), Angolans (interior West Central Africa), Igbo (from the Bight of Biafra), Senegambians, and Congolese (interior West Central Africa) made up the predominant ethnicities enslaved in British North America. In the Chesapeake, the Igbo outnumbered all other ethnicities, with the Akans having significant numbers there as well. Senegambians and others from West Central Africa and Sierra Leonians filled out the enslaved population in the Chesapeake. The Low Country of Georgia and South Carolina reversed the specific ethnicity trends of the Chesapeake slave population. Whereas the Chesapeake had more Biafrians, the Low Country had more people from interior West Central Africa. The dominant ethnicities in the Low Country, in descending order of total numbers, were as follows: (1) Congolese, (2) Angolans, (3) Senegambians, and (4) Akans. In the later part of the 18th century, planters from the Low Country brought in substantial numbers of Sierra Leonians that had a significant impact on the development of the slave society at the beginning of the 19th century. Senegambians and a mix of the closely related Fon, Ewe, and Yoruba (Bight of Benin) dominated the Louisiana slave society of the early and mid-18th century while it was under French control. During the late 18th century, after the Spanish gained control of Louisiana, the Congolese, the Angolans, and other West Central Africans arrived in even greater numbers to not only provide additional African diversity to black society but also stifle trends toward a common black racial identity. By the early 19th century, a majority of Africans in Louisiana were Congolese/Angolan. Specifically, 35.8 percent of the slaves brought to Louisiana between 1720 and 1820 were from West Central Africa. Most of the slaves who went into the northern colonies were creoles (that is, they were born into slavery somewhere else in the Americas or were taken from Africa to somewhere else in the Americas to be "seasoned"). Being "seasoned" meant that the slaves were made to accept their enslavement, taught English, and possibly taught a new skill. After being "seasoned" by their initial owners, usually somewhere in the Caribbean, these creoles were sold down the line to the northern colonies of British North America.

The Colonial North

Although the first Africans arrived in Virginia in 1619, official slavery in British North America began in Massachusetts. In 1641, the colony of

Massachusetts passed its first slave law allowing the enslavement of lawful captives and those sold to the colony as slaves, but banning the enslavement of any free people already in the colony. Thus, this law allowed African slaves to be brought to Massachusetts and sold, but, slavery never became popular in Massachusetts or the rest of New England, and thus few Africans ended up in the North. New England merchants eventually participated heavily in the international slave trade, and many a New England fortune was made in doing so.

In the Mid-Atlantic, New York acquired a significant number of slaves to primarily work in the harbor while it was still a Dutch colony. New Jersey, which began as a Swedish colony before it was seized by the Dutch, had some slaves from its beginning as a colony, and this continued after it became an English colony. Quickly after its founding, Pennsylvania allowed slaves to be brought in to supplement its indentured workforce, but slaves never became a major component of that workforce.

In the North, creole slaves tended to work in small numbers and primarily in households as servants or as extra hands for the family farm or business. Sometimes, owners hired out their slaves into skilled trades such as carpentry, printing, smithing, and tailoring. They also might be rented out to work in the maritime industry. Slaves in the North usually did not have their own quarters and typically lived in the slaveholders' homes. This fact limited their ability to make their own families. Because most slaves in the North were creoles when they came and had little opportunities to form large social networks with other blacks, they quickly lost their African identity and tended to become more like their white colonial counterparts in their social and cultural orientations. In the 19th century, the descendants of these slaves became many of the free, black elite that led the struggle for abolition of slavery in the South and social inclusion for all blacks in the United States.

The Chesapeake

In contrast to Massachusetts, slavery in Virginia began piecemeal. Although Africans to Virginia did not come there willingly in the first half of the 1600s, they did not immediately become slaves. Most, if not all, became indentured servants like most of the whites coming in from England, and they had the potential to gain their freedom. Some Africans eventually owned their own plantations and had their own indentured servants. Their status was still less than that of whites, however. The Virginia courts and legislature gradually diminished this status further until slavery and African heritage became synonymous by 1662.

As the 17th century progressed, elite Virginians developed a racialized form of slavery because of the failure of indentured servitude to provide the needed labor required by the growing of tobacco, and because the increasing number of freed indentured servants became a threat to the social and economic order of the colony as land for freed servants became more limited and social mobility became more circumscribed. The elite

Scene on an American tobacco plantation, 1725. (JupiterImages)

wanted to limit relationships between Africans and white indentured servants as they formalized the colony's slave system to prevent the two
groups (which had much in common) from uniting and overthrowing the
established order. As a result, elite Virginians passed laws against intermarriage and intermingling between whites and black slaves at the same time
they promoted white solidarity through the degradation of blacks. Maryland followed Virginia's lead and developed its own racialized chattel slave
system in the late 17th and early 18th centuries.

As the slave system in the Chesapeake stabilized in the 18th century,
the growing, harvesting, and curing of tobacco dominated the lives of the
enslaved. Slaveholders employed a system of gang labor in which groups
of slaves were supervised closely by overseers to ensure the correct growing and handling of the expensive and delicate cash crop of tobacco. This
system gave the slaves little time to themselves during the peak planting
and harvesting seasons for tobacco. In the little spare time that they had,
they grew small gardens, raised chickens, trapped small game, and fished.

In the Chesapeake, slaves started families and took care of their elderly
among the slave quarters, but most were not content to settle for a limited
social network on their solitary plantations. Most traveled by night to visit
friends and families on other plantations despite white restrictions against
doing so. Many married spouses from other plantations, which created an
interlocking kinship network in the Chesapeake that worked to reinforce
African ethnic identities (of which 40 percent were Igbo), especially in the

colonial period, and later to promote an African American consciousness during the Revolutionary era. The Chesapeake landscape facilitated the creation of these kinship networks because the plantations were a maze of fields with varying shapes and sizes bordered by forests that provided cover for the nighttime journeys of slaves between the plantations. These networks would be broken up in the early 19th century, however, as plantation owners from the Upper South began to sell their slaves to other southern states because of the changing economy in the Upper South and the rising cost of slaves.

The Georgia and South Carolina Low Country

Colonists from Barbados and other English colonies in the Caribbean settled South Carolina in 1670, and they brought with them the plantation economy they had developed in the West Indies. The plantations these early colonist established grew primarily rice and indigo. In 1732, Georgia was founded as a military buffer for South Carolina against the Spanish in Florida and the French in Louisiana. Although slavery was originally banned in Georgia, that ban was lifted by 1751, and Georgia's economy quickly imitated that of South Carolina. Georgia raised rice, indigo, and Sea Island cotton on large plantations primarily located on the barrier islands off the coast. Georgia and South Carolina planters preferred to import African slaves from West Central Africa. Therefore, Congolese and Angolans made up the largest ethnicities (40 percent combined) among the slaves found on colonial Low Country plantations. Low Country planters preferred these West Central Africans because many grew rice in their homeland.

The growing of rice required little direct supervision of slaves by whites because of the nature of its growth cycle and its durability. Therefore, the Low Country implemented the task labor system for its slaves. Slaves were given a daily task to accomplish that guaranteed the successful planting, tending, or harvesting of the rice crop depending on the season. When the slaves accomplished these tasks, the rest of the day was theirs to do with as they wished. This gave the slaves time to raise their own gardens and farm animals, hunt, and fish. It also allowed them to build, repair, and improve their living quarters, and they could better take care of their families' needs and socialize. In some cases, slaves were able to create food and craft surpluses that they could barter or sell in local markets.

Because Low Country plantations tended to be quite large, planters seldom had the need to sell their slaves, and this tended to preserve slave families. As a result, generations of families lived and died on the same plantations. Thus, slave society remained fairly stable in the Low Country. Low Country slave society, therefore, preserved more African elements than anywhere else in North America. During the colonial period, West Central African predominance in the Low Country coupled with the stability of slave society on the plantations actually provided a common racial identity built on ethnicity as opposed to other areas where ethnic diversity prevented this development.

Louisiana

From its inception in the late 17th century until the Spanish took control in 1769, French Louisiana imported 18,928 slaves. The Spanish continued importing slaves until they turned the colony back over to French rule in 1800. After the United States bought Louisiana in 1803, African slave importation continued until the ban on importation began in 1808.

After the Spanish took over Louisiana, large numbers of Americans began to move into Louisiana at an ever-increasing pace that continued until the United States gained control, which caused an even greater increase in the flow of Americans and their slaves into the region. Many of the slaves brought in by Americans were from different African ethnicities, or were descended from different African ethnicities, than those already in Louisiana. Those slaves imported into Louisiana from Africa during the Spanish period tended to be different ethnicities from those brought in by Americans and those imported during the initial French colonial period. These differences in ethnicity prevented the development of an African American racial consciousness until the 1820s. Furthermore, a number of small, Maroon communities of runaway slaves sustained themselves in the many swamps and bayous of Louisiana during the French colonial period, which also limited the growth of an African American identity.

The French intended to establish a plantation economy in colonial Louisiana, which used slaves to produce tobacco. Yet despite their hopes, the French neither had enough colonists move to Louisiana nor did the government provide enough funds to sustain anything more than a basic frontier exchange economy that tied Native Americans, whites, and blacks together for their mutual benefit. The stunted nature of Louisiana's economy affected Africans and African Americans significantly.

Blacks contributed to this frontier exchange economy first through their labor in the limited plantation economy that existed during the French era and second through a wide range of jobs and enterprises that sustained the exchange economy in an ancillary fashion. They worked as boatmen, hunters, peddlers, and soldiers. Blacks hunted, fished, gardened, and raised small farm animals to exchange with whites in formal and informal markets found in New Orleans and other towns of Louisiana. African Americans also worked in the deerskin trade as freemen, runaways, and slaves. The deerskin trade was vital to French Louisiana, because it kept most regional, Native American tribes allied to the French and enemies with the British, and, with few exceptions, the deerskin trade and its resulting alliance system prevented Native wars against the French in Louisiana.

After the French turned control of colonial Louisiana over to the Spanish, the frontier exchange system that dominated the early colonial economy shifted toward rapid commercialization of the deerskin trade and a full-scale plantation economy. Cotton, sugar, and indigo crops joined tobacco and deerskins as the primary exports from Louisiana. The African American population became more diverse with the influx of Americans and their slaves and with the increased importation of slaves from Africa. The plantation economy began to limit black interactions with whites. Whites restricted black gardening, hunting, and marketing activities and passed slave codes to restrict the movement of slaves off of plantations. The increased white presence and slave codes brought an end to free Maroon communities and forced blacks to restrict their social interactions to plantation communities. Thus, African ethnic identity was initially reinforced at the expense of common black identity and an American identity.

Because of the dominance of the Fon, the Ewe, and the Yoruba influence in French colonial Louisiana and their significant presence in the port city of New Orleans, the voodoo religious system spread widely among free and enslaved blacks throughout the region. The voodoo belief system created a unique identity and social consciousness for blacks in Louisiana that lasts into the 21st century, and in the colonial period, it reinforced the African identity of Louisiana's black inhabitants. The voodoo religious system diminished during the 19th century as Louisiana became part of the United States and numerous other belief systems were introduced to the region. By the end of the 19th century, voodoo became associated more with magic than religion.

The American Revolution

The American Revolution brought the unfulfilled promise of freedom for most African and African American slaves as white Americans claimed for themselves God-given rights they continued to deny both free and enslaved blacks. The American Revolution did change the lives of many Africans and African Americans, however, by changing the nature and form of black society and culture. Specifically between the years of 1770 and 1810, many slaves received their freedom, especially in the North where state after state gradually began banning slavery after the American War for Independence. This period saw an increase in American-born blacks and fewer arrivals of slaves from Africa to the United States, because of the abolition of slavery in the North and the banning of the slave importation into the United States in 1808. This increase in American-born blacks led to the localized development of an African American society and culture that was more uniquely American and less African in nature. By the 1820s, the African American population finally eclipsed the population of those born in Africa. In the years during and immediately after the American Revolution, whites demonstrated more tolerance of blacks, free and enslaved, than they did before the American War for Independence. Ultimately, the Revolutionary era created African American institutions and social patterns that influenced African American life throughout the

19th century. Older regional differences expanded as blacks, free and enslaved, in the North, the Upper South, the Low Country, and Louisiana developed new relationships with whites influenced by the size and nature of black populations in those regions.

Although a small number of free blacks existed in the colonies before the American Revolution, most whites did not want their numbers to increase. As the War for Independence dragged on, many Loyalists and Patriots recognized the need to enlist blacks into their respective armies. To entice slaves to fight, both the British and the Patriots promised freedom to those slaves who served. Large plantation owners in the South resisted the enlistment of slaves into Patriot forces. In the Upper South, Maryland permitted the limited enlistment of slaves and began to conscript free blacks, and North Carolina and Delaware allowed free blacks to serve in Patriot forces. Virginia allowed some slaves to enlist. In Georgia and South Carolina, where the large number of slaves caused southerners there to fear slave rebellion, slaves were absolutely forbidden from joining the military. With smaller slave and free black populations, northern states had less fear from slave rebellion, and as a result, they more readily embraced the enlistment of blacks. Rhode Island went so far as to recruit a black regiment.

At the end of the war, the British took thousands of slaves to Canada, Great Britain, the West Indies, and even Africa where they gained their freedom. Thousands of other slaves freed by the British remained in

Engraving depicting the shooting of British Major John Pitcairn by an African American soldier, Peter Salem, at the Battle of Lexington during the Revolutionary War. (Bettmann/Corbis)

America and maintained their freedom after the war by moving to areas far from their place of enslavement. Additionally, Patriots freed thousands for their service in the military, and owners or state legislatures freed many others. Furthermore, many slaves ran away during the chaos of the war, with most disappearing into free black populations and maintaining their independence after the war.

Because of the rhetoric of freedom and liberty espoused by the American Revolution, northern states began to see the need to abolish slavery. The New England states led the way by being the first to free their limited number of slaves. The Mid-Atlantic states followed suit as soon as it became apparent that the flood of immigrants into the region after the war easily replaced the loss of slaves as a source of cheap labor.

The Upper South continued to manumit many of its slaves after the Revolutionary era because of changes in the economy and the persistence of evangelical Christianity, but these elements did not bring about full abolition. A shift from dependence on labor-intensive tobacco toward a more diverse agricultural economy that included cereals began to limit the need for slave labor in the region. The growth of larger cities and towns in the Upper South such as Baltimore and Richmond accelerated changes in the economy of the Upper South as these urban economies became more dependent on flexible wage labor rather than expensive slave labor. Many of the freed slaves in the Upper South migrated to these expanding cities and towns because of the increased number of economic opportunities, and as a result, these growing urban areas provided havens for runaways that could disappear among the growing number of freed blacks. Finally, the continued influence of the Great Awakening supported revolutionary rhetoric by promoting equality of all men before the eyes of God. This led to a small antislavery movement in the Upper South that further stimulated manumission.

Despite all these changes, slavery persisted in the Upper South. It also flourished and expanded in the Deep South because of the invention of the cotton gin in 1793, which sped up the ability to produce upland cotton. Because upland cotton could be grown throughout the South, but especially in the Deep South, slavery became extremely profitable. This fact coupled with the beginning of the ban on importing slaves in 1808 drove up prices on slaves. This, in turn, brought resurgence to the institution of slavery in the Upper South as slaveholders found an economic niche by providing slaves for the Deep South. The selling of more and more slaves from the Upper South to the Deep South broke up more and more families and scattered relatives throughout the region. This impacted not only the slave communities but also the free black communities in the Upper South because most of these free blacks still had family members that were enslaved.

Because of Revolutionary ideology, some whites began to develop new concepts of race relations, and this led to a brief period during and immediately after the Revolutionary era in which the barriers created to keep free blacks in their place were partially eroded. These erosions included new laws to prevent the kidnapping and enslavement of free blacks and

Olaudah Equiano (1745–1797)

A manumitted slave, Olaudah Equiano's autobiography encouraged the British government to make the international slave trade illegal in 1807. According to his autobiography, Equiano was born in Nigeria into an important family, but he was kidnapped at an early age and sold as a domestic slave to an African village in a nearby region. From there, Equiano was sold to Europeans. Some scholars question whether or not Equiano actually was captured in Africa or was born into slavery in the Americas. Regardless of whether or not this aspect of his autobiography is true, Equiano was able to capture the horror and brutality of the slave trade, the Middle Passage, and the slave institution in his narrative in vivid detail.

According to his autobiography, Equiano was not bought by planters in the West Indies because he was too small to work on the sugar plantations. Therefore, Equiano was eventually sold in Virginia. During his lifetime, he was sold many times over from one slaveholder to another. His initial holder in Virginia was Michael Pascal, a lieutenant in the British Navy. Equiano received naval training while held by Pascal, and at one point, Pascal sent him away to school to receive an education. Eventually, Robert King, a Quaker merchant from Philadelphia, bought Equiano and had him trained as a gauger of weights and measures. Equiano used this position as a way to acquire money, and he bought his freedom in 1766. Shortly afterward, he returned to England. While in England, Equiano became a fixture in the abolition movement that was growing rapidly there. After several adventures in the Arctic and the Caribbean, Equiano set out to write an account of his life. *The Interesting Narrative of the Life of Olaudah Equiano, or Gustavus Vass, the African* was first published in1789. Because Equaino traveled so much as a slave in North America and the Caribbean, his narrative demonstrated that the vicious nature of slavery that began with the capture of slaves in Africa and continued under horrible Middle Passage to the Americas permeated all of the British holdings in America. Because of the vivid detail Equiano provided, his narrative contributed greatly to the abolition campaign in Great Britain, which eventually outlawed slavery in the British Empire in 1807, and helped lay the foundation for a nascent abolition movement in the United States in the early 19th century.

the easing of some manumission codes as well as decreased hostility by whites toward blacks especially in the North. Because of this, a reorientation of black communities allowed some to prosper economically, and an elite class emerged in black communities that soon began to lead these communities. These elites led the charge in demanding an end to slavery and greater liberties for blacks who already had their freedom. In response to the easing of some restrictions on their lives in some places, free blacks led by these new elites began to advance economically, become better educated, and even challenge continued restrictions on their freedom in the North and the continuation of slavery in the South.

Yet despite the progress made toward egalitarianism caused by the rhetoric of the American Revolution, most whites continued to support restrictions on the free black population of the North and stricter slave codes in the South as well as tighter control of free blacks in that region. The restrictions on free blacks eventually began to increase, especially after 1800, as the number of free blacks began to grow. This led to limitations on free black mobility, restraints on business opportunities, and denial of any political rights in the North and the South.

Free blacks began to resist white obstructions to their freedom in one of two ways. Some abandoned relationships and any connections with slaves. These actions included the cessation of demands calling for the abolition of slavery. Although not totally limited to the region, this adjustment was prominent in the Deep South where the smaller number of free blacks were at greater risk for white retaliation. Over time, some of the economically successful elites in the North also employed this approach as they sought inclusion for themselves in American society.

Other blacks in the North and the Upper South responded by strengthening their communities, free and enslaved, from the inside. They created organizations and places where they could educate their children, entertain themselves, protect themselves, and worship freely away from the influence and hindrance of white society. Free blacks established African churches, fraternal societies, and schools that led to the creation of a new African American society and culture that united the black community in the face of white oppression. This process advanced rapidly in the North because of the region's greater ethnic homogeneity. In the Upper South, it gained momentum as fewer and fewer Africans were brought in from overseas, especially after 1808.

African American communities created these institutions more rapidly toward the end of the 18th century and at the beginning of the 19th, but as time went by, opposition to the formation of African American churches and schools in the Upper South came under increasing attack by white southerners as fear of slave insurrections increased during the second and third decades of the 19th century. This fear extended to free blacks not just the enslaved and ultimately led to bans against any gatherings by blacks, free or enslaved. Yet despite white opposition to these institutions and any organization within black communities, some of these organizations persisted in the Upper South well into the 19th century. In the North, these institutions continued to grow and proliferate because white northerners had little to fear from black communities and many welcomed this self-imposed segregation from white society.

Although some viewed black institutions as imitations of the same white organizations, black institutions embraced and embellished a growing African American culture that was distinctive from that of the larger, white culture. Influenced by their African heritage and adjusting to the historical realities of the early 19th century, these African American organizations remained at the center of black culture and society well into the 20th century. These institutions provided training, education, and social and cultural orientation opportunities that strengthened family life, gave solidarity to black communities, and allowed the next generation to improve on the advances of the previous generation. By the 1820s,

Paul Cuffe (1759–1817)

Paul Cuffe was an African American abolitionist, patriot, and successful businessman. Born on Chuttyhunk Island, Massachusetts, in 1759, Paul Cuffe was the son of a manumitted slave father, known as Kofi, and a Native American mother. A member of the Ashanti tribe in Western Africa, Kofi was captured by slavers at the age of ten and brought to America. Cuffe's mother, Rose Moses, was a member of a branch of the Wampanoag tribe that lived on Martha's Vineyard.

Paul Cuffe educated himself and made his fortune in the whaling and shipping industries in the Americas and Europe. His business started out as a small trading business during the American Revolution, but eventually it expanded to include a shipyard and a large fleet of merchant vessels. Despite his status as a wealthy individual, Cuffe worked to improve the condition of all blacks in America, both free and enslaved. At one point in 1780, Paul Cuffe and his brother refused to pay taxes in Massachusetts, because as African Americans, they were not allowed to vote. They were briefly jailed for this act of civil disobedience, but in 1783, the Massachusetts legislature passed a law that enabled all male taxpayers to vote, white and black.

Cuffe eventually came to the conclusion that African American emigration back to Africa was the answer to problems for blacks in America, both free and enslaved. He began exploratory voyages to Sierra Leone in 1809. In addition to bettering the condition of African Americans, Cuffe, a Quaker, hoped to bring enlightenment to the continent of Africa through his colonization plan as well as economic development. After being delayed by the War of 1812, Cuffe, in December 1815, took his first group of emigrants to Sierra Leone in Africa covering the cost of the voyage for most of them himself. He hoped to make these voyages an annual event, but his declining health prevented him from continuing the colonization effort. Although some African Americans believed as Cuffe did that they would never be civil, economic, or social equals with whites in the United States and supported his colonization efforts, most African Americans opposed the idea. Cuffe died in 1817 and should be known by history for his efforts as an African American leader and as one the first advocates of Pan-Africanism.

however, the solidarity of African American communities would begin to divide as many of the elites continued to seek inclusion in American society.

By the 1820s, the number of slaves born outside the United States fell below that of those born in the United States. At that time, the development of African American society, culture, and identity among slaves in the South occurred. From that point forward, the African influence decreased and the American influence increased. The influence of Africa remained strong among slaves and runaways and those free blacks who remained connected to slave populations. As a result, two visions of the black future in America developed after the 1820s. One looked toward inclusion in America, hoping that eventually the promise of liberty would be extended to them because of the influence of Christianity and the rhetoric of freedom. The other vision saw the hypocrisy inherent in American society during the early 19th century and recognized that American racism would not accept anyone of African descent as equal. Therefore, they continued to develop their own African influenced institutions and organizations and attempted to preserve their communities and their African heritage apart from white society. Even after the end of slavery in the South, this divide among African Americans continued to affect black society throughout the rest of the 19th century and into the 20th century. It manifested itself at the turn of the 20th century as some chose to follow the leadership of Booker T. Washington and his focus on developing black economic independence first and the acquisition of civil rights later and others chose to follow W. E. B. Du Bois and his pursuit of immediate civil equality.

References and Further Reading

Berlin, Ira. "The Revolution in Black Life," *Beyond the American Revolution: Explorations in the History of the American Radicalism.* DeKalb: Northern Illinois University Press, 1976, 351–377.

Berlin, Ira. "Time, Space, and the Evolution of Afro-American Society on British Mainland North America." *American Historical Review* 85 (1980): 44–78.

Berlin, Ira. *Many Thousands Gone: The First Two Centuries of Slavery in North America.* Cambridge, MA: Harvard University Press, 1998.

Berlin, Ira. *Generations of Captivity: A History of African-American Slaves.* Cambridge, MA: Harvard University Press, 2003.

Brown, Kathleen M. *Good Wives, Nasty Wenches, and Anxious Patriarchs: Gender, Race, and Power in Colonial Virginia.* Chapel Hill: University of North Carolina Press, 1996.

Davis, David Brion. *Inhuman Bondage: The Rise and Fall of Slavery in the New World.* New York: Oxford University Press, 2006.

Genovese, Eugene D. *Roll, Jordan, Roll: The World the Slaves Made.* New York: Pantheon, 1974.

Gomez, Michael A. *Exchanging Our Country Marks: The Transformation of African Identities in the Colonial and Antebellum South.* Chapel Hill: University of North Carolina Press, 1998.

Greene, Lorenzo Johnston. *The Negro in Colonial New England, 1620–1776.* New York: Columbia University Press, 1992.

Isaac, Rhys. *The Transformation of Virginia, 1740–1790.* Chapel Hill: University of North Carolina Press, 1982.

Jordan, Winthrop D. *White over Black: American Attitudes toward the Negro, 1550–1812.* Chapel Hill: University of North Carolina Press, 1968.

Kulikoff, Allan. *Tobacco and Slaves: The Development of Southern Cultures in the Chesapeake, 1680–1800.* Chapel Hill: University of North Carolina Press, 1986.

Lepore, Jill. *New York Burning: Liberty, Slavery, and Conspiracy in Eighteenth-Century Manhattan*. New York: Knopf, 2005.

Morgan, Edmund S. *American Slavery, American Freedom: The Ordeal of Colonial Virginia*. New York: Norton, 1975.

Morgan, Philip D. *Slave Counterpoint: Black Culture in the Eighteenth-Century Chesapeake and Lowcountry*. Chapel Hill: University of North Carolina Press, 1998.

Patterson, Orlando. *Slavery and Social Death: A Comparative Study*. Cambridge, MA: Harvard University Press, 1982.

Usner, Daniel H., Jr. *Indians, Settlers, and Slaves in a Frontier Exchange Economy: The Lower Mississippi Valley Before 1783*. Chapel Hill: University of North Carolina Press, 1992.

Free Blacks in Antebellum America | 2

Shelby Callaway

The American practice of associating slavery with race made the existence of free black people a thorny issue for antebellum America. Free blacks had no place in the free versus enslaved and black versus white dichotomy that had come to shape the legal, economic, and social makeup of antebellum America. In the early 19th century, American free blacks took their place in American society and formed a distinctly African American culture. Distinct from slave culture and more than a darker skinned variation on white culture, African American culture and society grew out of the free black communities and institutions of the 1800s. These communities and their leaders were almost always centered on black Christian churches. The church was the most important element of free black society; it produced most of the social and political leaders, founded schools, started mutual aid societies, and contributed to a more distinct and unified African American consciousness and culture. Understanding the antebellum history of the black church is the starting point for understanding the social and cultural history of free blacks in the antebellum period and its formation as a unique culture in American history.

Churches

Slaves had been exposed to Christianity in the colonial period and some of the free blacks who emerged from that population were members of white churches. The formation of the independent black church can be traced back to the religious revivals at the turn of the 19th century. The Second Great Awakening, a revival that spread throughout America in the early 1800s, was fueled by emotional preaching and revival camp meetings. The charismatic and evangelical theologies were a reaction to the conservatism, formalism, and "Englishness" of the Anglican Church. Although the traditional Anglican Church placed an emphasis on dry, religious catechism and featured academic sermons on the nature of the trinity or similar esoteric, complex topics; the evangelical denominations, particularly Methodists and Baptists, called for a revival of a simpler "primitive" church.

Conversion, direct connection with God, emotionalism, and piety were the hallmarks of evangelical theology. This simple and powerful doctrine was especially convincing to free blacks, slaves, and poor whites who did not, and often could not, understand the complex theologies of the older churches. Moreover, these groups on the bottom of society liked the egalitarian nature of the Methodists and Baptists.

Traveling preachers spread the gospel and converted white and black, slave and free. Importantly, besides salvation and membership, preaching positions in these denominations were open to free blacks in the early 1800s. The more stoic denominations like Anglicans and Presbyterians required a certain level of education and instruction before one could be ordained a preacher. The evangelical sects had much less stringent requirements, and thus the door was opened to most anyone who was a convincing preacher, regardless of education or color. A black person could become a preacher in a mixed-race church if he demonstrated skill in preaching and winning souls. Moreover, early in the 1800s, the theology of both Methodists and Baptists espoused a strong current of antislavery feeling. Antislavery, plus spiritualism, made the Methodists and Baptists appealing to blacks, and both denominations' membership rolls swelled with new black members. In some places, black members soon outnumbered the white members of the congregation.

Early on, blacks and whites attended the same churches where both could be ordained. Indeed, black preachers sometimes spoke to majority white audiences, and sometimes both blacks and whites represented their joint churches at larger church synods or association meetings. This may have been the most integrated that mainstream Protestant churches have ever been in America. Unfortunately, this egalitarian feeling did not last long. Despite the democratic, fraternal movement among evangelistic churches in the late 18th and early 19th centuries, church members were not equal. Many congregations, though integrated, had segregated seating, relegating black members to back corners and galleries. Even in churches with black majorities, the white members held all of the important offices in church administration.

Although the congregations of mixed evangelical churches were sometimes composed of both slaves and free blacks, black preachers were almost always free. These free black preachers eventually grew tired of the discrimination they faced in church, and they led the drive to create independent churches for black members only. This drive was based on the desire to escape racist church members and a desire to found independent black churches where they would be able to preach their own messages. Free black leaders wanted the power to influence church decisions and develop their theology along lines that reflected their unique culture, free of white oversight and religious doctrines that stressed the importance of obedience and deference to whites. The desire to be free of white oversight became a recurring theme in most all aspects of free black communities.

The demographics of free black society in the antebellum period are important. Free blacks have always lived in America, whether West Indian migrants, mulattos, or freed slaves. There also existed, particularly in the Lower South, a caste of free mulattos who formed the upper crust of free black society. This group strove to pass for white and was treated differently from newly freed black slaves by white society. This light-skinned caste saw itself as racially distinct from smaller middle and lower classes of darker-skinned blacks who were mostly composed of recently freed slaves who often still had connections with enslaved family members and friends.

The situation changed moving north, where there were fewer mulattos and fewer slaves. Thus, for most of the antebellum period, most of the blacks in the North were lower class and free. The free blacks of the North and Upper South were a far more homogenous group than the free blacks of the Lower South. The mulatto, free black population in the South drifted to the North throughout the 19th century, removing what might have been a source of leadership for southern, nonmulatto free blacks. This demographic difference explains why northern free blacks did more to help unify and direct the course of African American culture and society as it emerged in the antebellum period. The best educated and wealthiest northern free blacks were not busy trying to break into white society as they were in the South, because they had no hope of succeeding. Because all blacks were shunned regardless of caste by northern white society, free blacks were naturally more concerned with the plight of black people as a whole, instead of their particular caste within free society. Moreover, in the North, an increasing number of European immigrants in the antebellum period competed for the same menial jobs as free black workers. Any solidarity between free blacks and poor whites that may have existed because of their similar circumstances evaporated when they began to compete for jobs, further sharpening free black identity. Nationwide, cities held the largest numbers of free blacks, particularly cities in the Upper South. Escaped slaves fled to cities to take advantage of their relative anonymity and try to pass for free, this combined with a higher tendency for urban slaveholders to free their slaves made free blacks a more solidly urban group than either whites or slaves. The cities where most free blacks could be found were in the Middle Atlantic States, on the borderlands ringing the South, or within the South clustered around state lines.

The clustering of free blacks on state lines can be traced to the legal situation they faced in the South. The ideals of the independence movement and the Revolutionary War had pricked the conscience of many slaveholders who manumitted their slaves, particularly in the Upper South. The growth of the cotton industry and the money it brought in the 19th century dispelled the worries about black liberty some of the post-Revolutionary whites had felt in the South. As slavery grew, the ability of masters to free their slaves decreased. By the 1830s, it took approval from

John Carruthers Stanly, Free Black Slaveholder (1774–1856)

Born a slave, John Carruthers Stanly went on to become the largest black slaveholder and the wealthiest black man in North Carolina. That a man of Stanly's background could and would become a slaveholder illustrates some of the challenges facing the free black community in the 19th century.

Born in 1774 to a black slave woman and her white owner, Stanly was sold and educated by his owners and taught barbering. By 1795, he was operating a thriving business and was manumitted by his owners who cited his faithful service as cause for his release. Stanly's barbering business did so well that by 1805 he was able to purchase and free his wife and five children. This in itself is a remarkable though not uncommon story. Educated and skilled slaves often were able to save enough money to emancipate themselves and loved ones legally by purchasing and then freeing them.

Stanly, however, purchased many more slaves and did not free them. Beginning with two male slaves, who he trained to run his barbering business, Stanly expanded into real estate speculation, cotton, turpentine, and slave trading. By 1830, he owned three plantations, employed three white overseers, and owned 163 slaves, more than double that of the next largest black slaveholder. Stanly treated his slaves much like any other white slaveholder neither being cited for excessive kindness nor cruelty. He did not take pains to ensure slave families remained together and sold and traded slaves indiscriminately.

Although, he did eventually free some of his long-serving slaves such as the two barbers he first purchased.

Stanly was viewed by the white population as an ideal representative of the free black society, and he was cited as an example by proponents of black suffrage in the debates surrounding a new constitution in North Carolina in 1835. Owing to his mixed racial heritage and success, Stanly was allowed some acceptance in white society. He was even allowed to purchase his family a pew, albeit in the back, in the local Presbyterian Church. Coincidentally, it was Stanly's backing of his white half brothers' failed business ventures that eroded his fortune, eventually reducing him to only seven slaves.

The obvious question is why a free black man, particularly one who had been a slave himself would own slaves? Most free blacks worked within the system, purchasing slaves and freeing them or joining abolitionist societies, while some advocated revolutionary rejection of the entire slavery system, and ran away or led slave revolts. John Stanly was a member of a small population of free blacks that accepted the system and attempted to benefit from it. Free black slaveholders were rare, but not unheard of. While the majority of freed blacks were predictably and vehemently antislavery, the existence of slaveholders among this group raises a host of questions about the nature of slavery and black identity.

the state legislature in most southern states to free a slave, even if their owner was willing. Eventually, this would become a wholesale restriction on manumission in some states in the South. Moreover, if a slave was successfully freed, most states prohibited him from living in the state he had been a slave. Although benevolent slaveholders could get around these restrictions, the laws reflect a fear about what was to be done with the freed

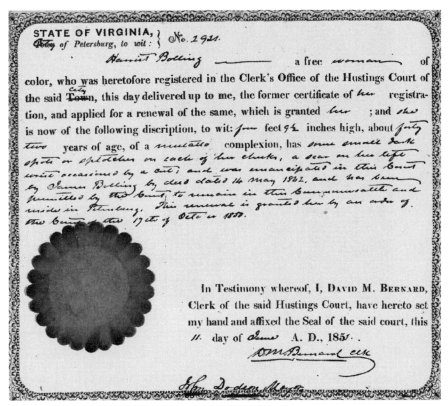

Certificate of freedom of Harriet Bolling, Petersburg, Virginia, 1851. This certificate indicates that the forty-two-year-old mulatto, Harriet Bolling, was freed by James Bolling in 1842. Freeborn blacks could stay in Virginia, but emancipated African Americans generally were required to leave the state. This certificate states that the court allowed Bolling 'to remain in this Commonwealth and reside in Petersburg.' (Library of Congress)

slaves. Whites feared keeping them around lest they incite other slaves or try to join white society, and thus free blacks had to leave or stay enslaved. Because of the legal hassles, many free blacks found it convenient to live near state borders so they could move quickly when state harassment grew too intense. Of course, all freedmen did not live on the borders of states. Many never moved away once freed. Most would have been unable to fathom leaving the small world they inhabited, moving through a hostile South to begin life somewhere else. What to do with freed slaves was a big concern, particularly for the cities into which they flocked. In general, free blacks wished to be left alone and whites wished them to disappear or remain slaves.

The desire to be left alone inspired free black leaders to form independent African churches. There was, of course, no universal, unified black experience in any area and so there was no unified black church either. Existing class differences between and among free blacks and slaves carried over into religious life, and there were different patterns in

Richard Allen (1760–1831), founder and first bishop of the African Methodist Episcopal Church. (Payne, Daniel Alexander. *History of the African Methodist Episcopal Church*, 1891)

different regions of the country. There is no precise moment when free black churches became the center of free black cultural awareness and social life, the process was halting and took different paths throughout the country. In the North for example, free blacks were a more cohesive group and able to more easily form churches. Moreover, northern white congregations were happy to see them go. In 1797, some of the black members of the Methodist church in Baltimore left to form a black Methodist church. Soon after its establishment, the mixed congregation Methodist Episcopal Church lost most of its black members as they flocked to the new church. After similar moves by free black congregations in other cities, the independent, African Methodist Episcopal (AME) denomination was founded in 1816 and led by its first bishop Richard Allen. The AME Church shared most of its theological principles with the white Methodists, including a hierarchical, Episcopal system of administration. The AME church administration became a conduit through which many free black leaders rose to power in the antebellum period. Baptist churches were also popular with free blacks. Because they were not organized in a hierarchy like the Methodist churches, but in confederate associations, blacks were allowed the freedom to form their own Baptist churches and still remain part of the Baptist association. The first African Baptist Church was founded in Boston in 1805, and the Baptist movement spread throughout the black community, winning converts and swelling church roles in a way similar to the success of the AME.

Perhaps the most important contrast between the black and white churches was the strong antislavery stance of the AME Church and African Baptist Church. Recall that the evangelical white churches in the

South had been antislavery in the late 18th century. As slavery increased in social and economic importance to white members through the 19th century, the southern churches toned down their antislavery stance. In 1844, the debate over slavery split the Methodist Episcopal Church into northern and southern branches, depending on their side in the debate. In 1845, the Baptist convention also would split.

The independent black churches faced different challenges in the North and South. Northern whites shared the southern whites' racist opinions and welcomed the blacks leaving their churches, while southern whites feared independent congregations led by free black preachers would incite existing slaves to revolt. The failed 1822 black revolt in Charleston, South Carolina, led by Denmark Vesey included in its organizers some members of the Charleston AME church. This fact combined with slave preacher Nat Turner's famous and bloody slave insurrection in Virginia fed southern fears about the dangers of independent black churches and unsupervised meetings between free blacks and slaves. Repressive legislation was passed throughout the South regulating black religious meetings and requiring white preachers or white trustees to be present at black gatherings to prevent and report any rebellious ideas being spread.

While these limitations eventually were loosened throughout the antebellum period, black churches were largely restricted to cities for fear of what might happen if independent black churches could influence rural slaves. The AME church was outlawed throughout the South after the Vesey revolt, and increasingly repressive laws regulating or outlawing all independent black churches were enacted. Eventually, the white congregations' fears about separate black churches were surpassed by their desire to get blacks out of their midst. This as well as unrelenting pressure from free blacks led to a number of African churches being formed in the 1840s that were sponsored by the semi-independent white Baptists and Methodists. Southern white churches reasoned that, if blacks were insistent on their own churches, they would do well to guide the formation of these churches. To prevent inflammatory preaching by free black preachers, white wardens and preachers monitored the black churches. Churches with white oversight, if not exactly independent, were still congregations of exclusively free blacks and slaves and so remained the valuable base from which to launch most all other free black social movements, both North and South. In the North, the independent churches moved ahead by leaps and bounds, but the movement was retarded in the South. Besides the opposition of whites, free black society was different in the Lower South and worked against the interests of a free black church. The Lower South had the largest existing social and cultural divisions between free blacks—a distinction was made between freed black slaves, mulattos, and even mulattos with various skin tones. Thus the free Negro elite, who often were mulattos, did not join free Negro churches, preferring to try for acceptance at white churches. Particularly in New Orleans and other areas where Spanish and French influence had created a large mulatto population, mulattos had long enjoyed a measure of acceptance not extended to dark-skinned free blacks and so did not associate with them. Moreover, the greater presence of the Catholic Church and its more tolerant racial policy in the Lower South gave free blacks an alternative to founding their own churches. Thus, while free blacks in the Lower South were lighter skinned and typically better off economically, their churches took longer to develop and were founded largely after the Civil War when northern black churches sent missionaries to the South.

Black churches were characterized by highly charismatic services. Shouting, singing, clapping, weeping, fainting, laughing, and dancing were all aspects of the black church services. While these elements might be found in both white and black evangelical churches, black churches were cited as having the most enthusiastic worshipers. Indeed, the loud enthusiasm of black church services lasted long after the evangelical fervor inspired by the Second Great Awakening had faded from white services. In black worship, emotional outbursts and singing becoming an integral part of the service. The distinctive style of worship used by black congregations demonstrated more than simple stylistic preference, it was a method of communicating with the spiritual world and being attuned to its needs. The characteristic enthusiasm of worship in black churches incorporated aspects of African culture blacks had managed to retain. It combined with protestant evangelism and formed a unique kind of church in which charismatic emotionalism created a distinctly African American worship experience that sought to connect the spiritual and temporal world through charismatic sometimes frenzied worship.

The free black church was shaped by the experience of slavery. Free blacks, often former slaves, made up most church leaders so there was a strong antislavery undercurrent in the theology of the black churches. In churches led by whites, the message to blacks was that they were to be obedient to their masters and patiently suffer their naturally inferior position on earth in anticipation of rewards in heaven. This was the message that had long been preached on plantations and by white preachers trying to use religion as a control on the enslaved population. Obedience remained a favorite topic of white preachers throughout the antebellum period. Christian free blacks, however, did not accept only the teachings handed down by white overseers. Old Testament stories like that of Moses leading the Israelites out of slavery in Egypt were popular for free black preachers. Black theology incorporated a strong element of divine justice—that is, while inequalities and injustice exist on earth, God sees all and will set all things right in time. To free blacks, this meant not only eventually reaping rewards in heaven for suffering on earth, but also actual divine intervention on earth, setting right wrongs. This concept was developed by black church leaders to mean that good Christians should do God's work by setting right these wrongs. The worldly problem most often mentioned was slavery, and black churches were on the forefront of the abolitionist movement throughout the antebellum period.

The church legalized marriages, births, and deaths; it encouraged discipline, education, and reciprocity, and it provided a refuge from the white-dominated world. Because of the reluctance of blacks to trust white authorities, disputes between members and even punishment for crimes were often dealt with by the church councils. Black churches hung on despite regulation, destruction, and outlaw status to become the bedrock of the black community. They produced schools and social organizations aimed at black preservation and elevation and always with an eye toward ending slavery. Perhaps most important, the church gave free blacks a sense of common purpose and unity providing a somewhat insulated organization through which free blacks could organize their interests and begin to fight for a respectable place in society.

Schools

Education has always been the way for Americans to advance economically and socially. Free black people in the antebellum period knew this and tried to find ways to educate their children and themselves. Early mixed schools went the way of the early mixed churches; after the Revolutionary flush of egalitarianism disappeared, blacks were increasingly discriminated against and left mixed schools. Some sympathetic whites, such as the Quakers, established schools for black students that gradually were taken over by free blacks who wished to be in control of their own education. Segregation became the norm and public schools for black students sprung up in the 1820s in centers of free black society like Boston and Philadelphia. As with black churches, most black schools were staffed by white teachers. The black community worked to have them replaced by black teachers and founded normal schools for educating black teachers toward the end of the antebellum period. Even so, city public schools often refused employment of black teachers. Public funds were predictably short or refused for black schools throughout the nation, despite free blacks paying school taxes. In the cities, abolition societies sponsored schools as part of their efforts to make freed slaves useful members of society. Teaching technical skills that would provide the formerly rural agricultural workers the knowledge they needed to find work in the cities was the abolitionists' goal. While maintaining the fight for public education, most blacks turned to newly formed African churches that supported Sunday schools and day schools to educate black children. As the memberships of free black churches increased throughout the 19th century, so too did enrollment in church schools. Besides this primary education, some larger churches founded secondary schools. In areas that did not have a strong black church, wealthy free blacks sometimes founded schools themselves.

Free blacks knew the importance of education for self-improvement, and they had a desire to combat the negative stereotypes held by most whites that they were naturally slow witted and suited for manual labor rather than intellectual pursuits. In the North, schools were segregated and black schools were underfunded. In the South, whites often opposed black education all together for the same reasons they opposed independent black churches. Education could make free black people question their situation as second-class citizens in a country that espoused egalitarian and democratic values. The same fears about black conspiracy and rebellion that plagued black churches affected schools, and laws were passed prohibiting the education of free blacks in the South. Even so, most southern whites did not mind some education of free blacks as keeping them entirely benighted left them as public wards. White churches sponsored some schools for blacks, while black churches operated clandestine schools even when prohibited by law. In education, as they had done with religion, free blacks formed their own institutions because of their desire to be their own masters and as a reaction to white harassment in mixed schools. Schools run by blacks for blacks provided self-help, an empowering concept for people who came from so disadvantaged a starting place. Free blacks knew they could not expect help from the government or poor whites, although petitions to the government did not stop throughout the antebellum period. White people in the North might be members of abolition societies and feel strongly about ending slavery, but the freeing of slaves was a different matter from the care of black people after they were freed. The question of what was to become of freed black slaves produced some interesting answers.

Free Black Communities

One seeming obvious solution for what was to be done with the growing free black population was to move them away from white society. Various plans were introduced for exporting them to colonies on the western border territories, Haiti, or more often back to Africa. Plans for repatriation of blacks to Africa had been entertained throughout the 18th century. Originally a humanitarian effort to alleviate the evils of slavery, in the 19th century the plan became more of a scheme to get rid of unwanted free blacks who were seen as useless or dangerous, or both.

The American Colonization Society was established in 1817 to help free blacks colonize Africa. The society with the help of the U.S. government acquired land and started a settlement in West Africa that would become Liberia. President James Monroe—for whom the capital of Liberia, Monrovia, was named—shared the opinion of many whites that free blacks would only suffer discrimination and hardship if left in white society. Thus, the best thing for them was removal. Leaders of the free black community, particularly in the newly founded AME church, organized the resistance to white efforts encouraging emigration. Most free blacks argued that their ancestors had settled this country, if involuntarily, and their labor had helped build it. While they did not relish the poor treatment they received in America, it was now their home. Moreover, the free black population did not wish to abandon the black slave population, a group to whom they remained attached, to their fate in bondage. The sense of unity with their brothers in bondage is an important aspect of free black communities in the antebellum period.

Even so, some blacks tired of the injustice and oppression they faced in America did go back to Africa. By 1860, the American Colonization Society had resettled nearly 12,000 blacks in Liberia. Liberia gained its independence in 1847 and was truly administered by black leaders. This combined with the growing injustices free blacks faced in the 1850s made

Painting of the Liberian senate by Robert K. Griffin, ca. 1856. (Library of Congress)

emigration less shunned by some leaders. Indeed, some who had long encouraged staying in America and fighting for equality and abolition grew doubtful that equality would ever be achieved in America and formed the African Civilization Society. This was a black organization that encouraged leaving in a spirit of disdain for American failures to live up to its stated convictions. Even with the growth of the emigration movement, most free blacks remained committed to staying in America. This commitment illustrates that the black community was not simply a transplanted African community; they had become truly African American, blending elements of both cultures to form a new one. In 1827, the first newspaper owned by black Americans, *Freedom's Journal* began publication under Samuel Cornish. The paper was distributed throughout the North and voiced the concerns of free black society, particularly antislavery and self-help. *Freedoms Journal* encouraged free blacks to resist the urge of emigration. The paper was another element unifying the growing African American society, which was committed to self-preservation, equality, and the abolition of slavery.

Despite, and sometimes in response to, the efforts of free blacks, throughout the antebellum period, any civil rights they might have enjoyed throughout the Revolutionary period eroded. The Fugitive Slave Act, passed by Congress in 1793, prohibited helping escaped slaves and required slaves to be returned to their holders. The Fugitive Slave Act was updated in 1850 and made more stringent. The new law left little recourse for blacks accused of being escaped slaves to defend themselves and granted fugitive slave hunters wide authority. The erosion of rights culminated in the well known *Dred Scott* decision of 1857, which ruled that black Americans, slave or free, were not citizens of the

James Forten (1766–1842)

One of the wealthiest men in Pennsylvania in the early 19th century, black or white, James Forten had the means and the drive to become a successful businessman, a leader of the free-black community in Philadelphia, and a leading abolitionist. James Forten was born to free black parents in Philadelphia in 1766. He had some formal education but was forced to find work when his father died. During the War for Independence, Forten served in the Continental Navy as a powder boy onboard a privateer. His ship was captured by the British though he was offered freedom in England. Forten's patriotism kept him from accepting the offer and he remained a prisoner for seven months until he was released. Upon his return to Philadelphia in 1786, Forten was hired by his father's former employer as a sail-maker's apprentice. He learned the business and was quickly promoted to foreman. When the shop's owner retired 1798, he sold it to Forten who later invented a mechanism for more efficient handling of the large sails. His invention and business sense helped Forten grow the business to become one of the largest and most profitable sail lofts in Philadelphia. Forten became one of the wealthiest men in America, employing many workers both black and white.

While he lived in grand style, Forten devoted most of his fortune, by the 1830s, to the causes of abolitionists and equal rights. As a free black man of means raised in Philadelphia in the days before the Revolution, Forten was inundated in the rhetoric of liberty, patriotism, and equal rights. In 1813, Forten began his public career when he wrote an anonymous pamphlet called "Letters from a Man of Colour." The pamphlet, denounced a bill being considered in the Philadelphia legislature that required the registration of all black people arriving in Pennsylvania. Forten saw the bill as an affront to the rights of black Pennsylvanian's and pointed out that free blacks were not necessarily a burden to the white community. Perhaps because of his eloquent denouncement, the bill was not passed.

Later, Forten became one of the major financial backers of William Lloyd Garrison's abolitionist paper, *The Liberator*. Besides providing funding, Forten wrote letters to the paper published under the name "A Colored Philadelphian." Forten wrote about abolition and encouraged free blacks to resist calls by the American Colonization Society to return to Africa. Early in his life, Forten had considered the colonization plans for free blacks as a possible solution to the problem of equal rights. After he saw how strongly the free black community in Philadelphia opposed such plans for expatriation, he too fought against the removal of blacks from the country he had fought to create.

James Forten and his family were active in the early abolitionist movement and took part in the founding and financing of numerous abolitionist organizations and societies. Throughout his public career, Forten remained a respected member of the black and white communities. Forten kept up his business and his fight against slavery until his death in 1842 at age seventy-five. He is remembered as one of the first, key figures of the Philadelphia free black community that generated so many leaders during the struggle against slavery.

United States. African American communities in the North reacted with fierce anger to the increasing oppression they faced in the late antebellum period. In Boston, Fredrick Douglass vowed to defy and attack any fugitive slave hunters who entered Boston. The black community in Boston prevented any such extraditions by working together to hide or rescue blacks who were accused of being escaped slaves. In some places, free black societies were formed in some northern cities specifically to prevent slave hunters finding their quarry.

Social Organizations

The formation of social organizations by free blacks also got under way in the antebellum period. To provide for the black community, free blacks formed social organizations and fraternal orders that provided communal values and another layer of connectedness between and among the free black community and its leaders. The Free African Society of Philadelphia was probably the first such organization, founded in 1787 by Richard Allen and Absolam Jones, later founders of the AME church. It provided benefits to widows and children, sponsored education, supported abolitionist societies, and paid death benefits to its members. Only intemperate or immoral people were excluded. This exclusion illustrates the desire of the free black leadership to be taken seriously and thus have their causes taken seriously.

Prince Hall, a Revolutionary war veteran and free black, established the first African Masonic lodge in Boston in 1787. Interestingly, Hall was granted a charter by the British order of Masons after being rejected by the American order. The Free African Society was typical of the kinds of community-based African benevolent societies that arose anywhere free blacks lived. The African Masonic lodge was a more rare organization as observing the secret societies arcane rituals required more money and time than many middle-class free blacks had. Still, the Masonic reverence for Egypt and Africa made it popular.

Benevolent societies grew strongest in the North where there were more free, middle-class black men, who had something to loose in the event of a natural disaster, epidemic, or white harassment. For these free black men, many of whom were the leaders of their communities, the societies offered a kind of insurance in the event of tragedy. Importantly, black women formed benevolent societies independent of the men. Benevolent societies and fraternal orders typically collected membership dues that were used to provide necessary assistance to the destitute, infirm, widowed, and orphaned. Most stressed abolition of slavery, self-reliance, leadership development, and Christianity. In the South, which enacted legal restrictions on blacks congregating, mutual aid societies managed a respectable membership. While some whites feared any independent black meeting, it was difficult to justify attacking organizations that cared for widows and buried the dead.

Benevolent societies could take a number of forms. Some were built around specific trades or social interests. Also, different societies catered to the needs of the varied economic circumstances of free blacks. Despite differences in specific benefits provided, nearly all provided burial benefits. Black burials often were involved, lavish productions that went on for several days and featured eating, singing, and religious services. The importance placed on burial and correctly tending to the dead was a holdover from African cultural practices. While African cultural elements certainly influenced black funerary practices, the realities of black life also had an influence. In the South, where other gatherings were often under observance by white authorities, funeral proceedings were left to the black people. Thus, one of the reasons black funerals went on for so long was that they were an occasion for blacks to congregate unobserved. This explains the jubilant feeling at many black funerals. The Christian belief that the deceased had gone to a better place combined with the fun of a large, unobserved gathering made funerals one of the most important social events in black culture. As such, even the poorest free blacks were often members of some kind of society that provided for burial costs and cemetery plots.

Not all free black societies had such lofty goals as abolition of slavery and self-reliance. The Brown Fellowship Society had been formed in Charleston in 1790 by brown- or light-skinned mulatto men who stressed their free ancestry, high social rank, mixed blood, and toleration of slavery. They felt they had more in common with white society than with newly freed blacks. The example of the Brown Fellowship Society sharpens the image of free blacks in the antebellum period. Both the Brown Fellowship Society and the Free African Society sought to protect members in times of trouble and were important for the social hierarchy of their communities, even though their goals were different.

When discussing the free black communities of antebellum America, it should be clear that all free people of color were not members of that cultural group. Mulatto societies often traced their heritage to Spanish and French occupation of the southern United States and had different interests than these free black communities. The free black society that emerged during the antebellum period was composed primarily of former slaves and their children. Some had escaped bondage and many had been freed in the heady days during and after the Revolutionary War. The ideals of liberty and fraternity introduced by the war and the subsequent evangelical religious revivals were not forgotten by these free black Americans.

The names free blacks gave their institutions—such as the Free *African* Society, the *African* Methodist Episcopal Church, the *African* Civilization Society, and others—illustrate their connection with slavery and Africa. These people remembered the promise of the late 18th century and strove to make it a reality in the face of mounting legal and physical opposition. They did not forget their African culture or revolutionary American ideals and merged the two into a distinctly African American society. Antebellum free blacks did not try to escape their African roots and never lost solidarity with Africans in bondage. People like Richard Allen, Fredrick Douglass, Prince Hall, and Sojourner Truth fought for the rights of all black people, free and enslaved. Churches, schools, social organizations, the abolition societies, and the Underground Railroad all grew from and influenced the unique African American society that was forged in the antebellum period. Similar to the Revolutionary War, the impending Civil War would once again raise the hopes of black Americans but leave them only partly fulfilled.

References and Further Reading

Berlin, Ira. *Slaves without Masters: The Free Negro in the Antebellum South.* New York: Pantheon Books, 1974.

Horton, James Oliver, and Lois E. Horton. *In Hope of Liberty: Culture, Community, and Protest Among Northern Free Blacks, 1700–1860.* New York: Oxford University Press, 1997.

Rael, Patrick. *Black Identity and Black Protest in the Antebellum North.* Chapel Hill: University of North Carolina Press, 2002.

Reiss, Oscar. *Blacks in Colonial America.* Jefferson, NC: McFarland & Company, Inc., 1997.

Schweninger, Loren. "John Carruthers Stanly and the Anomaly of Black Slaveholding." *North Carolina Historical Review* 67 (April 1990): 159–192.

Sweet, John Wood. *Bodies Politic: Negotiating Race in the American North, 1730–1830.* Baltimore: Johns Hopkins University Press, 2003.

Still Rising: An Intricate Look at Black Female Slaves

Crystal L. Johnson

3

The last time I talked to my grandmother (Birda Robinson), prior to her passing, I asked her to take me down memory lane. Birda was an eighty-year-old black woman who had lived a hard and yet fascinating life that I, as a young black woman and granddaughter, wanted to know and understand. Birda was a woman with an eighth-grade education who on two separate occasions had the spirited tenacity and guts to take her children and leave abusive men. In all, Birda raised and supported six children, my father being the eldest, and instilled in not only her children but also her grandchildren a sense of honor, duty to family, and inner strength. I specifically want to emphasize the words honor, duty, and strength because of the significance they had in one of the stories my grandmother told me that night. The story of my dad, Birda, and school I had heard many times before, but to hear it from her brought an understanding of the overwhelming importance my grandmother had in all of our lives. The story as told by Birda went like this:

> While at work, [mind you her second job] I received a call from Charles William's school [the middle name only used when trouble was a coming]. The principal of the school asked me to come down because Charles William had gotten into trouble. Taking off early from work I went to your father's school, and after hearing what he had done, basically hanging out with the wrong people at the wrong time, I asked Charles William's principal who would normally be called in these situations if a parent was not around? The principal said the juvenile detention department. [Upon hearing this, my grandmother replied] "Well Mr. Principal, the next time Charles William acts like a fool and without the common sense God gave him, you call that department because I have two other children who can't afford me missing work because of his foolishness."

That night my grandmother went on to tell me that my father not only asked to go to another school, but he also let her know he would never again embarrass her or his family again. My grandmother was the embodiment, in my very biased opinion, of the black woman still rising. If one were to compare her life to that of the black female slave similarities continuously overflow.

Too often strong young black women forget the essence of the black female slave. The African American community erases the importance of the female slave, and in doing so commits a grave injustice to our history, but more important, to one of the most significant elements of American history. I stated earlier that I went down memory lane with my grandmother. I did that specifically to understand and appreciate the significance of her life. To truly comprehend that significance, I as a young black woman must decisively know why the black female slave was, and still is, relevant to the African American community. The black female slave embodies numerous categories, which when comprehended transcend through time and generations.

The enslaved female wore various hats within the institution of slavery. Constance A. Cunningham in *The Sin of Omission: Black Women in Nineteenth Century American History* referred to these hats as "the crucial roles women were expected to balance" (1990, 278). This essay looks critically at four roles that leading historians feel the black female slave embodied during and after slavery. The first role was that of an oppressed object or piece of property. Assessing this role demonstrates

A woodcut in *Pictures of Slavery* published in 1834, depicts an African American slave sitting on a balance as slave traders put weights on the other side of the balance to determine her weight and price. (Corbis)

how the emasculating of these slave women's femininity was refocused into a survival mechanism that these women channeled throughout the slave community. The second role was that of resistant foe that so many slave women assumed during slavery. Were these women complacent with their status or did they have a hidden agenda that mirrored resistant men like Nat Turner? Third, these women were the center of the slave family, and this role affected the men of the slave community significantly. Did these men feel more demasculinized or did they accept a matrilineal family? Finally, many slave women wore the role of survivor throughout slavery.

The Emasculation of Slave Women

> A brisk likely country-born Negro wench about eighteen or nineteen years of age, who is a good Spinner; with a child, about eighteen months old (Wolloch 1997, 244).
>
> She's never been 'bused and will make de good breeder (Wolloch 1997, 244).
>
> Yous am de portly gal and Rufus am de portly man. De Massa wants you-uns fer to bring portly chillen (Wolloch 1997, 245).

The above three statements are indicative of the first role that the black female slave had forced upon her. The black female slave endured sheer cruelty when viewed as an object or as a piece of property. These women's sense of feminine identity was stripped from them and replaced by the deplorable notion of the black female slave as a breeder and a commodity to sell, buy, or trade at will.

Sexual exploitation proved to be the most common way to objectify the black female slave. It was not uncommon for white men to rape the black female slave, whether out of pleasure or the need to increase profits, through the natural expansion of the slave population. White men did not think of their actions as immoral—for how could the white man be morally wrong to a piece of property? "Cose back in de days," Sarah Fitzpatrick wrote, "when I come long us wimmin could't help it ef a white man wanted to take up time wid us" (Wolloch 1997, 245). The goal for many black women living within the institution of slavery was survival. In many respects, these women had no choice but to succumb to the sexual advances of white masters and overseers.

The black female did try to assert some control over her own body and femininity. Rose William within her narrative emphasized the want to have control when she tells of her initial rejection of Rufus. William wrote,

> After I's in, [the bed] dat nigger come and crawl in de bunk with me 'fore I knows it. I says, What you means, you fool nigger? He say for me to hush de mouth. Dis am my bunk too . . . Git out, I's told him . . . Hush yous big mouth and stay 'way from dis nigger, dat all I wants (Wolloch 1997, 245).

Louisa Picquet (1828–1896)

Louisa Picquet was born in 1828 in Columbia, South Carolina, to Elizabeth Ramsey, a cook and seamstress, and John Randolph, Elizabeth's white master. Looking eerily like Mr. Randolph's other child by his white wife, Picquet, her mother, and her brother were sold to Mr. Cook of Monticello Georgia. As a child, Picquet was hired out by Cook as a nurse or nanny to pay off increasing gambling debts. At the age of thirteen, Picquet was separated from her mother who was sold to a Mr. A. C. Horton of Warton, Texas, while Picquet was sold by the sheriff in Georgia to a Mr. Williams of New Orleans. Picquet remained with Mr. Williams until his death and became at the age of sixteen his mistress, bearing him four sons. In 1849, upon the death of Mr. Williams, Picquet gained her freedom and moved to Cincinnati, Ohio, with two of her sons. Picquet eventually earned enough money to purchase her mother's freedom in 1860 and went on to publish the saga of her life within the book—*The Octoroon: Inside Views of Southern Domestic Life, 1861.*

The life of Louisa Picquet reflects in numerous ways the roles that black female slaves were forced to endure within slavery. Picquet was exposed to the fear of rape, the escalation of sexual violence, and the overall sexual exploitation that was considered the norm within the institution. Picquet was direct in the telling of her trials within slavery. She unveiled to her readers the horrific essence of what life was like for her and many other slave women. She gave a prime example of this when she wrote of her

initial encounter with Mr. Williams. She revealed to the reader that her purchase was for sheer satisfaction. Mr. Williams stated to her, "[I am] getting old, and [I] thought [I] buy [you], and end [my] days with [you], if [you] behave [I will] treat [you] well, but, if not, [I will] whip [you] almost to death" (Loewenberg and Bogin 1976). With that simple verbal communication, Mr. Williams dictated how Picquet was an oppressed object or piece of property to use at will. Picquet's control over her body was taken from her in that moment, and in its place, the keen understanding that she had one choice in that situation—to survive.

Louisa Picquet did survive the peculiar institution of slavery and went on to showcase in her book the injustices, cruelties, and appalling realities of slavery. She highlighted the many roles black female slaves bore during slavery, but also reflected on insightful issues within the slave community. In only being one-eighth African American, Picquet's memoir brings to light the issue of mixed racial heritage. She expressed the hypocrisy and immorality of white Christian slaveholders who sing praises to God on Sunday and then rape their slaves to produce offspring.

Louisa Picquet survived being sold off twice and becoming the concubine of Mr. Williams. She gained her freedom, married Henry Picquet, and purchased her mother's freedom. Writing down her experiences in her own words, though, is why she remains so important to understanding black female slaves within the institution of slavery.

Even though Rose asserts her authority over her own body, she does so only when confronted by the advances of a black male slave. The harsh reality, however, was that the control over their bodies that the black female tried to gain quickly dissipated in the arrogance of the white slave master. The idea of the black female slave as property was perpetuated not out of truth, but rather out of fear and need. The black female slave feared the deplorable consequences that she and her family would be subjected to if she did not comply with the demands of the master. In addition, black female slaves turned a negative situation into what could be viewed as a positive outcome. While some complied out of fear, others accepted the advances of white masters out of the material rewards that could be attained. The promise to be freed at a later date and the ultimate promise of her family remaining intact enticed black female slaves to give into the lustful wants and desires of her master and the peculiar institution of slavery. The ensuing outcome of that compliance, though, was the lost of her feminine identity and the inescapable trap of the white slave owners "licentious passion" (Berry and Blassingame 1982, 118). For many slave women, the acceptance of this "licentious passion" was a psychological construct. These young girls and women were a product of an environment in which the mother passed down to the daughter the understanding of accepting the reality of their existence and learning the technique of survival.

Although the black female slave endured the vain nature of the white master, her spirit remained intact. Some reactions were indicative of the black female slave perceiving that justice would prevail over injustice. Sarah Fitzpatrick was one such black female slave who believed justice, not necessarily social, but definitely religious justice would prevail. Fitzpatrick stated in a Tuskegee interview, "I looks at it lack dis, I'd say, well ya been hard on me Mr. White-man but I ain't gonna treat ya bad, 'cause God is always 'bove de debel" (Wolloch 1997, 254). The religious fortitude of women like Sarah Fitzpatrick sustained the psyche of black female slaves and made it possible for these women to bear the deplorable environment of slavery. These women conveyed the idea of matrifocality, the notion that women as mothers were the focal point of the slave family. As Deborah Gray White contended, these slave women were "more central . . . to [the] family's continuity and survival as a unit" (White 2000, 275). Slave women were willing to place before any other person or concern the slave family unit, and in doing, so established a mother-child familial bond that took precedent within the slave community. The protecting of the family was more important for the slave woman than any type of personal benefit. The black female slave, while being mentally, physically, sexually, and socially oppressed created a foundation upon which surviving these grave deeds was attainable. Survival of the slave community deemed to have more importance in the mind of the black female slave. Sojourner Truth once posed the question "Ar'n't I a Woman?" The black female slave would probably answer, "yes," but with the selfless understanding that her children, husband, and community had to be set in front of her need to be a "woman." The natural existence of pride for these slave women was moved to the periphery, and in its place, the daunting task of maintaining the slave family.

The Resistant Foe

The black female slave as a resistant foe, while not highly advertised as a role the black female embodied was a realistic role for black women during slavery. At first glance, the average person may conclude that the black female slave was of a docile, nonviolent, and nonresistant nature. Black female slaves, on the contrary, encompassed not only the wits, but also the desire, to resist the immoral atrocities of slavery. From the boarding of the slave vessels to the settling into slave quarters, African and black women participated and assisted in slave insurrections. Deborah Gray White in *Ar'n't I a Woman?* (1999) depicted the African woman as the "lookout" or as Angela Davis put it, "the socializers of resistance" (1990, 293). The African woman easily fit into the role of assistant to resistance, for the white captains of these slave ships did not perceive her as a threat. "The natural assumption [was,]" White stated, "that women could be overpowered" (White 1999, 64). The insignificance placed on the African woman as a resistant foe proved harmful many times over to the proposed profits to be made on these slaves within the institution of slavery. As Dr. Bell, a physician on board the Thames vessel, a vessel on which a revolt took place, stated, "had the women [truly] assisted them [the men], in all probability your property here at this time would have been small." (White 1999, 64). African women were just as prone to resisting their condition as African men were for they were not content with the notion of losing their freedom, home, and way of life.

Resistance by the black female slave came in many forms during enslavement, especially for those black female slaves who were not successful in escaping or who did not die during vessel revolts. The behavior of the black female slave, especially with regard to sexual exploitation, proved a significant if not subtle way of resisting. To the bewilderment of fellow slaves, masters, and overseers, as White chronicled, "women fought back despite severe consequences" (White 1999, 64). Slave women would violently resist the sexual advances of their white masters and overseers. Many times, these women took the only recourse available to them, that of fighting off their attacker. White noted a prime example of this resistance when a slave woman [Ms. Loguen] was attacked. Instead of complying with the sexual advances of her attacker, "she picked a stick and dealt her would be rapist a blow that sent him staggering" (White 1999, 64). Such resistance is fascinating for it challenges the notion of the black female slave as the helpless victim with absolutely no control. With the emergence of these overt forms of resistance, the black female slave lessened the blow of objectification that she as a whole was subjected to on a daily basis.

With these drastic forms of resistance came harsh punishments. From killing the resistor to selling them on the auction block, both men and women who participated in violent resistance took the chance of suffering extreme consequences. For some slave women, the price for violent resistance was too high, but the desire and need to resist was still felt. Thus, more subtle ways of resisting were used. Some of the less overt forms of resistance included the use of poison, self-mutilation, work slowdowns, sabotaging the harvest, the feigning of illness, or faking pregnancy by slave women. These forms of resistance, while subtle, did not go unnoticed. For instance in 1751, the South Carolina Legislator wrote, with regard to poisoning as a resistance act, "that in case any slave teach or instruct another slave in the

Harriet Jacobs (1813–1897)

Harriet Ann Jacobs was born in 1813 in Edenton, North Carolina, to Delilah—daughter of Molly Horniblow and Daniel Jacobs. At a very early age, Jacobs's mother died and her grandmother's mistress—Margaret Horniblow took her into her household. Upon Margaret's death, Jacobs, at the age of twelve was willed to the five-year-old niece of Margaret. Thus, Mary Matilda Norcom, or Miss Emily as she was called, owned her first slave at the tender of age of five. Because of Miss Emily's immature state, her father Dr. James Norcom (Dr. Flint) held ownership of both Harriet Jacobs and her brother John S. Jacobs.

From her initial arrival, Jacobs encountered the sexual advances of Dr. Flint, for his intent was simple—to make her his concubine. Jacobs perceived this environment as unbearable and chose to engage in another sexual relationship with a Mr. Samuel Tredwell Sawyer (Mr. Sands) to escape the licentious desires of Dr. Flint. She noted in her book *Incidents in the Life of a Slave Girl*, "I would rather drudge my life on a cotton plantation, 'til the grave opened to give me rest, than live with an unprincipled master" (Jacobs 1987). In engaging in a sexual relationship with Mr. Sands, which produced two children—Joseph and Louisa Matilda, Jacobs circumvented a system of sexual exploitation.

Jacobs's defiant rejection of Dr. Flint led to her being sent out to work on a cotton plantation several miles from Edenton and her children, an action Jacobs made peace with once she knew her children were safe. In a sense, Dr. Flint taking this measure created an opportunity for Jacobs to escape slavery in its entirety. Dr. Flint eventually sold Jacobs's children to a slave trader who was working on behalf of Mr. Sands. Mr. Sands returned Ben and Ellen to Jacobs's grandmother. Here in lay Jacobs's opportunity and future pursuit of freedom. Jacobs over the next seven years lived within the confines of her grandmother's attic, where she read the bible, sewed, watched over her children, and wrote letters to Dr. Flint to misdirect him. This bold act was reflective of Jacobs as a resistor. While this resistant nature was not violent, it did serve the purpose of regaining control over her life and the lives of her children.

Harriet Jacobs eventually escaped slavery at the age of twenty-seven, living as a fugitive slave for ten years. This status did not deter her, but rather encouraged her to move forward and eventually write her life story. *Incidents in the Life of a Slave Girl* is a provocative account of life for the slave girl and woman.

knowledge of any poisonous root, plant, herb, or other poison whatever, he or she, so offending, shall, upon conviction thereof suffer death as a felon" (Cole 1978, 41). While these resistant mechanics were subtle in nature, the benefactors of the institution of slavery knew the harsh ramifications that could come from such antics, and at the center of many of these antics stood the black female slave. From the periphery, the black female slave, through her overt and subtle resistant actions, empowered herself and took what little control she could over her life. The black female slave within her community, as Davis noted, had been "assigned the mission of promoting the consciousness and practice of resistance" (1990, 293). In retrospect, the role of resistor propelled the black female slave to the center of not only her own family unit but also the slave community.

The Center of the Family

While the role of resistor empowered the black female slave, the one significant role that has passed from generation to generation is that of the black female being the center of the family. This statement is not to suggest that the black male slave did not have a proper place or role within the slave family, but rather that the self-reliance and self-sufficiency embodied by the black female slave contributed to a female solidarity and independence that helped the slave family survive the institution of slavery.

The black female slave laid the foundation for future black women to stand at the center of their families, a foundation built due to force and not want, for the black female slave was "thrust by the force of circumstances into the center of the slave community" (Davis 1990, 293). "She was," as Davis stated, "essential to the survival of the community" (1990, 293). The black female slave created a matriarchal family that provided emotional, mental, and physical support to not only her family but the slave community as well.

Children served as a poignant example as to why black female slaves were at the center of the family unit. Black women, unlike men, were less likely to run away and escape to the North, for in doing so, they would have to abandon their children. Such an act, even with the compensation of freedom, was deemed impossible for the black female slave. While not all slave men left, the void created by the departure of the men who did leave the slave family propelled black women into a multifaceted position.

Slave family in a cotton field near Savannah, ca. 1860. (Bettmann/Corbis)

The black woman became to the family a mother, father, provider, and protectorate.

Even in late age, the black female slave had significance. As a caregiver to the community of slave children, black women served as wise elders and nurturers. These women were there, as White pointed out, "fer de lil' chilluns and babies" (1999, 116). Both the young and older black female slave were "strong, industrious, pious [women who were] loved by their children" (Berry and Blassingame 1982, 77).

The black female slave took on the role of center in the family out of need more than want, and in doing so, the black male slave did take a secondary role within the family unit. The formation of the strong woman had its origins in the slave era, but the beginnings of the endangered black man started, ironically, with the elevation of the slave woman. Slowly the black male slave was stripped of his manhood in that he was unable to take on the traditional male roles in the family. The black male slave was not the protectorate or provider for the black slave family. Whether due to the absence of the black male, his notions of freedom in the North, or the psychological limitations that the institution of slavery inflicted on the black male, the black male had no agency within his own family. This lack of agency within the family unit would come to be problematic in later decades and movements.

The Survivor

The most difficult role for the black woman to take on was that of survivor. This role, however, has transcended over many generations and thus has created the strong black woman of the 21st cnetury. The psychological, sexual, and mental anguish suffered by the black female slave created a woman with thick skin. For the black female slave, the plantation was a "psychological battleground" (White 1999, 116) on which survival was based on wits, control, and patience. The black female slave embodied these different attributes and became a significant part of American history. In looking back on their foremothers, young black girls and women can begin to grasp the concept that their own passions, desires, quirks, and strengths come from these women before them who stepped into these complicated roles. It took phenomenal women to endure the pains, tribulations, and daily injustices of the institution of slavery. These women had the will to survive a barbaric institution, and it is left up to the black girls and women of this century to embrace the multiple roles generated during slavery.

In embracing these roles, black women recognize the sacrifices and internalize the true identity of the black woman. I am forever grateful to my grandmother for awakening in me the desire to understand my past and the capability to continue to rise to the ever-growing challenge to maintain a true identity through the use of significant black female roles. When reflecting on the many life stories my grandmother told me as a child, teenager, and young black woman, I recognize her and the black

Slaves of Confederate General Thomas F. Drayton at his plantation on Hilton Head Island, South Carolina, May 1862. (Library of Congress)

female slave with great respect, as phenomenal women who did not stop rising to the many challenges and harsh realities in their lives. Hopefully, the black woman of the present and future will continue to face challenges before them.

References and Further Reading

Berry, Mary, and John W. Blassingame. *Long Memory: The Black Experience in America*. New York: Oxford University Press, 1982.

Cole, Johnetta. "Militant Black Women in Early U.S. History." *The Black Scholar* 9, no. 7 (April 1978): 41.

Cunningham, Constance A. "The Sin of Omission: Black Women in Nineteenth-Century American History." In *Black Women in United States History*, ed. Darlene Clark Hine. New York: Carlson Publishing, 1990.

Davis, Angela. "Reflections on the Black Woman's Role in the Community of Slaves." In *Black Women in United States History*, ed. Darlene Clark Hine. New York: Carlson Publishing, 1990.

Jacobs, Harriet. *Incidents in the Life of a Slave Girl*. 1861; rpt., ed. Jean Fagan-Yellin, Cambridge, MA: Harvard University Press, 1987.

Maryland Gazettel. "Skilled Slaves in Maryland: *The Maryland Gazettel*, 1748–1763." In *Early American Women: A Documentary History, 1600–1900*, ed. Nancy Wolloch. New York: McGraw-Hill, 1997, 244–245, 254.

White, Deborah Gray. *Ar'nt I a Woman? Female Slaves in the Plantation South.* New York: W. W. Norton, 1999.

White, Deborah Gray. "Gender Roles and Gender Identity in Slave Communities." In *Major Problems in African American History,* vol. 1, *From Slavery to Freedom, 1619–1877,* ed. Thomas C. Holt and Elsa Barkley Brown. New York: Houghton Mifflin, 2000, 268–276.

Safety in the Briar Patch: Enslaved Communities in the Nineteenth-Century United States

4

Karen Wilson

Enslaved communities were composed of enslaved people, also called slaves or bondpeople, who either lived together or came together from various locations to sustain and protect themselves under one of the most brutal systems of slavery ever conceived. Such a community of enslaved people is also known as a *slave quarter community*. In the late 18th century, slave quarter communities existed in the northeastern United States, as well as in the American Southeast, Southwest, and West. These communities existed in rural, primarily agricultural settings as well as in urban areas.

It was tremendously hard on people to sustain a sense of their own humanity and their communal relationships while living in the midst of a system that regarded them as less than human. Enslaved people maintained slave quarter communities on large plantations on which 50 or more people were enslaved. They also maintained them by keeping up social and familial ties, when possible, with family, friends, and biological or fictive family members (friends who were considered as close as family) who lived on or were sold to farms or plantations within close proximity. These bonds were often useful in defining protective responses to the constant threat of the hazardous and oppressive slaveholding society of which they were a part. Much of this protection was found in secrecy. By the 19th century, the enslavement that was winding down in the North had become a way of life in the South. Slavery had grown and changed in response to contemporary economic realities (now called the Market Revolution). The Market Revolution required that great amounts of raw materials, including cotton, rice, and sugar, be supplied to manufacture goods in factories housed, for the most part, in northern cities. This change in economic conditions forced a change in the expectations about enslaved people.

Five generations of a slave family in Beaufort, South Carolina, 1862. (Library of Congress)

Rather than intelligent and self-reliant (as many enslaved during the 17th and 18th centuries were expected to be), the 19th-century slave was expected to labor efficiently, ceaselessly, and mindlessly—like a machine—to cultivate and harvest whatever raw materials the Market Revolution required. Overseers and masters often used violence to force submission to the rigors of this ceaseless labor. Slavery, however, required more than ceaseless labor—it required consent to a permanently subhuman status.

Slaves in the 19th century were supposed to have been childlike, dependent, and wholly incapable of original thought. This slave was to have no ability to read or to write, no leadership potential, and no interest in the world outside of the farm or plantation on which he or she lived. For many slaveholders, the perfect slave had no morality and no religion. Such perfect slaves had no familial ties and no marital or communal relations—no friends. This 19th-century slavery decreed that a slave's only interest was to please his or her master and to have children for which they had no feeling. Because enslaved persons actually were human—with all of the intelligence, emotions, talents, failings, and desires of humankind—the requirements of this new kind of slavery were impossible to fulfill.

This new kind of slavery required a new set of responses on the part of enslaved individuals and communities. First, enslaved communities taught enslaved people never to trust their enslavers. Enslaved communities also taught their members to keep what happened inside their community to themselves. Furthermore, they shaped the "Sambo" mask: a shuffling, often stupid, eye-rolling, childish, and heedless *persona*, or personality, designed to be shown, when necessary, to the society that wished to enslave them. Inside enslaved communities, however, individuals were quite different.

Secrecy was an important characteristic of life in the slave quarter community. Few who were not members of such communities were privy to information on their socio-cultural and political realities. People who had been enslaved before the Civil War tell us that they preserved this secrecy to protect themselves and each other—preserving their communities as sanctuaries from a dangerous and often unpredictable world.

This chapter is organized in four major sections. First, it will begin by briefly examining the different sources of information that help us to understand what went on in communities where enslaved people lived. Such sources show us that although they were sometimes difficult places, slave quarter communities were also centers of psychological and emotional protection, political training, cultural continuity, and cultural change. Second, it will briefly examine intercultural contact, continuity, and change on the continent of Africa and the ways in which those African cultural mores were refreshed, continued, and transformed in the United States. Third, it will explore the broad aspects of intentionally secretive slave quarter communities, including their existence as both physical and psychological spaces; their social organizations including familial, extra-familial, and cross-communal connections; their specific occupational, religious, and recreational activities; and the attitudes of their inhabitants as revealed in such cultural expressions as song, story, and dance. Finally, the article will consider the role of enslaved people in moving forward the agenda of their own freedom so effectively that President Lincoln was compelled to respond with their emancipation.

Sources of Information on Slave Quarter Communities

Where do we garner information through which we can approximate a realistic sense of the slave quarter communities of the 19th-century United States? Such information comes from a variety of sources. Some sources outside of enslaved communities include individual and societal written records such as court and other legal proceedings, the correspondence and personal journals of planters (both men and women), plantation business accounts, and contemporary newspaper articles. Each of these sources can provide a range of views culled from the observations of those who lived outside the slave quarter community. Such sources tell us not only about the slave quarter community, but also about how that community was perceived by others.

Sources from inside enslaved communities or connected to them provide information from a wide range of experiences, ideas, and perspectives. Such sources include interviews with formerly enslaved people and narratives written by them in a range of situations and circumstances; essays, legal petitions, and correspondence during and after enslavement; records of religious and social societies such as churches and lodges; and by newspapers, novels, stories, operas, poetry, and other journalistic, literary, and artistic forms produced by free antebellum and postbellum African American communities.

Enslaved people left eloquent testimony of their experiences. Song, story, dance, and other forms of artistic creation reflect the interests, issues, philosophies, and intellectual activities of enslaved people. Songs open a window into the work lives and attitudes of enslaved people. Stories of enslaved communities show even more clearly the challenges enslaved people faced and the strategies they used to respond to those challenges. Black dance illustrates an array of social and cultural choices that were distinctly different than those espoused by the mainstream Euro-American community.

Finally, the testimony of the generation born within fifty years after emancipation sheds important light on the culture of the slave quarter community. Those born after enslavement were raised by parents and grandparents, aunts, uncles, and extended family members who had undergone enslavement and whose lives in freedom continued the ideologies, theologies, and cultural practices that had served them so well in enslavement. The generations born in the earliest decades of emancipation, then, were nurtured in communities that preserved traditions developed during enslavement with less of the pressure of secrecy than their elders had known—at least before the iron fist of Jim Crow segregation began the attempt to control the movements of black people, along with their dreams. Their testimony is invaluable in understanding and appreciating the brilliant cultural practices that slave quarter communities produced.

Locations

Enslaved communities existed in every original colony and, later, throughout much of the United States. Slave labor and ingenuity built such New England states as Massachusetts, Rhode Island, Connecticut, New Hampshire, and Vermont. The Mid-Atlantic States of New York, New Jersey, Pennsylvania, Maryland, and Delaware also utilized enslaved labor for a time. Southern states, including North and South Carolina, Georgia, Alabama, Kentucky, Tennessee, Arkansas, Virginia and West Virginia, Mississippi, Florida, Louisiana, and eventually Texas, came to slavery early or late, but eventually depended on slave labor. Enslaved people also labored as far West as California: some of the miners who worked the California gold fields were enslaved.

In the first quarter of the 19th century, however, some 200 years of direct enslavement was winding down in most northern regions.

Emancipation appeared on the books in New York State in 1799; however, the law that was created instituted a freedom so gradual that manumission, or complete freedom, did not occur until the latter half of the 1820s more than a quarter of a century later. Most northern states eventually renounced slave labor. Although even when overt slavery was gone from the North, the race-based policies, practices, and institutions that slavery had engendered continued to affect and to poison those societies for many generations. Just as northern slavery was losing steam, however, southern slavery was regaining momentum.

Many of the regions in which slavery continued included both rural and urban settings. On large plantations, slave quarter communities could hold 300 or more people, although many enslaved communities were not that large. Much rural, or country, slavery tended to take place on smaller farms with most slaveholders owning fewer than twelve slaves. On such small holdings, many enslaved people, or bondpeople, ate and were housed with planter families. In such a situation, when bondpeople wished to create and sustain community with other enslaved people—as they often did—they had to create that community by connecting groups from a number of smaller farms or households into an extended community. City households often had such small groups of slaves.

Bondpeople in cities seem to have enjoyed more "freedoms," or small occasions for independence, than rural slaves on large plantations. Still, there was a marked difference between "freedoms" and true freedom or the legal right to govern yourself. Both in urban and in rural settings,

Slaves gin cotton. The invention of the cotton gin led to increased production of the cotton crop in the American South, which caused an expansion of slavery in the region. (Library of Congress)

Slavery in the Northern United States

State	Mass.	N.H.	N.Y.	Conn.	R.I.	Pa.	N.J.	Vt.
European settlement	1620	1623	1624	1633	1636	1638	1620	1666
First record of slavery	ca. 1629	1645	1626	1639	1652	1639	ca. 1626	ca. 1760
Official end of slavery	1783	1783	1799	1784	1784	1780	1804	1777
Actual end of slavery	1783	ca. 1845	1827	1848	1842	ca. 1845	1865	ca. 1777
Percent black 1790	1.4%	0.6%	7.6%	2.3%	6.3%	2.4%	7.7%	0.3%
Percent black 1860	0.78%	0.15%	1.26%	1.87%	2.26%	1.95%	3.76%	0.22%

Source: From Douglas Harper, "Introduction," *Slavery in the North*, http://www.slavenorth.com (accessed June 20, 2008).

individuals and disparate groups stayed connected through informal information networks, often called, "the grapevine."

The Grapevine: Communication Networks Linking Enslaved Communities

Enslaved individuals and communities developed numerous ways to collect information and distribute it. These networks functioned in various ways and, like grapevines, could turn up anywhere. The grapevine surged with information supplied by many, distributed by many, but controlled by none. Historian Steven Hahn approximates that more than 10 percent of the enslaved could read. Some bondpeople collected or delivered information for the grapevine when they traveled for work. These included enslaved artists or artisans like blacksmiths, seamstresses, or musicians whose skills might be lent or "hired out" to planters or other persons in the vicinity who then paid their master to utilize their skill or ability. Others were trusted to deliver messages or materials over long or short distances. Others responsible for the spread of information included sailors—both enslaved and free—who could travel widely and collect regional, national, or international goods or information that found their ways into enslaved communities. Longshoremen and others who had access to those sailors spread information as well.

Often, household workers listened to planter's discussions while they ate dinner or virtually anywhere else in the house. One woman reported crawling under the house so that she could hear her "master" read the newspaper aloud at night, then shared the news. Field people were also involved. One enslaved community in Arkansas constructed a map of their plantation collecting information on the part of the plantation where each worked, then correlating that information by using the stars as a guide. The entire map was eventually recorded on a quilt.

Bondpeople often lived in areas where planters, their families, their employees, and their society were in control. There were also times and spaces in which enslaved people were in control, and white people seldom entered those spaces. These were times and spaces in which black people, their kinship networks, their mores, their rules of interaction, and their cultural practices dictated appropriate behavior. We refer to these times and spaces as black space and time, or "the Quarters." "The Quarters" could be as large as a brush or "hush arbor," a place far from planter's hearing in which enslaved people could meet in private to talk or to worship and pray. It might be as small as a pantry, if one were truly alone. It could even be defined by a black person's mind. Black people made choices that were appropriate to their own needs and desires when space and time was under African or African American control.

Refreshing the African Cultural Connection

Culture is made up of those social behaviors developed by a group over time in response to age-old questions. The answers that form a group's culture come in response to such questions as how will we eat, how and where will we find shelter, how will we communicate, or how did the world come to be? The foods that a community eats, the kinds of homes they find or construct, the languages they speak, and the philosophies and theologies they develop are their answers to those questions and constitute their *culture*. When African peoples flowed into slave quarter communities in the United States, many different African cultures flowed with them. When they arrived in the United States, some of those cultural practices continued, some did not continue, and some transformed. It is, however, important to realize that African people made choices to change, to blend, or to keep their cultural practices according to their needs. Such continuities or discontinuities in cultural practice illustrate diaspora or the ways culture adapts when any people or peoples leave that place they consider their "homeland." When Africans and their descendants spread across the Western Hemisphere, their cultures underwent such a diasporic process.

Some enslaved people knew—and could identify—the African nations from which they or their parents, grandparents, or great-grandparents had been taken. Others did not have such specific knowledge. Still, these African descended communities made consistent cultural choices based on *aesthetics*, or cultural guidelines, which had emerged from the range of cultural traditions that they knew. The traditions they knew included those of Native American and European nations; however, the guidelines that guided cultural choices in the slave quarter were most often African. Choices made by individuals and by communities could respond quickly to the needs of their specific situations. The guidelines for making such choices changed much more slowly.

These African cultural mores, and the aesthetics they represented, were supplied with new African ideas and information in a number of ways. Although the slave trade was outlawed in 1808, Africans were smuggled into the United States for the purposes of enslavement and labor as late as 1865. Years after enslavement was over, formerly enslaved people spoke either of their own memories of Africa or of the practices of parents or grandparents who had been born there. Furthermore, port cities such as Charleston, South Carolina, and Wilmington, North Carolina, provided access to information and cultural artifacts from the African continent over the shipping lanes. Masks for the John Canoe celebrations in Wilmington, North Carolina, and such surrounding towns as New Bern, Fayetteville, and Southport were supplied in this manner. Although some enslaved persons experienced "seasoning" in the Caribbean, and other newly enslaved African arrivals reached the United States directly, new arrivals to United States slavery continually supplied new and different African cultural information. Seasoning was a period designed by slaveholders to break down new slaves, to teach the newly enslaved European languages, or to accustom Africans in other ways to their newly enslaved status.

Historians often cannot be certain of the cultural groups of enslaved people because, no matter where they were purchased along the African coastline, enslaved people could have been forced to walk hundreds of miles before reaching coastal markets or staging areas. The African cultures that informed enslaved African American communities, however, appear to have come primarily from the regions of West and Central Africa. According to historian David Richardson, the British slave trade operated primarily through six staging areas on the West African coast: present day Senegambia (then known by Europeans as Senegal and The Gambia), Sierra Leone, the Gold Coast, the Bight of Benin, the Bight of Biafra, and West Central Africa. The peoples of the Kongo/Angola regions of West Central Africa were among the first African peoples to arrive in British North America. They brought with them some of the earliest African traditions to influence the Western Hemisphere after European contact. In the 19th century, later groups of African people brought to the United States for the slave trade included peoples from such regions as Senegambia, the Niger Delta, the Cross River region east of the Niger, and regions reaching across into Sudan. These peoples included Malinke and other Mande language speakers, the Sereer, the Fulbe, peoples of the Akan city states such as Ashanti, Fante, and Akwamu and Igbo peoples, Wolof peoples, and those of Sierra Leone. Sometimes such groups shared linguistic families or realms of spiritual practice reflecting years of historical connection and prior contact. Often, individuals and national groups had had contact for military, political, economic, or social reasons. Such historic connections helped lay the foundations of community-building for enslaved people in the United States. In some cases, such as that of the Oyo Yoruba and the Fon of Dahomey, such contact went on in different ways for more than 100 years before contact continued in the Western Hemisphere.

Social Organization and Religion in the Slave Quarter Community

Although many states recognized neither the marriages of enslaved people as legal unions nor the bond between mother and child as sacrosanct, enslaved families and communities did recognize them as such. The African American spiritual "Sometimes I Feel Like a Motherless Child" expresses the pain of being sold away from mother and home. Formerly enslaved people spoke of the pain and devastation such sale could cause. Often families could do nothing to stop a child's sale, but there were instances in which a parent could and did fight such a sale successfully. One such mother, Isabella, fought for and achieved the return of her young son, Peter.

Religious observation brought certain members of enslaved communities together. Enslaved communities included people of a range of religious convictions ranging from nationally or ethnically based spiritual practices, to Islamic adherence, to a Christianity that was deeply influenced by pan-African ideologies and theological approaches.

While she was enslaved in upstate New York, Isabella became involved in the Methodist Church. She, along with many other enslaved people, found a flexibility in that church that left room for them to practice a new-found Christianity in ways that seemed most good and appropriate to themselves. Although enslaved people across the United States were attracted to such Protestant denominations as Baptism and Methodism, many of their worship practices were strikingly similar. These included *ring shout*, a combination of singing, rhythm, and movement in which certain

Slave wedding, ca. 1820. (Art Media)

Isabella (ca. 1797–1883)

Born Isabella on the Van Wagener estate in upstate New York ca. 1797, Isabella was no stranger to the loss of family through sale. As a child, she and her siblings had been sold away from their parents. As an adult, ten of her own children were sold away from her. In 1827, her one remaining child, six year old Peter, was sold to a nearby farmer to work as a page. When Peter proved too young for his intended employment, he was returned to Isabella's master. Her master then broke the law and his promise to her by sending Peter to Georgia as a wedding present for his daughter. In her distress, Isabella appealed to her mistress who responded, "Such a fuss over a little nigger!" Isabella's fears were, however, well founded. The daughter's husband abused Peter and later brutally murdered his wife.

As, female, Black and enslaved, Isabella had no legal standing in the courts of the United States. Still she was determined to effect the return of her son. She managed to hire three consecutive lawyers to secure his release and finally had Peter returned to her in 1828, one year after the laws of New York State had pronounced she and her son free. Her former owner did not respond to this decision well. He was averse to letting such a good, strong worker go and tried to convince her that she owed him more time as a slave. As a result, Isabella eventually took her son and left the farm effectively stealing themselves. Later, they moved to Lower Manhattan in New York City, a very culturally African area. In later years, Isabella became an activist for women's rights, civil rights, and the abolition of slavery. She is best known to many by the name she took later in life, Sojourner Truth.

members moved around a counterclockwise circle while others sang a "runnin' sperichil," clapping, slapping, and stomping in complex and compelling rhythms. In this setting, the *shouter* was the person who moved around the circle to the enthralling rhythms.

As opposed to the governing guidelines of lift, lyricism, and synchrony associated with European classic dance, the guidelines governing African classic dance styles included movement that is grounded ("get down, get down") and radiating from the hips, bent knees—and similar angularity around the body, a subtle bounce in the upper torso, driving rhythm that shows in the movement of the body, and improvisation. In some cases, each major part of the body will respond to a different part of a complex rhythm while facial features may well remain calm and a bit detached. Although the movement approximated dance according to African aesthetic guidelines, it was not considered dance, however, unless the shouter's feet crossed in the process. Once someone's feet crossed, that person was not only thrown out of the circle, they were thrown out of the church. Both movements that were accepted in the shout and those that were not accepted clearly reflected African ideals of movement.

The process leading to membership in the enslaved Christian church was not an easy one and involved prayer "in the wilderness," time on the "mourner's bench," and a deep and heartfelt confession of faith.

I've been in the valley praying all night,
All night—all night,
All night—all night.
Give me a little more time to pray.

Often, this time was followed by a revival during which the new converts were baptized in long white gowns by the pastor and deacons of the church. Simon Brown reported that a deacon "holding a long staff built like a cross" would start the proceedings as the church community sang when he was enslaved in Virginia,

Wade in the water, children;
Oh, Wade in the water, children;
Wade in the water, children;
God's going to trouble the water.

Historian Margaret Washington (Creel) asserts that these demands reflected those necessary to join a range of African associations responsible for spiritual leadership, social and artistic appropriateness, and political monitoring. These same practices gave bondpeople opportunities to express their attitudes toward new problems like slavery, a challenge they faced on a daily basis.

The following African American Spiritual, "I an' Satan Had a Race," came from the Port Royal Islands off the coast of Georgia, ca. 1863. This spiritual, created during slavery, expresses a number of attitudes held by this enslaved community.

I an Satan had a race Hallelu, hallelu
Win de race agin de course
Satan tell me to my face
He will break my kingdom down
Jesus whisper in my heart
He will build 'em up again.
Satan mount de iron grey;
Ride half way to Pilot-Bar.
Jesus mount de milk-white horse.
Say you cheat my fader children.
Say you cheat 'em out of glory.
Trouble like a gloomy cloud
Gader dick an' tunder loud.

White was the color of spiritual purity among many African peoples well before widespread European contact. Satan—representing slaveholders—rides an iron-grey horse in this metaphorical race while Jesus rides a milk-white steed on behalf of the slave herself. She won the race, although the course was set up for her to fail. Satan blatantly threatened to tear down this person's "kingdom" or self-worth. Jesus is, however, on the side of the righteous and quietly assures her that he will rebuild what the devil—the master or mistress, and the system he or she represents—has attempted to destroy, while accusing him of cheating the blessed children of his father. This song calls for justice. It establishes that—at least in this community—enslavement was considered the work of the devil. The effect of white presence in black lives was often devilish and difficult and the effect on black families was a case in point.

Simon Brown spoke of the trouble he encountered when he fell in love with Ellen, the woman he later married. She was beautiful and two white brothers wanted her. They ambushed Simon and beat him within an inch of his life. He was able, however, to recover and fight back and, because he had his master's support, he was finally able to marry Ellen. Everyone was not so fortunate.

Brown states that marriage ceremonies for enslaved people were often not taken seriously by white communities. Rather than the preacher, the master often conducted the ceremony. Although "jumping the broom" may have reflected earlier African wedding practice, 19th-century slaves did not like to do this. Brown testified that in the 19th century slaveholders made enslaved people "jump the broom" so that they could laugh at them (Faulkner 1993, 12). After slavery, formerly enslaved people often remarried each other in a church when they could. Many who had been parted by sale looked for each other for years. Black newspapers such as the *Chicago Defender* (founded 1905) carried columns through which people could look for lost spouses and children well into the 20th century.

Brer Rabbit Saves His Children: Teaching Strategy and Infolded Leadership

The rabbit trickster, Brer Rabbit, was featured in stories collected throughout the slaveholding South. Brer Rabbit was a kind of "everyman," and stories about him tell us much about the ways in which enslaved individuals and communities saw themselves. Many stories about Brer Rabbit involve his children. Enslaved communities taught their inhabitants what was important through songs and stories, some of which we still have. These stories and songs were teaching tools that were passed down through generations. They helped individuals and communities learn how to interact with an oppressive society. The also helped people learn the ideas behind organizing and executing social action, when necessary. At the turn of the 20th century, formerly enslaved storytellers in Society Hill, South Carolina, recounted a number of teaching stories that were told during slavery. "Brer Rabbit Rescues His Children" is one such story.

In "Brer Rabbit Rescues His Children," Brer Rabbit's children are tricked into entering a trap and are taken by his enemies. He discovers them held captive with a number of their missing neighbors in the cave of Brer Lion and Brer Gilyard, the dragon. Brer Rabbit is able to outsmart the stronger creatures and free his children and friends by creatively combining the contributions of animals with widely differing talents and abilities. Brer Rabbit then arranges for the far stronger animals to use their strength against each other. He plans strategies that are hidden—or "infolded"—and carries them out in ways that make these two dangerous animals use their strength to ultimately defeat each other. This story taught that successful leaders need not be able to overpower enemies alone. The intelligent combination of community members' different strengths could overcome a much stronger enemy. This was important because slaveholders had more resources than enslaved people, including weapons and the legal license to use them. Enslaved people used stories to teach that, if used wisely, their intelligence and creativity could overcome the masters' brute, or institutionalized, force.

Activities in the Slave Quarter

As difficult as enslavement was, bondpeople still found time to exercise their humanity by taking part in human activities when they were able. The categories of activities in the slave quarter community were not unlike those of other communities in the 19th-century United States and included communal and individual religious observance. Family and friends also came together for taffy pulls, quilting bees, dances, and communal singing.

One major difference between enslaved African descended communities and free European communities was the undeniable presence of sound. Sound filled enslaved working communities for two reasons. Song was encouraged by slaveholders, because it let planters know where enslaved people were, even when they could not see them. The enslaved people sang at the demand of the planter and overseer that they not be silent. According to the formerly enslaved statesman, abolitionist, and civil rights activist, Frederick Douglass, "a silent slave is not liked by masters or overseers. *'Make a noise,' 'make a noise,'* and *'bear a hand,'* are the words usually addressed to the slaves when there is silence amongst them. This may account for the almost constant singing heard in the southern states" (Douglass 1855, 74). Certainly, silent people could easily hide and might run away. For this reason, singing and other forms of music making were an almost constant occurrence when plantation administration was in attendance.

African American folklorist and educator Robert Russa Moton offered another important reason that enslaved people were required to sing. Moten and a group of African American folklorists from the Folklore Society of Hampton Institute wrote,

> In the work songs the rhythm sets the time of the work on which all are engaged, and the beating of feet, the swaying of the body or the movement of the arm may be retarded or accelerated at will by the leader. They thus formed a useful auxiliary to the plantation discipline and may be said to have had an economic value to carrying on the productive labor of the South. (Moton 1895, 50)

Not only did music let the plantation administration know where enslaved people were, it also encouraged and coordinated the work that made the slave system profitable.

Other reasons for the generation of music and others forms of sound in enslaved communities were more organic to Africans and their descendants. Music played a much larger role in the lives of enslaved Africans and their descendants than it did in the lives of their enslavers. For many of the peoples whose cultures informed that of the enslaved community, music and other appropriate forms of sound accompanied many of the events of daily life. Musicologist Francis Bebey writes, "music is an integral part of the life of every African individual from the moment of his birth" (Bebey 1975, 8).

One important example of the relationship of song to work and fun occurred in such harvest festivals as *corn shucking*. At harvest time, competing groups of workers from different plantations would have a contest to see which workgroup was fastest at shucking, or opening, the most corn. Each workgroup had a leader who sang to regulate the work, to encourage the workers to greater feats of shucking, and to make improvised jokes and thrusts at the opposing team(s). When the shucking was over, the enslaved women would have prepared a great feast for the enslaved workers. After the feast, there was a big dance with a fiddler and caller presiding. Corn shuckings were great events for the planters and the enslaved community—and a time of great fun and frolic. Much of the fun was built around food.

The foodways of Africans and their descendants reflected European, Native American, and African cooking methods applied to the foods they encountered in the new world. Maria Franklin has found that enslaved Afro-Virginians, for instance, often chose "poorer" cuts of meat and vegetables that responded well to all day cooking. They also augmented this diet. Franklin argues that archaeological "evidence indicates that they hunted, fished, gardened, raised livestock, and collected shellfish, wild berries, and nuts for their families" to augment foods that were distributed to them. She adds, "If you've ever had greens, black-eye peas or ham hocks, you've had a taste of the culinary ingenuity that enslaved Africans contributed to Southern foodways" (Franklin 2002, 88).

Self-Emancipation: Pushing the Agenda of Freedom

When Union armies began marching across the southeastern United States, enslaved people watched carefully. When they were certain that the presence of this military force represented an opportunity for freedom, people began to leave their enslavement. First, they began to leave in trickles of a few at a time, but soon, they were leaving in floods. Some of the earliest Union generals to witness slaves escaping to Union lines returned them, vowing that they had no intention of relieving southern planters of their "property." Others with more abolitionist leanings accepted them as liberated individuals. Still others took the self-liberated

African American contrabands arrive at Union lines, 1863. (Image by David B. Woodbury. Library of Congress)

slaves as "contrabands" or the "spoils of war." Enslaved people never stopped coming. Soon their numbers were so large that the government had to decide what to do with them. Their presence certainly proved a boon to the Union armies for they brought their skills and their labor with them. Their labor supported the North as surely as their absence crippled the South. Contrabands served the Union Army in whatever ways they were allowed, including as cooks, ditch diggers, nurses, seamstresses, laundresses, and valets. Sometimes they served as spies for the North. From the moment of their arrival, some enslaved people wanted to fight for their own freedom.

It took several years before the Union Army accepted the offers of formerly enslaved men to fight. Eventually some 200,000 African American men took up arms as soldiers during the Civil War—although they were not paid as much as Anglo soldiers and often did not receive their pay at all. Nurse, teacher, and seamstress Susie King Taylor traveled with the Thirty-third Regiment, First South Carolina Volunteers and wrote of her experiences some years later. She said that the nights were worse than any other time: that was when the Confederate soldiers would come looking for black soldiers. It was terrifying for many of these black Union soldiers—some of whom had been born free but most born enslaved—to go out against former enslavers to uncertain outcomes night after night. Mrs. Taylor testified, however, that the regiment never lost a man. She and Thomas W. Higginson, the white commander of the regiment, reported that men held a Ring Shout to prepare themselves to meet the "Secesh" or Confederate forces. In the midst of the Shout, the men encouraged each other: "Stand up to 'em brudder." "Hol' 'em brudder."

Susie King Taylor (1848–1912)

The book by nurse, teacher, seamstress, and camp cook Susan King Taylor, *Reminiscences of My Life in Camp,* may be the only account by a formerly enslaved African American woman of what she and many other "colored women did during the war." She was born Susan Baker in Liberty County, Georgia on August 6, 1848. Taylor and her mother, Hagar, were enslaved by Valentine Grest, a Swiss-born farmer. Taylor's grandmother was free and maintained a separate residence in the city of Savannah, Georgia. Grest was her guardian, and Taylor required a signed pass by him to travel the city at night. Grest gave Taylor's mother permission to send her and her brother to stay with their grandmother in Savannah.

While the children lived in Savannah, their grandmother made clandestine arrangements for them to learn to read and write. Soon, Taylor was forging Grest's signature on passes for her grandmother. When the Union forces began to fire on Fort Pulaski, Taylor was sent to her mother in the country. Two days after Fort Pulaski fell, her uncle took his family of seven and Susie to St. Catharine's Island and the protection of the Union Army.

She was thirteen years old when General Whitmore asked her to use her literacy skills to teach newly freed men, women, and children how to read and write, and she quickly agreed. Susan King Taylor became the first person to openly teach enslaved people in Georgia. Her activities give us an idea of the kinds of contributions made by African American women to the well-being and success of the Union forces during the Civil War.

Enslaved people in the 19th-century United States led complicated lives. On one hand, they were expected to be childish, subhuman, and dull. Knowing themselves to be otherwise, they arranged to be seen outside of the slave quarter as the outside world wished to see them. This mask hid a society that flourished in secret. This society was at times dangerous and contentious for its members, but it was also intelligent, creative, and strong.

References and Further Reading

Bebey, Francis. *African Music: A People's Art.* New York: Lawrence Hill & Co., 1975.

Douglass, Frederick. *Narrative of the Life of an American Slave [1845] in Autobiographies.* New York: Library of America, 1996.

Faulkner, William. *The Days When the Animals Talked: Black American Folktales and How They Came to Be.* New York: African World Press, 1993.

Franklin, Maria. "The Archaeological Dimensions of Soul Food: Interpreting Race, Culture, and Afro-Virginian Identity." In *Race and the Archaeology of Identity,* ed. Charles E. Orser, Jr. Salt Lake City: University of Utah Press, 2002, 88–107.

Granger, Mary. *Drums and Shadow: Survival Studies among the Georgia Coastal Negroes.* New York: Forgotten Books, 2007.

Hahn, Steven. *A Nation under Our Feet: Black Political Struggles in the Rural South from Slavery to the Great Migration*. New York: Belknap Press, 2003.

Moton, Robert Russ. *Southern Workman*. Hampton, VA: Folklore Society of Hampton Institute, 1895.

McKitrick, Eric L. *Slavery Defended: The Views of the Old South*. Englewood Cliffs, NJ: Prentice-Hall, 1963.

Morgan, Edmund S. *American Slavery, American Freedom: The Ordeal of Colonial Virginia*. New York: W. W. Norton, 1975.

Stampp, Kenneth. *The Peculiar Institution: Slavery in the Ante-Bellum South*. 1956; rpt., New York: Vintage Books, 1999.

Stuckey, Sterling. *Going Through the Storm: The Influence of African American Art in History*. New York: Oxford University Press, 1994.

Uncovering the True Relationship between Masters and Slaves | 5

Jennifer Hildebrand

M ost slave masters believed that their slaves were childlike and happy, and that they relied on the institution of slavery to survive. They insisted that their slaves could not possibly take care of themselves and that they needed their masters, who functioned in the role of father to slaves of all ages. Slaves had a different perspective. Most of them were not happy. They did not enjoy the long hours, the lack of autonomy, or the abuse that was a part of the institution of slavery. They knew that their masters and mistresses were exploiting their labor rather than caring for them. How can we reconcile two such different understandings of slavery? It is only possible to understand the relationship between master and slave if we delve into the primary sources that both master and slave have left behind, listening to the voices of both parties.

The Slaveholder's Perspective

Historically in the United States, masters represented Africans and their descendants as inferior, childlike, and dependent. This representation served several purposes. In the early years of the United States, slavery and the presence of persons of African descent helped Americans define their own identity. The majority of the people who first came from Europe to the area that would become the United States were English; most of them continued to think of themselves as English until the American Revolution (and a few continued to think of themselves as English even after that eruption). As the newly independent "Americans" set about to create a new nation, they had to develop a new system of politics, and their crafting of the Constitution and Bill of Rights often receives attention. But socially and culturally, these new Americans also had a new identity to create. What did it mean to be an American? The negative representation of Africans and their descendants actually made it easier for them to answer that question because it allowed them to employ a strategy that we might call binary self-definition. They examined Africans and their descendants in the United States, and, using a racist and ethnocentric standard, they found them to be different—opposite, even—from the idealized images they had of themselves. So if their dark-skinned slaves were inferior, they, with their white skin, were superior. Their slaves were dependent; they were independent. Their slaves were lazy; they were hardworking.

Stereotyping their slaves as children incapable of self-care allowed masters to portray themselves as all-powerful—just as a father was generally imagined to be within the 18th- and 19th-century family. According to this ideology, often referred to as paternalism, slave masters—these pseudo-fathers—loved and protected their slaves as they would their own children. Their slaves, in return, loved them and willingly offered their loyalty. Masters explained the supposed inferiority of their slaves by arguing that it was "natural," a result of some sort of ingrained racial characteristic (a completely false assertion). Their racism led them to conclude that African cultures were "primitive" or "uncivilized." The belief in the inferiority of persons of African descent, combined with the myth of their happiness under the paternalistic care of their masters, allowed slaveholders to represent slavery as a benevolent institution.

Having convinced himself that this father-child relationship really did exist, the master had to work hard to ensure that reality did not ever rise up to prove him wrong. Masters argued, for example, that if they did not

The owners of a plantation visiting the slave quarters. The illustration depicts benevolent slaveholders and grateful, happy slaves. (North Wind Picture Archives)

provide food, their slaves would go hungry; if they did not provide clothing, their slaves would have nothing to wear. But this truly was not the case. Slaves could have provided for themselves if they were not forced to labor constantly for the master. So the master had to create a situation in which his myth became reality. Many masters forbade their slaves to plant any sort of garden in which to grow their own food, and they did not give their slaves enough time off to allow them to hunt or fish for the meat that would sustain their families. Of course, slaves were never paid a salary, so purchasing necessities was not an option. So the master certainly did provide the slaves with the only food they had—but only because he made it impossible for them to get it in any other way. Attaining clothing for oneself or one's family presented a similar obstacle, and once again, masters stepped in, providing for their slaves and asserting that without their support, the slave would not survive. By making it impossible for slaves to support themselves, masters created a self-fulfilling prophecy.

Especially during and after the 1830s, as abolitionists began a concerted fight against slavery from the North and as slave runaways and rebels maintained a steady resistance from within the South, slaveholders put a lot of effort into defending their ownership of other human beings. An educator, Virginian Thomas R. Dew emphasized the economic necessity of protecting slavery as an institution. He argued that if the slaves were freed, their owners must be compensated for their loss of "property." Additionally, he said, the prejudices of the American people meant that African-descended persons could not stay here. They would have to be sent to Africa. Compensation and transplantation would bankrupt the state, according to his calculations. Thornton Stringfellow, a Virginia minister, put considerable effort into demonstrating what he believed to be Biblical support for the peculiar institution. He argued that God sanctioned slavery, and that Jesus recognized its validity. James Henry Hammond, once governor of South Carolina and a U.S. senator, presented a defense based on the necessities of labor, arguing that every society needed "a class to do the menial duties, to perform the drudgery of life" (Hammond in McKitrick, ed., 122). Defenders of slavery dragged science into the debate as well. "Scientist" Samuel Cartwright argued (quite wrongly, we now know) that Africans and their descendants belonged to a different species of man, so enslaving them could not really have a moral taint.

While slaveholders, who wanted desperately to justify their ownership of human beings, embraced many of these arguments, the assertion that slavery was in fact a paternalistic, benevolent institution seemed to remain most popular among them. Declarations of the master's love for his slave—and more importantly, of the slave's love for his master—became commonplace. John Pendleton Kennedy, born in Baltimore, Maryland, and later the United States Secretary of the Navy, demonstrated the southern belief in the permanent childlike state of persons of African descent: "The Negro . . . in his true nature is always a boy, let him be ever so old." Kennedy added that a person of African descent was "dependent upon the white race; dependent for guidance and direction even to the obtaining of

James Henry Hammond (1807–1864)

James Henry Hammond was born in 1807 in South Carolina. He would later serve the state as a representative (1835–1836), the governor (1842), and a senator (1857–1860). As he would later advise his son, Hammond believed it better to choose a rather homely wife with a fortune rather than an attractive woman without one. Following his own advice, upon his marriage, Hammond became the owner of 147 slaves. In his official positions representing the state of South Carolina, Hammond advocated for slavery passionately and was a leading proponent of the belief that slaves were happy and carefree.

If one is seeking to debunk the myth of the happy, well-cared-for slave, of which Hammond was a leading proponent, one need look no further than the plantation of James Henry Hammond. Especially during the early years of his reign as master, Hammond's slaves died in significantly high numbers, leading historian Carol Bleser to suggest that Hammond really did believe the opinion that he articulated in his "Mud Sill Speech." Hammond argued that every society needed an inferior group to do the hard work, and he apparently saw this working class as dispensable. Bleser's implication is that he quite literally worked them to death. Though he did not consider the loss in human terms—the loss of a life—he did consider the economic costs of replacing slaves who died under his care. For this reason, he sometimes called in doctors and sometimes played doctor himself. According to historian Drew Gilpin Faust, Hammond's slaves had little faith in the efficacy of his medicines, often trying to conceal their illnesses or to treat themselves using cures that had an African heritage.

The female slaves living on Hammond's property were almost certainly miserable. Hammond took a slave woman as his mistress in 1839, eight years after he married his wife, Catherine. Later, he would take the slave woman's twelve-year-old daughter as his mistress as well. Hammond's records reveal that several of the slaves on his plantation were of mixed race, and in at least one case, he named the white father, a stable hand. It seems highly unlikely that slave women entered into such relationships of a free will.

Hammond's slaves rebelled. He reported fires on his plantation that may well have been started by his slaves. His slaves ran away—they made fifty-three attempts between 1831 and 1855. Hammond refused to see such resistance as a condemnation of slavery as an institution. Bleser found that even in his personal papers, where historians often expect to find a public figure's "real" thoughts, he continued to preach the blessings of slavery.

his most indispensable necessities. Apart from this protection he has the helplessness of a child" (quoted in Elkins, 132). Hammond went so far as to assert that by enslaving them, masters had "elevated" their slaves "from the condition in which God first created them." Slaves were, moreover, "happy, content, unaspiring [*sic*], and utterly incapable, from intellectual weakness, ever to give us any trouble by their aspirations" (Hammond in McKitrick 1963, 123). The only danger facing slaves came from those persons intent on abolishing the institution, he proclaimed: "I believe our slaves are the happiest 3 millions of human beings on whom the sun shines. Into their Eden is coming Satan in the guise of an abolitionist" (quoted in Stampp 1999, 430).

The Slaves' Reality

The voices of the master class survived slavery in a number of ways—in letters and diaries, autobiographies, plantation records, and court records. It is often harder to find the voices of the enslaved, but it is certainly not impossible. In a small number of cases, a slave managed to escape, and then told his or her story in an autobiography. Some persons who were enslaved when the Civil War ended had a chance to provide an oral history of their lives to writers employed by the Works Progress Administration in the 1930s, during the Great Depression. Though we recognize that a lot of time passed between their experience as slaves and their retelling of the story, historians have found their testimony relatively reliable and extremely valuable when trying to piece together the story of the enslaved. Other sources, which require the historian to read with a bit more caution and creativity, include the songs and folktales that the slaves shared during the days of slavery. Some of these were written down by masters who overheard them, and others were preserved within the family and retold by the descendants of slaves. All of these sources give us a much wider window into the institution of slavery, and allow us to balance the interpretation of slavery that the master provided against that of the enslaved.

Today, when we consider the violence of the master class, the theft of the profits of one's labor, and the supposed ownership of another person, it is clear that the slaves must have hated slavery. But the masters worked hard to convince themselves that the master-slave relationship was a positive one. Fortunately, the enslaved told us—through both their words and their actions—that they despised the peculiar institution. Slaves ran away from their masters, especially when they were threatened with physical harm or a sale away from friends and family. Slaves plotted and even rose up in rebellion against their masters. The rebellion led by Nat Turner and the

Illustration of a runaway slave, part of a larger piece printed as a memorial to the American Anti-Slavery Society, 1838. (Library of Congress)

conspiracies of Gabriel Prosser and Denmark Vesey are the best known, but historian Herbert Aptheker argued that more than 250 plots or actual uprisings occurred during slavery. On an everyday level, resistance was commonplace as well. Slaves showed their displeasure with the master-slave relationship by stealing from the master, by "accidentally" breaking the master's tools, by working slowly, and by generally disobeying, whenever possible, those rules that aimed to completely control the slave's body and mind.

The songs and folktales of the enslaved testify about their dislike for their masters and for the institution of slavery. Sometimes the complaint was explicit. In a spiritual called "Hold the Wind," slaves sang:

> When I get to heaven, gwine be at ease,
> Me and my God gonna do as we please
> Gonna chatter with the Father, argue with the Son,
> Tell um 'bout the world I just come from. (quoted in Stuckey 1994, 6)

The message is quite clear: in heaven, the slave will be "at ease," no longer forced to work from sunrise to sunset. Moreover, when he or she meets up with God and Jesus, the slave owner had better watch out, because the slave is going to tell them *exactly* what sort of things really went on during slavery. Other songs allowed the slaves to say just how hard they were worked by their masters, and just how tired they felt:

> I'll walk in de graveyard, I'll walk through de graveyard,
>   To lay dis body down.
> I'll lie in de grave and stretch out my arms,
>   Lay dis body down. (quoted in Stuckey 1994, 12)

Such lyrics testified to the exhaustion of the slave and the longing for peace. The rest that the enslaved longed for could only realistically be expected after death.

Slaves observed their masters carefully, and they knew their masters much better than their masters knew them. So they knew exactly how much protest they could voice in front of their masters. Masters, who wanted so badly to believe in the paternalistic myth of the happy slave, did not want to hear their slaves singing about their displeasure or their exhaustion. So if the master was near, the enslaved would employ a system of double meanings. Cloaking their own sufferings in a tale from the Bible, for example, led their masters to think that they were singing about a story that they heard from the minister. But slave songs with Biblical themes usually expressed their religious beliefs *and* their distaste for slavery. Songs about small David defeating powerful Goliath had a special meaning to the powerless slave. When the slaves sang, "Joshua fit [fought] the battle of Jerico / An' de walls come tumblin' down," we can understand today, as masters could not or would not, that slaves were envisioning the invisible walls that held the slave on the plantation tumbling down

Denmark Vesey (1767–1822)

In Charleston, South Carolina, Denmark Vesey planned a slave uprising for 1822. His plot was remarkable for many reasons. Though it failed, its reach was reputedly widespread, involving thousands of slaves. Perhaps more interesting, however, is the fact that Vesey was a free man.

In 1781, Captain Joseph Vesey purchased Denmark Vesey, who was roughly fourteen. Joseph Vesey was a slave trader, and he soon resold Denmark. When it became clear that Denmark was not well—he had epilepsy—he was returned to the captain as defective property. He spent the next two years as the captain's personal slave, traveling with him aboard slave ships and seeing the horrors of the Middle Passage firsthand. Then Joseph settled in Charleston, and Denmark remained with him for the next seventeen years. During Denmark's trial, Joseph would testify that he had always been a loyal slave, perhaps demonstrating that slaves, of necessity, hid their displeasure from their masters, and that masters wanted desperately to believe that their slaves were happy.

In a remarkable shift of luck, Denmark Vesey won $1,500 in a lottery in 1800. He used his winnings to purchase his freedom ($600) and to open a carpenter's shop. Vesey established himself as a skilled and reliable blacksmith. He bought a nice house. As he rose to a level of prominence in the African American community of Charleston, Vesey, with several other free blacks, established a black Methodist church that flourished.

Why did a free, relatively prosperous man risk life, limb, and property by leading a revolt against slavery? The simple answer is that though no longer a slave, he still hated slavery. His children remained enslaved. The economic downturn of 1819 meant that he had to see slaves auctioned off by indebted masters, often separating family and friends. Moreover, he found that freedom from slavery did not bring him freedom from prejudice and restrictions put in place by the ruling white race. Fearing the sort of message that was disseminated in a black church, Charleston's whites closed it four years after it opened. Vesey drew inspiration from a successful slave revolt that established the independent island of Haiti in 1804 and from the Bible. Joshua, chapter four verse twenty-one, was one of his favorites: "And they utterly destroyed all that was in the city, both man and woman, young and old, and ox, and sheep, and ass, with the edge of the sword."

Vesey recruited thousands of enslaved and free African Americans from urban Charleston and the neighboring plantations, drawing on African and Christian religious practices to inspire them. The conspiracy was planned for July 14, 1822, but George Wilson, an enslaved man, revealed it to his master. Vesey moved the date up to mid-June, hoping to catch the master class unaware, but the authorities found out. In the panic that followed, soldiers flooded Charleston's streets. More than 100 people were arrested, and a lengthy trial revealed the depth and intricacy of the plan. Denmark Vesey was hanged with thirty-six others, having given his life as a freed man because of his hatred of the relationship between master and slave.

around them. The rescue of Egypt's slaves by Moses must have been a particular favorite of the enslaved, and when they sang "Go down, Moses, 'Way down in Egypt land, / Tell ole Pharoah, To let my people go," the song had both a religious and a very personal meaning (Johnson and Johnson 1954, 65–67, 56–58, 51–53). By employing this system of double meanings, by masking their own hatred of slavery in the stories of the Bible, slaves managed to avoid being punished by masters who did not want to hear their complaints. They also managed to give voice to their own frustrations and to create a valuable historical record.

The folktales that slaves shared among themselves also allowed them to protest against the slave-master relationship without upsetting their masters. Many of the tales that slaves told featured a cast of animals. Brer (an abbreviation of Brother) Rabbit often starred in these tales, and in many cases he represented the slave. Smaller than his foes, Brer Rabbit used his wits to survive much as the slaves had to rely on their own mental dexterity to survive and resist slavery. William Faulkner's "Brer Tiger and the Big Wind" provides an excellent example. In this tale, Brer Tiger owned a large plot of land with a pear tree that never stopped producing fruit and a spring that never ran dry. One year, rain did not come to Brer Tiger's neighborhood. Though he still had his pears and his spring, his neighbors' crops were not growing, and their creeks and springs had dried up. But Brer Tiger would not share his bounty—much like the slave masters who would not share their bounty with their slaves, even though it was the labor of the slaves that produced it.

Brer Rabbit had no choice. Working in concert with the other small creatures in the area, they managed to trick big, strong, Brer Tiger, who had a mouth full of sharp, powerful teeth, into believing that a big wind—a cyclone or a tornado—was headed straight for them. The other, smaller animals pretended to be afraid, and they begged Brer Rabbit to tie them to a tree so that the wind would not blow them away. Instantly, Brer Tiger stepped in and demanded that Brer Rabbit tie him up first. The implication, of course, was that Brer Tiger believed that his life was more important than the lives of the other creatures around him—just like a master thought his life was more valuable than his slaves' lives. With Brer Tiger tied quite snugly to a tree, the other animals were free to feast upon his pears and to fill their buckets with his water (Faulkner 1993, 89–94). Such a tale conveys clearly the slaves' disgust at their masters' greed. But in many cases, a slave could have told the tale right in front of his or her master. The masters had worked so hard to convince themselves that their slaves were uneducated, silly, childlike beings, that all they heard were cute stories about fuzzy animals. Because they believed their slaves were unintelligent, masters became quite deaf to the ways in which slaves voiced their critique of the peculiar institution.

When we listen to the voices of the enslaved, it is clear that they were not the simple, backward, uncivilized beings that their masters insisted they were. The slave-master relationship was much more complicated than masters believed. We can discern the level of civilization from which the enslaved came when we reflect on the abilities that they brought with them to the area that would become the United States. Studying the early years of the colony of South Carolina, historian Peter Wood described a number of skills possessed by African slaves: the aptitude to build effective fortifications; knowledge of the flora and fauna of South Carolina (which was quite similar to that of West Africa, the region of origin for most of

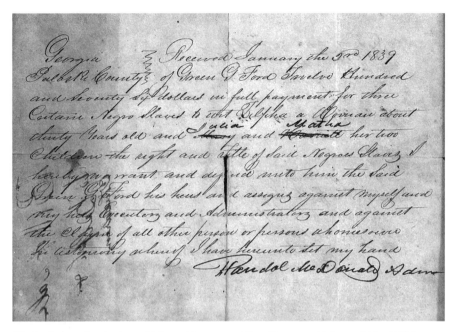

Bill of sale for a female slave of 'about thirty years old' and her two children, sold for $1,274.
(Valdosta State University Archives and Special Collections)

South Carolina's slaves); detailed knowledge about the medicinal qualities of certain plants; the ability to weave baskets, boxes, and mats from the grasses of South Carolina; familiarity with swampland and knowledge about building and maneuvering canoes in the swamps; sophisticated fishing techniques, including the ability to poison streams with an herbal agent that made the fish lethargic, so that they might be picked up by hand, yet without poisoning the eater of the fish; the raising of livestock, upon which the livelihood of Africans and Europeans in South Carolina rested in the early years; the cultivation of rice, a crop with which many West Africans were familiar; and, finally, the knowledge to create the mortar, pestle, and fanning basket used to husk the rice after harvest (Wood 1974).

Wood concluded that slaves were not "passive objects of white instruction." Instead, they brought knowledge with them from Africa and shared it among themselves. "Occasionally," Wood added, they "ended up teaching their masters. Africans . . . proved knowledgeable and competent in areas where Europeans remained disdainful or ignorant" (1974, 161). African skills thus proved crucial to the success of many of the southern colonies. Rather than helpless and dependant slaves, Wood revealed masters who were, in many ways, dependent on the knowledge and skills of their slaves. But the contribution of Africans to the emergence of the United States of America goes further. According to historian Edmund Morgan, at the time of the American Revolution, the colonies "desperately needed the assistance of other countries," and they managed to purchase that assistance—with the profits from tobacco, a crop "produced mainly by slave labor." Morgan concluded that "to a large degree it may be said that Americans bought their independence with slave labor" (1975, 5). The fact that African knowledge and skill in addition to African labor were necessary to the survival and evolution of the United States disproves the masters' notion of the helpless, hapless, dependent slaves.

We also learn far more about the role of violence in the master-slave relationship when we listen to the voices of the enslaved. Masters did not deny that they used corporal punishment to make their slaves behave as they wanted. They argued that a slave, just like a child, needed to be corrected now and then. But their descriptions rarely portrayed the full extent of this violence. A much truer picture can be found in the autobiography of Frederick Douglass, a slave who managed to escape to freedom in the North. Consider this description of a beating administered by his master, Captain Anthony, to Douglass's Aunt:

> Master . . . would at times seem to take great pleasure in whipping a slave. I have often been awakened at the dawn of day by the most heart-rending shrieks of an aunt of mine, whom he used to tie up to a joist, and whip upon her naked back till she was literally covered with blood. No words, no tears, no prayers, from his gory victim, seemed to move his iron heart from its bloody purpose. The louder she screamed, the harder he whipped; and where the blood ran fastest, there he whipped longest. He would whip her to make her scream, and whip her to make her hush; and not until overcome by fatigue, would he cease to swing the blood-clotted cowskin. (1996, 18)

Douglass wanted to emphasize the fact that such beatings were common and occurred every day: he provided the above description in the first chapter of his autobiography, in which he described his own childhood, to emphasize to his readers that such horrors were quite familiar even to a child.

Douglass also wanted to explain to his readers that masters administered such beatings frequently. They did not mete out physical punishments on a rational basis and only when absolutely necessary, as they often claimed in their public statements. Douglass asserted that violence by masters and their hired overseers often went beyond a mere corrective. In fact, Douglass asserted, "killing a slave, or any colored person, in Talbot [C]ounty, Maryland, [was] not treated as a crime, either by the courts or the community." Douglass presented the case of Thomas Lanman, who "killed two slaves, one of whom he killed with a hatchet, by knocking his brains out. He used to boast of the commission of the awful and bloody deed. I have heard him do so laughingly" (1996, 31). Apparently, no bond existed that could protect a slave from an angry master, and even the rational knowledge that killing his slaves meant wasting the money that he invested in them could not stop Lanman's thirst for blood.

Neither the gender of the slave nor the gender of the slave owner precluded violence. Douglass described the actions of Mrs. Giles Hicks, who owned Douglass's cousin—until Mrs. Hicks killed her. His cousin was "a young girl between fifteen and sixteen years of age," and Mrs. Hicks

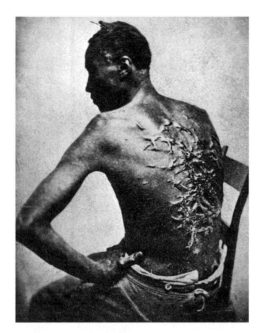

The original caption on this 1863 photo-graph of a slave read: 'Overseer Aarayou Carrier whipped me. I was two months in bed sore from the whipping. My master come after I was whipped; he discharged the overseer.' (Bettmann/Corbis)

mangl[ed] her person in the most horrible manner, breaking her nose and breastbone with a stick, so that the poor girl expired in a few hours after-ward. . . . The offence for which this girl was thus murdered was this: She had been set that night to mind Mrs. Hicks's baby, and during the night she fell asleep, and the baby cried. She, having lost her rest for several nights previous, did not hear the crying. They were both in the room with Mrs. Hicks. Mrs. Hicks, finding the girl slow to move, jumped from her bed, seized an oak stick of wood by the fireplace, and with it broke the girl's nose and breastbone, and thus ended her life. (1996, 31)

Mistresses, as well as masters, did not hesitate to turn to violence when seized by anger, and neither master nor mistress allowed any of the rules of humanity or religion—"Thou shalt not kill"—to govern them when pas-sion was aroused.

Gender also factors into a discussion of master-slave relationships in another way. For many enslaved women, rape at the hands of their mas-ters was an oft-endured violation. Though little literature exists as yet to address the fact, we must assume that sexual violence was not always lim-ited to female victims. We do have testimony from the enslaved regarding the rape of female slaves; however, the general societal rules regarding dis-cussions of sexual matters during the 19th century, when slave narratives were written, prevented such discussions from being graphic. In a chapter entitled "The Trials of Girlhood," escaped slave Harriet Jacobs explained the challenges that she faced upon turning fifteen—"a sad epoch in the life of a slave girl." It was at that time, she related, that

> My master began to whisper foul words in my ear. Young as I was, I could not remain ignorant of their import. . . . He tried his utmost to corrupt the pure principles my grandmother had instilled. He peopled my young mind with unclean images, such as only a vile monster could think of. I turned from him with disgust and hatred. But he was my master. I was compelled to live under the same roof with him—where I saw a man forty years my senior daily violating the most sacred commandments of nature. He told me I was his property; that I must be subject to his will in all things. My soul revolted against the mean tyranny. But where could I turn for protection? No matter whether the slave girl be as black as ebony or as fair as her mistress. In either case, there is no shadow of law to protect her from insult, from violence, or even from death; all these are inflicted by fiends who bear the shape of men. The mistress, who ought to protect the helpless victim, has no other feelings towards her but those of jealousy and rage. The degradation, the wrongs, the vices, that grow out of slavery, are more than I can describe. (Jacobs 2001, 26)

Jacobs wrote enough to make her suffering at the hands of her master clear. She explained that the knowledge of the master's sexual offenses was all too common among slave children, especially girls: "Even the little child, who is accustomed to wait on her mistress and her children, will learn, before she is twelve years old, why it is that her mistress hates such and such a one among the slaves." The knowledge of the master's behavior is soon made worse by her personal experience of it:

> Soon she will learn to tremble when she hears her master's footfall. She will be compelled to realize that she is no longer a child. If God has bestowed beauty upon her, it will prove her greatest curse. That which commands admiration in the white woman only hastens the degradation of the female slave. (Jacobs 2001, 26)

Finally, Jacobs informed her reader, "I cannot tell how much I suffered in the presence of these wrongs, nor how I am still pained by the retrospect" (Jacobs 2001, 27).

Historiography: How Historians Write about Slavery

Slaves hated slavery. Most who read that statement today acknowledge it as a common fact, but fifty years ago, in many schools across the United States, the message given to students was quite different. For almost 100 years after slavery ended, historians continued to write about that "peculiar institution" as if it had been a positive good for society and especially for the slaves held in bondage. During the first half of the 20th century, U. B. Phillips's conclusions, presented in *American Negro Slavery* (1918), reigned supreme. Phillips believed that the master was superior in knowledge and capability. He did not believe that the enslaved brought any knowledge or skills to their masters' plantations. He summarized his position by repeating a phrase often heard among planters: "a negro was what a white man made him." Phillips thought African-descended persons were likely to copy the European-descended persons that he considered to be culturally, religiously, and intellectually superior. This "imitative" tendency, combined with the power that a master held over a slave, led him to conclude that slaves "became largely standardized." He believed that this "standardized" slave was generally happy, open to Christianity, highly superstitious, glad to accept a subordinate position, and very loyal to his or her master (1966, 291). Phillips's account of slave-slaveholder relations clearly bore the racist stamp of slaveholders. His scholarship is problematic because he listened only to the voices of the slaveholders. Today, his work tells us a lot about masters' and mistresses' perceptions of slavery, but it tells us little about the real relationship between master and slave.

In 1903, W. E. B. Du Bois published *The Souls of Black Folk*. The essays in this volume contain enough sensitivity to African and African American cultural traits to demonstrate that enslaved Africans had much knowledge to exchange with their masters. But in 1903 and for many years later, most historians were no more ready to listen to this argument than slaveholders had been willing to acknowledge just how much they learned from their slaves. In 1943, Herbert Aptheker began, in *American Negro Slave Revolts*, to counter the idea that slaves were happy. Using a carefully derived definition of revolt, Aptheker found that the supposedly happy American slaves had arisen against their masters approximately 250 times. Still, mainstream history clung to the nostalgic image of the happy slave who was devoted to his or her master.

By the mid-1950s, however, American society was beginning to change. African Americans banded together to fight the racism that still existed in the United States, tackling especially the prejudice that took the form of segregation and disenfranchisement. As activist African Americans refused to have their voices silenced, some historians became convinced that these activists' ancestors might not have been easily silenced, either. Kenneth Stampp's *The Peculiar Institution* (1956) broke some important new ground in terms of historians' understanding of the relations between master and slave. He argued that if the slaves seemed like children, it was only because their masters forced them to behave in such a way by denying them opportunities for independence. He emphasized that any challenge to the master's belief in the subordination of a slave was often punished with the sort of violence that Frederick Douglass described. Any time slaves played along with the master's stereotypes, perhaps fearing punishment if they complained, the master could revel in the happiness and loyalty of his slaves. Stampp dismissed the notion of the happy slave as "folklore" and insisted that it "must not be mistaken for fact" (1999, 7).

Historians proved unwilling to relinquish the stereotype of the happy slave immediately, however. Stanley Elkins's *Slavery: A Problem in American Institutional and Intellectual Life* (1959) took a slightly different path than that followed by Stampp. Elkins argued that the helpless slave who depended on his paternalistic master really did exist—but only because of the brutality of the institution of slavery. Elkins found that Africans were not weak or backward when observed among their own ethnic groups on the African continent. Instead, it was the horror of capture, the long march to the sea, sale, and the Middle Passage (the journey from the African continent to the Americas) that left the slave *tabula rasa*, a blank slate, ready to soak up whatever information the master felt he or she needed. Elkins attributed the creation of this blank-minded slave to the violence often overlooked by those who embraced the stereotype of the happy slave. But he nonetheless insisted that the initial shock of enslavement and the internment-camp-like conditions of the plantation left the slave so psychically wounded that she or he had nothing to contribute to the social formation of the United States. Though a departure from the benevolence emphasized by Phillips, Elkins's story remained one in which the relationship between the master and the slave was controlled completely by the master.

Historians continued to reexamine and retell the story of the master-slave relationship. In 1968, Sterling Stuckey published an article entitled "Through the Prism of Folklore" in the *Massachusetts Review*. In it, he turned to the folklore and songs of the enslaved. He argued that if we wanted to know what slaves thought, we should listen to their voices. Of course, that was a difficult task to undertake. Obviously, masters did not want their slaves taking time away from work to write their own histories. Moreover, masters realized that literacy brought power, and they wanted their slaves as powerless as possible. This does not mean that the enslaved failed to tell their stories, however. Many African groups emphasized the sharing of stories and histories orally instead of in writing. It is possible that many of the enslaved might have chosen to tell their life stories in spoken or sung words even if they had had access to literacy. So we need to look to songs and folktales to find them. Masters did not object when slaves sang—indeed, they often believed (incorrectly) that it showed that slaves were happy. Neither did masters object when slaves told folktales—again, this was often seen as evidence of contentment, or at least of the childlike nature attributed by paternalistic masters to their slaves.

Many of the songs and tales of slaves have been recorded. Because masters did not believe them to be subversive, they saw no reason to try to suppress them. Stuckey suggested, then, that we use those songs and tales as our prism. Before, historians looked at slaves using one single, undifferentiated beam of light: masters' accounts. But when you shine a light through a prism, it refracts, and you see all of the colors of the rainbow: red, orange, yellow, green, blue, indigo, and violet. The lives of slaves are just the same. If we only look at the single ray of light that the masters saw, then all we see is plain, white light. But when we use folklore as a prism to refract the lives of the enslaved, we see so much more. When we listen to their voices, we hear about their lives that existed outside of the watchful eye of the master. We hear about their family values, their religious beliefs, the way they spent their (little) leisure time, their remembrances of Africa. We also hear that, no matter what the master thought, they did not like slavery, and in most cases, they did not much care for their masters, either.

Conclusion

Twenty-first-century historians agree that slavery was a coercive, brutal institution. But they also know that the psychic and spiritual strength of enslaved Africans and their descendants was stronger than the horrors of the peculiar institution. Despite the unequal power relationship that existed between master and slave, the relationship between the two was not one-sided. Africans and their descendants contributed much to the cultural and social life of the United States. Though the exchange of ideas between slave and slaveholder may not have been equal in terms of the power of the contributors, Africans and their descendants brought customs, traditions, and knowledge of extreme and lasting value to the relationship between master and slave. Twenty-first-century historians still have a big job ahead of them: they need to continue to explore the voices of the enslaved to ensure that we represent America's history accurately.

References and Further Reading

Aptheker, Herbert. *American Negro Slave Revolts*. 1943; rpt., New York: International Publishers, 1993.

Bleser, Carol, ed. *Secret and Sacred: The Diaries of James Henry Hammond, A Southern Slaveholder*. 1988; rpt., Columbia: University of South Carolina Press, 1997.

Douglass, Frederick. *Narrative of the Life of an American Slave*. 1845; rpt., in *Autobiographies*, New York: Library of America, 1996.

Du Bois, W. E. B. *The Souls of Black Folks*. New York: Oxford University Press, 2008.

Elkins, Stanley M. *Slavery: A Problem in American Institutional and Intellectual Life*, 3rd ed. 1959; rpt., Chicago: University of Chicago Press, 1976.

Faulkner, William. *The Days When the Animals Talked: Black American Folktales and How They Came to Be*. New York: African World Press, 1993.

Faust, Drew Gilpin. *James Henry Hammond and the Old South: A Design for Mastery*. Baton Rouge: Louisiana State University Press, 1982.

Jacobs, Harriet. *Incidents in the Life of a Slave Girl*. 1861; rpt., New York: W. W. Norton, 2001.

Johnson, James Weldon, and J. Rosamond Johnson. *The Book of Negro Spirituals*. New York: Da Capo Press, 1954.

McKitrick, Eric L. *Slavery Defended: The Views of the Old South*. Englewood Cliffs, NJ: Prentice-Hall, 1963.

Morgan, Edmund S. *American Slavery, American Freedom: The Ordeal of Colonial Virginia*. New York: W. W. Norton, 1975.

Phillips, U. B. *American Negro Slavery*. 1918; rpt., Baton Rouge: Louisiana State University Press, 1966.

Stampp, Kenneth. *The Peculiar Institution: Slavery in the Ante-Bellum South*. 1956; rpt., New York: Vintage Books, 1999.

Stuckey, Sterling. *Going Through the Storm: The Influence of African American Art in History*. New York: Oxford University Press, 1994.

Wood, Peter. "'It Was a Negro Taught Them': A New Look at Labor in Early South Carolina." *Journal of Asian and African Studies* 9 (1974): 160–179.

"Yes, We All Shall Be Free": African Americans Make the Civil War a Struggle for Freedom

David Williams and Teresa Crisp Williams

6

"I can just barely remember my mother." That was what Tom Robinson, born into slavery on a North Carolina plantation, told an interviewer for the 1930s Federal Writers Project. He was only ten years old when he was sold away from his mother shortly before the Civil War started.

> But I do remember how she used to take us children and kneel down in front of the fireplace and pray. She'd pray that the time would come when everybody could worship the Lord under their own vine and fig tree—all of them free. It's come to me lots of time since. There she was a'praying, and on other plantations women was a'praying. All over the country the same prayer was being prayed. (Berlin 1995, 275–276)

The Civil War served only to make such prayers more expectant and intense. In her reminiscences of the war years, former Savannah slave Susie King Taylor wrote vividly of the excitement among her neighbors: "Oh, how those people prayed for freedom! I remember, one night, my grandmother went out into the suburbs of the city to a church meeting, and they were fervently singing this old hymn,—"

> Yes, we all shall be free,
> Yes, we all shall be free,
> Yes, we all shall be free,
> When the Lord shall appear—

Suddenly, she recalled, local lawmen burst in and arrested the entire congregation for "planning freedom." They further accused the slaves of singing "the Lord" instead of "Yankee," as King recalled, "to blind any one who might be listening" (Taylor 2006, 8).

Susie Baker King Taylor, an escaped slave from South Carolina, joined the Thirty-third U.S. Colored Troops as laundress, teacher, and nurse during the Civil War. (Library of Congress)

But enslaved blacks were not simply waiting either for God or the Yankees to give them freedom. They were taking it for themselves. Though Lincoln's Emancipation Proclamation is often cited as having "freed the slaves," it only grudgingly recognized what blacks had themselves already forced on Lincoln's government. That document, as Professor Ira Berlin points out,

> heralded not the dawn of universal liberty but the compromised and piecemeal arrival of an undefined freedom. Indeed, the Proclamation's flat prose, ridiculed as having the moral grandeur of a bill of lading, suggests that the true authorship of African American freedom lies elsewhere—not at the top of American society but at the bottom. (Berlin 1995, 279)

"They Learn to Feel Very Independent"

Slaveholder Laura Comer illustrated Berlin's point when she wrote in her diary, "the servants are so indolent and obstinate it is a trial to have anything to do with them" (Williams, Williams, and Carlson 2002, 138). Slaves resisted slavery by feigning ignorance or illness, sabotaging plantation equipment, and roaming freely in defiance of the law. As for forced labor, what work slaves did was done with measured effort. Some refused to work at all. A plantation mistress wrote of one of her slaves: "Nancy has been very impertinent. . . . She said she would not be hired out by the month, neither would she go out to get work" (Williams, Williams, and Carlson 2002, 138). Another woman wrote to her husband, "We are doing as best we know, or as good as we can get the Servants to do; they learn to feel very independent" (Williams, Williams, and Carlson 2002, 138).

One slave who had learned his letters forged a pass and made his way from Richmond north to federal lines. Another slave journeyed 500 miles writing his own passes along the way. Some slaves did not have quite that far to go. In northern Missouri, the free state of Iowa was right next door. So common was it for slaves to cross the border during the war that many slaveholders either moved south or had their slaves "sold down the river." Joe Johnson was a Missouri slave who feared that fate. So he hid his family in a wagon, slipped past the slave patrols, and kept going until he reached the Iowa border. For slaves in Texas, the route to freedom most often led south to Mexico.

Many escaping slaves found it simpler and safer to stay close to home. After a severe beating, one Georgia slave ran away and dug out a sizeable cave in which he took up residence. A short time later, under cover of night, he crept back to his old plantation, packed up his wife and two children, and took them back to his cave where they all lived until the war's end. In most cases, fugitives banded together for mutual support and protection. They sustained themselves by living off the land and making raids against local plantations—often the very plantations on which they had labored without pay for years.

Those slaves who did not escape gave aid and comfort to those who did. They funneled food and supplies to their fugitive friends and relatives, passed information to them, and provided a much-needed support network. It would have been difficult if not impossible for many fugitive bands to operate effectively without such support. The same was true for bands of white deserters, draft evaders, and their families who also depended on local slaves for support. Like so many other enslaved blacks, Jeff Rayford did whatever he could to help deserters hiding in the Pearl River swamp of Mississippi. Another Mississippi freedman recalled carrying food to hideouts where women and children had taken up residence. In Jones County, Rachel Knight, a slave of both white and black ancestry, was a key ally of the deserter gang led by Newton Knight, her owner's grandson. She supplied food for the men and served as a spy in their operations against local Confederates.

John Kellogg, a Union prisoner escaping through the Georgia mountains with the help of local blacks, was impressed by what he called the slave "telegraph line." Slaves near Carnesville told Kellogg and his comrades of Union troop movements, some at a distance of a hundred and 50 miles, between Chattanooga and Atlanta. The information was essential to planning the safest route back to federal lines. Union prisoner James Gilmore, who slipped out of Richmond's Libby Prison and made it back to safety with the help of Virginia blacks, made his gratitude clear in a manuscript he authored shortly after the war. Gilmore's publisher, Edmund Kirke, was eager to get it into print. "It tells," Kirke said,

> what the North does not as yet fully realize—the fact that in the very heart of the South are four millions of people—of strong, able-bodied, true-hearted people,—whose loyalty led them, while the heel of the "chivalry" was on their necks, and a halter dangling before their eyes, to give their last crust, and their only suit of Sunday homespun, to the fleeing fugitive, simply because he wore the livery and fought the battles of the Union. (Williams 2005, 341)

Harriet Tubman, famous for her prewar service on the Underground Railroad, headed a ring of spies and scouts who operated along the South Carolina coast. Mary Louveste, an employee at Virginia's Gosport Navy Yard where the Confederacy's ironclad warship *Virginia* was under construction, smuggled out plans and other documents related to the new secret weapon. She carried the material to Washington, D.C., where she placed it in the hands of Secretary of the Navy Gideon Welles. There was even a black Union spy in the Confederate White House. Mary Elizabeth Bowser, an associate of unionist Richmond socialite Elizabeth Van Lew, worked as a maid at the presidential residence. She funneled anything worthy of note to Van Lew who passed the information on to the Federals at City Point.

Very often intelligence came from escaping slaves who related news of fortifications, military movements, and Confederate troop strength. One evening near Fortress Monroe, six Virginia slaves arrived behind federal lines with detailed information on Confederate deployments in the region. There were two earthworks guarding approaches to the Nansemond River

> about one-half mile apart—the first about four miles from the mouth—both on the left bank. . . . Each mounts four guns, about 24-pounders. . . . The first is garrisoned by forty men of the Isle of Wight regiment, the second by eight. One gun in each fort will traverse; the chassis of the others are immovable. (Williams 2005, 343)

Increasingly, in groups large and small, slaves made their way to Union lines. In what historian W. E. B. Du Bois called a general strike against the Confederacy, slaves by the tens of thousands simply threw down their tools, packed up their meager belongings, and walked off the plantations. As early as summer of 1861, at least 15,000 slaves escaped to the Federals. A year later, in North Carolina alone, one Confederate general estimated that slaves worth at least $1 million had run off. By late summer 1862, Georgia slaves numbering 20,000 had fled to the Union forces occupying the state's coastal regions. The farther south Union armies advanced, the more slaves sought their promise of freedom. In December 1864, when Sherman's army moved through Georgia, a single column reported 17,000 blacks trailing behind.

That so many bondsmen and women took flight to follow Sherman was more a reflection of their desire for freedom than of any love they had for Union troops. Few were under any illusion that "Uncle Billy," as Sherman's men affectionately called him, held any great affection for them. If any did, they were quickly disappointed. On December 3, 1864, with Confederate cavalry hot on their heels, Sherman's men pulled up their pontoon bridges after crossing Ebenezer Creek near Savannah, leaving more than 500 terrified refugees stranded on the opposite bank. Some, with children clinging to their backs, jumped into the swollen creek and drowned trying to reach freedom.

"I Will Speak upon the Ashes"

Such cruelty among white northern soldiers reflected attitudes that were just as common back home. The *Christian Recorder* noted that in wartime Philadelphia it was "almost impossible for a respectable colored person to walk the streets without being insulted" (Gallman 1994, 139). The same was true for public transportation. Even a soldier's pass offered Harriet Tubman no protection from abuse. On a train heading home to Auburn, New York, from the Virginia front, she encountered a conductor in New Jersey who was sure her pass was forged or stolen. He could not conceive that a black woman might get such a pass any other way. When Tubman refused to vacate her seat, four men grabbed her up, dumped her in the baggage car, and there she was held until the train reached Auburn.

Legal ground for blacks in the Midwest was shaky. Illinois voters, by a majority of two to one, amended their constitution in 1862 to keep blacks from settling there. The next year, when Indiana passed a law barring blacks from entering the state, Sojourner Truth, a long-time crusader for African American liberation, set out for an Indiana speaking tour. Authorities arrested her several times, but she kept to her mission. After a crowd at Angola threatened to burn down the hall in which she was scheduled to speak, she defiantly proclaimed, "Then I will speak upon the ashes" (Truth 1991, 140).

Though denied the rights of full citizenship, the North's black population was ready to assume what was generally held to be one of the ultimate responsibilities of any citizen. When Lincoln called for volunteers in April 1861, blacks held a mass meeting at Boston's Twelfth Baptist Church and announced their willingness to "stand by and defend the Government with 'our lives, our fortunes, and our sacred honor.'" Even the women were ready to take the field "as nurses, seamstresses, and warriors if need be" (Quarles 1989, 26–27). Similar offers came from blacks all over the country.

But Lincoln refused to accept their services. Though differing with Confederates on the issue of disunion, Lincoln was largely united with them in his racist views. Blacks, he thought, simply could not make good soldiers. "If we were to arm them," Lincoln said, "I fear that in a few weeks the arms would be in the hands of the rebels" (Williams 2005, 351). Nor did he want to make slavery a war issue. In his first inaugural address, Lincoln stated flatly that he had no purpose, directly or indirectly, to interfere with slavery in the states where it existed.

Despite Lincoln's effort not to make slavery a war issue, blacks themselves forced the question by refusing to stay put. The farther south Union armies advanced, the more self-emancipated blacks flooded to Union lines, and it was impossible to re-enslave them. They simply would not submit. By the war's second year, it became clear to Lincoln that Union victory would inevitably mean the end of slavery. Blacks were seeing to that whether whites liked it or not. So Lincoln tried to get in front of the issue by calling for gradual emancipation, government compensation for slaveholders, and—in a policy that amounted to racial cleansing—the deportation of blacks to Africa, or to the Caribbean, or to Central America, or almost anywhere as long as it was out of the United States. Congress agreed. In its *Report on Emancipation and Colonization*, the U.S. House of Representatives plainly stated that "the highest interests of the white race, whether Anglo-Saxon, Celt, or Scandinavian, require that the whole country should be held and occupied by these races alone" (Blight 1989, 122). As a first step toward that goal, Congress allocated $600,000 to transport and colonize blacks out of the country.

Among the most disappointed at such words was author, editor, and former slave Frederick Douglass. "If the black man cannot find peace from the aggressions of the white race on this continent," Douglass pointed out, "he will not be likely to find it permanently on any part of the habitable globe. The same base and selfish lust for dominion which would drive us from this country would hunt us from the world" (Blight 1989, 142).

"A Necessary War Measure"

In spite of Lincoln's efforts to control the issue, events affecting the role of blacks in the conflict began moving beyond his control from the earliest days of the war. The pressures blacks had been putting on Union forces in the field demanded an immediate response. The first significant reaction came in May 1861 when General Benjamin Butler, commanding federal troops in Virginia, realized that it was futile to turn back escaping slaves. They would not stay away. So he declared them "contraband of war" and put them to work building fortifications. Lincoln let the move stand because the slaves were not technically free, just confiscated property. Congress supported that interpretation by passing the First Confiscation Act.

Then on August 30 the Savannah-born and Charleston-raised General John C. Frémont, commanding the federal Department of the West, issued the war's first true emancipation proclamation, freeing all slaves held by pro-Confederates in Missouri. Lincoln canceled the order and fired Frémont. However, blacks kept coming and pressure kept building. In April 1862, General David Hunter, headquartered on the South Carolina coast, freed all the slaves in his area of operations and created the war's first black regiment, the First South Carolina (later the Thirty-third South Carolina Regiment, United States Colored Troops). Lincoln rescinded this order, too, and relieved Hunter of his command.

There was pressure for emancipation on the home front as well. The North's small abolitionist minority had been applying pressure from the war's beginning with little success. But news of black refugees flooding into Union lines sparked a new concern among white northerners. If the war ended with slavery intact, would the slaves go back to their former owners? Yankee troops had already tried—and failed—to force them back. George Boutwell, former governor of Massachusetts, warned in the summer of 1862 that if slavery were not abolished, the North would soon be overrun by black fugitives.

Pushing for a policy of racial containment, northern whites from a broad range of political stripes pressured Lincoln to keep blacks in the South. Republicans and War Democrats in Congress, who increasingly tended to support ending slavery as a war measure to weaken the Confederacy, put pressure on Lincoln as well. Some even argued that escaping slaves ought to be enlisted and put on the front lines. Battle and desertion had depleted Union ranks, and few white volunteers were willing to fill them. In the summer of 1862, Congress forced Lincoln's hand. It passed the Militia Act, authorizing black enlistment under white officers, and the Second Confiscation Act, divesting pro-Confederate slaveholders of their slaves. The Second Confiscation Act left in doubt the future of blacks in the United States as it called for their deportation. It left no doubt, however, that Congress meant to deprive the Confederacy of slave labor and keep black migration to the North in check.

Although the Act's intent was clear, its enforcement proved unwieldy. Determining the difference between those slaveholders who had engaged in disloyal acts and those who had not was almost impossible. Moreover, Lincoln thought that to enforce the act might cause more white soldiers to desert. Forced emancipation might even push the remaining loyal slave states of Missouri, Kentucky, and Maryland out of the Union. Lincoln worried that an emancipation announcement coming after a string of military defeats in the summer of 1862 would make his government look weak and desperate. The Battle of Antietam changed that. On September 22, just days after the Army of the Potomac turned back a Confederate advance near the western Maryland village of Sharpsburg, Lincoln issued his preliminary Emancipation Proclamation. Effective January 1, 1863, slaves held in areas still in rebellion against the United States would be free.

The Proclamation was a tentative document that freed only slaves it could not immediately reach; slaves in the loyal slaveholding states and parts of Confederate states already under Union control were not affected. It was "a necessary war measure," Lincoln wrote, meant primarily to undermine the rebellion. It called for black colonization, Lincoln's ultimate solution to the "negro question." To ease enforcement, it went further than the Second Confiscation Act in promising freedom to all slaves held in rebellious regions, not just those held by rebellious slaveholders. Most important, it turned the Union Army into a force for liberation and called for blacks themselves to join that force.

Robert Smalls (1839–1915)

In May 1862, enslaved South Carolinian Robert Smalls ran the transport steamer *Planter* with its cargo of ammunition and artillery out of Charleston harbor and turned it over to the blockading Federals. Smalls was a skilled seaman whose owner had hired him out as assistant pilot on the ship. When he learned that General David Hunter, commanding the Federals at Beaufort, had freed all the slaves in his area of operations, Smalls laid plans to escape. On the night of May 12, after his captain and white shipmates went ashore, Smalls and a few other black crewmen fired up the boilers and headed for a nearby wharf where they picked up family members. Then they headed down the harbor and past Fort Sumter. Guards at outposts along the way, and even those at Sumter, suspected nothing because Smalls knew all the proper signals. In the darkness, no one ashore could tell that the crewmen waving to them were all black.

Once past Sumter, Smalls ordered full steam and made for the Federals, hoping they would see the old sheet he had hoisted as a white flag of truce. As Smalls approached the first Union vessel he sighted, the startled seamen brought their guns to bear on the *Planter*. A member of the federal crew later recalled:

> Just as No. 3 port gun was being elevated, some one cried out, "I see something that looks like a white flag;" and true enough there was something flying on the steamer that would have been *white* by application of soap and water.

As she neared us, we looked in vain for the face of a white man. When they discovered that we would not fire on them, there was a rush of contrabands out on her deck, some dancing, some singing, whistling, jumping; and others stood looking towards Fort Sumter, and muttering all sorts of maledictions against it, and '*de heart of de Souf*,' generally. (McPherson 1982, 157)

As the *Planter* came alongside, Smalls stepped forward, took off his hat, and called out, "Good morning, sir! I've brought you some of the old United States guns, sir!" (McPherson 1982, 157). Smalls' daring feat was in part what led General David Hunter, commanding Union-held coastal regions of South Carolina, Georgia, and Florida, to create the U.S. Army's first black regiment, the First South Carolina. The *Planter* was put in Union service and Smalls continued as the vessel's pilot. In 1863, after running the steamer beyond the reach of Confederate guns despite his captain's order to surrender, Smalls was placed in command of the *Planter*.

After the war, Smalls served several terms as a congress member from his overwhelmingly African American district in South Carolina. In 1899, he was appointed customs collector for Beaufort with a $1,000 annual salary plus 3 percent commission fees. He held that position until 1913. Two years later, he died of natural causes in the home where he and his mother had once been held as slaves.

"The Heroic Descendants of Africa"

The Emancipation Proclamation had its intended effect on African American men. They flooded into recruiting offices across the North and flocked to Union lines across the South, tens of thousands of them eager to enlist. Frederick Douglass was among the most enthusiastic supporters of black enlistment. Two of his sons joined that rush along with more than 200,000 other black men who served in the Union armed forces. More than 80 percent of those who enlisted were from the southern states. Another 200,000 blacks served as laborers, teamsters, cooks, launderers, carpenters, nurses, scouts, and in many other capacities for the Union forces. Nearly all had been slaves. But no longer. Nevertheless, so strong was prejudice against their military capabilities among most Union officers that it seemed as if black soldiers might never be used for any but menial tasks. In some regiments, the colonel was "Ole Massa." Squads were work "gangs" and their officers "nigger drivers" (Wilson 2002, 39). The soldiers may as well have been slaves.

Still, some white commanders of black regiments were committed to earning respect for their men and pushed hard for combat assignments. They made the most of their opportunities when they came. On May 27, 1863, the Louisiana Native Guard, composed for the most part of recently freed blacks, participated in an assault against Confederate fortifications on the Mississippi River at Port Hudson, 25 miles north of Baton Rouge. In an after-action report, one of the Guard's white lieutenants admitted that he had entertained some fears as to his men's "pluck." "But I have now none," he added.

> Valiantly did the heroic descendants of Africa move forward cool as if Marshaled for dress parade, under a most murderous fire from the enemies guns . . . these men did not swerve, or show cowardice. I have been in several engagements, and I never before beheld such coolness and daring. Their gallantry entitles them to a special praise. And I already observe, the sneers of others are being tempered into eulogy." (Berlin et al. 1992, 440–441)

The notion that blacks lacked the discipline for soldiering was dealt a major blow on July 16 when the Fifty-fourth Massachusetts fought off a Rebel charge on James Island just south of Charleston, South Carolina.

U.S. Colored Troops at Port Hudson, Louisiana, 1864. (National Archives)

The regiment lost nine killed, thirteen wounded, and seventeen missing in action—but it held fast. "It is not for us to blow our own horn," Corporal James Henry Gooding wrote back home to Boston, "but when a regiment of white men gave us three cheers as we were passing them, it shows that we did our duty as men should" (Gooding 1991, 38).

An even tougher test came two days later when the Fifty-fourth spearheaded an assault on Fort Wagner, which guarded the southern approach to Charleston harbor. Though the effort to take Wagner failed, it was not from a lack of trying. Six hundred men of the Fifty-fourth went in on the assault. Forty percent of them were captured, killed, or wounded. One of the most severely injured was Sergeant William Carney, who had retrieved a U.S. flag and carried it back with him despite wounds to his head, chest, right leg, and arm. He became the first of twenty-three black soldiers awarded the Congressional Medal of Honor during the war.

Opposition to using blacks in the army continued to crumble as Pennsylvania, Ohio, Michigan, Indiana, Illinois, Connecticut, and New York organized black troops by the thousands. In the army, too, attitudes were changing. Much as they had resisted it, most white soldiers gradually came to accept emancipation and blacks in the army as a necessary part of the war effort. Some even took pride in it. One officer from Wayland, Massachusetts, had been described by those who knew him as "a bitter pro-slavery man, violent and vulgar in his talk against abolitionists and 'niggers.'" But after serving with blacks in Louisiana, he was so impressed that he returned home a committed abolitionist. On a train bound for Boston, as a black soldier in uniform stepped onto the car, someone yelled: "I'm not going to ride with niggers." The officer, in full uniform, rose from his seat for all to see and called out: "Come here, my good fellow! I've been fighting along side of people of your color, and glad enough I was to have 'em by my side. Come and sit by me" (Williams 2005, 373).

Everywhere they could, blacks were taking full measure of their hard-won freedoms. One black soldier spoke with pride about how he had,

> "for once in his life . . . walked fearlessly and boldly through the streets of
> [a] southern city! And he did this without being required to take off his cap
> at every step, or to give all the side-walks to those lordly princes of the sunny
> south, the planters' sons! (Williams 2005, 375)

"Slavery under a Softer Name"

Former slaves were taking more than freedom as their birthright. They were taking land, too. Planters often hastily left their lands as the Yankees closed in, leaving their slaves behind as well. When that happened, slaves frequently assumed that the land on which their families had lived and worked, sometimes for generations, was now theirs. After Charles Pettigrew fled his Bonarva plantation in North Carolina, resident blacks divided the land and livestock among themselves and kept on farming. So did former slaves on nearby Somerset Place. When Yankee troops showed up at the Mississippi plantation of Joseph Davis, the Confederate president's brother, Davis was long gone and former slaves were running the place.

Unfortunately for former slaves, the notion that they held title to their land was false. As far as the federal government was concerned, the plantations were "abandoned" lands subject to federal confiscation, to be sold or leased for nonpayment of taxes. Blacks protested vigorously at the injustice of such a policy. If they had no land, how could they be free? They had worked the land all their lives. The land, they insisted, was theirs by right, but the government was not listening to former slaves. In 1863, federal authorities began selling or leasing confiscated plantations, usually to favored clients. Many wound up in the hands of northern investors and cotton textile companies. Some went to army officers and government officials. What little was left went to those few freedmen who could afford to buy a little acreage. In South Carolina's Sea Islands auctions, the smallest parcels went to groups of freedmen who pooled their scarce funds for the purchases.

Most plantations remained in the hands of planters, who quickly renounced any Confederate loyalties when Union armies arrived. Those who had the opportunity to do so before January 1, 1863, when the Emancipation Proclamation went into effect, kept title to their land *and* their slaves. In areas reclaimed for the Union after that date, slaves were technically free. But, in fact, the new freedom looked much like the old slavery. Federal policy governing plantations, whether owned or leased, called for keeping blacks on the land as contract laborers or sharecroppers. Though nominally free, nothing but freedom was given to them. Supplies from plantation stores were doled out on credit, but with interest rates controlled by the planters. Those rates, which reached as high as 200 percent, were designed to make their debt total more than any income workers could produce. Inevitably, when crops were harvested and sold, the workers' profit share rarely covered their debt.

Thus, freed people were trapped in debt slavery, sometimes called the new slavery, and it was backed by federal force. Government-sanctioned contracts forbad workers to leave the plantations without their employer's permission. Provost marshals were authorized to round up vagrant blacks and to discipline those who resisted the new labor arrangement. It seemed to African Americans and white sympathizers alike, as historian Eric Foner put it, "that the army was acting more like a slave patrol than an agent of emancipation" (Foner 1988, 55).

Lincoln did little to reassure those who questioned his commitment to slavery's permanent abolition when, in December 1863, he issued his "Proclamation of Amnesty and Reconstruction." Claiming Constitutional authority to issue reprieves and pardons for offenses against the United States, Lincoln declared that any Confederate state would be allowed to reestablish a federally recognized state government when a number of its citizens—totaling at least 10 percent of those who had voted in the 1860 presidential election—took an oath of loyalty to the United States and promised to abide by congressional acts and presidential edicts regarding slavery.

Lincoln's Ten Percent Plan, as it came to be called, did not quite settle the issue of slavery's future in the seceded states once they were readmitted. As Lincoln himself declared, all acts and edicts of the federal government in reference to slavery, including the Emancipation Proclamation, were war measures subject to being modified or declared void by the Supreme Court. Nor did Lincoln's plan insure any legal protections for newly freed African Americans. Wendell Phillips, a long-time abolitionist from Boston, complained that Lincoln's plan restored "all power into the hands of the unchanged white race." Phillips pointed to the newly reconstructed government in Louisiana where, with Lincoln's backing, General Nathaniel Banks was forcing blacks into unjust labor contracts, and debt slavery, at the point of federal bayonets. "Such reconstruction," wrote Phillips, "makes freedom of the negro a sham, and perpetuates slavery under a softer name" (Williams 2005, 381).

"I Was Not for Mr. Lincoln"

Among those most upset with Lincoln was Frederick Douglass. He blasted the Ten Percent Plan as "an entire contradiction of the constitutional idea of the Republican Government." After promising freedom for the slaves and asking them to fight for the Union, Lincoln was now prepared to "hand the Negro back to the political power of his former master, without a single element of strength to shield himself" (Blight 1989, 182–183). That reality drove Douglass, along with allies like Wendell Phillips and Elizabeth Cady Stanton, to break with the Republicans and support the newly formed Radical Democratic Party. In May 1864, party delegates met in Cleveland and nominated John C. Frémont as their candidate in that year's presidential campaign. The convention's platform called for equality under the law regardless of race, distribution of confiscated rebel plantations to soldiers and resident former slaves, and abolishing slavery permanently by constitutional amendment.

Few party members had any real hope that Frémont could win the November election. The more politically astute hoped only that the threat of a splinter party might force Republicans either to dump Lincoln at their upcoming convention or at least make their party platform more friendly to blacks. It did neither. When the allied Union Party, composed of Republicans and a faction of war-supporting Democrats, met on June 7 in Baltimore, Lincoln easily won the delegates' support. As for their platform, the only plank it had in common with Frémont's party was its call for an anti-slavery amendment.

Despite backing from Lincoln and the Union Party, as well as passage in the Senate, the amendment's sponsors could not muster the two-thirds vote in the House necessary to get it passed and sent to the states for ratification. There was too much fear among House Democrats. Many of them had been elected in 1862 on platforms opposing abolition. Now another election year was upon them, and "abolitionist" was still a dirty word among large segments of the northern electorate—so much so that even

Elizabeth Garey (1822–ca. 1890)

In March 1871, during the throes of Reconstruction, the U.S. Congress established the Commissioners of Claims Act whereby southerners loyal to the Union during the Civil War could petition for reimbursement of property taken or destroyed by Union troops. Having been recently widowed, one woman in Savannah, Georgia, made such a petition. Her name was Elizabeth Garey (sometimes spelled Geary).

Garey was born in McIntosh County, Georgia, in 1822, the daughter of a white man of property and a black woman. She grew up to be a free woman and married a free black man, William Garey, also of mixed heritage. He was a respected carpenter; she was a sought-after seamstress and baker of pies, cakes, and breads. They established a residence with an adjacent kitchen and grocery store in Darien, raising seven children.

On June 11, 1863, black Union soldiers led by white officers made their way upriver to Darien and disembarked with orders to take what they could and set fire to the town. It was not long before the entire town was consumed by the raging fire leaving only three dwellings and a church left standing. Garey and her family fled to the woods and hid in various abandoned homes as did other families, black and white.

Throughout their ordeal, the Garey's remained loyal to the Union. When a Federal transport vessel, the *Darlington*, approached the burned town, Rebels opened fire. Garey's husband sent word of the Rebels' location to Union troops. Reinforcements were called on to successfully scatter the Rebels. Local whites heard of the Garey's warning and threatened them with hanging. White friends interceded for them, but to little avail. On the morning of July 5, they were able to get word to a Union gunboat that came upriver and took Garey and her family on board. It was about this time that two of her sons began service with the Union armed forces.

Garey and the rest of her family fled to Beaufort, South Carolina, as refugees, employed by the Federals in nursing, sewing signal flags, cooking, and providing carpentry services. While in South Carolina, Garey was responsible for saving the life of Susie King Taylor, the only African American woman to write a narrative of her wartime experiences. Taylor was traveling by boat one cold December night in 1863 when the boat capsized. The few survivors floated with the current calling out for help. Were it not for the insistence of Garey that someone was in trouble, William Garey, Garey's son, would not have pulled them from the cold waters.

When the Commissioners of Claims Act was created in 1871, Garey was a widow living with her sons. Her claim consisted of a list of items destroyed or taken and their values. Among the items listed was a milk cow valued at $50, a grocery store worth $50, a house worth $2,500, and furniture from the parlor and bedrooms valued at $500, much of which was later seen in officers' tents. Her total claim came to $3,400. After considering Garey's testimony, the Commission allowed a reimbursement of $30.

some of the amendment's backers began calling themselves "emancipationists" as a signal that they supported only nominal freedom, and no more than that, for enslaved blacks. Whatever its implications, the amendment could not threaten white supremacy.

That assurance was not enough to sway House Democrats in the summer of 1864. Nor did it carry much weight with the party as a whole. At their August convention, Democrats refused to support the abolition

Frederick Douglass, leader in the abolition movement (1818–1895). (Library of Congress)

amendment. Even their support for maintaining the Union was considerably vague. They adopted a platform promising to halt the fighting, call a convention of all the states, and restore the Federal Union. The question of whether any Confederate state would willingly participate in a convention was left aside entirely. So was the question of slavery, although the Democratic nominee, George McClellan, did say that any state returning to the Union under his administration would receive a full guarantee of its constitutional rights. McClellan's implied message was that the right to hold slaves would be safe.

It was too much for many of the Radicals. Some began encouraging Frémont to drop out of the race. As weak as Lincoln was on anything but nominal freedom for blacks, he at least seemed committed on that point. McClellan, on the other hand, seemed bent on preserving slavery as a constitutional right. That was the last thing Frémont and the Radicals wanted. Lincoln's reelection chances improved with the fall of Atlanta on September 2, 1864, but fear remained that Frémont still might draw enough Radical votes to give McClellan the presidency. After meeting in mid-September with a delegation from the White House, Frémont suspended his bid for the presidency and threw his support to Lincoln. "It became evident," Frémont later explained, "that Mr. Lincoln could not be elected if I remained in the field" (Williams 2005, 385). He may have been right. After one of the most racist campaigns in U.S. history—with Democrats charging that Lincoln wanted not just freedom but also social and political equality for blacks, and Republicans denying the accusation at every turn—Lincoln won the popular vote in November by no more than a questionable 10 percent margin.

Though they had succeeded in keeping McClellan out of the White House, the Radicals were not enthusiastic about giving Lincoln a second term. "When there was any shadow of a hope," wrote Frederick Douglass, "that a man of a more decided anti-slavery conviction and policy could be elected, I was not for Mr. Lincoln" (McFeely 1991, 234). Still, Lincoln did stand by the party platform. A month after his reelection, Lincoln pushed the House to approve the Senate's emancipation amendment. Taking the election's outcome as a referendum, House members finally granted approval in a lame duck session on January 31, 1865. The proposed Thirteenth Amendment ending slavery went out to the states for ratification with Lincoln's blessing. But that was as far as Lincoln was willing to go. He stuck to his Ten Percent Plan, as did his successor, Andrew Johnson, and left the fate of free blacks largely in the hands of former slaveholders. What freedom blacks could wrest out of that relationship would be of their own making.

References and Further Reading

Berlin, Ira. "The Slaves Were the Primary Force Behind Their Emancipation." In *The Civil War: Opposing Viewpoints*, ed. William Dudley. San Diego: Greenhaven Press, 1995.

Berlin, Ira, Marc Favreau, and Steven F. Miller, eds. *Remembering Slavery: African Americans Talk about Their Personal Experiences of Slavery and Freedom.* New York: New Press, 1998.

Berlin, Ira, Barbara J. Fields, Steven F. Miller, Joseph P. Reidy, and Leslie S. Rowland, eds. *Free at Last: A Documentary History of Slavery, Freedom, and the Civil War.* New York: New Press, 1992.

Blight, David W. *Frederick Douglass's Civil War: Keeping Faith in Jubilee.* Baton Rouge: Louisiana State University Press, 1989.

Browne, Junium Henri. *Four Years in Secessia: Adventures Within and Beyond the Union Lines.* Hartford, CT: O. D. Case, 1865.

Foner, Eric. *Reconstruction: America's Unfinished Revolution, 1863–1877.* New York: Harper and Row, 1988.

Gallman, Matthew. *The North Fights the Civil War: The Home Front.* Chicago: Ivan Dee, 1994.

Glatthaar, Joseph T. *Forged in Battle: The Civil War Alliance of Black Soldiers and White Officers.* New York: Free Press, 1990.

Gooding, James Henry. *On the Altar of Freedom: A Black Soldier's Civil War Letters from the Front,* ed. Virginia Matzke Adams. Amherst: University of Massachusetts Press, 1991.

McFeely, William S. *Frederick Douglass.* New York: W. W. Norton, 1991.

McPherson, James. *The Negro's Civil War.* Urbana: University of Illinois Press, 1982.

Quarles, Benjamin. *The Negro in the Civil War.* 1953; rpt., with introduction by William S. McFeely, New York: Da Capo, 1989.

Taylor, Susie King. *Reminiscences of My Life in Camp*. 1902; rpt., with introduction by Catherine Clinton, Athens: University of Georgia Press, 2006.

Truth, Sojourner. *Narrative of Sojourner Truth*. New York: Oxford University Press, 1991.

Williams, David. *A People's History of the Civil War: Struggles for the Meaning of Freedom*. New York: New Press, 2005.

Williams, David, Teresa Crisp Williams, and David Carlson. *Plain Folk in a Rich Man's War: Class and Dissent in Confederate Georgia*. Gainesville: University Press of Florida, 2002.

Wilson, Keith P. *Campfires of Freedom: The Camp Life of Black Soldiers during the Civil War*. Kent, OH: Kent State University Press, 2002.

African Americans during Reconstruction (1863–1877) 7

Dawn J. Herd-Clark

Reconstruction, the period immediately after the Civil War (1861–1865), was initially a period of substantial changes for African Americans living in the former southern slave states. Beginning in 1863, with the implementation of President Abraham Lincoln's Ten Percent Plan for reconstructing the South, Reconstruction lasted until 1877, when the last of the federal troops were removed from the former Confederate states. During Reconstruction, African Americans, many of whom had been enslaved their entire lives, had an opportunity to experience freedom for the first time. This freedom allowed some African Americans to receive an education, own land, vote, and hold political office for the first time in their lives. By the end of the 19th century, however, freedom for African Americans living in the South would be limited because of racism and discrimination by southern whites and neglected by other segments of the American population. The rights African Americans fought to achieve during Reconstruction would be lost until the modern civil rights movement of the 1950s and 1960s.

Freedom

There had always been a free African American population in the antebellum South, although their rights were limited by southern prejudice. During the Civil War, the number of free blacks increased as slaves took the liberty of liberating themselves as Union troops approached. Even more slaves sought their freedom once President Abraham Lincoln announced the Emancipation Proclamation, stating "all persons held as slaves within any State or designated part of a State, the people whereof shall then be in rebellion against the United States, shall be then, thenceforward, and forever free." The institution of slavery was abolished in 1865 with the ratification of the Thirteenth Amendment, stating "neither slavery nor involuntary servitude, except as punishment for crime whereof the part shall have been duly convicted, shall exist within the United States, or any place subject to their jurisdiction." Once free, former slaves (known as freedmen) began to live their version of the American dream; unfortunately for many, it would soon become a nightmare.

When former slaves received, or sometimes took, their freedom, many had the ability for the first time to decide their own fate. Many freedmen took the liberty of walking off the plantations they had been enslaved on just because they could; during the institution of slavery, for a slave to leave their plantation they had to have permission from an authority figure to do so. Many of the freedmen who left the plantations on which they had lived and worked were in search of loved ones. During the institution of slavery, many black families were divided when relatives were sold westward because of American expansion. After the Civil War, former slaves sought their loved ones to help families reconnect. As former slaves reconnected with family members, they needed a place to live, thus land ownership became a priority for freedmen.

Property Ownership

There were black property owners in the antebellum South, however, their numbers were relatively small. During Reconstruction, freedmen, who left their former owners, wanted a place to live and land of their own to cultivate. Acquiring land for freedmen was a difficult task. One way freedmen secured land was by taking it from their former owners. As Union troops approached, many white southerners fled for their lives, leaving all their material possessions, including land. Many freedmen took this opportunity to declare the land their own and began to grow crops on it. Another way freedmen acquired land was through the assistance of the federal government. On January 16, 1865, Union General William T. Sherman issued Special Field Order No. 15, which states

> the islands from Charleston, south, the abandoned rice fields along the rivers for thirty miles back from the sea, and the country bordering the St. Johns river, Florida, are reserved and set apart for the settlement of the negroes now made free by the acts of war and the proclamation of the President of the United States.

Through Special Field Order No. 15 freedmen could acquire forty-acre plots of land from Charleston, South Carolina, to Jacksonville, Florida, as well as the use of Army mules; the motto "forty acres and a mule" came from this order. Although freedmen resisted the efforts to do so, President Andrew Johnson returned most of the land to the southern white landowners, and freedmen were either forced to sign labor contracts or get evicted off the land.

Although land ownership was the goal for most freedmen, sharecropping became their reality, as well as the reality for many southern whites. Under the sharecropping system, one rents another's land and shares the crop as payment for use of the land. Freedmen had hoped that their proceeds from sharecropping would fund the purchase of their own land. Unfortunately, that was rarely the case. Instead, it became a cycle of debt. Freedmen would enter into a sharecropping contract, but they lacked the initial supplies to harvest a crop. Thus, they frequently had to borrow such items as seed and farm tools, or family provisions, such as flour or sugar, until their crop was harvested. Therefore, they started their season in debt. Additionally, the only person to extend credit to freedmen was the landowner, who had inflated prices as well a high interest rates. If the harvest was bountiful, the sharecropper might break even, but that was often difficult to prove because freedmen often were illiterate and lacked the ability to view the landowner's credit records. The sharecropper's harvest could fail because of a drought or a boll weevil infestation; the sharecropper would thus be in debt until the next year. This cycle of debt had the potential to last for decades. This left freedmen legally tied to the land until they could pay off their debt. Compounding the sharecropping problem was the convict lease system. If one was in debt and attempted to leave without paying it, they could be arrested and jailed for doing so. If one was incarcerated in jail, a company could purchase his or her labor from the state. The convict worked during the day, usually uncompensated, while returning to the jail at night. The convict lease system was deadly and affected mostly, although not solely, African American men. To assist the freedmen with their labor contracts, as well as other issues pertaining to the South after the Civil War, the federal government created the Freedmen's Bureau.

Freedmen's Bureau

To assist the federal government with the landownership issue in the South, as well as other tasks that needed to be addressed during Reconstruction, on March 3, 1865, the Bureau of Refugees, Freedmen, and Abandoned Lands, more commonly known as the Freedmen's Bureau, was created. General Oliver O. Howard, after which Howard University is named, was the noted leader of the Bureau. The Freedmen's Bureau dealt with Civil War refugees, those both black and white who were displaced by the war; freedmen, the 4 million former southern slaves; and abandoned lands, land that southern whites left as they fled from the South and the advancing Union Army. Additionally, the Freedmen's Bureau served as a missing person's bureau, assisted with southern education, negotiated labor contracts, solved legal disputes, provided food and clothing rations, established hospitals, and worked with former African American military personnel to help them secure back pay from the government. To assist Howard, Freedmen's Bureau agents were hired. To become an agent, one had to have been an officer in the military. Therefore, few agents were African American.

Howard and his agents had the enormous task of assisting with the rebuilding of the South after the Civil War while confronted by limited financial resources as well as a resentful southern white population. Despite their hostility toward freedmen and the organization designed to assist with their transition to freedom, many southern whites also received aid from the Freedmen's Bureau. Southerners looking for lost loved ones could register the name and last know location of relatives and, with the Freedmen's Bureau assistance, possibly become reunited. During Reconstruction, freedmen had the ability to be financially compensated for their labor. This made it necessary to create labor contracts. Because most freedmen were illiterate, they relied on the Freedman's Bureau agents to help them negotiate their compensation contracts. When labor contracts were unclear, as well as property disputed, southerners had access to the Freedmen's Bureau courts, which ideally were less biased than that of the traditional southern court system. After the Civil War, southerners, both black and white, needed food and clothing because of the severe devastation wrought by the war. The Freedmen's Bureau distributed these items to those in need. Medical treatment was also badly needed among southerners. During the institution of slavery, slaves did not have access to medical care, and as a result, they had many medical needs that needed attention. Additionally, both blacks and whites needed medical attention because of war wounds. The Freedmen's Bureau hospitals provided badly needed medical care for all southerners.

African American Civil War veterans badly needed their back pay from their prior military services. The Bureau assisted with this endeavor as well. With Abraham Lincoln's assassination by actor and southern sympathizer John Wilkes Booth on April 14, 1865, his vice president, Andrew Johnson, became president. Although he was not fond of wealthy southern whites, he disliked freedmen even more. Initially he vetoed funding for the Bureau, but Congress overrode it. He constantly undermined the Freedmen's Bureau, however, and it ceased operating in 1872. Recent historical scholarship has been critical of the Bureau in its endeavors to redistribute land, supervise labor contracts, and solve legal disputes, but most historians praise its efforts in the field of education.

Education

If they could not have land, freedmen wanted an education to increase the economic opportunities available to them. During the institution of slavery, it was illegal to educate a slave. Additionally, many slaveholders believed that an education ruined a "good slave." Once blacks received their freedom, they tried to secure an education. The Freedmen's Bureau was an invaluable ally in that fight. Although the Freedmen's Bureau provided funding to establish schools, it did not absorb the entire expense. For a community to secure a Freedmen's Bureau school, they had to

Students and teachers pose outside the Freedmen's Bureau school in Beaufort, South Carolina, ca. 1865. (Corbis)

demonstrate a financial commitment to the education facility. While the Freedmen's Bureau helped provide the schoolhouse, freedmen were required to pay, house, and feed the teacher. What is most remarkable about this feat is that despite the fact that freedmen had little financial capital, they pulled their meager resources together for the purpose of educating themselves and future generations. The Freedmen's Bureau laid the groundwork for public education in the South after the Civil War. Although the Freedmen's Bureau was not alone in helping to educate freedmen, they were significant.

Another prominent organization to assist with the education of freedmen was the American Missionary Association (AMA). The AMA grew out of the defense of the Amistad Africans from 1839–1841. In 1846, as an interdenominational abolitionist organization, it soon began to work with Native Americans and immigrants, as well as its foreign missions department. When the institution of slavery was abolished in 1865, the organization began to focus primarily on the education of freedmen. From its early endeavors in African American education, the AMA assisted in establishing many noted institutions of higher education, including Atlanta University (1865), Fisk University (1866), Howard University (1867), and Hampton University (1868). The Freedmen's Bureau and the AMA, as well as other religious groups, worked together to help freedmen secure an education.

Various religious organizations sent teachers to educate freedmen. The teachers, frequently white women from New England, saw educating freedmen as an aspect of their missionary work. They wanted to teach freedmen to read so that they could be better Christians and read the

Charlotte Forten Grimké (1837–1914)

Education was a top priority for freedmen during Reconstruction. To educate the 4 million former slaves, a dedicated band of teachers, both African American and white, committed their time and talents to do so. One such educator was a woman of African descent, Charlotte Forten Grimké. Born Charlotte Forten to a prominent free black family in Philadelphia, Pennsylvania, in 1837, her charitable act of educating freedmen consumed her life's work until her death in 1914.

At a young age Grimké became familiar with the dreadful plight both free and enslaved African Americans faced on a daily basis. Her paternal grandfather, James Forten, Sr. was a wealthy sail maker and active abolitionist. Her parents, Robert Bridges and Mary Woods Forten, also well known in the abolitionist movement, instilled in her an obligation to assist those who were enslaved. To help prepare Grimké for her life's work, she was initially educated at home by tutors. She moved to Massachusetts to enroll in Higginson Grammar School, in Salem, to live with family friends and prominent abolitionists Charles and Sarah Redmond, because of Philadelphia's segregated school system. Despite being the only nonwhite student enrolled at Higginson, Grimké excelled in her studies. After completing grammar school, Grimké enrolled in Salem's Normal School and eventually became a teacher in Salem, Massachusetts, the first African American teacher hired, as well as a member of the Salem Female Anti-Slavery Society.

Tuberculosis forced Grimké to return to Philadelphia, where she began to develop her skills as a poet in various abolitionist publications. With the onset of the Civil War, Grimké wanted to assist slaves in securing their physical and mental freedom, and in 1862, she relocated to St. Helena Island, South Carolina, where she taught former slaves to read and write. While there, Grimké continued to write and her diary, *Life on the Sea Islands*, was published by *Atlantic Monthly* in 1864. The work of educating freedmen took a physical toll on Grimké; she left after two years. However, it did not stop her ability to assist freedmen. She worked endlessly to recruit teachers to help educate freedmen.

In 1873, Grimké became a clerk with the U.S. Treasury Department. On December 19, 1878, Forten wed Francis J. Grimké, a Presbyterian minister. Grimké assisted her husband while he served as the pastor of the Fifteenth Street Presbyterian Church. The couple gave birth to one daughter, Theodora Cornelia, who died as an infant in 1880. Because of her ailing health, Grimké returned to Massachusetts later in life and died in 1914. Grimké left a legacy of civil rights activism, including the education of her people.

Bible, as well as convert them to their denominations. When these teachers went to the South, they frequently were alienated by the southern white community, and some were physically attacked. Most religious denominations participated in educating freedmen. The American Baptist Home Mission Society founded Shaw University (1865), Northern Methodists established Bennett College for Women (1873), and the Episcopalian Church created St. Augustine's College (1867). Although freedmen appreciated the northern missionaries, they preferred teachers who were African Americans. Thus, as the African American population became more educated, they began to fill the teaching positions in schools for freedmen.

The efforts of all the missionaries and educators during Reconstruction were invaluable, because the South was reluctant to allocate adequate state funds for their education.

Education for freedmen was deemed necessary to improve their circumstance in society. All freedmen, regardless of age, wanted an opportunity to learn. Older African Americans wanted to learn how to read the Bible before they died, while younger African Americans were eager to take advantage of the new opportunities afforded to them. Since southern states would not support black education, missionary organizations did. Because these various denominations did not receive federal or state funding, they had to charge tuition. Freedmen had to use their meager resources to educate their children as well as themselves. Because most freedmen did not have the financial resources to pay their tuition in cash, most schools during Reconstruction allowed alternate payment forms. Students frequently brought items to barter for their education. These items included such things as green beans, corn, eggs, and chickens. Schools often allowed students the opportunity to work off their tuition by assisting the school in some capacity. Students cleaned the campus buildings, served the food, and even assisted with the construction of buildings to defray the cost of their education expenses. Parents truly sacrificed for their children to receive an education; they not only paid some form of tuition, but also lost the labor of their child while he or she was at school.

Although freedmen children went to school, it does not mean that they were excused from work. They had to labor around their school schedule. It was expected that they would get up early in the morning to assist the family in some work capacity, then walk the mile or two, or even further, to school, complete their studies, walk home, work with their families until nightfall, complete their homework, and then go to sleep. While at school, the curriculum varied but usually included reading, writing, and arithmetic, as well as some form of industrial education. Manual training taught students some form of labor that they could perform with their hands. Examples of this training included that of carpentry for boys, domestic science for girls, and agriculture for both genders. This education proved invaluable as freedmen made greater strides at defining themselves during Reconstruction. One institution that freedmen turned to during this tremulous time is the church.

The Church

The church rose to prominence in African American society during Reconstruction as the oppressive forces facing freedmen increased. Religion played a prominent role in the lives of those of African descent from Africa's earliest days. Africans, before being brought to America, had traditional religious values. By the 19th century, most African Americans transferred their religious fervor to Christianity. Under the institution of slavery, religion served as a coping mechanism for those who were enslaved. Despite the fact that the sermons preached black subordination, slaves knew differently and prayed for their freedom. Once they received their freedom, the church emerged as the center of the African American community. It was one of the few institutions controlled by blacks and free of white supervision. Most freedmen joined either the Baptist or Methodist church because of their autonomy. Churches allowed African Americans to hold leadership positions, speak publicly, and organize through the various ministries of the church, including the music ministry, Deacon or Deaconess Board, or the sick and shut-in ministry. These church leadership roles prepared African Americans for the political arena; many elected officials were members of the clergy.

Politics

In the antebellum South, African Americans could not vote. Once they received their freedom, they chose to be politically active. They understood the power of voting in the United States. African American men gained the right to vote with the passage of the Fifteenth Amendment to the U.S. Constitution, which was ratified in 1870. Radical Republicans supported this legislation once they implemented their plan of Reconstruction in 1867. Once African American men secured this right, they began to actively engage in politics, especially in that of the Republican Party. Blacks aligned themselves with the Republican Party because of their belief that Abraham Lincoln "freed the slaves." With the inclusion of black men in politics in the South, African Americans began to get elected into political office. Although African American women did not gain the right to vote until the Nineteenth Amendment in 1920, they expressed themselves politically during Reconstruction. They rallied for candidates of their choice, encouraged the men in the family to vote, and, when necessary, armed themselves to ensure that their men could cast their ballots. Black

African American males vote in the United States for the first time following the passage of the Fifteenth Amendment, enacted on March 30, 1870. (Library of Congress)

Hiram Rhoades Revels (1822–1901)

During Reconstruction, African Americans fought to exercise their political rights, a long-sought-after goal throughout the 19th century. Once African American men were guaranteed the right the vote via the Fifteenth Amendment, in 1870, they began to help shape post—Civil War America politically. One such individual to do so was Hiram Rhoades Revels. Revels is noted in history as the first person of African descent to serve in the U.S. Senate, filling the seat left vacant when Jefferson Davis joined the Confederate cause.

Revels, of African American and Native American descent, was born free in 1822, in Fayetteville, North Carolina. He then moved to Lincolnton, North Carolina, in 1838, to serve as a barber apprentice for his brother, Elias Revels. Upon Elias' death, in 1841, Revels became the manager of the barbershop. Wanting to secure an education, Revels moved to Indiana, a free state, to do so and attended Beach Grove Quaker Seminary in Liberty, Indiana. In the early 1850s, Revels met and married the former Phoeba A. Bass, and they raised six daughters. Revels continued his education in Ohio and Illinois, while also becoming an ordained minister in the African Methodist Episcopal (AME) Church. His service to the church led him to preach in Ohio, Indiana, Illinois, Tennessee, Kentucky, Missouri, and Kansas. Eventually, he settled in Baltimore, Maryland, where he served as the principal of a school and led a church.

When the Civil War began in 1861, Revels recruited African American soldiers from Maryland to serve with the Union Army. During the war, he moved to Missouri to open a school for African Americans, while continuing to recruit African Americans for the Union Army. Revels assisted the Union Army by serving as the chaplain for a free black regiment of soldiers from Mississippi.

At the conclusion of the Civil War, Revels settled in Natchez, Mississippi, where he continued his pastoral duties and began to play an active role in politics. Initially elected an alderman in 1868, his ability was noted by both blacks and whites. He then won a seat as a state senator from Adams County, Mississippi, and then, in 1870, he was elected to the U.S. Senate, to become the first person of African descent to do so. Revels took his Senate seat on February 25, 1870, after his credentials were initially challenged, and served until March 4, 1871. An able senator, Revels introduced several bills and presented numerous petitions.

Upon his return to Mississippi, Revels became the first president of Alcorn College, Mississippi's first state-supported institution of higher education for African Americans, from 1871 until 1874 and from 1876 until 1882. Although Revels was a college president, it did not stop his political activism. During his first term as president of Alcorn College, Revels served as the secretary of state ad interim Mississippi in 1873.

Upon his retirement from Alcorn College, Revels moved to Holly Springs, Mississippi, to preach, edit the *Southwestern Christian Advocate*, the official newspaper of the AME Church, and teach theology at Rusk College. Revels died of a stroke on January 16, 1901, thus bringing his life of political activism to a close.

men held various national, state, and local elected positions and were actively participating in politics; however, white Republicans dominated the party's agenda.

The proportion of black elected officials correlated with the number of African Americans in the state, and thus states with the largest population of blacks had the most black officeholders. The U.S. Senate saw two noted African Americans: Blanche K. Bruce and Hiram Revels represented Mississippi during Reconstruction. The House of Representatives saw fourteen black men from North Carolina serve during Reconstruction. One African American, Pinckney Benton Stewart (P. B. S.) Pinchback, served as the governor of Louisiana for one month during Reconstruction; however, Pinchback was not elected to the governorship. Pinchback initially started out as a Louisiana state senator and was named senate president pro tem. He became the acting lieutenant governor when the elected lieutenant governor, also an African American, Oscar Dunn, died while in office. When Louisiana Governor Henry Clay Warmoth was impeached and removed from office for election violations, P. B. S. Pinchback was named acting governor. African Americans were elected to state houses as well. In Mississippi and South Carolina, they accounted for a majority of the representatives. Other elected positions reached by African Americans during Reconstruction included superintendent of education, coroner, mayor, and sheriff.

During the first half of the 20th century, most Americans believed that these African American elected officials were dishonest, were corrupt, and overspent their budgets. Thus, these officials caused the South further economic turmoil, hindering its financial recovery from the Civil War. Columbia University's William A. Dunning, in his 1907 work *Reconstruction, Political and Economic: 1865–1877*, argued that southern whites were prepared to work with the North during Reconstruction; however, freedmen, carpetbaggers, and scalawags caused turmoil in the South, both politically and economically, thus furthering the decline of the South. Dunning's graduate students helped form the Dunning School, advancing his ideas about Reconstruction. One of the first scholars to dispute the Dunning School was William Edward Burghardt Du Bois; he did so in his 1935 work, *Black Reconstruction*. The Dunning School was further refuted in the 1950s, which also coincided with the modern civil rights movement, by noted revisionist historians such as Kenneth Stampp. These and other historians concluded that African American elected officials during Reconstruction were no more corrupt than their white counterparts, whether they were Republicans or Democrats.

Concerning the alleged fiscal mismanagement of African American elected officials during Reconstruction, they did increase government spending, but the expenditures were necessary. Black elected officials spent funds on the implementation of a public education system in the South. Because of what became formally known as Jim Crow Laws, separate education facilities were required for black and white southerners, thus further increasing government expenditures. African American elected officials also appropriated funds to rebuild the South after the Civil War. Because the Civil War was primarily a defensive war for the South, most of the battles took place throughout the South, causing severe destruction. White southerners expected the local, state, and federal governments to fund this rebuilding process, and doing so increased the budgets of these African American elected officials. These and other expenditures caused African American elected officials to overspend their budgets.

As black elected officials helped to advocate their plight, southern whites attempted to thwart their political advances through various methods. The South soon began to implement a poll tax (a tax one had to pay to vote). This was difficult for many freedmen, as well as poor whites, to pay. Because many southerners were not paid their wages in legal tender, they lacked the funds to pay to vote. Additionally many freedmen needed their meager funds to pay rent or educate their children. Another tactic used to prevent freedmen from voting included literacy tests. During literacy tests, voting registrars required potential voters to read or interpret a portion of the state or U.S. Constitution. African Americans were often given the difficult portions of the Constitution to read or interpret, while whites attempting to register were given easier passages or not given the test at all. The grandfather clause was another method used to disenfranchise African American men. The grandfather clause stipulated that if either your father or grandfather could vote before 1867 then you were exempt from education or taxation qualifications to vote. Because African American men could not vote until the passage of the Fifteenth Amendment to the U.S. Constitution in 1870, the grandfather clause further hindered their ability to vote. The grandfather clause was declared unconstitutional by the U.S. Supreme Court in the 1915 court case *Guinn v. United States*. This ruling was significant because it was the first legal victory for the National Association for the Advancement of Colored People (NAACP), a civil rights organization formed in 1909. Fear and intimidation were used to stop African Americans from exercising their Fifteenth Amendment rights. It was not uncommon for a lynching to take place around election time, serving as a warning to potential African American voters. These and other tactics were used to stop African Americans from making progress during Reconstruction.

White Opposition to Black Advancement

As freedmen began to advance themselves in southern society, many southern whites resented their progress and tried to thwart it whenever possible. One formal organization to do so was the Ku Klux Klan. Formed in Pulaski, Tennessee, in 1866, the fraternity of former Confederate soldiers soon evolved into an organization to keep freedmen "in their proper place." Notorious for their night rides, Klan members, dressed in their hooded white outfits, committed arson, and used public whippings, rape, and murder to intimidate freedmen and their supporters. Although the Klan was the most visible and best documented of these organizations, it was not the sole one. There were also the Knights of the White Camellia, the White Brotherhood, and the Whitecaps, among others. To curb the acts of the Klan and similar organizations, the Enforcements Acts of 1870 and 1871 were passed by Congress. These laws assisted freedmen and their allies when their civil rights were violated. The 1870 act made it illegal to wear masks or disguises and protected the civil rights of all Americans. The

Illustration from 1874 depicting the White League and Ku Klux Klan shaking hands over cowering African Americans. On April 13, 1873, in Colfax, Louisiana, a group of white men (including members of the White League and the Ku Klux Klan) clashed with African Americans at the Colfax courthouse ostensibly over a contested local election. The massacre eventually led to the 1875 Supreme Court case, *United States v. Cruikshank*. (Library of Congress)

1871 act, also known as the Ku Klux Klan Act, made it a crime to interfere with African American political rights, including voter registration, office holding, or jury service. It also made it easier for the U.S. district attorney to use federal courts to prosecute state officials, as well as individuals, for such violations. Although there were some Klansmen prosecuted under these measures, African American civil rights, as well as that of their supporters, were still violated.

Black codes, initially formed in Mississippi and South Carolina, were laws that southern African Americans had to follow that stopped them from exercising their civil rights and kept them as a cheap labor force for the South's agricultural economy. Although similar to slave codes, laws that slaves had to abide by, black codes did guarantee certain liberties that slave codes had not, including the right to marry, own land, and sue and be sued. Despite these new liberties, black codes also contained other provisions that were detrimental to the freedom of African Americans. One black code allowed African American children to be apprenticed out to families if the state deemed necessary to do so, without the consent of the child's parents. Another black code required freedmen to have written employment for the forthcoming year. If laborers left before they completed their contract, they forfeited all previously earned wages. Other black codes included vagrancy laws, bans on alcohol usage, and laws against owning firearms. Black codes were designed to allow any white person to enforce them, thus keeping southern blacks as close to the institution of slavery as possible and ensuring the South a cheap labor source. Because of these difficult conditions for southern blacks, many freedmen attempted to leave the South.

Civil Rights Act of 1875

As Reconstruction drew to a close, Congress made one last attempt to protect the rights of southern African Americans with the passage of the Civil

Rights Act of 1875. The initial goal of the legislation, proposed by Radical Republican Senator Charles Sumner and House member Benjamin Butler, was to allow African Americans access to public accommodations, including schools, churches, cemeteries, and hotels, without regard to race. Specifically it stated

> that all persons within the jurisdiction of the United States shall be entitled to the full and equal and enjoyment of the accommodations, advantages, facilities, and privileges of inns, public conveyances on land or water, theaters, and other places of public amusement; subject only to the conditions and limitations established by law, and applicable alike to citizens of every race and color, regardless of any previous condition of servitude.

Although it passed the Republican-controlled Senate in 1874, House Democrats weakened the final version of the legislation by deleting its ban on discrimination in churches, cemeteries, and schools. Additionally, the provisions that were kept were not enforced and, in 1883, the U.S. Supreme Court declared the legislation unconstitutional, stating that Congress could not regulate individual entities. The Civil Rights Act of 1964 dealt with many of the issues that the Civil Rights Act of 1875 had attempted to address.

The End of Reconstruction

The period known as Reconstruction came to an end in 1877 due to a dispute over the presidential election of 1876. During the election of 1876, the Republican Party ran former Union Army office and Ohio Governor Rutherford B. Hayes, and the Democratic Party selected Samuel J. Tilden, a well-known reformer and New York governor. The initial election results indicated a win for Tilden by nearly 300,000 popular votes; however, election returns from Louisiana, South Carolina, Florida, and Oregon were unclear. The combined total of twenty electoral votes in these four states were in dispute; Tilden needed one electoral vote to become the president of the United States, while Hayes needed all twenty of the disputed electoral votes. Because the U.S. Constitution had not made a provision for settling such an issue, it was agreed that Congress should intervene in the matter. The Republicans dominated the Senate and supported Hayes, and at the same time, the Democratic-controlled House of Representatives supported Tilden. To settle the disputed election returns, Congress created a special electoral commission. Composed of five senators, five representatives, and five justices of the U.S. Supreme Court, the commission included five Republican and Democratic congress members, as well as two Republican and Democratic Supreme Court Justices. The last justice selected was to be an independent; however, a justice who was a Republican sympathizer was selected and the vote, 8–7 in favor of Rutherford B. Hayes, fell along party lines. For Hayes to become president, many compromises were made, including the removal of federal troops from the South, the appointment of at least one southerner to Hayes' cabinet, funding for southern railroads, and federal appropriations for southern internal improvements. Once military troops were removed from the South, freedmen were left to defend themselves from the hostility of southern whites.

Post-Reconstruction Blacks

In 1896, the U.S. Supreme Court handed down the *Plessy v. Ferguson* decision legalizing segregation. Southern African Americans had to endure the legacy of Reconstruction until the modern civil rights movement of the 1950s and 1960s, culminating with the 1954 *Oliver Brown et al. v. Board of Education of Topeka et al.* decision, the Civil Rights Act of 1964, and the Voting Rights Act of 1965.

References and Further Reading

Anderson, James D. *The Education of Blacks in the South, 1860–1935.* Chapel Hill: University of North Carolina Press, 1988.

Click, Patricia C. *Time Full of Trial: The Roanoke Island Freedmen's Colony, 1862–1867.* Chapel Hill: University of North Carolina Press, 2001.

Du Bois, W. E. B., and David Levering Lewis. *Black Reconstruction in America, 1860–1880.* New York: Free Press, 1998.

Faulkner, Carol. *Women's Radical Reconstruction: The Freedmen's Aid Movement.* Philadelphia: University of Pennsylvania Press, 2004.

Foner, Eric. *Forever Free: The Story of Emancipation and Reconstruction.* New York: Vintage, 2006.

Foner, Eric. *Freedom's Lawmakers: A Directory of Black Office Holders During Reconstruction.* Baton Rouge: Louisiana State University Press, 1996.

Foner, Eric. *Reconstruction: America's Unfinished Revolution, 1863–1877.* New York: Harper & Row, 1988.

Franklin, John Hope. *Reconstruction after the Civil War.* Chicago: University of Chicago Press, 1961.

Gerber, Richard A., and Alan Friedlander. *The Civil Rights Act of 1875: A Reexamination.* New Haven: Connecticut Academy of Arts and Sciences, 2008.

Holt, Thomas. *Black over White: Negro Political Leadership in South Carolina.* Urbana: University of Illinois Press, 1979.

Holzer, Holder, Edna Greene Medford, and Frank J. Williams. *The Emancipation Proclamation: Three Views.* Baton Rouge: Louisiana State University Press, 2006.

Jenkins, Wilbert L. *Climbing up to Glory: A Short History of African Americans during the Civil War and Reconstruction.* Wilmington, DE: Scholarly Resources, 2002.

Litwack, Leon. *Been in the Storm So Long.* New York: Vintage Books, 1980.

Perman, Michael L. *Emancipation and Reconstruction, 1862–1879.* Arlington Heights, IL: Harlan Davidson, Inc., 1987.

Rabinowitz, Howard N, ed. *Southern Black Leaders of the Reconstruction Era.* Urbana: University of Illinois Press, 1982.

Stampp, Kenneth M. *The Era of Reconstruction, 1865–1877.* New York: Vintage, 1967.

Trelease, Allen W. *White Terror: The Ku Klux Klan Conspiracy and Southern Reconstruction.* Baton Rouge: Louisiana State University Press, 1995.

Williams, Heather Andrea. *Self-Taught: African American Education in Slavery and Freedom.* Chapel Hill: University of North Carolina Press, 2007.

Wilson, Kirt H. *The Reconstruction Desegregation Debate: The Politics of Equality and the Rhetoric of Place, 1870–1875.* East Lansing: Michigan State University Press, 2002.

African American Responses to Early Jim Crow

Mary Block

T he term "Jim Crow" originated as early as 1832 in the title of a black face minstrel show performed by a white man named Thomas "Daddy" Rice. Rice covered his face with charcoal paste or burnt cork to make it black, and then he danced and sang his act on stage for the amusement of white audiences. Daddy Rice's show consisted of racist, stereotypical caricatures of black men. In 1841, Massachusetts' abolitionists usurped the term and applied it to the segregated railway cars in the state. "Jim Crow" came to signify the car set aside for African Americans. Scholars are not certain as to how the phrase Jim Crow came to be synonymous with the complex series of racial laws and traditions that southern whites developed to ensure their racial, legal, political, and social supremacy. We do know that the first southern laws dubbed "Jim Crow" pertained to the segregated railroad cars and so the term seems to have carried over from its earlier popularized usage. The phrase's meaning and common usage expanded by the turn of the 20th century as segregation expanded beyond railroad cars.

The Jim Crow system entailed not only the customary and legal racial segregation and political disenfranchisement of African Americans, but also the violent and brutal tactics that whites employed to gain and maintain dominance over blacks. The function of Jim Crow was to maintain white supremacy through the denigration and humiliation of African Americans. Although Jim Crow is associated with the South and the southern way of life, it also existed in the North and the West. We tend to attribute the system of Jim Crow almost exclusively to the South because the vast majority of African Americans lived in that region and so it was most ubiquitous there, and also because white southerners implemented it with a savagery and viciousness unparalleled in the other regions of the country.

Ground-level whipping post, above which is a platform for the pillory, presently occupied by two African American men; a ladder leans against the platform, a group of men loiter in the background, ca. 1889. (Library of Congress)

Laws mandating racial segregation and black disenfranchisement originated in the North, where states had abolished slavery by the 1820s, mostly through gradual emancipation laws. A majority of northern whites shared the belief with their southern counterparts that white folks constituted a superior race of people and justified segregation and disenfranchisement on the grounds that blacks were innately inferior and therefore could not meet the vital responsibilities of citizenship. Some scholars have noted that southern legislatures modeled their respective post–Civil War Jim Crow statutes on the North's antebellum discrimination laws. Most northern states had barred free blacks from voting, office-holding, and jury service, and mandated the separation of the races in public schools and public accommodations. Blacks were discriminated against in employment. These discriminations were not uniform in all northern states, and they were not enforced consistently from jurisdiction to jurisdiction.

Northern free blacks did not suffer the indignity of Jim Crow laws quietly or passively. In Massachusetts, free blacks formed organizations that actively agitated to improve their condition. Free black men and women primarily from the Boston area formed the Massachusetts General Colored Association in 1826, an all-black antislavery organization. In 1833, they merged with William Lloyd Garrison's New England Anti-Slavery Society and fought not only for an end to slavery, but also for an end to racial discrimination. The group began its antidiscrimination campaign with an attack on the Massachusetts law banning interracial marriages and succeeded in convincing the state legislature to repeal it in 1843.

The Abiel Smith school, the first school in Boston for African Americans. (Kevin Fleming/Corbis)

One of the primary goals of free blacks regardless of region was access to public education. Most northern public schools were segregated, a circumstance to which free blacks willingly acquiesced. African Americans often preferred segregated schools because of racial prejudice against their children. Initially, the parents of Boston's free black children refused to send them to white schools because of the poor treatment they received from white students and teachers. Instead, they created private schools; however, because many could not afford the tuition required to attend them, some hired private tutors and others remained illiterate. The patchwork system of educating black children proved unsuccessful, and in 1800, the parents of some black children petitioned the Boston School Committee to establish a publicly funded school for black children. The committee refused. Hearing of their plight, however, a number of prominent, sympathetic whites offered financial support to the private schools. This system remained intact until 1818 when the Boston School Committee assumed control for primary education of Boston's free black children and built them a school.

William Cooper Nell, who became one of Boston's most prominent African American abolitionists, was educated in the segregated system. Nell decided in 1840 that segregation was incompatible with democracy, and he along with several prominent white abolitionists petitioned the Boston School Committee to integrate the primary schools. At the same time, Nell and a group of militant free blacks turned their attention to the railroad companies, which had a policy of requiring black and white passengers to sit in separate cars. Nell and the other abolitionists usurped the widely popular and thus familiar caricature of "Jim Crow" and applied it as a moniker for the railway car set aside for blacks. To protest racial segregation on the trains, a group of black activists purchased tickets, took their seats in the white car, and refused to go to the Jim Crow car after being ordered to do so. An angry mob of whites intervened and violently removed them from the train. These African American activists then petitioned the state legislature to outlaw the Jim Crow cars, but the lawmakers refused to bar the practice. Undaunted, the activists pressured the railroads to end voluntarily the practice of racial segregation on intrastate trains until they finally succeeded in 1843.

Emboldened by their victory with the railway companies, the activists returned their attention to the Jim Crow public school system the following year. In 1844, Boston had 117 primary schools, but only one for black children. The School Committee asserted that black children constituted only 2 percent of the total student population and, therefore, did not need more than one school. The committee also noted that black children used the same textbooks as white students and a few African American students had been admitted to the public high school. Nell and his associates noted that the reason only a handful of black students had been admitted to the high school was because the education they received in the segregated school was so woefully inferior to that of whites they could not qualify academically for high school. The Boston School Committee members, all of whom were white, tried to blame the discrepancy on the innate intellectual inferiority of blacks, but the activists would have none of it and blamed the institutional failures on racial segregation.

When their efforts with the Boston School Committee failed, the activists petitioned the state legislature, a strategy that also failed. They organized mass meetings to protest segregation, and even resorted to a boycott of the black school. Not receiving any satisfaction, the group decided to challenge Boston's Jim Crow school system in the courts. The irony was that blacks initially had insisted on a segregated education for their children and then midway through the century, they insisted on integration. The change in attitude was the direct result of the substandard education pupils at the all-black school received. To challenge the policy of Jim Crow schools, Benjamin Roberts brought a lawsuit against the City of Boston on behalf of his five-year-old daughter Sarah and hired the renowned lawyer and abolitionist Charles Sumner to argue his case. Sumner used an 1845 state law that forbade anyone from preventing a child from attending public school.

In his petition to the Massachusetts Supreme Judicial Court, Charles Sumner employed several lines of argument against segregated schools. Four times Benjamin Roberts had tried to enroll his daughter in the white school near his home, and each time the white school principal refused to admit the child. Sumner asserted that Sarah had to pass by five white schools on her way to the black one, which he charged only exacerbated the injustice inherent in segregation. Forcing Sarah Roberts to attend an all-black school of inferior quality when other schools were closer to home violated her right to equal protection under the law as guaranteed in the Massachusetts constitution. Separating children in primary schools based on race or skin color, insisted Sumner, created a caste system that violated a basic tenet of the state constitution's promise that all of the state's citizens were "born free and equal." Segregation based on skin color was inherently unequal and was not only a violation of Sarah Roberts' personal rights, but also a violation of the human rights of all free blacks in Massachusetts, which the state constitution expressly forbade.

The Boston School Committee responded that racially based discrimination in public education was legal, and it had the authority to assign African American children to segregated schools. The committee, however, based the crux of its argument on the fact that it had not violated the state law forbidding anyone from preventing a child to attend school, because it had in fact provided a publicly funded school for all of the city's black children.

Writing for the state supreme court, Chief Judge Lemuel Shaw rejected each of Sumner's assertions and upheld the School Committee's authority to mandate segregation in Boston's primary grades. Shaw noted that racially based discriminations were consistent with local custom. As for all person's being equal before the law, Shaw observed a manifest difference between an ideal of equality and the lived reality of it. "When this great principle" of equality before the law "comes to be applied to the actual and various conditions of persons in society," wrote the judge, "it will not warrant the assertion, that men and women are legally clothed with the same civil and political powers, and that children and adults are legally to have the same functions and be subject to the same treatment." According to Judge Shaw the only guarantee of the state constitution's free and equal clause was "that the rights of all, as they are settled and regulated by law, are equally entitled to the paternal consideration and protection of the law, for their maintenance and security" (*Roberts v. City of Boston*, 5 Cush. [Mass.] 198, 206). The law was based on reality and American society tolerated and sanctioned racial discrimination. Thus, segregated schools were permissible under the state constitution. The School Committee provided the African American children of Boston with a place where they could be educated and, therefore, was not in violation of state law.

The case of *Roberts v. City of Boston* (1849) is important to an understanding of the black response to Jim Crow. This ruling established a critical precedent for bolstering Jim Crow laws and customs, which meant that the Jim Crow system was legally acceptable and could flourish in America. The fact that one of the most influential judges of the antebellum era rendered the decision only added to its prestige and other judges employed its rationale to uphold racially discriminatory laws in their jurisdictions. Indeed, when the justices of the U.S. Supreme Court were asked to rule on the constitutionality of Louisiana's Jim Crow law, they turned to this precedent. Once black Americans understood the legal rationale for racial discrimination as provided in this case, they could prepare to attack its underlying assumptions in future challenges. This case is important because it illustrates the commitment that African Americans had to achieving equality before the law and in American society.

Undaunted by this ruling, black Bostonians turned their gaze toward the state legislature. If the state's highest court would not hold that segregation was contrary to the state's constitution, then they would fight until they convinced lawmakers to pass laws expressly banning such policies. After a long fifteen-year struggle, they succeeded. In April 1855, legislators passed a statute that outlawed segregation in the public schools.

Racial prejudice and discrimination, however, continued in the Bay State. Massachusetts did not allow African Americans to join the militia, and in Boston, places of amusement such as theaters were mostly segregated and those that admitted blacks made them sit in a segregated section. Black Bostonians frequently challenged Jim Crow practices and on occasion succeeded in compelling theater owners to alter their policy. When two prominent black activists found themselves summarily tossed out of one of Boston's most popular playhouses, they brought criminal charges against the agent and the police officer who had assaulted them. After the criminal court found the two white men guilty, the black activists brought a civil suit against the theater, which they also won. Realizing that African Americans would continue to fight against theater owners' policy of Jim Crow seating, a few capitulated and allowed blacks to sit amid whites, but most continued the practice of segregation.

Black Bostonians scored another huge victory in 1865, when after years of agitating for an antidiscrimination law in public accommodations, state lawmakers enacted one in May, just one month after the Confederate states had to surrender to the United States. The 1865 law banned racial discrimination on account of race or color in hotels, places of amusement, public conveyances, and public meetings. With the enactment of this law, Massachusetts became the first state in America to pass civil rights legislation, and it remained the only state with such a law until 1873 when New York passed its first. The Massachusetts laws served as the model for the federal Civil Rights Act of 1875. But these laws did not stop white Americans from being prejudiced toward African Americans, and blacks in Boston and elsewhere in the North encountered racial hatred wherever they went, a fact that only impelled them to continue to fight.

Northern free blacks never stopped trying to defeat Jim Crow whenever it reared its head. In Massachusetts, black activists returned to the state legislature and asked for a stronger antidiscrimination law. In 1885, lawmakers responded with new legislation that prohibited discrimination in unlicensed as well as licensed public establishments and fined businesses that did not comply. Still, Black Bostonians had to return to demand an even more stringent antidiscrimination law only a decade later. Lawmakers obliged and increased the fine to $300 and added a new provision that made jail time possible for noncompliance. The law took effect June 4, 1895, the same day it was signed into law.

Boston's free blacks were not the only ones to fight against Jim Crow laws and practices. New York had the largest population of free blacks in the North. Those free African Americans who lived or worked in Brooklyn had access to public transportation, but New York City excluded them from trains and trolleys and, despite having to pay full fare, they could ride only on the outside platform of horse-drawn cabs. In the mid-1850s, two free blacks, a teacher named Elizabeth Jennings and a Heidelberg-educated Presbyterian minister named J. W. C. Pennington, challenged the racially discriminatory practice in the cabs. They purchased tickets and sat inside the cab and refused to leave when ordered to do so. They brought suit against the city after being forcibly removed, and they won, thus securing for all free blacks the right to ride in the public, horse-drawn carriages in New York City.

Northern free blacks were not the only ones fighting racial discrimination. Free African Americans in the West also sought access to public education and equal citizenship. Between 1852 and 1860, California's black population grew from 962 to 4,086, and by 1910, it had reached 21,645, which amounted to about 1 percent of the total population. Most black Californians lived in urban centers, especially San Francisco, the state's largest 19th-century city, and Sacramento. They worked primarily in the service and manual labor sectors. Most western blacks migrated from northeastern states and had higher literacy rates and incomes when compared to free blacks in the South. Black Californians had their own newspapers and some operated their own businesses. Despite the fact that the California Constitution of 1849 banned slavery in the state, an estimated 300 slaves worked in the gold fields and an undetermined number worked as domestics. Although white officials proved unwilling to challenge slaveholders property rights within the state, the free black community was more than willing to utilize legal and extralegal means to secure the freedom of bondsmen and women and many slaves were able to escape slavery thanks to the tireless efforts of California's free blacks and white abolitionists.

Most white Californians did not want slavery in their state, yet they actively supported racially discriminatory legislation and, indeed, California had a number of Jim Crow laws on the books. Lawmakers banned interracial marriages and even black homesteading. Persons with as little as one-sixth African blood could not vote, hold public office, serve on juries, or testify against whites in court. The state had its own fugitive slave law and the governor asked lawmakers to ban black immigration into the state. Clearly, despite having entered the nation as a nonslave state, white Californians did not want African Americans living within their borders.

Laws denying black Californians basic civil rights prompted them to call a series of conventions to plan a civil rights campaign protesting the state's Jim Crow laws. The Jim Crow laws were not harsh enough to prevent the development of an African American community in the urban centers or to halt the growth of a small, but influential middle class. Black Californians of all classes understood that they had to stand together to fight discrimination. They formed the Franchise League in 1862 to campaign for the vote and to end restrictions on black testimony in courts. They met with limited success when the state legislature repealed the restriction on testimony in 1863. Emboldened by this small victory, they pressed on with their efforts.

During the Civil War, black Californians attacked segregation on public transportation, especially the streetcars, which had a habit of excluding blacks. William Bowen brought a lawsuit against the San Francisco streetcar after he was ejected from one in May 1863. He asked for $10,000 and a jury awarded him $3,999 in damages. Charlotte Brown had filed an antidiscrimination lawsuit the previous month after she too had been thrown off a public conveyance. The judge in her case instructed the jury that excluding blacks from public transportation violated state law, but the jurors awarded her only five cents in damages, an amount equal to the fare. After Brown was excluded from yet another streetcar, she brought another lawsuit, and the second time the jury awarded her $500 in damages. These victories were not enough to get the streetcars to change their racist practices, and thus the black activists pressed on until 1893 when they achieved passage of an antidiscrimination law.

Black Californians waged a similar campaign to integrate the public schools. When the state initially began to develop its public school system, the earliest laws made no mention of race, and thus, in the arena of public education, it appeared that the state did not discriminate. Yet, when black parents tried to enroll their children in public school, the principals turned them away. In May 1854, San Francisco opened the first "colored school," but this was a private institution that received no state funds. In 1860, the white school superintendent told the San Francisco school board that African American children needed better education facilities, and it contributed monies to help them build a new school, which opened four years later. Sacramento opened a private school for black children in 1855, and the city helped them to build a schoolhouse the following year.

For most of this time, the state had no law mandating segregated schools. The system had developed on its own in accordance with custom and the wishes of many black parents who understood that their children would meet with discrimination and a hostile learning environment should they attend schools with white children and teachers. Still, some black parents agitated to have their children admitted to the public schools, which impelled the state to pass the first public school segregation law in 1863. The law barred not only black students from the white schools, but also excluded Asian and Native American children. The law allowed, but did not require, local school boards to establish separate schools for nonwhite children. Many white Californians looked at the public school law with great discomfort as it forced them to equate their state's Jim Crow schools with the Confederate South. Public disapproval by whites as well as blacks led lawmakers to weaken some Jim Crow legislation, such as the law prohibiting blacks from testifying against whites in courts of law. In 1866, state legislators changed the Jim Crow school law to mandate that school boards create publicly funded schools in districts with ten or more black, Asian, and Native American children.

Not all black Californians, however, thought their children should have to attend Jim Crow schools, and some parents attempted to enroll their children in the white schools, albeit with little success. The parents of Mary Frances Ward sued Noah Flood, the principal of the Broadway Grammar School in San Francisco, because he would not admit their child to the white school. The Wards asserted that school segregation based on race violated the constitutional rights of African Americans. In the case of *Ward v. Flood* (1874), the California supreme court employed the rationale set forth in the *Roberts* decision and held that to deny a black child access to public education was indeed unconstitutional, however, the state of

California did not do this. The state provided black children equal access to public education, and the mere fact that the state required black children to attend a separate school was not a violation of the state or the federal constitution.

Black Californians did not like the court's response and sought legislative relief, and there they succeeded. By the end of 1875, several California school districts, such as Oakland, Sacramento, and Vallejo, had integrated. San Francisco, the largest school district, also integrated and, by 1880, the state stopped requiring that black students attend Jim Crow schools. It appears that economics played the primary role in the shift in attitude. In the 1870s, California saw a period of economic depression and high unemployment and the taxpayers were willing to integrate the schools to keep taxation low. Although black children had won the right to attend schools with white students, the state still mandated a Jim Crow school system for Asian and Native American children. Even though black children could attend school with whites, discrimination in housing and neighborhood patterns meant that most California school children went to separate schools all the same.

Jim Crow arose in the North and spread to the West and affected all parts in between, but nowhere was it so pervasive and so brutal as in the American South. Following the Civil War, much of the rest of the nation was moving away from a Jim Crow system of segregation. Illinois repealed its ban on black migration into the state and allowed blacks to sit on juries and testify in courts. New York City, San Francisco, Cleveland, Cincinnati, and Philadelphia abandoned the practice of Jim Crow streetcars. Even as northern states repealed some of their most egregious Jim Crow legislation, social separation remained, as did segregation in most public accommodations, such as public schools, restaurants, hotels, parks, and beaches. Whites in all regions continued to think of themselves as a superior race and that belief fueled the rationale for racial prejudice, although in many places outside the South, the discrimination was more rooted in custom than in law. As punitive and degrading as Jim Crow was in the North and the West, however, it was never as bad as it was in the South. Jim Crow laws and customs were never so oppressive or as sadistically and savagely enforced as they were in the former Confederate States.

Emancipation for southern blacks occurred in stages, but slavery formally ended on January 31, 1865, with the ratification of the Thirteenth Amendment to the U.S. Constitution, which abolished the institution throughout the nation. The United States entered a period of its history known as the Reconstruction era that lasted from 1863 to 1877. Four million bondsmen and women celebrated and proclaimed that their "Day of Jubilee" had arrived. Immediately, the former slaves began creating their own institutions and communities. The freedmen and women forged their own understanding of emancipation, which included participation in the democratic process. They insisted on the full rights of citizenship with all its trappings: the right to a publicly funded education, the right to vote and hold public office, and the right to sit on juries. In addition, they demanded the legal right to marry, own land, make contracts, sue and be

African American kindergarten class at Whittier Primary School in Hampton, Virginia, ca. 1899.
(Library of Congress)

sued, and testify in court against whites. They formed benevolence societies to care for the sick, the elderly, and the indigent. Those who had resources or were highly resourceful opened their own businesses.

The freedmen and women established their own churches and, equally important to them, they established their own schools. They understood how vital it was to be able to read, write, and perform basic math. In spite of the economic hardship that having a child in school posed to black families who needed all the producers they could get, black parents insisted that their children get an education. Many parents themselves attended night schools. Like their northern counterparts, southern African Americans preferred segregated schools. Blacks understood that knowledge was power and their everyday lived experience told them that they had to be educated at least enough to prevent exploitation by whites. Blacks believed wholeheartedly that education was the means to maintaining their freedom and to uplifting their race, and they embraced it with eagerness and enthusiasm. An education not only could protect them from whites, but also could open new doors of opportunity for them.

Charlotte Hawkins Brown who was born in Henderson, North Carolina, but grew up in Cambridge, Massachusetts, returned to the South at the turn of the century as a teacher. She opened her own school and employed a curriculum similar to the ones used in the Massachusetts schools. In an age in which so many thought that African Americans need only learn an agricultural trade, Hawkins Brown taught her students spelling, reading,

Charlotte Hawkins Brown (1883–1961)

Charlotte Hawkins was born in Henderson, North Carolina, in June 1883, and her family moved to Cambridge, Massachusetts, when she was five years old. She received her primary education in the Allston Grammar School in Cambridge, Massachusetts, and graduated from Cambridge English High. Hawkins had the good fortune to have had a chance encounter with Alice Mitchell Palmer, a renowned Massachusetts educator, who became her college financial sponsor and mentor. Hawkins married Edward Brown in 1911.

In 1901, after a year of junior college, Brown migrated to Sedalia, North Carolina, to teach at a school for poor, rural blacks. Her job came to an end after only a year when her sponsors decided to close that school, but at the urging of the local black community, she ventured to open a new one. With financial help from her friends in the North, Brown purchased 200 acres of land and raised two buildings on the campus. She established a board of trustees that consisted entirely of African Americans and named her school the Palmer Memorial Institute in honor of her friend and mentor.

Brown's school was unique in the South because it had a traditional academic program modeled after the public schools of Massachusetts. She taught spelling, reading, writing, arithmetic, and personal hygiene in the primary grades and literature, grammar, geography, history, and agriculture in the secondary grades. She encouraged those students who aspired to college to learn French and civil government. In an era in which Jim Crow intensified and southern whites were hostile to black education that included anything more than agriculture, Hawkins succeeded admirably. She received several honorary degrees, including at the doctoral level and thus became eligible to call herself Dr. Brown.

Brown did not limit her considerable abilities to education. She became involved in the community and participated in a number of professional organizations such as the National Association of Colored Women, an umbrella organization for state and local women's clubs. Dr. Brown retired in 1952 after fifty years of teaching, and she died in January 1961 after a long illness. She is buried on the campus of the school she loved and to which she gave so much.

writing, and mathematics. Her curriculum included classes in drama, literature, music, history, geography, and French. Several of Hawkins Brown's pupils went on to attend college. She was so successful that she was able to forge a biracial coalition of northerners and progressive southerners to keep her school afloat financially. So pleased were southern blacks with their chance to receive a formal education, that when a general in the U.S. Army visited a school and asked the pupils what message he could tell their friends up North, one young student stood and proudly proclaimed, "Tell them we are rising." And rise they did.

Having won their freedom, southern blacks were determined to resist white efforts to control them. This resistance took many forms and often was subtle but sometimes obvious. Many left the farms they had worked as slaves and set off to find loved ones who had been sold away. As free men and women, they no longer needed permission to leave the plantation. Some stepped off simply because they could. Former slaves refused to work for former masters who had been excessively cruel and moved on to other places in search of better wages and working conditions. As free laborers, many southern blacks insisted on setting their own work hours, and they refused to sign labor contracts they felt were exploitative. They refused to work in gangs and demanded pay for nonfarming chores. Unless they had to, women and children did not work in the fields. A few freedmen and women burned the homes and barns of their former masters, but such instances were rare. Some demanded outright ownership of the land that they had worked as slaves, whereas others were willing to wait until they could purchase land of their own. The former slaves were determined to forge successful lives for themselves and refused to let whites deny that to them.

The right to vote and to participate in the democratic process was every bit as important to African American southerners as getting an education. Blacks and whites formed Union Clubs, which were organizations that registered black men to vote (neither white nor black women had that right) and taught them how to read and cast a ballot. On Election Day, African Americans went to the polls in throngs. Voting was a dangerous act for African Americans in the South as many were murdered for it. In some instances, black women accompanied their men to the polls carrying large hickory sticks to ensure that they got to the polls unmolested and that, once there, they voted for the correct candidates. Naturally, blacks supported politicians who supported them and with the help of black votes such candidates were elected overwhelmingly to the state governments of

Robert Smalls was a slave whose exploits for the Union during the Civil War won him national recognition; he was later elected as a Republican to five nonconsecutive terms in the U.S. House of Representatives. (Library of Congress)

the former Confederacy. Once in office, these politicians established new state constitutions that guaranteed blacks political and civil rights on par with whites, including the right to vote, hold public office, and sit on juries. The new state charters removed most legal disabilities and outlawed such punishments as whippings, which many saw as a vestige of slavery, but they typically avoided the question of integration in public accommodations. Scores of black men were elected to office, especially at the local level. Some African American men such as Robert Smalls of South Carolina, Blanche Bruce and P. B. S. Pinchback of Louisiana, and John Lynch of Mississippi made careers for themselves in national politics, while most others served in state and local offices.

Southern whites were appalled at the political and social advancements of blacks and acted swiftly and violently to reassert white supremacy. The Ku Klux Klan, originally a benign fraternal society, morphed into a large paramilitary organization bent on reinstituting white supremacy through acts of terrorism, and other similar vigilante groups arose to terrorize southern blacks and any whites who aided them. During the Reconstruction era, the Klan began a "Reign of Terror" against the freedmen and women that was so bloody the federal government had to step in to stop it. The Ku Kluxers, as they were known, targeted black politicians and civic leaders, and they murdered blacks by the score. The reality for southern blacks was that any of them could at any time experience the sadism and savagery of southern white supremacists. For example, Klansmen nearly beat to death a 103-year-old African American woman and a paralyzed black man. A white mob in Georgia beat a freedman to death with such brutality that his daughter who had witnessed the murder died a short time afterward. In Mississippi, angry whites disemboweled a black man in front of his wife who had just given birth to twins. Such was life for black southerners after emancipation.

Congress formed a committee to investigate these atrocities and the public record of their findings reveals the horrific struggles that blacks endured. Investigators found that white terrorist groups burned black churches, homes, and schools. They beat and sometimes lynched teachers and well-educated blacks. They drove black landowners off of their property or, if they refused to leave, murdered them. They broke down the doors of private homes in the middle of the night, dragged African American men out of their beds, and beat them in their own front yards, all because they had voted or were registering and training other blacks to vote. They would beat and rape the wife or daughter of a politically active African American man to send him a message. The function of these acts of terror was to compel blacks to submit to white supremacy. Yet despite the sadism and brutality of southern whites, African Americans continued their political activities and their fight to gain the full rights to which all American citizens are entitled.

Not all altercations between southern whites and African Americans were physically violent, although all of them were clearly intended to humiliate and degrade. It was common, for example, for a group of whites to force a black man they encountered on a public street to dance before letting him pass. On occasion, they might force alcohol down his throat until he could hardly stand. If the mob was large enough, they might accost two black men and make them fight each other, all for the amusement of the white spectators and for the humiliation of the blacks who had to submit. Rather than compel submission, however, white supremacists inadvertently impelled many young African American men and women to fight the Jim Crow system rather than give in to it. Letters, memoirs, and recollections from youths who experienced or witnessed white brutality during the Reconstruction and Jim Crow eras reveal a resentment that fueled a rage to defeat rather than submit to white supremacy.

Jim Crow did not wash over and blanket the South all at once like a tidal wave; rather, it came unevenly in fits and starts. The South's era of Jim Crow began to take hold over the course of the 1880s and lasted until the mid-1960s. The South's Jim Crow era coincided with its lynching era, which lasted from the 1880s through the 1930s. As had been the case in slavery days, violence was one of the primary mechanisms of white control over blacks in the Jim Crow South. At the same time that many blacks were losing their civil and political freedoms, however, others in some states and in some areas within states continued to enjoy a degree of social and political autonomy. The rural South increasingly revealed its penchant for sadism and racial hatred, while urban centers continued to offer some opportunities for African Americans. In some southern towns, blacks could sit in restaurants, theaters, and saloons alongside whites into the first decade of the 20th century. In many urban areas, they continued to hold minor public offices such as watchman or policeman. Black children had access to publicly funded education, albeit in segregated schools.

As the South limped along in its slow crawl toward urbanization, both blacks and whites migrated to the cities in search of employment, opportunity, and amusement. In the cities, a small but influential black middle class emerged, one that embraced certain white values such as the nuclear family, male-headed households, respectability, thriftiness, and temperance. Black businessmen increasingly played an important role in community affairs, and African Americans came to engage in virtually every arena of the local economy. Urban middle-class women also played a vital role in their communities. Women's contributions consisted of operating mission and benevolent societies through which they tended to the orphaned, the poor, the widowed, and the infirm. They created literary societies and established musical and theater groups to bring culture to their communities.

A rapid influx of African Americans into the cities of the South coupled with a rising black middle class and an increasing militancy among black youths who had been born after slavery signaled trouble to some. Southern whites began to develop a mythical nostalgia for the good old days of slavery when blacks knew their place and those that stepped out could be dealt with easily and quickly. This younger generation of African Americans appeared insolent and uppity. Worse, these youths seemed to white southerners to be ambitious and impatient to gain access to the fundamental freedoms to which American citizens were entitled. These young men and women not only aspired to basic rights, but also sought equality between the races. White southerners responded to this perceived threat to their traditional way of life by searching for more effective ways to control blacks, especially the young, uppity ones. Out of this hysteria came a demand for racially discriminatory legislation, which in turn produced the racial caste system known as Jim Crow. By the start of the 1890s, southern states were well on their way into an era rife with racial hatred and violence and the reascendance of white supremacy.

Tennessee has the distinction not only of bequeathing the nation the Ku Klux Klan, but also the first Jim Crow law. In 1881, the state legislature enacted a law that mandated separate railroad cars for blacks and whites. The law specified that the separate accommodations had to be equal. Blacks who paid a first-class fare had to sit in a Jim Crow car, but one ostensibly with the same first-class accommodations that whites enjoyed. Railroads did not like these laws because separate cars were expensive for them to maintain. Often, they got around the laws by providing separate though far-from-equal accommodations.

There was a manifest difference between the first- and second-class cars on trains. Ladies and gentlemen sat in the first-class car. The cars had clean, plush, soft seats. They had clean floors and air as neither spitting nor smoking was allowed, and they provided ice water to passengers. In fact, first-class cars were also known as the "ladies car" because of the level of behavioral decorum required of the passengers. White ladies often traveled the trains unescorted. Many white southerners were disturbed at the thought that an unaccompanied white woman might have to sit next to a black man on a public train. Second-class cars, on the other hand, had hard, filthy seats when they provided seats at all. Often, the second-class car was merely the baggage car with a curtain strung across it to divide the luggage from the passengers. The air was rife with tobacco smoke and the floors filthy and sticky from tobacco juice. The trains provided no water to passengers in this car. The white men who typically rode in the second-class cars were unrefined to say the least. They often gambled, cursed, and drank as they rode the rails. Second-class cars apparently had no rules mandating good behavior. It is not difficult to understand why African American ladies and gentlemen would not wish to ride in the second-class car.

African Americans did not like the Separate Car Law because they knew that separate was seldom if ever equal. Many blacks challenged the Separate Car Laws by bringing lawsuits against the railroads whose duty it was to enforce them. Blacks struggled to achieve and maintain white standards of respectability, and those blacks who had gained such status were deeply offended when states suggested that they too should have to ride in the Jim Crow car. They understood requiring dirty and poor blacks to do so, but not themselves. A black newspaper editor in Savannah, Georgia, called on his readers to challenge the laws. He instructed them to call the conductor's bluff if ordered to the Jim Crow car. Sixteen-year-old Mary Church took that advice. When the conductor directed her to remove herself to second class, she showed him her first-class ticket and refused to budge. He insisted she leave first class and Church offered to remain in her seat, but said she would get off the train at the next stop so she could wire her father who would hire a lawyer and sue the railroad company. The conductor allowed Church to remain in the ladies car until she reached her destination. Lawsuits were the other reason why railway companies disliked the Separate Car Laws. Increasingly, over the course of the 1880s, southern African Americans were compelled to sue the railroad companies in courts of law.

One of the first respectable African Americans to challenge the legality of Tennessee's Jim Crow law was a Memphis schoolteacher named Ida B. Wells. Wells purchased a first-class ticket and took her seat in the ladies car. The conductor asked her to leave, and when she refused, he forcibly dragged her into the Jim Crow car. Wells sued on grounds that she was a lady and thus entitled to ride in the ladies car. She also asserted that the second-class car was a smoking car and did not provide equal accommodations. Wells won her case in the Shelby County Circuit Court, which awarded her a $500 judgment, but the railroad appealed the judgment. The Tennessee Supreme Court reversed the lower court's ruling and took the word of the railroad company that the separate accommodations were equal. Without any evidence to sustain the claim, the Supreme Court charged that Wells had boarded the train for the purpose of causing a disturbance. This ruling by the state's highest court meant that so long as a federal court did not say otherwise, the 1881 Tennessee law was valid. The court's ruling did not settle the matter so far as black Tennesseans were concerned. They continued to fight the law, but without success.

After the Tennessee law survived a court challenge, other southern states began enacting similar Jim Crow car laws. Between 1881 and 1891, ten states passed such laws. Mississippi lawmakers passed one in 1888 that was challenged by a railway company. The case went to the U.S. Supreme Court, which in 1890 ruled that the law did not violate the Interstate Commerce Clause and thus was constitutional. With the blessing of the U.S. Supreme Court, the rest of the southern states enacted their own Separate Car Laws. At the same time that legislatures of the former Confederacy passed Separate Car Laws, they also began a debate about disfranchising blacks. In Tennessee, for example, through vote fraud and violence, Democrats captured control of the legislature in 1888 and swiftly began passing laws that prohibited or limited African Americans' right to vote. By 1890, they had succeeded in cutting the black vote by half.

That same year, whites in Mississippi voted to amend the state constitution to disenfranchise blacks and poor whites. Legislators added a literacy clause that required that voters be able to read a section of the state constitution. The test's administrators were white and few blacks passed the test, even those that could read. Poor whites, on the other hand, seldom failed and were allowed to vote. Black Mississippians resisted the state's efforts to disenfranchise them. One newspaper editor called on the black churches to hold night schools to teach blacks to read so they could pass the test. They also challenged the law in court. The case advanced all the way to the U.S. Supreme Court. In the case of *Williams v. Mississippi* (1898), the Court ruled that literacy tests did not violate the equal protection clause of the Fourteenth Amendment because the law affected illiterate blacks and whites equally and thus did not discriminate based on race. Attorneys for the black plaintiffs pointed out that in the course of the debate over amending the U.S. Constitution, state legislators acknowledged that the purpose of the effort was to disenfranchise blacks. The Supreme Court held that the intent of the constitutional change was irrelevant.

One of the main reasons for southern whites' effort to disenfranchise blacks was that this younger generation of African Americans raised outside of slavery was increasingly unwilling to defer to whites. Black's non-subservient demeanor did not cause lawmakers to pass Jim Crow legislation, but it did lead to the perception that segregation was the solution to the problem of an ever-increasing tension between blacks and whites. Preventing blacks from voting certainly decreased their political power and thus their ability to hinder southern whites' efforts to deny them basic civil and political rights. That is why once the Supreme Court ruled that in certain instances whites could bar blacks from voting, southern lawmakers began enacting a new round of discriminatory statutes. They passed poll taxes that required voters to pay a tax to vote. Blacks were the most likely group to be unable to pay, but as the law conceivably affected poor whites just the same, they knew it would survive a constitutional challenge, and they were right. Some states went so far as to institute morals directives, which empowered the local registrar to determine whether a voter was of good character before allowing him to vote.

As the 19th century neared its end, Jim Crow spread beyond the railroad cars and into the train stations. States began requiring separate waiting rooms for blacks and whites. From there segregation, spread into the courthouses of the South, where rules barring blacks from testifying against whites and sitting on juries prevailed. So fanatical were white supremacists about separating the races that they put two Bibles in every courthouse, one for whites to swear on and another for blacks. Jim Crow began to settle over the South like a large black cloud and, increasingly, southern blacks found themselves disenfranchised and excluded from the democratic process. Where laws failed, violence was employed to enforce the Jim Crow system, but it was also through violence that white supremacists regained control of governments in the South. The two went hand in hand in establishing and perpetuating the Jim Crow system.

African Americans resisted all efforts to encroach on their rights and tried to push back against whites limiting their rights, particularly in public spaces. They were determined to prevent whites from excluding them from the market place. Trains and train stations and even courthouses are a different kind of public space from the marketplace in the sense that they are not consumer driven. The reality is that even white segregationists wanted African American dollars. Despite their virulent white supremacy, white southerners competed for the black consumer and that is one reason why segregationists were never able to achieve perfect separation of the races. Blacks understood this, and used the new consumer culture to their advantage and to help mitigate some of the worst aspects of the Jim Crow system.

Southern whites had drawn a color line and expected blacks to adhere to it; the problem was that no one, black or white, knew exactly where that line was. This was especially true in the marketplace. For example, blacks and whites rode together on the streetcars, and although signs stated that blacks had to sit in the back and whites in the front, this separation did not prevent contact between the two groups. The uncertainty of where the line was drawn, of course, often resulted in friction at best and violence at worst. How could a white supremacist be certain that when an African American bumped into him, it was an accident? Indeed, such bumping and jostling may have been intentional and part of that testing of boundaries. When intentional, it was also a form of resistance to the Jim Crow system.

In the countryside, whites were able to exert more control over blacks. In the marketplace, general store owners even determined what items an African American could purchase by limiting the amount of credit they would give. Rural shopkeepers insisted that blacks adhere to rules of deference such as making them wait until all the white customers had been helped before allowing blacks to purchase their items. This system remained intact until the age of the mail order catalog, and then those blacks who could pay with cash purchased items without having to suffer degrading treatment. Both the Montgomery Ward and the Sears catalogs found their way into the homes of black southerners. Mail ordering became even more viable an alternative for blacks after 1898 when the U.S. Postal Service introduced free rural delivery. Being able to bypass the local merchant who previously had controlled the mail made it even easier for blacks to make shopping a more dignified and private affair. Mail order shopping became an act of resistance to the Jim Crow system in rural areas.

In the cities, on the other hand, white merchants faced competition not only from other white storeowners, but also from African American businessmen. This made racial separation difficult if not impossible. Outside streets, sidewalks, and town squares tended to be crowded and inside stores teemed with consumers, especially on Saturday afternoons when most people ventured into town to do their shopping. Public water fountains and restrooms were fairly easy to segregate, as were theaters. Restaurants, diners, and cafés tended to be segregated, with notable exceptions. The Choke 'Em Down Lunch Room in Belle Glades, Florida, for example, fed people of both races. But in the case of stores and shops, racial ordering simply proved difficult if not impossible. In businesses where blacks shopped in large numbers, white storeowners tended to serve customers in turn rather than risk losing black dollars. Blacks knew they could go down the street to another merchant who would treat them better to win their patronage. Even in stores and shops where signs mandating segregation were displayed, they were honored more in the breach as owners did not want to offend their black customers. Black consumerism also was a form of resistance to the Jim Crow system, especially when blacks threatened white shopkeepers with boycotts or simply took their business elsewhere.

Men stand in front of the S. J. Gilpin shoe store in Richmond, Virginia, ca. 1899. (Library of Congress)

Southern whites managed to achieve a high degree of segregation in some mostly rural spaces, but they were less successful in others, especially urban areas. Whites had their greatest success at instituting Jim Crow schools and at the polls, but they were less triumphant in certain kinds of public accommodations and on public conveyances. From the standpoint of the law bolstering the Jim Crow system, segregation on public conveyances is where southern whites had their greatest 19th-century success. In 1890, Louisiana lawmakers passed a Separate Car Law that required all intrastate trains to have separate but equal first-class cars, one for blacks and another whites. The law stipulated that blacks could not enter the white car and conversely whites could not be seated in the Jim Crow car. New Orleans had a powerful and militant group of Afro-Creoles that determined to challenge the law. They formed a civil rights organization, the Citizens' Committee to Test the Constitutionality of the Separate Car Law. They immediately condemned the law as class legislation and a violation of their constitutional rights.

The committee chose Homer Plessy, one of their members, to violate the law so they could test its constitutionality. They selected Plessy because he was an octoroon, meaning he was one-eighth black and seven-eighths white. Plessy easily could have passed for white and the members wanted him because they also wanted to highlight the irrationality of white notions of race. The group raised money and hired Albion W. Tourgee, a white northern lawyer and champion of black civil rights who also had experience challenging Jim Crow laws in higher courts. Tourgee took the case

Homer Adolphe Plessy (1863–1925)

Homer A. Plessy was born March 17, 1863, in New Orleans to a French-speaking, free black family. His father died when he was five and his mother apprenticed him to a shoemaker. In 1879, Plessy began his own business in the trade making leather boots and shoes to order. Plessy belonged to a community unique to New Orleans known as Afro-Creoles. These men and women were highly educated, free blacks that had enjoyed the privileges of freedom dating back to the Crescent City's era as a French colony. Plessy, as a businessman, joined a benevolent society that provided medical and funeral expenses to its members. In 1888, he wed Louise Bourdenave.

In 1890, Plessy joined the Citizens Committee, an organization devoted to challenging Louisiana's Separate Car Law. The law required intrastate railways to provide separate but equal first-class cars. It barred blacks from entering the white car and whites from the black car. Plessy was an octoroon, which meant that he was one-eighth black and seven-eighths white, and anyone who did not know that he had some African ancestry would not recognize that he was not white. Plessy had one great-grandparent who was black and that, according to Louisiana law, made him a person of color. The Committee chose him to violate the Separate Car Law because they wanted not only to challenge the law on grounds it violated the Thirteenth and Fourteenth Amendments, but also to highlight the absurdity of the state's notion of race.

Plessy purchased a first-class ticket on an intrastate train and was arrested shortly after he took his seat. He was jailed, but released after Committee members paid his $500 bond. His criminal trial was postponed until the Supreme Court decided whether the law was constitutional, which it did in May 1896. On January 11, 1897, the Supreme Court having upheld the constitutionality of the Separate Car Law, Homer Plessy pleaded guilty to violating the law and paid the $25 fine. He returned to his shoemaking business and appears to have lived a long and happy life with his family. He died on March 1, 1925, and is buried in the St. Louis Catholic cemetery on Basin Street in New Orleans. His tombstone is simple and bears no words to honor his brave act of civil disobedience in protesting an unjust law.

pro bono. The committee's goal was to take the case all the way to the U.S. Supreme Court. Plessy purchased his ticket and then sat in the whites-only car. The entire scenario was staged. The group had a sheriff there to arrest Plessy before the train left the station, which he did. In his notes, the sheriff admitted that he could not tell to which race Plessy belonged. With the help of a friendly judge named John Howard Ferguson, the case moved quickly through the state courts and wound its way into the federal system. The committee also had help from the railroad company, which did not want the added expense of a separate first-class car.

Plessy argued in the state courts that the law was unconstitutional and therefore he could not be convicted of its violation. The state court suspended his criminal case until the federal courts could decide on the law's validity. The Supreme Court handed down its ruling on the matter in May 1896. The court's vote was 7–1 to uphold the Louisiana Separate Car Law. One justice did not participate. Justice Henry Billings Brown of Michigan wrote the decision for the court. Brown's ruling relied heavily on the reasoning set forth in Boston Judge Lemuel Shaw's ruling in the *Roberts* (1849) school segregation case. Justice Brown asserted that race was a matter for the states not the federal government and concluded that the police powers of the state allowed them to segregate intrastate railways if they so desired. The Louisiana law, according to the justices, did not violate the Thirteenth Amendment because it was not a form of slavery. It also did not violate the Fourteenth Amendment's privileges and immunities clause because it affected both races equally and, therefore, did not discriminate against one race. Separate accommodations were constitutional so long as they were equal.

The lone dissent in this case came from Kentuckian John Marshall Harlan, a former slaveholder. Marshall was no champion of black civil rights, but he did insist that the Louisiana law did not pass constitutional muster. Iterating the theory of government espoused by the vast majority of the constitution's framers, Harlan wrote that the function of government was to protect the rights of the people and not to oppress them. If, as his esteemed colleagues insisted, it really was lawful for states to segregate based on race, then it logically followed that they could discriminate based on religion or some other criteria. Harlan concluded his dissent asserting that the federal constitution was color-blind and could neither create nor tolerate social classes among its citizens.

The *Plessy* decision and its "separate but equal doctrine" stood as a precedent for upholding Jim Crow legislation for the next several decades until the Supreme Court overturned it in the 1954 case of *Brown v. Board of Education at Topeka, Kansas*. The *Plessy* case symbolized a victory for white supremacy, and in its wake, even more Jim Crow legislation pervaded the South. What is more, with the taint of legitimacy, Jim Crow began a slow crawl northward and into the national psyche.

Scholars have noted that at the turn of the 20th century, the nation's regions reunited in favor of overseas imperialism and southern white supremacy and its segregationist tendencies moved North into the rest of the country. Northern academics began to devise racist theories that they passed off as science. These theories asserted that blacks were biologically, intellectually, and morally inferior to whites and became popular despite all the evidence to the contrary. Jim Crow legislation intensified in the early 20th century and continued well into it. Wherever it reared its head, African Americans stood up in opposition. Despite court rulings, legislation, brutality, and violence, black Americans persisted against great odds in both resisting and fighting the Jim Crow system. Not until the passage of the Civil Rights Act in 1964 and the Voting Rights Act in 1965 did the support mechanisms of the South's system of Jim Crow crumble.

References and Further Reading

De Graaf, Lawrence B., Kevin Mulroy, and Quintard Taylor, eds. *Seeking El Dorado: African Americans in California.* Seattle: University of Washington Press, 2001.

Fireside, Harvey. *Separate and Unequal: Homer Plessy and the Supreme Court Decision that Legalized Racism*. New York: Carroll & Graf, 2004.

Hale, Grace Elizabeth. "'For Colored' and 'For White': Segregated Consumption in the South." In *Jumpin' Jim Crow: Southern Politics from Civil War to Civil Rights*, ed. Jane Daily, Glenda Elizabeth Gilmore, and Bryant Simon. Princeton, NJ: Princeton University Press, 2000.

Litwack, Leon. *Trouble in Mind: Black Southerners in the Age of Jim Crow*. New York: Alfred A. Knopf, 1998.

Lofgren, Charles A. *The Plessy Case: A Legal-Historical Interpretation*. New York: Oxford University Press, 1987.

Omori, Kazuteru. "Race-Neutral Individualism and Resurgence of the Color Line: Massachusetts Civil Rights Legislation, 1855–1895." *Journal of American Ethnic History* 22, no. 1 (Fall 2002): 32–58.

Wormser, Richard. *The Rise and Fall of Jim Crow*. New York: St. Martin's/Griffin, 2003.

"Their Plows Singing beneath the Sandy Loam": African American Agriculture in the Late-Nineteenth-Century South

9

Mark D. Hersey

In a world dominated by cookie-cutter suburban houses, interstate high-ways, cable television, and high-speed Internet, it is easy to forget that less than a century ago most Americans lived either on farms or in small, isolated rural communities. For most Americans, the rural world of the late 19th and early 20th centuries is nearly unfathomable. It is a world they think about—if indeed it ever crosses their minds—only in a passing, nostalgic way, perhaps in the rustic country scenes so fashionable on holiday greeting cards.

What is true of Americans generally is more true of African Americans specifically. Indeed, terms like "urban" and "inner city" are often used interchangeably—even if inaccurately—with "African American" and "black." The identification of African Americans with cities, however, is a recent one. In the late 19th century and well into the 20th century, most black Americans lived in rural areas and worked as farmers. For that matter, most African Americans lived in the rural South and most worked land that did not belong to them.

African Americans lived and farmed in virtually every state. In some states—like New York—African Americans had been tilling their own land for decades when the Civil War came to a close. Abolitionist John Brown, for instance, had purchased land in New York's Adirondack Mountains in part to provide new homes for fugitive slaves. There, despite the unlikely and unfavorable location, African Americans sought to scrape a living from the land.

In other states, African American farmers were relatively new arrivals in the late 19th century. Kansas, for instance, became the most popular destination for black refugees from the South during the late 1870s. The largest all-black community west of the Mississippi River—a community known as Nicodemus—was established in the northwestern portion of the state in 1877, and within a few years, it boasted a population of roughly 600. The largest migration of African Americans to the Sunflower State, however, came in 1879. Fleeing the poverty and racial violence of the South, thousands of black migrants known as Exodusters flocked to Kansas in the space of only a few months that year, hoping to work a piece of land they could call their own. It was, as historian Nell Irvin Painter argued, "the most remarkable migration in the United States after the Civil War" (1992, 184).

Even so, most African Americans remained in the South, and the majority found themselves caught in an economic system that more or less trapped them in a position of debt peonage. The various sorts of farm tenancy that marked the South from Reconstruction through World War II emerged out of two principal factors: the economic devastation that attended the South in the aftermath of the Civil War and prevailing social mores of the region.

In thinking about the economic situation of the South after the Civil War, it is worth remembering that the Union victory had rendered all Confederate currency worthless and any loans made to the Confederate government void. The Union blockade of the South had interrupted the region's commerce, most notably by all but eliminating cotton exports, a significant blow indeed considering the fact that cotton had been not only

An African American man cultivating cotton with a horse-drawn plow in North Carolina, ca. 1902. Following the Civil War, the South continued to be an agrarian economy, relying on cotton and tobacco as its two major crops. Many African Americans fled the South in the early 20th century to pursue opportunities for a better life provided by industrial jobs in the North. (Library of Congress)

the region's but the nation's most valuable export on the eve of the Civil War. Furthermore, most of the fighting had taken place in the South. Both armies had foraged, and by 1864, the Union Army had embraced a policy of literally waging war on the land itself, a policy best remembered in the famous campaigns of Generals William T. Sherman and Philip Sheridan. Thus, in the wake of the war, many southern planters found their fences pulled down, livestock diminished, and outbuildings destroyed. But perhaps the biggest blow to the South's economy had come with the emancipation of the slaves. The economic loss incurred with the dissipation of southern slave wealth was considerable indeed. In Alabama's Black Belt, for instance, planters were paying roughly $1,300 per slave in the late 1850s, a figure that translates to more than $25,000 in early twenty-first-century dollars.

The abolition of slavery, of course, did not alter the prevailing racial biases of the region. In the decades before secession, slaveholders had responded to abolitionist complaints not by arguing that slavery was an unfortunate necessity but rather by insisting that it constituted a moral good. Citing "scientific" studies that concluded that blacks were inferior to whites, the *Montgomery (Alabama) Daily Mail*, for instance, claimed that "it was only necessary to treat the subject of African slavery in a scientific and temperate manner in order to uproot the errors that prevail upon the subject in the North" (Jordan 1957, 97). *DeBow's Review*, a popular southern journal, maintained that slavery had "elevated" African Americans "from the depths of barbarism and brutalism to a degree of civilization and usefulness, and happiness" (1855, 455). These deep-rooted prejudices remained a central part of the thinking of southern whites, and in so doing, facilitated their rationalizing of an economic system that proved grossly exploitative of the freedmen and their children.

To the prevailing social mores of the region and its economic devastation can be added the fact that Reconstruction ushered in a period in which African Americans had substantive, albeit short-lived, political power. Refusing to work in anything approximating or recalling slavery, such as working in a gang under an overseer, African Americans played a role in shaping the system of tenant farming that emerged. Most African Americans, of course, had little in the way of capital and so could not afford to buy land—a prospect many whites sought to limit in any event by refusing to sell land to blacks. African Americans could insist, however, on living in family units and tilling the soil in a way that was considerably more autonomous than what they had known under slavery.

Some locales flirted with a system of wage labor, but in general, it was quickly abandoned for a number of reasons. To begin with, white landlords tended to be cash poor. Additionally, they recognized their need for a reliable labor force at certain times of the year, most especially at harvest, when, for example, a single heavy rain could ruin all of the cotton already on the boll. Planters simply could not risk having to scramble for labor if their hands quit at inopportune times. Likewise, the former slaves had no desire to rely on seasonal wages that could leave them unemployed for long stretches or, worse, take them away from their families by forcing them into migrant labor. When the experimenting in the years immediately following the Civil War had come to a close, the result was a compromise of sorts: a system of tenant farming best remembered for its well-documented system of sharecropping and crop liens.

In return for the use of the land and, often, seed, mules or horses, and farm equipment, a sharecropper agreed to give a certain percentage of the crop—usually between 25 and 50 percent, depending on how much in the way of seed, fertilizer, and farm equipment had been advanced—to the landowner from which he rented the land. In some ways, it seemed like a fair agreement. Living with his family in a cabin on a plot of perhaps twenty or forty acres (twenty being the most a cotton farmer with a one-horse equipment could reasonably expect to till), the sharecropper had a good bit of autonomy, the more so as white landlords increasingly moved to towns and cities, becoming absentee landlords over the course of the late 19th century. There was, however, a significant catch.

Tenants of all kinds, and sharecroppers in particular, tended to lack the requisite capital to provide essential supplies like food and clothing for their families before the harvest. As the two biggest staple crops of the plantation regions, cotton and tobacco, were not edible, tenants were compelled to be advanced such supplies by merchants (though in some regions the distinctions between landlords and merchants was fairly murky) in exchange for a lien on their crop at harvest. (A lien is simply a legal term meaning the right to take or hold the property of a debtor to guarantee payment.) The merchants frequently charged exorbitant interest rates—60 percent in some cases. Along with the landlords, they had priority over tenants in collecting money earned from the sale of the tenants' crop. The result of such an arrangement was a system in which the interest from debts accrued in bad years more than negated the profits tenants might earn in good years.

By the mid-1870s, most African Americans in the South's plantation regions found themselves economically dependent on whites for many of the essentials of day-to-day life, and more or less perpetually in debt. Black tenants could do little about the situation. There were few jobs for them outside the region, and the legal racial hardening that culminated in the Jim Crow legislation that appeared around the turn of the century was reflected throughout the nation. Violent, or even vocal, resistance carried with it the threat of white violence, and, because credit markets were profoundly local, African Americans who refused to treat whites deferentially or who insisted on becoming economically independent could have difficulty securing the very advances they needed to feed their families. Indeed, when black farmers did have good years—the kind of years that could free them from this endless cycle of dependence and debt—they still could fall prey to the whims of their white creditors, whose records by and large were the only ones local judicial authorities recognized. White creditors could, then, cook the books so to speak if they were willing (and they often were) to turn to corruption to keep a black tenant from climbing the agricultural ladder from tenant to independent yeoman.

For most of the late 19th century, then, the African American tenant farmers of the South found themselves in a peculiar position. In many regards, they could operate independently. In the plantation regions, for instance, they often lived in small, all-black farming communities (made up often times of the tenants on a given plantation) and so had little interaction with their white landlords. This physical separation provided a measure of security as it reduced the occasions on which an inadvertent violation of racial etiquette might touch off racial violence. One tenant from a community known as New Rising Star in Alabama's Macon County hinted at this when he explained to sociologist Charles S. Johnson, "You won't find a white family between here and Red Gap—that's up the road six or seven miles—so we don't have no trouble" (1941, 17).

Even those African American tenants whose daily experience brought them into contact with whites, however, could live with their families and benefit from their labor. They had the freedom to change creditors, and so they were not bound to a single landlord or plantation, even if the local nature of the credit market tended to prevent their moving too far. Tenants were free to fish, hunt, and gather firewood on the property they worked, and as of the late 19th century African Americans were still free to vote.

The appearance of autonomy, however, was misleading. Tenants were obliged to plant what their creditors wanted, and neither the landlords nor merchants had any interest in allowing tenants to plant anything other than staple crops like cotton and (to a lesser degree) corn, which could be used as forage for draft animals. Only staple crops brought the landlord a significant return on his investment, and the merchants had little reason to encourage the planting of vegetables as doing so would reduce the amount of food the tenants needed to be advanced. Even their behavior was circumscribed to the extent that if they wanted to be advanced funds for food and clothing they had to acknowledge white authority.

Among the results of such a system was the rise of King Cotton. Southern fields turned white with the bolls of cotton to an extent they never had in the antebellum years. Before the Civil War, cotton had been the most planted crop in the states of the Deep South, but there had been substantially more acres in other crops combined than in cotton. By the 1880s, however, two-thirds of the cultivated land in places like Alabama's Black Belt was sowed with cotton. The triumph of a cotton monoculture proved devastating both to the land and the people who worked it.

When Booker T. Washington moved to Alabama's Black Belt to take up his duties as the first principal of Tuskegee Institute, he was struck by the conditions black tenants faced in what he termed the "plantation districts." Whole families were sleeping in one-room cabins without windows and eating almost nothing but "fat pork and cornbread"—a diet conducive to diseases like pellagra—he reported in *Up from Slavery* (2003). These families "would as a general thing, proceed to the cotton field" after breakfast. "Their one object seemed to be to plant nothing but cotton," he wrote of the African American farmers he came across, who with "few exceptions" were tenants with their cotton crop "mortgaged." As a consequence, he

African Americans pick cotton, ca. 1899. (Library of Congress)

added, "in many cases cotton was planted up to the very door of the cabin" (Washington 2003, 92–94).

The conditions Washington encountered around Tuskegee differed but little from those in other areas of the Cotton Belt. Black tenants had every incentive to plant as much cotton as they could (after all, the profits from the crop were necessary if they hoped to escape the crippling dependency of tenancy) and, essentially, no incentive to care for soil they did not own and from which they could be removed (or at least forced to pay higher rents for) at the whim of a landlord. While cotton is not an especially demanding crop in terms of the nutrients it draws from the soil, the repeated plowing of cotton fields year after year opened the soil to erosion. As King Cotton tightened his grip, the deleterious effects of its reign became increasingly visible in the land itself.

By the early 1880s, southerners were lamenting the diminished fertility of the Cotton Belt's soils. One state report in Alabama, for instance, noted with considerable insight that this was due to "the bad system prevailing in [the plantation] sections . . . viz., large farms rented out in patches to laborers who are too poor and too much in debt to . . . have any interest in keeping up the fertility of the soil" (Smith 1884, 64). Most assessments, however, were less charitable toward the black tenants of the region. In 1886, for example, Alabama's first commissioner of agriculture accounted for the sorry condition of the Black Belt's soils by laying the blame at the feet of black tenants, whom he claimed were "wholly unqualified" for "the position of independent tenants" and consequently, "almost invariably fail" (Betts 1886, 18–19). Continuing, he asserted that the problems of the Black Belt could be accounted for in large measure by the fact that whites in the state's principal plantation region tended to "congregate in towns . . . leaving the lands for the most part to the exclusive possession of the negroes." In doing so, whites were "relieving" African Americans "from the moral restraint of the presence of the superior race, as well as from their industrial supervision and control" (Betts, 1886, 8). The implication was clear: in the absence of white oversight, the denuded soil of the Black Belt was the best that could be expected of a predominantly black labor force.

In fact, the agricultural problems of the South were not only blamed on the region's black farmers but also reinforced racial stereotypes. In *The Souls of Black Folk* (1997), W. E. B. Du Bois explained how the logic of racial animosity became circular and self-perpetuating. African American tenants "are careless," Du Bois noted, "because they have not found that it pays to be careful; they are improvident because the improvident ones of their acquaintance get on about as well as the provident" (1997, 128). But most of all, Du Bois added, "they cannot see why they should take unusual pains to make the white man's land better" (1997, 128). Du Bois concluded, "On the other hand, the white land-owner . . . shows his Northern visitor the scarred and wretched land; the ruined mansions, the worn-out soil and mortgaged acres, and says, This is Negro freedom!" (1997, 128).

One obvious solution to the declining soil fertility was the application of commercial chemical fertilizers, which began to proliferate in the 1860s. It was a solution that southerners embraced wholeheartedly; indeed, some states established departments of agriculture to both regulate these commercial fertilizers and to promote their extension and use. Colloquially referred to as "guano"—though little Peruvian guano (a particular kind of bird excrement) was actually imported after the Civil War—commercial fertilizers were adopted as a kind of cure-all for the South's agricultural woes.

White landlords and merchants, however, were reluctant to advance much in the way of commercial fertilizer to their black tenants. In part, they suspected that black tenants were incapable of properly applying the fertilizer, but more significant were their economic calculations. Not only were chemical fertilizers expensive, but their application held out two distinctly unappealing possibilities from the landlords' perspective. On the one hand, commercial fertilizers did not guarantee banner yields. Misapplication, drought, or insect pestilence, for example, could ruin the crop anyway, leaving the tenant in too deep a hole for the landlord to expect to recover his investment. On the other hand, properly applied in a good year (seasonally and for the market) the fertilizers could produce a banner crop, enabling the tenant to escape from under his creditors' thumbs. Consequently, as one state geological survey reported in 1883, "It may be said, in general terms, that in the great cotton-producing areas," where African American tenant farmers predominated, "the use of commercial fertilizers . . . is comparatively unknown" (Smith 1883, 112–114).

African American tenant farmers, then, faced some serious obstacles. Indeed, it might be argued that the entire social, political, and economic structures of the South were arranged to ensure that the region's black population would remain a cheap, pliable, and dependable source for agricultural labor. While the economic dependency of tenant farming shaped the lives of most African Americans in the region to a considerable degree, it did not define their entire existence. In fact, in many regards, their lives were little different from those of southern white farmers.

Like their white counterparts, and for that matter husbandmen throughout the nation, the life of black tenants was profoundly seasonal. The particular timing of planting and harvest, of course, depended on the climate and the crop. (A given crop might be planted later in the northern part of a state than in its southern reaches, for example, and different crops were planted and harvested at different times as the growing season for plants—say cotton and sugar—varies.) In a typical year in the Black Belt of Alabama and Mississippi, for instance, the year might begin with tenants settling into new cabins, and by February, the first of the previous year's stubble would be burned to clear the fields of weeds. In early March, the first crop, generally corn, might be put in the ground, and it was followed later that month by cotton, the principle crop of the region.

As the cotton germinated in April, there would be time to put a small number of other crops in—forage crops, sweet potatoes, and sugar cane to name some of the more prominent—before the time came to "chop" the cotton, which is to say thin out the number of cotton plants in the fields by hoeing under the least vital to leave the best plants with better access to water, sunlight, and nutrients. May and June were busy months spent primarily chopping cotton and fighting weeds to prevent them from choking out the cotton before it could be laid by. These efforts reached an almost feverish pace in mid to late June. "Cotton weather," wrote the African American novelist George Wylie Henderson in his novel *Ollie Miss* of the month of June. "Short hot nights and long hot days. Field hands had to work cotton fast" (Henderson 1973, 109–110).

With the arrival of what Henderson called "the sweet scent of the cotton blossoms" in July, however, the cotton crop was laid by, or left alone to allow the cotton bolls to mature. "Plowing and hoeing ceased . . . and field hands took their ease," continued Henderson. "Watermelons were ripe; late July days were long and lazy" (Henderson 1973, 110). By the middle of August, however, the pace of farm life quickened again as the cotton began to ripen. A single rain could lower the quality of the cotton and consequently the price a tenant would get for it, so picking it quickly was of paramount importance.

When a sufficient amount of cotton had been gathered, it would be taken to a local ginnery, which would extract the seeds (which could be sold for cotton seed oil) and bale the cotton. As this was done, the cotton would be graded based on its color, any impurities (such as cotton stalks) that might have been mixed in, and a number of other factors, and based on the price of that grade cotton in the world's cotton market, its value would be determined and a tenant's debts would be settled. Of course, intangibles—like race—could factor into the grade assigned a particular bale, and cotton brought by African Americans often received lower grades than the same caliber cotton brought by white farmers.

Whatever the price the cotton brought, its picking could stretch into December, and in many cases, the winter meant a move to another plantation with the faint hope that things might be better. By the time a tenant had settled in to his new situation, it was time to begin clearing the fields again, and seasonal rituals began once more. In such a way did the tenant farmers of the Black Belt seek to wring a living from the land.

Although most of their time was taken up with field work, black tenants were not automatons who miserably plodded their way through an endless succession of plowings, plantings, tendings, and harvestings. Their social lives were as varied as they were, but some sweeping generalizations can be made. Keeping in lockstep with the social norms of the late 19th and early 20th centuries, African American farming communities tended to be socially conservative. Pastors, for instance, wielded a disproportionate influence in these communities, and many attempted to impose bans on even seemingly innocuous activities like card playing and baseball. "Frolics," or dances that attracted young people and were often fueled by alcohol, drew particular condemnation, but such activities were commonplace nonetheless.

Henderson's *Ollie Miss* captured not only the seasonal rhythms of tenants' lives, but also its weekly flow: "From sun to sun, from Monday morning to Saturday noon!" Henderson wrote, the black farmers and their families worked. But "Saturday afternoons they went to ball games and picnics. Saturday nights they went to frolics. And on Sundays there was church. They could not sweat and sin the week long for nothing"

African American men, women, and children outside of church in Georgia, ca. 1899. From *Negro Life in Georgia, U.S.A.*, compiled and prepared by W. E. B. Du Bois. (Library of Congress)

(Henderson 1973, 109). To these activities might be added innumerable others: sewing, fishing, hunting, and, in literate families, reading to name but a few.

Many of these activities were not merely recreational. Clothes needed to be mended; fishing and hunting provided food for the table; and reading presented the possibility of anticipating market fluctuations and learning new ways to improve the farm economy. Indeed, for those few African American farmers who did manage to escape the seemingly endless cycle of dependence and debt—and in the counties of the plantation regions at the turn of the century the percentage of black landowners was usually less than 10 percent of the black population—such activities were veritable necessities if they hoped to avoid being drawn back into the quagmire of tenancy.

As Steven Hahn observed in his Pulitzer-prize-winning *A Nation under Our Feet*, black landownership in the South "almost always . . . demanded a protracted and precarious effort on the part of black households, and, often, extended black families" (Hahn 2003, 458). Sara Brooks, the daughter of black yeomen, recalled that her father worked for a timber company during the winter and weaved baskets from strips of white oak that he sold when he went to town. Her mother contributed to the family income by raising chickens and selling eggs. In fact, the entire family worked to make the farm as self-sufficient as possible. Her father supplemented their meat supply by hunting (primarily for opossums, which could be killed without the expense of guns or bullets), and Sara and her siblings hired on as day laborers at nearby plantations. Despite the hard life of a black homeowner, however, it offered considerably more autonomy than that of a tenant and the hope of a better life.

Economic independence mitigated many of the worst vicissitudes facing black farmers in the region, and its benefits led to a concerted effort on the part of black leaders to encourage tenants to make any sacrifice necessary to escape from tenancy. Booker T. Washington, for example, organized the Tuskegee Negro Farmers' Conference in 1892. Its success made it an annual event and other African American schools followed Tuskegee's lead in hosting such conferences. Local black leaders often organized "country meetings," which offered advice on better farming methods and ways in which tenants might move up the agricultural ladder. Community fairs provided an opportunity for black women to show off their domestic skills like cooking and needlework, men to display their prize crops, and speakers to expound on the necessity of escaping tenancy—all in an environment that afforded black families a form of inexpensive entertainment.

These efforts, however, often left much to be desired. The inaugural Tuskegee Negro Farmers' Conference, for instance, adopted a series of resolutions at its close, which were a mixed bag. One recommended that the South abandon its reliance on tenant labor, wishful thinking if ever there was. Another astutely encouraged tenants to raise as large a vegetable garden as their landlords would allow. Many, however, might well have been crafted by white southerners and included bringing an end to drinking, gambling, "and disgracing ourselves in many ways" and making sure that black women

The Tuskegee Negro Farmers' Conference

A number of late-19th-century organizations engaged in a variety of efforts to improve the lives of African American farmers, who increasingly found themselves trapped in a cycle of perpetual debt as tenants. The majority of these efforts proved half-hearted and ultimately abortive, as the issue of white supremacy prevented the Grange, the Farmers' Alliance, and the Agricultural Wheel from integrating black farmers as equals and genuinely taking up their concerns. Even the Morrill Act of 1890, which established black agricultural colleges, offered little respite. Federal funding for the schools was distributed by individual states, which diverted most of the money to the white land-grant institutions, leaving the black schools seriously underfunded.

Concerned that his school was not proving as helpful as it otherwise might, Booker T. Washington asked a number of "common, hardworking farmers" to come to Tuskegee in early 1892 so that he could learn more about their problems and hear their proposals about how Tuskegee might tweak its education programs to address the most pressing concerns facing them. To his surprise, more than 400 men and women showed up at Tuskegee on February 23 to participate in the inaugural Tuskegee Negro Farmers' Conference.

The conference's success encouraged Washington to make it an annual affair, and by 1898 attendance at the event had grown to more than 2,000. Other African American schools followed Tuskegee's lead in hosting similar events, and local black leaders loosely affiliated with the conference often organized "country meetings," which offered advice on better farming methods and ways in which

tenants might escape the quagmire of tenancy. By 1899, more than 150 local conferences were held throughout the South.

Although the conferences successfully identified many of the problems facing black farmers, they proved less astute at offering viable solutions to them. The first Tuskegee Negro Farmers' Conference, for instance, adopted a resolution that encouraged the South to abandon its reliance on tenant labor and tenants to raise a large vegetable garden. Unfortunately, white landlords had no interest in abandoning the tenant system and often forbid their tenants from having substantial gardens. Many of the resolutions adopted by subsequent farmers' conferences concluded with an expression of thanks to the white community for their support of black farmers. In part, such expressions were pragmatic sacrifices that needed to be made if southern whites were to continue to allow the meetings to take place at all, but there is no denying that these whites essentially asked African American tenants to shoulder the blame for their poverty, miserable living conditions, and the denuded condition of the land.

Even so, these efforts did make a difference in the lives of individual African American farmers and played a role in the increased landownership of black farmers in the early 20th century. Because it attracted thousands of visitors, the Tuskegee Negro Farmers' Conference drew national attention to the plight of black farmers, and, in fact, it helped lay the foundation for some of the organizations that played an important role in the civil rights movement of the mid-20th century.

behaved demurely (speaking "in a quiet tone of voice" in public and never wearing "their hair wrapped in strings") (Campbell 1936, 84–86).

Indeed, many of the resolutions adopted by subsequent farmers' conferences concluded with an expression of thanks to the white community for their support of the aims of black farmers. In part, of course, such expressions were pragmatic sacrifices that needed to be made if southern whites (and northern philanthropists whose funding was necessary to schools like Tuskegee Institute) were to continue to allow the meetings to take place at all. There is no denying, however, that such resolutions essentially asked African American tenants to shoulder the blame for their poverty, miserable living conditions, and the denuded land.

Even so and despite their obvious shortcomings, these efforts did make a difference in the lives of African American farmers. The Tuskegee Negro Farmers' Conference, for example, eventually attracted thousands of visitors each year, not only drawing national attention to the plight of black farmers but also laying the foundation for some of the organizations that played an important role in the civil rights movement of the mid-20th century. Perhaps the most useful example of the ways in which the efforts to improve the lives of impoverished black farmers bore real fruit can be found in the campaign of George Washington Carver, who took a position at Tuskegee in 1896.

Carver had grown up in the Midwest, homesteading in western Kansas before heading to Iowa where he became the first African American to earn an advanced degree in agricultural science. Recruited by Washington to Tuskegee, Carver was unprepared for what he encountered there. He was convinced, however, that God had chosen him to help lead his fellow African Americans out of the bondage of debt peonage.

Much of the scientific agriculture he brought with him—such as the use of up-to-date farm implements and the application of the best commercial fertilizers—made little sense in Alabama's Black Belt, where black families were simply too poor and too much in debt to seriously consider purchasing them. Consequently, Carver tweaked the principles of agricultural science to make them accessible: encouraging black farmers to collect and compost swamp muck and other organic debris to apply as a fertilizer; pointing out the richness of foodstuffs readily available for free in what many tenants overlooked as weeds—things like wild plums and dandelions; pleading with them to limit erosion by plowing crossways to hills and terracing wherever possible; providing specific details for the proper plowing and cultivation of various crops; proffering advice on inexpensive methods of food preservation; and attempting to induce tenants to diversify their crop production as much as was possible given their peculiar circumstances.

In the end, Carver's efforts failed to lift most black tenants from the depths of poverty in which they lived, but it would be wrong to dismiss them entirely. In the county in which Tuskegee was situated, for example, only 157 African American farmers out of roughly 19,000 black residents were working their own land at the turn of the century. By 1910, 507 black farmers in the county could claim to own the land they farmed. Thus, between the end of the Civil War and 1900, a total of 157 African Americans had found a way to become yeomen. In the single decade following 1900, that number more than tripled. And while the 1910 figure amounted to only 13 percent of black farm families, it was significantly

George Washington Carver (1864–1943)

Born a slave in the border state of Missouri toward the close of the Civil War, George Washington Carver never knew his biological parents. Adopted by his former owners, Carver was raised in a loving environment. Unfortunately, the education opportunities for African Americans were decidedly limited in Missouri, and so Carver headed to neighboring Kansas in search of an education. He remained in the Sunflower State for more than a decade, even homesteading on its western plains.

In the late 1880s, Carver moved to Iowa, where through a series of fortuitous relationships he became the first African American to enroll in the Iowa Agricultural College. There he studied under two future U.S. secretaries of agriculture and some of the most prominent agriculturists of the late 19th century. Among other things, his education introduced him to the nascent science of ecology.

Shortly before he became the first African American to earn an advanced degree in scientific agriculture, Booker T. Washington invited him to take charge of the new agricultural school at Tuskegee Institute. Carver, who had put his ambitions as an artist on hold to pursue an agricultural education, accepted the invitation, convinced that God had set him apart to be of service to black farmers.

At Tuskegee, Carver launched a campaign aimed at enabling black farmers to escape the crippling dependency of tenancy. Adapting the principles of scientific agriculture he had been taught in Iowa in such a way as to make them practicable for impoverished tenant farmers,

Carver attempted to persuade farmers that by abhorring waste and thinking ecologically (recognizing, in his words, the "mutual relationship of the animal, mineral and vegetable kingdoms"), farmers could satisfy many of their needs and wants with things they encountered everyday but either overlooked or neglected (Carver 1899). Indeed, while his campaign ultimately failed, a number of its facets anticipated the rise of ecological agriculture and the push for the application of "appropriate technology."

As part of his campaign, Carver conducted research on numerous southern crops, hoping to find one whose marketability would provide a viable alternative cash crop to cotton. His work with one of these—peanuts—thrust him into a position of national prominence and, in time, transformed him into an icon: the Peanut Man. Following his rise to fame in the 1920s, Carver's emphasis shifted from the plight of tenant farmers to the economy of the entire region. His efforts to find alternative uses for southern crops like sweet potatoes, peanuts, and soybeans made him a pioneer in the "chemurgy" movement, which sought to find industrial applications for agricultural products.

Although he is often credited with more innovations than he rightly merits, Carver's real significance lies in his environmental vision. Possessed of a deep religious appreciation for the natural world, Carver proved to be among the most farsighted reformers of the early conservation movement and a genuine innovator in natural resource use.

more than the 5 percent of farm families that had tilled their own land in 1900.

Unfortunately, World War I brought a close to Carver's campaign. With substantial job prospects available to African Americans outside the South for the first time, many black southerners fled to the cities of the North and West. For Carver's part, his reputation got a boost by calls for wartime conservation, and much of what he had preached to impoverished tenants as a matter of practical course suddenly became relevant for the entire nation. By the early 1920s, Carver had become a cultural icon—the Peanut Man—and he shifted his focus to the commercialization of his products for more than a decade before returning to his concern for impoverished tenants during the Great Depression.

Ultimately, the tenant system that emerged in the years following the Civil War remained in place through World War II, and for its duration, black tenant farmers carried on in much the same way. Indeed, the lives of black tenants in the late 1920s differed but little from those of the 1880s. Though the prospect of financial independence was comparatively bleak for most black farmers in the South, they continued to hope for better things, contribute to their communities, and follow the seasonal rhythms of their vocation, "their plows singing beneath the sandy loam" (Henderson 1973, 109).

References and Further Reading

Ayers, Edward L. *The Promise of the New South: Life after Reconstruction.* New York: Oxford University Press, 1992.

Betts, E. C. *Report of the First Commissioner of Agriculture of the State of Alabama.* Montgomery: Alabama Department of Agriculture, 1886.

Brown, James Seay. *Up Before Daylight: Life Histories from the Alabama Writers' Project, 1938–1939.* Tuscaloosa: University of Alabama Press, 1982.

Campbell, Thomas M. *The Moveable School Goes to the Negro Farmer.* Tuskegee, AL: Tuskegee Institute Press, 1936.

Carver, George Washington. "A Few Hints to Southern Farmers." *The Southern Workman and Hampton School Record* (September 1899).

Daniel, Pete. *Breaking the Land: The Transformation of Cotton, Tobacco, and Rice Cultures since 1880.* Chicago: University of Illinois Press, 1985.

Du Bois, W. E. B. *The Souls of Black Folk,* ed. with an introduction by David W. Blight and Robert Gooding-Williams. 1903; rpt., New York: Bedford Books, 1997.

Fite, Gilbert C. *Cotton Fields No More: Southern Agriculture, 1865–1980.* Lexington: University Press of Kentucky, 1984.

Glave, Dianne D. "'A Garden So Brilliant with Colors, So Original in Its Design': Rural African American Women, Gardening, Progressive Reform, and the Foundation of an African American Environmental Perspective." *Environmental History* 8 (July 2003): 395–411.

Grim, Valerie. "African American Landlords in the Rural South, 1870–1950: A Profile." *Agricultural History* 72 (Spring 1998): 399–416.

Hahn, Steven. *A Nation under Our Feet: Black Political Struggles in the Rural South from Slavery to the Great Migration.* Cambridge, MA: Harvard University Press, 2003.

Henderson, George Wylie. *Ollie Miss*. 1935; rpt., Chatham, NJ: The Chatham Bookseller, 1973.

Hersey, Mark D. "Hints and Suggestions to Farmers: George Washington Carver and Rural Conservation in the South." *Environmental History* 11 (April 2006): 239–268.

Johnson, Charles S. *Shadow of the Plantation*, with a new introduction by Joseph S. Himes. New Brunswick, CT: Transaction Publishers, 1996.

Jones, Allen W. "Improving Rural Life for Blacks: The Tuskegee Negro Farmers' Conference, 1892–1915." *Agricultural History* 65 (Spring 1991): 105–114.

Painter, Nell Irvin. *Exodusters: Black Migration to Kansas after Reconstruction—the First Major Migration to the North of Ex-Slaves*, with a new introduction by the author. 1977; rpt., New York: W. W. Norton, 1992.

Rosengarten, Theodore. *All God's Dangers: The Life of Nate Shaw*. Chicago: University of Chicago Press, 1974.

Simonsen, Thurdis, ed. *You May Plow Here: The Narrative of Sara Brooks*. New York: W. W. Norton, 1986.

Smith, Eugene Allen. *Geological Survey of Alabama: Report for the Years 1881 and 1882, Embracing an Account of the Agricultural Features of the State*. Montgomery, AL: W. D. Brown and Co., 1883.

Smith, Eugene Allen. *Report on the Cotton Production of the State of Alabama*. Washington, DC: U.S. Government Printing Office, 1884.

Washington, Booker T. *Up from Slavery by Booker T. Washington, with Related Documents*, ed. with an introduction by W. Fitzhugh Brundage. 1901; rpt., New York: Bedford/St. Martin's, 2003.

Wright, Gavin. *The Political Economy of the Cotton South: Household, Markets, and Wealth in the Nineteenth Century*. New York: W. W. Norton, 1978.

African Americans in the Nineteenth-Century West

10

James N. Leiker

The year was 1879. The failures of Reconstruction, in which African Americans hoped for relief from generations of binding oppression and slavery, had become evident, its hopes crushed in the federal government's withdrawal of Union troops from the former Confederacy two years before. As the northern public lost interest in the cause of black rights—a cause for which so many of its people had sacrificed—leaders of the once-defeated South asserted again the primacy of local rule, and with it, a system of legal and social subordination over millions of former slaves. In that year, more than 26,000 Exodusters, named from the biblical story of another people who fled bondage for a "promised land," headed to Kansas, searching for freedom and opportunities in the beckoning American West.

The great Frederick Douglass had dedicated his life to such principles, but he nonetheless described the "Kansas Fever" as unfortunate and ill-timed. For Douglass, the migration sent a pessimistic message that racial equality in the South was unfeasible, and that westward expansion would only produce restlessness and unsettlement: "The habit of roaming from place to place in pursuit of better conditions of existence is by no means a good one" (Douglass 1953, 335–338). Obviously, many African Americans disagreed. Three decades later, a young man named Oscar Micheaux bid farewell to Armour Avenue in Chicago, the destination of thousands of blacks during the Great Urban Migration of the early 20th century. With $2,340 in savings and Horace Greeley's words of "Go west, young man, and grow up with the country" ringing in his ears, Micheaux did indeed roam from place to place as a railroad porter before finally homesteading on a farm in South Dakota. He wrote, "So westward I journeyed the land of raw material, which my dreams had pictured to me as the land of real beginning, and where I was soon to learn more than a mere observer ever could by living in the realm of a great city" (Micheaux 1994, 47).

A portrait of the Shores family by homestead photographer Solomon Butcher, 1887. (Nebraska State Historical Society/RG2608/copy and reuse restrictions apply)

Micheaux's words describe a thoroughly American experience. In the century that preceded him, the United States expanded from its eastern origins to encompass the Great Plains, the Rocky Mountains, the Southwest, and the far Pacific coast, transforming a collection of Atlantic colonies into a continental power. That Micheaux represents an *African American* experience is less known. Western stereotypes perpetuated by popular culture—Stetson-wearing cowboys, blue-jacketed mounted soldiers, headdress-wearing Indians hunting bison—not only obscure the West's true diversity but also leave little room for a black presence (unless that presence is used as a parody, as in the case of the black sheriff in the movie *Blazing Saddles*). Although always a minority and at times even regarded as oddities, African Americans—long before the Exodusters, long before Micheaux—moved west in the 19th century, sometimes working in stereotypical "western" jobs such as ranching and soldiering, but more often engaged in mundane but important tasks such as building schools, establishing towns, and creating black communities that would champion the civil rights causes of the 20th century.

Blacks in the Early West

Indeed, the opening of the region, beginning with the United States' purchase of Louisiana in 1803, owes a partial debt to black history. Stretching from the Mississippi River to the Rockies, Louisiana became a holding of France in 1800, then under control of the military expansionist Napoleon

Bonaparte. Napoleon apparently had wanted Louisiana, along with France's Caribbean colony St. Domingue, to serve as the bases for a New World empire that he hoped to establish once his European conquests were complete. However, Napoleon's ambition outpaced his army's ability to subdue the locals. Since 1791, blacks on St. Domingue had fought a revolution against slavery and white rule. Led by Toussaint L'Ouverture, they renamed the island Haiti and successfully held off 25,000 French troops. Startled by his army's losses both to rebel forces and to tropical bouts with yellow fever, Napoleon decided to divest himself of his American properties. When President Thomas Jefferson's emissaries approached France seeking protection for U.S. traders on the Mississippi, its government responded with a surprising offer to sell the whole of Louisiana.

Establishing claim to the Louisiana Purchase and exploring its economic potential became the task of the U.S. Corps of Discovery—better known as the Lewis and Clark expedition—from 1804 to 1806. Mapping the northwestern rivers and trails, the expedition benefited from the presence of York, William Clark's black slave. Meriwether Lewis' journals document York's skills as a hunter, explorer, and barterer with Native Americans, who were fascinated by his dark skin. During his winter stay with the Mandan Indians in present-day North Dakota, York apparently allowed tribesmen to wet their fingers and try to rub off his color. Others like the Nez Perce, who painted themselves with charcoal in battle, regarded York as the bravest of his party because of his black skin, and turned to him as an interpreter. His ability to win the tribes' friendship was a useful asset, and by one account, Clark freed York when the expedition returned to St. Louis, after which he married and operated a dray service in Kentucky and Tennessee until his death.

Other black men crossed this same cultural frontier during the fur trade. Edward Rose, the son of a white trader and a black Cherokee woman, joined the Manuel Lisa expedition in 1806. During his first winter in the Bighorn River region, Rose lived and traded with the Crow (Absaroka) Indians, distinguishing himself as a warrior and diplomat. The Absarokas, and later the Arikaras in South Dakota, adopted Rose as a tribal member, and though he periodically worked for white traders, his loyalties remained primarily with Native Americans. In 1811, he brokered a deal between the Absarokas and the Astor Fur Company. As late as 1832, Rose continued to live with the Absaroka tribe, enjoying considerable status and following their polygynous custom of taking multiple wives.

Men like York and Edward Rose, who found acceptance among Indians, were exceptional examples. Most black westerners settled in established cities where they lived parallel with—and often segregated from—whites. Especially following the population boom of its gold rush and admission as a free state in 1850, California attracted African Americans into an array of service jobs, such as bootblacks, maids, and waiters. Some such as Mary Ellen Pleasant became prosperous entrepreneurs. Pleasant arrived in San Francisco as a cook in 1852 and soon owned three laundry businesses and had investments in various mining and real estate operations. With a population that reached more than 1,100 by 1860, black San Francisco soon

James P. Beckwourth (1798–1866)

Born in Virginia in 1798 to a slave woman and a white father, Jim Beckwourth moved with his master to Missouri at the age of twelve. After obtaining his freedom, he was apprenticed to a blacksmith in St. Louis and worked for a time as a hunter and lead miner before joining the Ashley fur-trapping expedition in 1824. For the next forty years, Beckwourth spent the better part of his life in the northern Rocky Mountains, hunting and trading beaver pelts and bison robes, and living with the Crow (Absaroka) Indians of Wyoming and Montana.

Fur traders often served as cultural mediators between the white and Native American worlds, conducting business, translating, negotiating treaties, and even intermarrying with Indians and raising families. Beckwourth was no exception, by his own account having at least five wives and siring at least two children among them. His familiarity with Native cultures and knowledge of mountain geography proved useful for U.S. expansion. In 1849, while journeying to California as a prospective gold-seeker, he lent his name to a trail through the Sierra Nevada Mountains that still carries the title "Beckwourth Pass."

Little would now be known about Beckwourth if not for his 1856 autobiography, *The Life and Adventures of James P. Beckwourth, Mountaineer, Scout, Pioneer, and Chief of the Crow Nation of Indians*. Published by Thomas D. Bonner, the book appeared at a time when the fur trade had become nearly extinct. Beckwourth, then nearing sixty, had built a lodge and trading post in the northern Sierra Nevadas, hoping to capitalize from the steady wagon traffic entering California in the wake of the gold rush. There he met Bonner and recited his adventures to him during the winter of 1854 and 1855. About Bonner, little is known except that he was a longtime agent of the New England Temperance Society, as well as a journalist who may have written under different pseudonyms. Bonner and Beckwourth seemingly hoped to profit from readers' fascination with mythic western figures like Kit Carson and Davy Crockett, and indeed, *Life and Adventures* shared much in common with dime novels and other sensationalist genres.

boasted numerous black-owned barbershops, bathhouses, clothing stores, and two joint stock companies. The rise of this thriving middle class led to a rich intellectual and political life. In 1849, three dozen San Franciscans formed the West's first black self-help organization, the Mutual Benefit and Relief Society, to assist recent black immigrants to California. Four years later, the Atheneum Institute was founded by former New Englanders to raise money for a library and to launch the West's first black newspaper, *Mirror of the Times*, in 1856. Hosting debates and lectures over abolitionist activity, the Atheneum Institute represented one of the first antislavery organizations west of St. Louis. Los Angeles and Sacramento also sported successful black communities that occasionally enjoyed friendly business and cultural relations with Latinos, Chinese, and even whites.

Blacks were a consistent if uncommon presence in the Spanish Southwest as well, dating back to the arrival of a Moroccan slave, Esteban, with the ill-fated Narvaez expedition of 1528. Stranded with a group of Spanish explorers that included Alvar Nunez Cabeza de Vaca, Esteban and his fellow

More than 500 pages in length, his memoir recounts how he became "chief" of the Crow nation; killed hundreds of bear, bison, and Indians; helped defeat the Seminoles in Florida; helped liberate California from Mexico; and had numerous love affairs with Spanish and Indian "princesses," one of them his wife's sister.

Despite obvious embellishment, not to mention vivid descriptions of violence, a close reading of *Life and Adventures* reveals a fondness and appreciation for Native Americans that was rare in frontier literature of the time. Beckwourth rebuked the alcohol trade as injurious to whites and Native Americans alike, and he particularly condemned the rapacity of colonizing settlers who occupied western lands with no respect for Native American sovereignty. Beckwourth ignored mention of his African American ancestry; with the exception of a scant reference to his slave mother in the opening chapter, he described himself as a white man representing white civilization. Though this may surprise contemporary readers, "blackness" may not have accounted for an important part of his

identity, not in the Far West where cultural divides of "white-Native" assumed more importance than racial ones of "white-black."

Whatever he and Bonner's intent, the book did little to elevate Beckwourth's economic fortunes. By 1859, Beckwourth's trading post had failed, and so he moved to a small farm south of Denver, Colorado, making his living as a farmer and fisherman. His skills as a tracker and his knowledge of Native cultures still earned him occasional employment. In 1864, he served as a reluctant scout on the infamous Chivington expedition in which a unit of the Colorado militia massacred a peaceful encampment of Arapahos and Southern Cheyennes at Sand Creek. No evidence suggests that Beckwourth participated in the attack directly. He died in Colorado a few years later. He is remembered mostly for his entertaining if highly exaggerated autobiography, which established his place in the pantheon of 19th-century frontier characters. The Texas folklorist J. Frank Dobie probably intended a compliment when he praised Beckwourth as "the champion of all western liars."

wanderers survived for eight years by posing as medicine men in their travels from Florida to Texas. Esteban apparently did for Cabeza de Vaca what York later did for Lewis and Clark, serving as a mediator with Indians. In 1539, Esteban guided a gold-seeking party into present-day Arizona and New Mexico where he met his death at the hands of Zuni villagers. People of African descent accompanied the Spanish to the northern reaches of New Spain in the 17th and 18th centuries both as slaves and as free persons. Occupying marginal status in the Spanish Empire, Afro-Hispanics often intermarried with Pueblo villagers and full-blood Spaniards. The 1750 Albuquerque census shows that out of some 200 households, more than fifty recorded at least one mulatto or mulatta spouse, while others recorded mixed-race servants. Similarly, in 1792, Spanish Texas reported 186 people of African descent from a population of 2,510. Considering that many free people of color chose to "lighten up" when dealing with census enumerators, these numbers actually may be much higher, illustrating a greater fluidity with regard to "race" in Spanish as opposed to English colonies.

Mexican independence from Spain in 1821 generally improved conditions for blacks. When the Mexican Senate abolished legal slavery in 1829, it did so in the hopes of encouraging black Americans to settle the Texas frontier, then under de facto control of nomadic raiders like the Comanches. The gradual arrival of Anglo Americans in Texas through the 1820s and 1830s exacerbated tensions with the Mexican government. Coming primarily from slaveholding states, whites in Texas defied Mexican law by transporting black slaves with them. In addition to the 30,000 Anglos who lived in Texas by 1836, some 5,000 African Americans lived there as well, only a small fraction of whom—about 150—were free. Such open defiance materialized in the revolution of 1836 that established the independent Republic of Texas, even though reabsorption by Mexico remained a possibility until the United States annexed it in 1845.

Every student of African American history is familiar with some thrilling story of a runaway slave who found freedom by escaping north. Few are aware of how thousands of Texas slaves sought freedom by fleeing south into Mexico. In 1855, Texas officials estimated that more than 4,000 black fugitives had fled their masters in the state's eastern Cotton Belt and crossed the harsh desert landscape, filled with raiding Indians, and escaped into northern Mexico through border towns like Eagle Pass. Hispanics in Texas sometimes aided runaways by sheltering them in homes and churches, causing several counties to outlaw communications between slaves and Mexicans. Texas Rangers, acting on the pretense of tracking hostile Indians, entered Mexico illegally to capture runaway slaves. One such group of schemers even conspired to capture Matamoros and create an independent, proslavery republic in the Lower Rio Grande Valley, essentially creating a buffer zone to discourage black flight. Accurate or not, Anglos in Texas and elsewhere in the Southwest came to perceive a Black-Hispanic alliance, as seen in the comment of a white migrant to the California gold fields in the 1840s: "It is notorious that the wooly-headed, thick-lipped African is regarded with more favor and affection than an American by the [Mexican] peons" (Lapp 1977, 33).

African Americans in the Indian Territory

Anglo settlement of California and Texas accompanied a variety of new ideas about race and land. Early explorers like Zebulon Pike and Stephen Long characterized the Great Plains and areas adjacent as "the Great American Desert," initially discouraging colonization by whites. By contrast, romantic assessments of Indians as toughened "noble savages" who could survive in any harsh environment led presidents from Jefferson to Van Buren to consider the assumed emptiness of the West an answer for the United States' convoluted racial problems. From this context came the establishment of Indian Territory in present-day eastern Oklahoma, what policymakers called "the permanent Indian frontier." In the 1830s, following a series of unsuccessful legislative challenges to removal, members of the "Five Civilized Tribes" were forced to leave their homes in the Southeast. Although thousands would lose their lives on "the Trail of Tears," many Cherokees, Creeks, Chickasaws, and others hoped that relocation west would permit greater autonomy from whites. In the mid-1840s, however, new ideas emerged under the banner of Manifest Destiny, which claimed that European Americans had a divine right to extend their institutions across the breadth of North America. Not only the nascent Indian Territory became fair game for settlement, but expansionists eyed the Mexican Southwest and California as well. What would be done with blacks, Native Americans, and Hispanics who already lived there remained an open question.

Black slaves endured removal side by side with their Native American masters, for whom slavery had become a profitable system of labor learned from southern planter elites. As with whites, only a minority of Native Americans practiced chattel slavery and did so in forms that varied considerably depending on tribal custom. With their high emancipation and intermarriage rates, the Seminoles appear to have been most tolerant in their treatment of blacks; in fact, their granting of sanctuary to runaway slaves in Florida became a leading cause of the U.S. Army's campaign against them in the 1830s. By contrast, tribes like the Creeks and Cherokees maintained strict slave codes, such as mandatory death sentences for slaves who killed Native Americans, and even attempted to prohibit inheritance for children of black–Native American unions. In 1824, a Cherokee warrior and wealthy farmer named Tarsekayahke (known colloquially as "Shoe Boots") appealed to his tribal council to recognize his five children as his free, legitimate heirs. Their mother, Doll, had been acquired by Shoe Boots as a slave in the 1790s and lived with him as his wife for thirty years.

Some slaveholding tribes like the Cherokees attempted to regulate the growing body of mixed-race people in their midst, which is more than can be said for white slaveholders who regarded the slave children of white masters as "black" and therefore undeserving of rights. But for most blacks in Indian Territory, full integration into tribal society—even for freedmen—proved unattainable. This inspired new efforts to create separate communities. The Black Seminoles were composed of an ethnic subgroup of the Seminole Nation. In 1850, facing hostility from neighboring tribes, particularly the Creeks, several hundred Black Seminoles fled the territory for Coahuila in northern Mexico, where they received land grants from the Mexican government in return for protecting the border from raiding nomads and American filibusters. Slave uprisings were common in Indian Territory. The largest of these occurred in 1842 when bondsmen from the Cherokee, Creek, and Choctaw nations—about three dozen total—launched a mass escape toward the Mexican border. The group killed a number of slave catchers and rode 300 miles onto the Plains before being captured by the Cherokee militia not far from the Red River.

The Issue of Slavery in the West

Clearly, by mid-century, slavery and race relations had become the most contentious issues of the day, provoked by the end of the Mexican War and the Treaty of Guadalupe-Hidalgo that brought the entire Southwest under U.S. control. Slavery brought for all Americans a crisis of conscience, perhaps more so in the West, where—unlike eastern states in which custom and geography helped determine individual positions—slavery had no historical boundaries. Utah became the only western territory north of the 36° 30′ line to legalize slavery in 1852. This may have been the consequence of Mormon leaders trying to disassociate themselves from abolitionism, which they recognized as a factor in the murder of their leader Joseph Smith. Oregon, settled mostly by migrants from midwestern states like Ohio and Indiana, passed a sequence of exclusion laws that ironically prohibited not only black slaves but also black freedmen from settling. These laws were seldom enforced against Oregon's small African American population, and exempted blacks and their descendants who lived there before such laws were passed. In California, the state legislature's ban on African Americans testifying in court prevented blacks from protecting their businesses, from suing, or even from identifying assailants. Even where slavery did not prevail, racial equality remained elusive, although at least one historian claims that black westerners had more economic and legal avenues open to them there than perhaps in any part of the country. Black westerners did not passively submit to discrimination. Mifflin Gibbs, a former bootblack who helped found the Atheneum Institute, joined with other Californians to successfully repeal the state's notorious "black laws." This opened the door for the aforementioned Mary Ellen Pleasant and two other African American women to sue a San Francisco streetcar company for rude and discriminatory treatment. They won.

The greatest western campaign against slavery occurred in Kansas. In the aftermath of Stephen Douglas' "popular sovereignty" doctrine, which allowed territorial voters to decide for themselves the question of slavery, Kansas Territory was besieged with extremists ranging from abolitionists to proslavery expansionists hoping to decide its eventual political fate, along with the vast majority of moderates who went there simply seeking land and hoping to avoid the controversy altogether. These moderates were disappointed. As factional violence ensued between pro- and antislavery forces, newspapers dubbed the region "Bleeding Kansas," an even more appropriate moniker after John Brown's well-publicized massacre of southern sympathizers near Pottawatomie Creek in 1856. Fed partly by its frontier character and distance from civil and military authorities, Kansas violence precipitated the larger national crisis that enveloped the nation in 1861. During these years, Kansas gained its reputation among southern slaves as a haven from oppression and slavery, a reputation they would remember during the Exodus movement. Several towns in northeast Kansas, most notably Lawrence and Topeka, became stops on the Underground Railroad. As of 1859, it was believed that nearly 300 fugitives had passed through Lawrence alone. "Jayhawkers" often attacked homes and plantations in neighboring Missouri, freeing slaves through armed force.

Kansas' reputation as "the free state" continued into the Civil War. U.S. Senator James Lane in 1862, refusing to wait for Lincoln's permission, organized the tricolor brigade of whites, Native Americans, and African

Americans, the first volunteer regiment in the Union Army to enlist people of color. But even white Kansans had their limitations. Following passage of the Wyandotte Constitution in 1859, which allowed for admission as a free state, legislators considered black exclusion laws similar to Oregon's. In 1860, a small total of 627 African Americans lived in Kansas; by 1865, the number had ballooned to 12,000, 9 percent of the state's total. Fear of being overwhelmed by a minority may explain the reluctance to extend suffrage rights to black men, which did not happen until the Fifteenth Amendment made it mandatory in 1870.

The complete story of the Civil War and Reconstruction in the West has been told elsewhere, but needless to say, the conflict divided communities there just as it did in the East. This especially was the case in Indian Territory, where many slaveholding Indians sided with the Confederacy. Although individual members of the Five Nations made significant contributions to the Union effort, the federal government after 1865 aimed to punish all tribes for the southern alliance. Some 7,000 African Americans and Afro-Indians gained their freedom during "Indian Reconstruction." A new set of imposed treaties required the tribes to grant full citizenship to their freedmen. Most, like the Seminoles, Creeks, and Cherokees, complied with these terms immediately by adopting ex-slaves as tribal members. Others like the Choctaws resisted this measure until 1885, and the Chickasaws even attempted to evict their freedmen through humiliating legislation.

With the Confederacy defeated, the United States turned more attention to the pacification of nomadic tribes. With their forces distributed thinly across the West, military leaders saw the advantage of befriending diverse groups and co-opting them into alliances. Such was the case with the Seminole Negro Indian Scouts, a group of about fifty Black Seminoles stationed in southern Texas. From 1870 to 1914, the Scouts assisted the Army by patrolling the Rio Grande and participating in campaigns against tribes like the Kickapoos and Lipan Apaches. Over time, bands of Black Seminoles joined the Scouts at their base near Fort Clark and established the nearby community of Brackettville. Surviving into the 21st century, Brackettville retains its unique cultural blend of African, Native American, and even Spanish heritages, as well as a strong military tradition bequeathed by Scout ancestors who helped secure the border.

African Americans in the Western Army

The western army provided recent freedmen some fresh opportunities. In July 1866, the U.S. Congress increased the size of the peacetime regular army by creating six new regiments composed exclusively of African Americans. In 1869, these six were reorganized and consolidated into two regiments of black infantry and two of cavalry. Impressed with the record of African Americans in the Civil War, Republican legislators saw military service as a useful means of uplifting former slaves and teaching them the responsibilities of citizenship. Consequently, each regiment was led by

African American soldiers of the Twenty-fifth Infantry with some members posing in buffalo robes proudly claiming their identity as buffalo soldiers, Fort Keogh, Missouri. (Library of Congress)

white officers and assigned a permanent chaplain (not a requirement for white regiments). History buffs often refer to blacks in the western army as "buffalo soldiers," a name apparently bestowed by the Plains Indians who equated their hair with the shaggy hump of a buffalo. However, the phrase seems anachronistic, not used widely by officers or enlisted men of the time.

African American men participated in all aspects of western conquest, serving in nearly every state and territory where prospective settlers demanded the Army's presence. As with white regiments, black infantry performed the less dramatic but onerous and even dangerous tasks of guarding railroad construction crews and payroll shipments, or constructing permanent buildings at fort sites. Cavalry regiments often spent weeks in the field, traveling on horseback as they tracked recalcitrant Native Americans or Mexican revolutionaries. When requested by civil authorities, fort commanders sometimes dispatched black troops to capture outlaws or suppress insurrections, as happened periodically in the case of labor unrest in mining camps. Though a rough form of respect characterized relations with white officers, black soldiers still endured discrimination. Even so, before the Spanish American War, blacks constituted 9 percent of the Army's total manpower with some of the highest reenlistment and lowest desertion rates, suggesting that the military offered to African Americans social and economic benefits that few civilian institutions could match.

Ironic, then, that black troops also struggled to gain acceptance by the very people they were employed to protect. Civil-military relations being generally poor, a number of explosive confrontations ensued, particularly when soldiers happened to be dark skinned. Civilians at Hays City, Kansas—a violent town along the Union Pacific frequented by prostitutes and gunfighters—waged an ongoing feud with black privates from adjacent Fort Hays. In 1869, three black infantrymen were accused of drunkenly killing a railroad watchman. While awaiting trial in the city jail, a mob of vigilantes seized the three and hanged them from a bridge, one of the earliest known lynchings in the state. Similar tensions erupted at Fort Concho, Texas, where a series of fights with cowboys and Texas Rangers caused black and white soldiers to cooperate in drafting a printed handbill that contained a dire message:

> We, the soldiers of the United States Army, do hereby warn cowboys, etc. of San Angelo and vicinity, to recognize our right of way as just and peaceable men. If we do not receive justice and fair play, which we must have, some-one must suffer, if not the guilty, then the innocent. It has gone too far, justice or death. (Leiker 1997, 3–17; 2002, *Racial Borders*, 90–91)

Even stationing black soldiers in nonwhite communities did not guarantee peaceful relations. From 1899 to 1906, violent outbreaks occurred in Mexican border towns like Laredo, El Paso, and Brownsville, often beginning with blacks being denied service in civilian businesses or being harassed by local police. But friendly and even loving relationships did sometimes develop as many African American men married and raised families with Native American and Hispanic women. In 1871, George Forniss, a soldier in the Twenty-fourth Infantry, married Cesaria Perazo, a marriage that lasted until her death in 1886. Six years later, Forniss began living with Severiana Tijernia, whom he eventually married and by whom he sired a daughter. Other buffalo soldiers intermarried with Cherokees and Black Seminoles, contributing to an increasingly complex multiracial population.

Black Cowboys

Besides soldiering, the postwar demand for beef drew many African Americans into the cattle industry. Twentieth-century popular culture, of course, made the mythic "cowboy" synonymous with the West, but in fact ranchers and herders accounted for only about 2 percent of all the region's workers, far outnumbered by miners and farmers. Before the war, slaves on Texas ranches learned the daily routine tasks of roping, branding, and breaking horses—all largely imports of Hispanic culture—and applied these skills as free laborers after 1865. Some black cowboys became local legends, such as Addison Jones, a bronco rider who inspired songs and poetry in West Texas, and "Bones" Hooks, a leader of the black community in Amarillo and co-founder of the Panhandle Plains Museum. Although ranching—like the military—included mostly masculine enterprises, women also worked with livestock. Johanna July, a Black Seminole who survived both a Native American attack and an abusive husband, gained fame as a tamer of wild horses from her home in Brackettville.

Henry Ossian Flipper (ca. 1850–1940)

Born into slavery in Georgia in the 1850s, Henry O. Flipper not only embodied the hope and promise of Reconstruction but his very life exemplified the opportunities and limitations of the post—Civil War West. Claimed by reformers as an example of what African Americans could attain given the right opportunities, he attended Atlanta University, and later, the U.S. Military Academy, becoming its first black graduate in 1877. A talented writer, he recorded the challenging social and academic experience of West Point in a book titled *The Colored Cadet at West Point* in 1878. At age twenty-one, he was assigned as second lieutenant, making him the first black commissioned officer in the U.S. Army.

Flipper's regiment, the Tenth Cavalry, had been created as part of an army expansion bill in 1866, one of a handful of regular army regiments that reserved enlistment for African Americans. Hence, Flipper and the enlisted men whom he led served in a capacity that many onlookers regarded as experimental, meant to determine whether blacks could make effective soldiers. From 1866 to the 1890s, African American soldiers participated in all aspects of western conquest ranging from Native American pacification to buttressing civil authority. Between 1878 and 1881, Flipper and the Tenth Cavalry served at western bases like Fort Concho, Texas, and Fort Sill, Indian Territory. A trained engineer, Lieutenant Flipper supervised multiple projects designed to improve the efficiency of these bases and their surrounding civilian communities, such as road construction and laying of telegraph lines. Flipper himself designed a drainage system that removed standing water from ponds to reduce malarial risk. His success in these efforts led to his promotion as acting assistant quartermaster at Fort Davis, Texas.

It was at Fort Davis that Flipper endured the most humiliating experience of his life. In 1881, he was brought before a court-martial board to answer charges of embezzlement. Funds had gone missing from the fort commissary, with prosecutors claiming that Flipper had taken the money and planned to abscond to Mexico. During a weeks-long trial held in the post chapel, Flipper claimed he had not stolen the funds but admitted to concealing their loss once he discovered them missing. The court-martial board acquitted Flipper of embezzlement, but found him guilty of conduct unbecoming an officer, leading to his dismissal from the U.S. Army. Maintaining he had been the victim of a racist conspiracy to frame and discredit him, he worked diligently—and unsuccessfully—to clear his name for the remainder of his days.

Blacks, Hispanics, and Euro-Americans worked together on the massive cattle drives of the 1860s and 1870s that herded millions of head from the southern plains to rail depots in Kansas, Colorado, and Nebraska. There was no glamour in working an overland trail, which meant months of sleeping outdoors and dealing with threats from outlaws, Native Americans, and stampedes for relatively low pay. Historians agree that the dangers of trail work, which required skill and mutual trust between the men, left no room for the sort of social hierarchy seen on southern plantations, and so tended to minimize racial divides. Such egalitarianism even continued at the end of the trail. "Cow towns" like Dodge City and Abilene seldom practiced racial segregation, and blacks usually stayed in the same hotels and drank at the same saloons (and patronized the same brothels) as white cowboys. Not

Historical debate over the Flipper trial continues today. Clearly, racism was well-entrenched in the U.S. Army, and several fellow officers at Fort Davis admitted to a personal dislike for Flipper. Whether this influenced the fairness of his trial remains an unsolved question. At the least, he had behaved negligently with company records and lied to a commanding officer, actions which—according to his defenders—may be attributed to his having panicked when the funds disappeared.

Between 1882 and 1919, Flipper—who never married—made his home in El Paso, Texas. Fluent in Spanish, he worked as a surveyor and mining engineer for private companies in the U.S. Southwest and northern Mexico. In the 1890s, he translated Spanish land deeds as an agent for the U.S. Department of Justice, and even authored a book on Spanish land laws and an essay on blacks in the Southwest. Businessmen and politicians in both countries came to regard him as an expert on the U.S.-Mexican border. During the chaotic Mexican Revolution of the 1910s, he drafted regular reports for a U.S. Senate subcommittee, headed by Senator Albert Fall of New Mexico, that documented property violations of Americans living south of the border. In 1916, at the age of sixty, he wrote a private manuscript titled "The Western Memoirs of Henry O. Flipper" describing his service with the Tenth Cavalry.

The 1920s saw an upturn in Henry Flipper's fortunes. In 1921, President Warren Harding appointed Senator Fall to the position of secretary of interior. Subsequently, Fall appointed Flipper to a job as special assistant, which meant his relocation to Washington, D.C. His friendship with Fall also secured for him some well-paying consulting positions with companies and agencies in Alaska and South America. Flipper retired in 1931, returning to Atlanta, Georgia—the state of his birth—to live with relatives. He died there in 1940, his dream of clearing his official military record unfulfilled.

In 1963, Professor Theodore Harris obtained legal rights to Flipper's "Western Memoirs" and published the manuscript under the title *Negro Frontiersman*. Harris' book drew historical attention to the Flipper case, just as the civil rights movement and Black Power likewise drew attention to other injustices involving race. In 1976, the Army Board for the Correction of Military Records reviewed Flipper's materials and ruled that his conviction and punishment were "unduly harsh and unjust." Finally, in 1999, President Bill Clinton provided Second Lieutenant Henry O. Flipper with a posthumous honorable discharge.

until the 1880s, when the arrival of railroads in Texas made the overland drives unnecessary, did towns like Dodge City close their red-light districts and provide a more "civilized" appearance by building schools, churches, and cultural centers. Not coincidentally, local segregation laws appeared simultaneously as western communities tried to shed their frontier image by adopting the mores of eastern cities.

No one experienced this transition from an agrarian to an industrial economy more acutely than Nathaniel or "Nat" Love. Born on a Tennessee plantation in 1854, Love worked as a sharecropper until age fifteen when he moved west to find work on ranches and cattle trails in Texas, Arizona, and New Mexico. Acquiring the pseudonym "Deadwood Dick" after winning a shooting contest in Deadwood, South Dakota, he recorded

Nat "Deadwood Dick" Love, African American cowboy (1854—1921). (Library of Congress)

his adventures in a 1907 memoir. Qualifying more as folklore than history, his autobiography contains exaggerated stories of Native American battles ("we had the satisfaction of making several good Indians out of bad ones"), hangings of rustlers, and supposed friendships with celebrities like Billy the Kid. Love concluded his yarn-spinning memoir with a surprisingly upbeat description of his postfrontier life (Love 1995, 42). In 1890, he took a job as a porter for the Pullman Company, serving white passengers in crowded rail cars while traversing the very plains over which he once herded livestock. Like the dime novelists whose work he imitated, Love projected an image of a "wild and woolly West" meant to titillate eastern readers.

African American Communities

Most African Americans who relocated did so not as individuals but as groups, often as part of extended families or even entire communities. Railroad agents and speculators who promoted western settlement, known as "boosters," often distributed pamphlets and other reports that embellished the region's agricultural potential. Booster literature played a role in the Exodusters migration of 1879–1880 when thousands of indigent southern refugees fled their homes in the Gulf Coast states, headed north in winter along the frozen Mississippi River, and finally turned west at

St. Louis. Lured to eastern Kansas by its liberal reputation and vague rumors of "forty acres and a mule," Exodusters who arrived there found disillusionment. Discovering no free land, a lucky few managed to purchase homestead claims or gain steady employment, but most congregated in Atchison and Topeka where they taxed the resources of local charity organizations. Some returned with heartbreak to the South, while others dispersed to nearby states like Colorado and Minnesota.

Middle-class African Americans, usually newspaper editors, also used "booster" tactics to attract blacks westward, although always with the warning that successful relocation required savings and hard work. Edwin P. McCabe, an attorney and land agent, launched a vigorous recruitment drive in the 1880s to attract blacks to Oklahoma. Here, in the developing Indian Territory, McCabe hoped to create a collection of all-black towns where African Americans could farm, educate their children, and prosper free from white interference. An early black nationalist, McCabe even believed that, with sufficient numbers, Oklahoma might join the United States as an all-black state. Though this obviously never transpired, the efforts of McCabe and other promoters resulted in the establishment of 28 black towns and an African American population in Oklahoma alone of 55,000 by 1900.

Black towns also appeared in Kansas, most having little or no connection to the Exodusters. In 1877, white investors attracted black members of a colonization society from Kentucky and Tennessee to a proposed site named "Nicodemus" after a legendary African prince who became the first American slave to buy his freedom. Located along the Solomon River, the site was described as having abundant game and fertile land for farming. But when the first settlers arrived, they saw a collection of crude dugouts on land with no timber or natural resources, causing several weary travelers to break into tears and others threatening to hang the investors. With perseverance, however, Nicodemus grew into a thriving community that by 1887 boasted more than 300 residents, a bank, churches, schools, and dozens of wheat farms. Its newspaper, the *Western Cyclone,* praised the town's optimistic attitude:

> We don't propose to say that we have discovered an Eldorado but to those
> who are anxious to better their condition and are willing to work and rustle,
> we invite you to come to Nicodemus. . . . Here you will encounter none of
> the prejudice you complain of so bitterly in the south, nor that cramped posi-
> tion you occupy further east" (*Nicodemus Cyclone* 1888).

Though its failure to attract a railroad terminal hastened the town's decline in the 1890s, Nicodemus, like Brackettville, continues to form the core of an active black community into the 21st century.

Similar ventures were attempted in the Far West. In 1908, a retired officer named Allen Allensworth founded a black settlement in California's lush San Joaquin Valley that, by 1920, had more than 200 residents. Despite a few triumphs, most black towns that began as isolated racial utopias failed for the same reason as did such white experiments. Dependent on rural values and small producer-based agriculture, town builders launched their enterprises just as America was becoming more urbanized and agriculture itself grew more industrial and capital intensive. Rural communities reported sizeable population losses at the turn of the century, and even thriving towns became victims of their own success as prosperous educated children drifted away to cities in search of better prospects.

Blacks in the Urban West

All westerners seemed to embrace their destiny as urbanites. Following the San Francisco model, new African American neighborhoods sprang up in cities like Denver, Lincoln, Salt Lake City, and Portland. From 1880 to 1900, every western state, Nevada excepted, saw an increase in black population, the largest in Montana, Nebraska, and Washington. African Americans' numbers in Colorado quadrupled during the period, even though the influx of blacks stayed proportionately lower than that of whites. Black newspapers like the *Seattle Republican* and organizations like the local Afro-American League aggressively promoted recruitment to Washington, praising the state's healthy climate and exceptional job opportunities. Black Seattle remained overwhelmingly male into the early 1900s, causing promoters to advertise the many domestic jobs available to black women as a way of achieving gender balance.

As urbanization proceeded apace, western cities—like their cow-town counterparts—also considered segregation, in most cases modeled on the de facto style of the North rather than the de jure style of the South. In "Free State" Kansas, the state legislature permitted cities with more than 15,000 people to practice local segregation of school districts; towns below that number—where few African Americans lived—could not segregate. Imbued with a frontier ethic that emphasized individual rather than group success, white westerners appeared to take the "separate but equal" concept articulated in *Plessy v. Ferguson* (1896) more literally than southerners, maintaining that African Americans had full rights to pursue economic advancement but not in ways that required mingling with whites. In opposing Jim Crow's westward march, black westerners aligned with the nation's growing militant African American middle class and their spokesman, W. E. B. Du Bois. By World War I, several western cities hosted chapters of the National Association for the Advancement of Colored People (NAACP), while thousands more in small towns and rural areas mobilized through the AME (African Methodist Episcopal) Church conference. When Montana approved an antimiscegenation law in 1909, editor Joseph B. Bass condemned the action in his newspaper, the *Montana Plaindealer*, earning him the scorn of fellow Republicans. As Helena's black population dwindled, so too did subscribers to Bass' *Plaindealer*, causing him to suspend publication in 1911.

In states where South and West converged, segregation assumed more complex qualities. In Texas, African Americans and Hispanics were equally liable to be excluded from public places or fall victims to lynching violence. Oklahoma saw a peculiar dynamic emerge as whites and blacks entered the state en masse during the land rushes of the 1890s. Alarmed at African Americans' growing assertiveness, many whites and Native Americans formed a common cause and lobbied for a host of Jim Crow and antimiscegenation laws that accompanied statehood in 1907. To fight discrimination within their tribal government, Afro-Cherokees appealed to federal authorities to have the tribe officially dissolved. Again, Indian nations differed in their dealings with blacks, both those who arrived after 1865 and those who descended from tribal freedmen. For a brief time, the Creeks encouraged blacks to assimilate and even join a short-lived movement to establish Oklahoma as an all-Indian state. Once state, federal, and tribal governments began classifying "Black Indians" and African-American immigrants as people of the same race, these groups gradually intermarried and steadily increased. Between 1910 and 1920, "blacks" in Oklahoma grew by almost 9 percent, in contrast to "Indians" whose numbers fell by almost one-quarter as more mixed-bloods identified themselves as white. Afro-Indians in the 21st century still fight for rights and recognition, both as people of Indigenous Nations and as oppressed minorities within those nations.

In 1909, some 200 blacks from Oklahoma did—for perhaps the last time—what black westerners had done for a century when faced with oppression: attempt a fresh start on a new frontier. Canada had long tried to lure American settlers onto its own western prairies, advertising the fertile soil of Saskatchewan and Manitoba as a natural haven for farmers and town builders. But when a group of African Americans arrived at the Saskatchewan border that fall, immigration supervisors reacted with surprise. Describing the new arrivals as "lazy, immoral, and altogether undesirable" as Canadian citizens, the Immigration Branch dispatched agents and reports to Oklahoma and parts of the South discouraging black emigration. Booker T. Washington even received packets explaining the inability of blacks to adjust to cold climates. Despite these efforts at exclusion, hundreds of African Americans persisted onto the Canadian Plains and made homes there, essentially becoming expatriates and developing new "Afro-Canadian" identities.

Conclusion

In 1890, the U.S. Census Bureau declared the "frontier"—spatially defined as less than two persons per square mile—closed. The West had been officially settled. Three years later, a University of Wisconsin professor named Frederick Jackson Turner expounded his "frontier thesis," an academic eulogy claiming that the availability of land had shaped Americans' sense of democracy and individualism, and with this "safety valve" now closed, the United States would next turn inward to address economic and political reform. Scholars long have challenged Turner's thesis, but its timing meshes with—and perhaps helps explain—the outrages imposed on African Americans in the 1890s: dramatic upsurges in lynchings, political disenfranchisement, and federal sanction of Jim Crow laws. As with

Micheaux's South Dakota homestead and the migration from Oklahoma to Canada, blacks still searched for "frontiers" to escape racism long after 1890. Yet no sooner had the struggle to settle the West concluded than a new struggle emerged to explain it. Fictions like Owen Wister's *The Virginian* and histories like Theodore Roosevelt's *The Winning of the West* portrayed the century past as a time of rugged masculinity, when brave Americans conquered a wilderness. Not surprisingly, African Americans joined this interpretive struggle, proclaiming that the heroic western stories claimed by whites belonged to blacks as well.

Oscar Micheaux exemplified this trend. After years of raising crops and living in a sod house, he wrote *The Conquest* in 1913. The book's hero, Oscar Devereaux—a thinly veiled alias—is a hard-working young black man who rises above his poor, unambitious relatives to become a Plains farmer. His previous short stories rejected, Micheaux paid the printing costs from his own pocket and traveled door to door among his white neighbors and black homes in the South promoting *The Conquest*. Its meager profits helped him start a small printing company that in 1917 published his third book, *The Homesteader*, which was another autobiographical account of his South Dakota experiences. A year later, with a budget of $15,000, Micheaux hired a cast of actors, leased a studio in Chicago, and self-produced a movie version of *The Homesteader*, which opened in theatres just as black veterans returned from World War I. Through the 1920s and 1930s, Micheaux wrote and produced dozens of novels and films, many of which espoused "western" themes of daring pioneers, economic self-determination, and stoic uplift in the face of white racism.

Frontier motifs likewise figured prominently in the Harlem Renaissance. Many artists of the 1920s New Negro movement originated from the West, such as Taylor Gordon from Montana and Aaron Douglass, born in Kansas and educated in Lincoln, Nebraska. Authors Ralph Ellison and Langston Hughes wrote about their childhood homes, respectively Oklahoma and Kansas, in *Invisible Man* (1952) and *Not without Laughter* (1930). (In the 1960s, when speaking to a young scholar seeking advice on writing black history, the elderly Hughes reminded him "Don't leave out the cowboys!") Even Hollywood showed some appreciation for the topic with the film *Harlem on the Prairie* (1937) and its three sequels, which placed a fairly light-skinned black actor named Herb Jeffries in cowboy garb and pitted his heroic character against dark-skinned villains. While most cultural representations of the West have been traditional masculine narratives, some assert a different perspective. Contemporary playwright Pearl Cleage's play *Flyin' West* tells the story of a matriarchal society centered in Nicodemus after the exodus, and of its "women warriors" who come to a friend's aid to prevent her abusive husband from stealing their property.

Despite these examples, most literature and film ignores the historical relationship between African Americans and the West. This is unfortunate because that story reveals valuable lessons about the connection of race to region. Racism certainly accompanied blacks during westward expansion, but that process drew them into a landscape so populated by multiple racial groups—Hispanics, Native Americans, and Asians—that new, complicated relationships had to develop that were, in some cases, bigoted and hierarchical and, in others, tolerant and egalitarian. Though most blacks in the 19th century heeded the admonitions of leaders like Douglass and Washington to remain in the South, a significant minority chose to risk safety and ostracism to embark for new homes in a region both attractive and frightening. These qualities, if nothing else, earned them the distinctly American compliment of being "pioneers."

References and Further Reading

Allmendinger, Blake. *Imagining the African American West*. Lincoln: University of Nebraska Press, 2005.

Athearn, Robert. *In Search of Canaan: Black Migration* to *Kansas, 1879–1880*. Lawrence: University Press of Kansas, 1978.

Billington, Monroe Lee, and Roger D. Hardaway, eds. *African Americans on the Western Frontier*. Niwot: University Press of Colorado, 1998.

Bonner, T. D. *The Life and Adventures of James P. Beckwourth: Mountaineer, Scout, Pioneer, and Chief of the Crow Nation*. Minneapolis: Ross and Haines, 1965.

Bowser, Pearl, and Louise Spence. *Writing Himself into History: Oscar Micheaux, His Silent Films, and His Audiences*. New Brunswick, NJ: Rutgers University Press, 2000.

Bringhurst, Newell G. "The Mormons and Slavery: A Closer Look." *Pacific Historical Review* 50 (1981): 329–338.

Burton, Arthur T. *Black, Red, and Deadly: Black and Indian Gunfighters of the Indian Territory, 1870–1907*. Austin, TX: Eakin Press, 1991.

Carroll, John M., ed. *The Black Military Experience in the American West*. New York: Liveright Publishing, 1971.

Chan, Sucheng, Douglas Henry Daniels, Mario T. Garcia, and Terry P. Wilson, eds. *Peoples of Color in the American West*. Lexington, MA: D. C. Heath, 1994.

Christian, Garna L. *Black Soldiers in Jim Crow, Texas, 1899–1917*. College Station: Texas A&M University Press, 1995.

Crockett, Norman L. *The Black Towns*. Lawrence: Regents Press of Kansas, 1976.

Dann, Martin. "From Sodom to the Promised Land: E. P. McCabe and the Movement for Oklahoma Colonization." *Kansas Historical Quarterly* 40, no. 3 (Fall 1974): 370–378.

De Graaf, Lawrence B., Kevin Mulroy, and Quintard Taylor, eds. *Seeking El Dorado: African Americans in California*. Los Angeles: Autry Museum of Western Heritage, 2001.

Dobak, William A. *The Black Regulars*. Norman: University of Oklahoma Press, 2002.

Douglas, Frederick. "The Negro Exodus from the Gulf States: Address before Convention of the American Social Science Association,

Saratoga Springs, September 12, 1879." In *The Life and Writings of Frederick Douglass*, vol. 4, ed. Philip Foner, 335–338. New York: International Publishers, 1955.

Durham, Philip, and Everett L. Jones. *The Negro Cowboys*. New York: Dodd, Mead, 1965.

Franklin, John Hope, and Alfred A. Moss, Jr. *From Slavery to Freedom: A History of African Americans*, 7th ed. New York: McGraw-Hill, 1994.

Hamilton, Kenneth W. *Black Towns and Profit: Promotion and Development in the Trans-Appalachian West, 1877–1915*. Urbana: University of Illinois Press, 1991.

Haywood, C. Robert. "No Less a Man: Blacks in Cow Town Dodge City, 1876–1886." *Western Historical Quarterly* 19, no. 2 (May 1988): 161–182.

Haywood, C. Robert. *Victorian West: Class and Culture in Kansas Cattle Towns*. Lawrence: University Press of Kansas, 1991.

Katz, William Loren. *Black Indians: A Hidden Heritage*. New York: Ethrac Publications, 1986.

Katz, William Loren. *The Black West*, 3rd ed. Seattle: Open Hand Publishing Co., 1987.

Lapp, Rudolph. *Blacks in Gold Rush California*. New Haven, CT: Yale University Press, 1977.

Leckie, William H. *The Buffalo Soldiers: A Narrative of the Negro Cavalry in the West*. Norman: University of Oklahoma Press, 1967.

Leiker, James N. "African Americans and Boosterism." *Journal of the West* 42, no. 4 (Fall 2003): 25–34.

Leiker, James N. "Black Soldiers at Fort Hays, Kansas, 1867–1869: A Study in Civilian-Military Violence." *Great Plains Quarterly* 17, no. 1 (Winter 1997): 3–17.

Leiker, James N. "Race Relations in the Sunflower State." *Kansas History, A Journal of the Central Plains* 25, no. 3 (Fall 2002): 218–222.

Leiker, James N. *Racial Borders: Black Soldiers along the Rio Grande*. College Station: Texas A&M University Press, 2002.

Littlefield, Daniel, Jr. *Africans and Seminoles: From Removal to Emancipation*. Westport, CT: Greenwood Press, 1977.

Love, Nathaniel. *The Life and Adventures of Nat Love, Better Known in the Cattle Country as "Deadwood Dick."* Lincoln: University of Nebraska Press, 1995.

Massey, Sara R., ed. *Black Cowboys of Texas*. College Station: Texas A&M University Press, 2000.

May, Katja. *African Americans and Native Americans in the Creek and Cherokee Nations, 1830s to 1920s*. New York: Garland Publishing, 1996.

Micheaux, Oscar. *The Conquest: The Story of a Negro Pioneer*. Lincoln: University of Nebraska Press, 1994.

Miles, Tiya. *Ties That Bind: The* Story *of an Afro-Cherokee Family in Slavery and Freedom*. Berkeley: University of California Press, 2005.

Mulroy, Kevin. *Freedom on the Border: The Seminole Maroons in Florida, the Indian Territory, Coahuila, and Texas*. Lubbock: Texas Tech University Press, 1993.

Nicodemus Cyclone (formerly *Western Cyclone*), January 20, 1888.

Painter, Nell Irvin. *Exodusters: Black Migration to Kansas after Reconstruction*. New York: Alfred A. Knopf, 1977.

Porter, Kenneth W. "The Seminole Negro-Indian Scouts, 1870–1881." *Southwestern Historical Quarterly* 55, no. 3 (January 1952): 358–377.

Roberson, Jere. "Edwin P. McCabe and the Langston Experiment." *Chronicles of Oklahoma* 51, no. 3 (Fall 1973): 343–355.

Savage, W. Sherman. "Slavery in the West." Reprinted in *African Americans on the Western Frontier*, ed. Monroe Lee Billington and Roger Hardaway. Niwot: University Press of Colorado, 1998.

Shepard, R. Bruce. *Deemed Unsuitable: Blacks from Oklahoma Move to Canadian Prairies in Search of Equality in the Early 20th Century Only to Find Racism in Their New Home*. Toronto: Umbrella Press, 1997.

Taylor, Quintard. *The Forging of a Black Community: Seattle's Central District from 1870 through the Civil Rights Era*. Seattle: University of Washington Press, 1994.

Taylor, Quintard, and Shirley Ann Wilson Moore, eds. *African American Women Confront the West, 1600–2000*. Norman: University of Oklahoma Press, 2003.

VanEpps-Taylor, Betti Carol. *Oscar Micheaux: A Biography*. Rapid City, SD: Dakota West, 1999.

Wickett, Murray. *Contested Territory: Whites, Native Americans, and African Americans in Oklahoma, 1865–1907*. Baton Rouge: Louisiana State University Press, 2000.

Wilson, Elinor. *Jim Beckwourth: Black Mountain Man, War Chief of the Crows, Trader, Trapper, Explorer, Frontiersman, Guide, Scout, Interpreter, Adventurer, and Gaudy Liar*. Norman: University of Oklahoma Press, 1972.

Woods, Randall B. "Integration, Exclusion, or Segregation? The 'Color Line' in Kansas, 1878–1900." *Western Historical Quarterly* 14 (1983): 181–198.

Black Indians: America's Forgotten People

11

Dixie Ray Haggard

Black Indians are an American people without a distinct, collective history. The tragic conquest of Native America and the horrific enslavement of Africans created these people. Black Indians managed to persevere and survive to the present day despite America's historic problem with accepting racial and cultural diversity. Because of the denial of racial and cultural plurality, however, Black Indians have continually had to negotiate their identity in the face of white, and sometimes Native and African American, denial of their dual heritage.

From the first arrival of Africans to North America in 1619 until the end of the 19th century, European colonists, and later white Americans, worked continually to prevent blacks and Native Americans from uniting against whites by playing the two groups against each other through the exploitation of racial differences and ethnic rivalries. White Americans used Natives as slave hunters and eventually turned some in the southern tribes into slaveholders. They also trained Africans and African Americans to hate and mistrust Native Americans to further antagonize potential relationships between these two groups. Thus, by creating real and fictional animosity between the two groups, white Americans successfully hid the cultural similarities between them. This allowed both groups to be exploited by white society until well into the 20th century. Yet despite the efforts of Europeans and Anglo-Americans, Africans and Native Americans intermingled from the very beginning.

Early Origins of Black Indians

In the American colonies, the original labor source was indentured servants of European descent. Over time, first African indentured servants and later African and Native American slaves replaced European indentured servants as the primary labor force in British colonial North America, especially in the South. This shift in the labor pool of the colonies introduced new people to the world through the intermixing of Africans, Europeans, and Native Americans. Thus, Africans and Natives first encountered each other on a significant scale through the experience of servitude and slavery. These interactions introduced new players to Native American–white relations, Black Indians. Black Indians were either people with both Native American and African/African American ancestry or black people that lived primarily within a Native American community.

Colonial Americans were uncomfortable with this intermingling, but it continued despite their attempts to prevent it. Colonists, and later Americans, implemented a caste system built on the concept of racial purity that sowed the seeds of confusion for Black Indians by denying them their dual identity. Within this system, any African ancestry made you black, and often this concept was used to force Black Indians to identify as African Americans and deny them their Native heritage. Alternately, Native Americans had to prove they had "enough Indian" ancestry in order to count as "real Indians" as the United States government began to provide food, clothing, shelter, education, and even money to honor treaty responsibilities. The situation resulting from these two facts led to Black Indians being classified as African Americans more and more with the passage of time. Nowhere was this fact more prevalent than on the East Coast of the United States.

The East Coast

From the Revolutionary era up through the early 19th century, African/African American and Native intermarriage increased rapidly. Close relations began in the colonial period because of the close contact between African and Native servants and slaves, but they continued over time as enslaved black males sought out free Native women to marry. This was partly because of the scarcity of African/African American women, especially in the northern colonies, but also because children inherited the status of the mother. Therefore, the child of an enslaved African/African American and a free Native woman would be free.

On the East Coast, social interactions between Natives and Africans/African Americans continued to be close into the 19th century as these groups were relegated to jobs that most whites did not want to do. The most prevalent of these occupations were in the fishing and whaling industries. While limiting people of color to menial jobs, whites also took advantage of the blending of Natives and Africans to detribalize the Native groups by eventually declaring Native tribes extinct and declaring the existing people as black or mulatto rather than Native. In this way, land that had been legally recognized as Native owned could be seized and redistributed among whites.

Black Indians found themselves under attack throughout the East Coast during the late 18th and early 19th centuries, even as northern

Mary Edmonia Lewis (1845–1890?)

Mary Edmonia Lewis was the first Black Indian woman to become famous for her art in the 19th century. Her mother was an Ojibway (Anishnaabeg) and her father was an African American, probably from the West Indies. Both of her parents died when she was a child. Edmonia Lewis and her brother, Samuel L. Lewis, lived with their mother's family as children in Niagara Falls. She learned the handicrafts of her people while young, and this may have been an early artistic influence. Twelve years older than Edmonia, her brother went west to seek his fortune, and he became a wealthy and prominent citizen of Bozeman, Montana. Samuel paid for Edmonia's education, first at New York Central College (a Baptist secondary school) in McGrawville, New York, and later at Oberlin College from 1860 to 1862. Oberlin College was the first institute of higher education in the United States to admit African Americans and women. While in school, she took up sculpting and decided on a career in art.

In 1862, Lewis moved to Boston, and while there, she studied under the master sculptor, Edward A. Brackett. She began attending abolitionist meetings at this time, and as a result, Lewis met famous abolitionists such as Frederick Douglass, William Garrison Lloyd, and Lydia Maria Child as well as other New England intellectuals. She also met Colonel Robert Gould Shaw before he and his unit, the Fifty-Fourth Massachusetts (the first all African American regular unit in the Union Army), were deployed to South Carolina during the Civil War. In 1864, Lewis sculpted a bust of Shaw to commemorate his and the Fifty-Fourth's courageous sacrifice at the battle of Fort Wagner. The sale of 100 copies of Shaw's bust along with continued monetary support from her brother generated the financial base she needed to go to Italy to continue to study and work.

In 1865, Lewis moved to Rome where she spent most of her active career and where she solidified her neoclassical style of sculpting in which she reflected the influence of classical Greek and Roman art. Numerous American and female sculptors worked in Rome during the period she lived there. This community of sculptors provided Lewis with the artistic and intellectual support she needed for her sculpting to prosper. Most of her subjects were famous abolitionists, and Lewis' American intellectual heroes usually were presented garbed in classical era robes rather than in contemporary clothing. However, Lewis' master work was *The Death of Cleopatra*, which portrayed the Egyptian queen after she was bitten by the asp. After disappearing in the late 19th and most of the 20th century, this piece can now be seen at the Smithsonian National Museum of American Art. Lewis had several prominent showings in the United States during the late 1860s and 1870s, but she faded from public view by the late 19th century. The date, place, and cause of her death are debated and uncertain.

states abolished slavery. In trying to control their slaves, prevent slave rebellions, stop southern slaves from running away, and prevent the threat to white racial purity in both the North and South, whites continually looked at the small, Native reservations in the region as places that undermined white authority and control. Many of the Natives in these communities actually were Black Indians that allowed free blacks to live among them. Whites were afraid that this intermingling of the races might spill over into white communities. As a result of this paranoia, white citizens repeatedly tried to get the states and national government to re-scind the Native reservations' tax-exempt status and investigate the threat these groups portended. Black Indian communities in Connecticut, Dela-ware, Maryland, Massachusetts, New Jersey, New York, Rhode Island, South Carolina, Tennessee, and Virginia lived in isolation from white com-munities. Unable to accept people so distinctly different from themselves, whites saw these societies as threats to dominant society's way of life and hegemony. Most whites denied these people their Native ancestry and used laws designed to control free blacks as checks on the perceived threat from these Black Indians. By classifying these people as blacks or mulattos, the federal government and the states detribalized these people and denied them the annuities and access to land that should have been guaranteed to them by treaties with the federal government.

Black Seminoles

The places little controlled by white society saw the greatest, peaceful interactions between Natives and Africans/African Americans. Nowhere was this true more than on the frontier. Africans and African Americans played crucial roles in the exploration of new territory and participated in the fur trade. At the same time, they played roles as negotiators, especially as social interactions increased. Although Black Indians were vital ele-ments of frontier history of the United States, these facts are rarely found in the histories written about the United States.

The Spanish term "maroon" was applied to independent commun-ities of escaped slaves. These communities did not exist for long in North America because slaveholders continually sought to break up these communities, often using Native Americans as slave hunters to do so. Maroon communities survived, however, under Spanish rule at Fort Mose near St. Augustine during the early 18th century and at the Negro Fort in the panhandle during the early 19th century. After Florida came under U.S. control, a maroon community continued to exist in Florida under the protection of the Miccosukee and Muscogee Seminoles until 1842. This maroon community came to be known as the Black Seminoles.

The Miccosukee Seminoles formed in the early to mid-18th century in northern Florida. Apalachee (originally a Florida tribe) refugees that lived among the Lower Muscogee Creeks in the first two decades of the 18th century made up the core of the Miccosukee Seminoles. By mid-cen-tury, some of these refugee Apalachees had moved back into Florida and merged with remnants of other Florida tribes to become the Miccosukee Seminoles. The Miccosukee Seminoles allied with the Spanish and the runaway slaves who lived at Gracia Real Santa Teresa de Mose, also known as Fort Mose. Fort Mose served as a successful maroon community and haven for runaway slaves from South Carolina and Georgia between 1738 and 1763. This began the long Seminole affiliation with runaway slaves. Fort Mose was abandoned when the Spanish gave control of Florida

A Black Seminole interpreter named "Gopher John," as illustrated in *The Exiles of Florida*, by Joshua Reed Giddings. Giddings was a member of Congress representing Ohio and an opponent of slavery. (Giddings, Joshua R. *Exiles of Florida*, 1858)

to the British at the end of the French and Indian War in 1763 and most of the inhabitants resettled in Cuba.

During the American Revolution, some Muscogee Creek immigrants from Alabama and Georgia began joining the Miccosukee Seminoles in northern Florida. Most of these immigrants were relatives of the Miccosukees who had earlier lived among the Creeks, and many were probably direct descendants of Florida tribes that no longer existed. As the American Revolution unfolded, Seminoles began raiding the Georgia frontier for supplies, horses, and cattle. They also began to free slaves who fled to Florida by the hundreds. At the end of the American Revolution, Spain regained control of Florida. At this time, Florida was populated by a growing Seminole population and a few hundred runaway slaves who laid the foundation for what later came to be known as the Black Seminoles.

During the War of 1812, the British, despite the fact that Florida was a Spanish colony, built a fort on the Apalachicola River in northwest Florida to encourage the Seminoles to ally with them and to recruit ex-slaves to serve alongside the Seminoles and the British. When the British evacuated in 1815, they left the fort in the control of approximately 300 former slaves. Eventually, 800 runaway slaves settled in the vicinity of what became known as the Negro Fort. In 1816, American forces under the command of Andrew Jackson destroyed the fort with 90 percent of the garrison being killed. The surrounding population of runaway slaves fled deeper into Florida and formed closer bonds with the Seminoles. At the same time, more and more Red Stick Creeks fled to Florida after earlier being defeated by Jackson in the Red Stick War (1813–1814). The Red

Sticks formed the core of the Muscogee Seminoles who now joined the Miccosukee Seminoles and the Black Seminoles in their resistance to the United States.

The relationship between the Native Seminoles and the Black Seminoles is unique in American history. The Black Seminoles adapted well to the region and proved valuable allies to the Native Seminoles. They cultivated rice as it was done in Africa as well as corn, sweet potatoes, vegetables, and cotton and lived in villages with their own chiefs separate from the Native Seminoles. Some intermarrying did occur, however. They also raised livestock, hunted, and fished. Many Black Seminoles became fluent in English, Miccosukee, Muscogee, and Spanish and became valuable translators for the Native Seminoles as well as interpreters of Anglo-American society, culture, and intentions. Native Seminoles and Black Seminoles soon united to keep Georgia slave hunters out of Florida. Both groups received weapons and other military supplies from the British who traded in Spanish Florida until the United States gained control of Florida.

The First Seminole War (1817–1818) broke out as Georgians calling themselves Patriots began attacking Native and Black Seminoles. The Seminoles responded by raiding Georgia plantations freeing hundreds of more slaves. Eventually, Andrew Jackson went back into Florida, destroyed several Seminole towns, seized Pensacola and St. Mark's, and executed two British citizens for inciting the Seminoles to attack the U.S. frontier. The U.S. government took advantage of this situation and demanded Spain turn Florida over to the United States if the Spanish could not control the Seminoles. In response, Spain sold Florida to the United States for $5 million.

After the First Seminole War, the United States tried to promote slavery among the Native Seminoles. Although Native Seminole leaders resisted these overtures by U.S. officials, this effort ultimately strained relations between Black and Native Seminoles. Yet despite the strain, Native leaders still took black wives, disallowed the selling of slaves within the various Seminole bands, and used blacks as military and diplomatic advisors and interpreters. Some 600 Black Seminoles moved farther south, however, being unsure of Native support and fearful of white slave hunters.

War broke out again between the United States and the Seminoles in 1835 and lasted until 1842 as the United States tried to implement its Removal Policy, which called for the forced removal of eastern tribes to Oklahoma and Kansas in the West. By the end of this war, the United States spent more than $40 million and lost 1,500 soldiers in battle. Black Seminoles proved to be valuable Seminole allies during this struggle, and the army quickly recognized their importance to the Seminole resistance. With the exception of approximately 500 Native Seminoles and a few, unknown number of Black Seminoles who never left Florida, the United States forced the Native Seminoles to relocate to Indian Territory in present-day Oklahoma. About 500 Black Seminoles accompanied the Native Seminoles.

The U.S. government removed the Seminoles west to territory controlled by the Muscogee Creek Nation because the U.S. government

John Horse (1812–1882)

A Black Seminole, John Horse served as a warrior, an interpreter, and, later, a leader for the Seminoles during the violent periods of the Second Seminole War, the Seminole Removal to Oklahoma, and the troubling times the Seminoles faced out west. He was the son of a Native Seminole named Charlie Cowaya (or Coheia) and an African woman who had either run away from her white owner or been purchased by Charlie Cowaya. Either way, Charlie Cowaya took her as his wife, and he did not treat her or his children by her as slaves. In Oklahoma, the Seminoles recognized Charlie Cawaya's intent by granting John Horse his freedom at that time. Cowaya seems to have been a corruption of "caballo," the Spanish word for horse, and this seems to be the reason the English derivation of John's last name is Horse.

John Horse worked as an interpreter for the Seminole leaders Micanopy, Osceola, and Alligator, and as a young warrior, he fought resolutely and courageously by Osceola's side during the Second Seminole War. In one famous incident in June 1837, John Horse, Osceola, Coacoochee, and Arpeika freed more than 700 Native and Black Seminoles from imprisonment near Tampa Bay just before these prisoners were to be deported to Indian Territory. After he, Coacoochee, and Osceola were deceitfully captured during peace talks and imprisoned at Fort Marion, John Horse and Coacoochee with sixteen other Seminoles miraculously escaped in November 1837.

Osceola was too ill to accompany them, and he later died in prison. John Horse fought in several more battles, but after the death of his first wife, a Native Seminole, a dejected John Horse chose to remove to Indian Territory in the spring of 1838.

In Indian Territory, John Horse became the primary leader of the Black Seminoles. He became an interpreter for the Army in 1839 to convince other Seminoles to remove to Indian Territory. In 1842, because Muscogee Creeks had settled on land promised to Seminoles in Indian Territory, conflict and tension arose between the Muscogee Creeks and Seminoles. This led to Muscogee Creeks kidnapping several Black Seminoles. In 1844, Washington declared that slave catchers could legally take Black Seminoles. Finally, by 1850, John Horse, Coacoochee, and many Black Seminoles had had enough fighting Muscogee Creek and white slave raiders as well as being treated poorly by the U.S. government. They migrated to Coahiula, Mexico, to get away from the threat of enslavement and abuse in Indian Territory.

After the Civil War, John Horse returned for a brief time to serve in the Seminole Negro Indian Scouts, a unit of the U.S. Army that served on the Texas frontier. John Horse finally returned to Mexico, and he died while traveling to Mexico City to garner additional land rights for his people in Mexico. To this day, descendants of these Black Seminoles live in Coahuila and others live nearby on the Texas side of the Rio Grande Valley.

considered the Seminoles part of the Muscogee Creek Nation. Because the Muscogee Creeks used chattel slavery, some among the Native Seminoles also began to adopt chattel slavery in Indian Territory. As Muscogee Creek and white slave catchers began kidnapping Black Seminoles, other Native Seminoles and Black Seminoles began to look toward moving to Mexico. At the same time, the U.S. attorney general decided that under U.S. law the Black Seminoles were still slaves. Finally, the Muscogee Creeks and whites began demanding that Black Seminoles disarm in the fall of 1849. In response, Black Seminoles and some Native Seminoles, totaling about 500 people, set out for Mexico. Slave catchers continued hunting those Black Seminoles who stayed behind in Indian Territory. For the next twenty years, the Black Seminoles in Mexico became a haven for Cherokee and Muscogee Creek runaway slaves before 1865 and freedmen after 1865, as well as some of those Black Seminoles who stayed behind in Indian Territory.

Mexico abolished slavery in 1829 and welcomed runaway slaves. As a result, the Black Seminoles were more than welcome in Mexico with the men serving in the Mexican Army. The United States, in 1856, recognized the Seminoles as an independent tribe, separate from the Muscogee Creeks and not governed by Creek law. In response, many of the Native and Black Seminoles decided to return to Indian Territory in late 1856. In early 1857, a smallpox epidemic broke out among those who remained in Mexico encouraging most of those who remained and survived the outbreak to head back to Indian Territory. However, numerous Black Seminole families stayed in Mexico.

Some of the remaining Black Seminoles in Mexico returned to Texas in 1870 because slavery had been abolished in the United States, and the army promised to hire the males and take care of their families. The army was willing to bring them back because it needed them to fight recalcitrant Natives from the southern Great Plains, and the military was not willing to depend on Texans who recently had served the Confederacy during the Civil War. The U.S. Army called the Black Seminole unit, the Seminole Negro Indian Scouts. This unit served with distinction until 1914, but they and their families faced constant discrimination. Whites in the state never accepted them and many former Confederates became outlaws, which

Black Seminole scouts on horseback. (Photographs and Prints Division, Schomburg Center for Research in Black Culture, The New York Public Library, Astor, Lenox and Tilden Foundations)

made them bitter enemies of this unit. The soldiers never received pensions they had been promised, and their families never received title to land that they had been guaranteed in Texas. Over time, some of these Black Seminoles returned to Mexico as others somehow managed to put down roots in Texas. Their descendants still occupy both sides of the Rio Grande Valley in Texas and Coahuila, Mexico.

The Rest of the Southeast

During the colonial period, white southerners exposed the Native tribes of the Southeast to chattel slavery. In fact from 1670 to roughly 1750, British colonials fueled an Indian slave trade that pitted one tribe against another in search of captives to be sold to the British for guns, ammunition, rum, and other trade items. Thus, from an early date, Natives and Africans mingled on the plantations of the South producing hundreds if not thousands of Black Indians. After 1750, some among the Cherokees, Chickasaws, Choctaws, and Muscogee Creeks began practicing a form of slavery with African slaves, but at this time, it was all together different from the chattel slavery practiced by white southerners. Often the only restrictions placed on these slaves were that they provide a portion of what they produced to their owners. These slaves, usually African males, often married into the tribe and the Natives considered their offspring to be free and equal members of the tribe.

However, the status of African slaves among these southern tribes changed after the United States gained its independence. During the George Washington administration, the United States developed a Native policy known as the Civilization Plan. Grounded in Enlightenment principles, the Civilization Plan hoped, through training and coexistence, to slowly accommodate Natives to Anglo-American lifestyle. Henry Knox and Thomas Jefferson, Washington's secretary of war and secretary of state, respectively, believed that it was in the best interest of Native Americans to give up hunting, which required vast space, and instead adopt the American yeoman-farmer lifestyle. (This policy ignored the reality that these people were already farmers when Europeans first came to North America.) This policy was well intentioned but naive. Eventually, when tribal officials were reluctant to give up land that stood in the way of America's progression to the West, federal traders were directed to open up credit lines to the tribes. In doing so, the government allowed Native debts to increase and eventually forced Native groups to pay off debts through land cession. Clearly, acquiring land was more important than the "civilization" of Native people.

In the Southeast, tribal members who participated in the Civilization Plan tended to adopt chattel slavery as well as the Anglo-American style of farming, and these people tended to be of mixed heritage, white fathers and Native mothers. The introduction of slavery divided the nation economically between the wealthy, elite minority and the poor majority that clung to traditional ways. The percentage of slaves among the Cherokees reached as high as 18 percent before Removal. The Chickasaws matched them at 18 percent with the Choctaws reaching 14 percent and the Muscogee Creeks topping out at 10 percent. These four tribes even adopted slave codes to keep their slaves in line. These codes included limits on slave travel, curfews, and prohibitions on learning to read and write. The Chickasaws treated their slaves almost as harshly as did white southerners, but the other three tribes tended to be less likely to abuse their slaves than white planters. Also, the Cherokees, Choctaws, and Muscogee Creeks tried to not break up families when they sold slaves.

Despite the assimilation of the mixed-blood elites (children of white males and Native females) and the effort of these elites to stop intermarriage between Natives and blacks, many traditional Cherokees, Chickasaws, Choctaws, and Muscogee Creeks continued to intermarry with slaves, free blacks, and runaway blacks, thus producing Black Indian offspring. Because these tribes were matrilineal, these Black Indians were considered full members of the nation, if the mother was a Native. Therefore, the issue of race and ethnicity continued to remain rather fluid among the Cherokees, Chickasaws, Choctaws, and Muscogee Creeks in the years before Removal.

In the 1830s, the U.S. government changed its Indian policy to one of forced removal of all eastern tribes to Indian Territory west of the Mississippi River in present-day Kansas and Oklahoma. The southeastern tribes were removed to Oklahoma. Removal created significant cultural, economic, political, and social disruptions among these people, and thousands died during these forced migrations that the Cherokees called the Trail of Tears.

In Indian Territory, slavery became more entrenched as whites continued to intermarry with these tribes in ever-greater numbers. Native slavery still remained milder than that of white southerners, however, and all five of the southern tribes, Cherokees, Chickasaws, Choctaws, Muscogee Creeks, and Seminoles (also known as the Five Civilized Tribes), eventually adjusted to the new territory and began to flourish, including the Black Indians in each nation. Ultimately, the Civil War engulfed Indian Territory and settled the slave question once and for all. To the detriment of all five of the southern tribes, the Civil War divided each nation over which side to take. By war's end, the region was decimated, and the U.S. government forced all of the tribes to emancipate their slaves. The Cherokees had already done so, and the Seminoles really had nothing to do because their slaves, in essence, were mostly free. The Muscogee Creeks moved quickly to comply. The Chickasaws and Choctaws resisted for decades, and once they freed their slaves, they resisted giving these freedmen equal status within their nation.

With the exception of the Seminoles, the freedmen of the Five Civilized Tribes, after emancipation, faced decades of discrimination and less-than-equal status among these tribes. Specifically, the four tribes challenged the freedmen's equal access to education, land, political participation, and occupational opportunity. Blacks among the Seminoles immediately began participating in politics, and Seminole freedmen and Black Seminoles established businesses, churches, and schools almost as soon. Freedmen began to build their lives among the other Civilized Tribes despite some opposition. Most decided to stay within their emancipating nation rather than venture out into the world dominated by whites, which was more openly hostile to freedmen. Black Indians and freedmen prospered among the Five Civilized like nowhere else. Despite the growing influence of whites among these tribes and increasing intermarriage between whites and the elites of the Five Civilized tribes, black prosperity encouraged more and more intermarriage between Natives of the Civilized Tribes and their freedmen, which greatly increased the number of biologically Black Indians in their midst.

Because some among the Five Tribes sided with the Confederacy, the U.S. government punished these tribes by taking a large percentage of the land guaranteed to them in Indian Territory by the removal treaties. Most of this land was given to western tribes as they were pacified and put onto reservations. This drastically increased the number of Natives living in Indian Territory as well as the number of different tribes. At the same time, it limited the power of any tribal government to actually control their own territory, the people who lived in it, and especially, any people who moved to it or through it. As a result, large numbers of outlaws descended on the territory and reeked havoc. Larger numbers of freedmen from the South also moved to Indian Territory to escape white intimidation and terrorism that grew in that region, especially after Reconstruction ended. Most stayed and married Native men and women. This led to a significant increase in the number of Black Indians living in Indian Territory, not only among the Five Civilized Tribes but also among the many western groups put onto reservations in the territory. They found greater safety and greater fulfillment living among Native people there. Although they faced some discrimination from some Natives in the territory and from the rapidly increasing white, immigrant population, Black Indians and freedmen living in Indian Territory found they had more status and rights there than anywhere else in the United States in the late 19th century.

The West

In the West beyond the Mississippi River, Africans were present in the very first explorations by the Spanish. The Spanish brought slaves with them when they first colonized New Mexico in the 16th century. This fact combined with the presence of an indigenous slave-raiding and exchange system already in place guaranteed that Black Indians probably appeared in the region soon after the Spanish arrival. Additionally, evidence now indicates that a Black Indian from Mexico played a significant role in the Pueblo Revolt of 1680. In all likelihood, Black Indians lived in considerable numbers among the Natives of the Southwest and southern Plains long before Anglo Americans found their way into the western frontier. However, clear documentation of Black Indians among western tribes does not begin until the 19th century.

The Black Indian presence in the history of the American West was first seen among fur traders primarily in the Rocky Mountains. In the early

19th century, the fur trade had become a significant business in the American economy. The first African Americans entered the West as lesser partners, employees, or slaves for white fur traders. These white traders found that negotiations with Natives went more smoothly when handled by Africans, probably because of negative contact with white imperialists for several centuries. Over time, the success of African Americans trading with Natives led to high wages and rewards for black traders who began to venture out on their own into the West. They quickly became some of the most trusted employees of the American fur companies. Many of the black traders began to live more and more among Native groups, took Native wives, and had Black Indian offspring. These Black Indians later played significant go-between roles as interpreters and negotiators as Americans flooded into the West during the second half of the 19th century.

Black Indians made their presence felt in the American West during the early 19th century on the southern Great Plains and in the Southwest. The Black Indians who probably lived among Natives in these areas since the 16th century were joined on the southern Plains by runaway slaves from Texas in the early 19th century. Runaways and Black Indians joined the Commanches, Kiowas, and Apaches who raided the Texas frontier from the time Texas gained its independence up to the end of the 19th century. Black Indians also were found living among California tribes just before the gold rush of 1849, and throughout the Southwest, Black Indians worked as gunrunners, interpreters, and traders with Native people, Mexicans, Texans, and the U.S. Army.

In the late 19th century, the Black Indian presence increased in the Southwest as freedmen moved into the area from and through Oklahoma and Texas and chose to side with Natives and their resistance to white control of the region. In some cases, freedmen and Black Indians became war leaders of Native bands because they best knew the tactics of white frontiersmen and the army, and they could exploit the weaknesses of these frontiersmen and the army. Ironically, in Texas, many of these hostile Black Indians fought against the Seminole Negro Indian Scouts whose fathers and grandfathers had earlier fought to preserve their and their Native Seminole allies' independence in Florida against the U.S. Army. These hostile Black Indians also fought Black Negro units in the U.S. Army made up of freedmen and commonly known in today's literature as buffalo soldiers. Thus, even at this late date, white America managed to pit Native against African American, Native against Black Indian, Black Indian against Black Indian, Black Indian against freedman, and freedman against freedman to maintain its hegemony over all people of color. When the U.S. Army finally pacified the Native people of the Southwest and southern Plains and consigned them to reservations, their Black Indian allies often accompanied them there and suffered with their Native allies, friends, and families. They took their place in an American history that has left Black Indians burdened by the weight of denigration caused by their dual heritage and, at the same time, confronted by a white America that denied them the benefits and security of that dual heritage.

References and Further Reading

Foster, Lawrence. *Negro-Indian Relationships in the Southeast*. Philadelphia: n.p., 1935.

Haliburton, Rudi, Jr. *Red over Black: Slavery among the Cherokee Indians*. Westport, CT: Greenwood Press, 1977.

Hammond, Peter B. "Afro-American Indians and Afro-Asians: Cultural Contacts Between Africa and the Peoples of Asia and Aboriginal America." In *Expanding Horizons in African Studies*, ed. Gwendolan M. Carter and Ann Paden. Evanston, IL: Northwestern University Press, 1969.

Katz, William Loren. *Black Indians*. New York: Simon Pulse, 1986.

Katz, William Loren, and Paula A. Franklin. *Proudly Red and Black*. New York: Maxwell/Macmillan, 1993.

Littlefield, Daniel F., Jr. *Africans and Seminoles: From Removal to Emancipation*. Westport, CT: Greenwood Press, 1977.

Littlefield, Daniel F., Jr. *The Cherokee Freedmen: From Emancipation to American Citizenship*. Westport, CT: Greenwood Press, 1978.

Lofton, John M., Jr. "White, Indian, and Negro Contacts in Colonial South Carolina." *Southern Indian Studies* 1 (1949): 3–12.

McLoughlin, William G. "Red Indians, Black Slavery, and White Racism: America's Slaveholding Indians." *American Quarterly* 26 (1974): 367–385.

Nash, Gary B. *Red, White, and Black: The Peoples of Early America*. Englewood Cliffs, NJ: Prentice-Hall, 1974.

Perdue, Theda. *Slavery and the Evolution of Cherokee Society, 1540–1866*. Knoxville: University of Tennessee Press, 1979.

Porter, Kenneth W. *The Black Seminoles: History of a Freedom-Seeking People*. Gainesville: University Press of Florida, 1996.

Porter, Kenneth W. *The Negro on the American Frontier*. New York: Arno Press and the New York Times, 1971.

Price, Edward T. "A Geographic Analysis of White-Negro-Indian Racial Mixtures in Eastern United States." *Annals of the Association of American Geographers* 43 (1953): 138–156.

Willis, William S., Jr. "Divide and Rule: Red, White, and Black in the Old South." In *Red, White, and Black: Symposium on Indians in the Old South*, ed. Charles M. Hudson. Athens: University of Georgia Press, 1971.

Wilson, Walt. "Freedmen in the Indian Territory During Reconstruction." *Chronicles of Oklahoma* 49 (1971): 230–244.

African American Leaders | 12

Paige Haggard

E ven at the dawn of the 19th century, it was obvious that slavery could not exist permanently in America and the efforts of African American leaders during this time changed the daily lives of slaves and freeman alike. They helped end the "peculiar institution" of slavery, ensured the freedom of blacks throughout America, and worked to bring justice to the oppressed population. Not only did these leaders change the lives of African Americans during the 1800s, their work sowed the seeds of the Civil Rights Movement that blossomed in the following century, thereby changing generations of lives.

Leaders of Slave Rebellions

On August 30, 1800, a slave blacksmith Gabriel, inspired by the principles of the American Revolution to free his fellow slaves, planned to weaken the Virginian slaveholders' power in an attack on Richmond. By setting fire to the warehouse district, the rebellion would distract the town's white population. Then the revolt would seize the armory and take the governor hostage. Weather delayed the rebellion's start and Gabriel ultimately was betrayed. He nearly escaped on the ship of a sympathetic captain; however, two slave shiphands turned him in. Seventy people were tried, forty-four were convicted, and more than twenty-five were hanged. Gabriel's organizational strategies and ideological framework were his legacy to future slave uprisings.

Charles Deslondes's insurrection in Louisiana followed less than a decade later. Like Gabriel, Deslondes planned to attack the state's economic center, in this case New Orleans. A combination of militia, angry slaveholders, and

U.S. troops crushed the ill-equipped army of men and women 35 miles outside the city.

The Denmark Vesey conspiracy in 1822 would have been America's most elaborate slave uprising. It is rumored that the plot involved the poisoning of wells and that the conspiracy went all the way up to South Carolina Governor Thomas Bennett's personal servants. Scheduled for Bastille Day, Vesey's plot centered on Charleston, the fifth-largest city in America. Vesey, a freed skilled laborer, planned to seize all arsenal and ships at port. Six infantry and cavalry companies of armed slaves would raze the city and annihilate its population. Vesey's insurgency would have been the largest slave uprising in U.S. history, involving as many as 9,000 slaves. Nevertheless, the plot leaked and 117 slaves were arrested along with eleven free blacks. Forty people were banished, and twenty-nine were hanged. Though Vesey's plan did not have a chance to start, its intimations shocked both Charleston and South Carolina to the core. More importantly, Vesey promoted negritude, the idea that blacks share a spiritual and cultural identity, a concept that would be critical for change in both this century and the next.

In 1831, the Nat Turner revolt shook the foundations of slavery in another part of the South, this time in Virginia. Turner had visions that led him to believe that God meant for him to lead his people out of slavery:

> I saw white spirits and black spirits engaged in battle, and the sun was darkened—the thunder rolled in the Heavens and blood flowed in streams—and I heard a voice saying, "Such is your luck, such you are called to see, and let it come rough or smooth, you must surely bare it." (Duff and Mitchell 1971, 6)

Nat Turner with fellow insurgent slaves during the Slave Rebellion of 1831. (Bridgeman Archive)

Taking a solar eclipse as a sign for the insurrection, he planned for the fourth of July, but when he fell ill that day, the rebellion was delayed until August 21. It involved sixty to eighty blacks and was quelled in forty hours.

These uprisings all voiced a fact that Martin Luther King Jr. would articulate a century later: "A riot is the language of the unheard" (King 1968). These revolts showed that slavery was criminal and the violence down South forced many black abolitionists to be less concerned with rhetoric and more active in their protests.

Leaders in the Free Black Community and the Abolition Movement

As the 19th century progressed, the number of free black voices protesting slavery increased drastically. The community's resistance to the American Colonization Society (ACS) encouraged this rise. ACS, founded in 1816, was a group working to colonize Liberia with free blacks. Many blacks cried in protest that ACS wanted "'to exile us from the land of our nativity'" (Ploski 1971, 14). It is not that the black community had not considered expatriatism. Paul Cuffe Sr., the richest African American in 1810, declared, "'Blacks would be better off in Africa, where we could rise to be a people'" (Thomas 1986, 31). But ACS as a group would not allow black leadership and the society depicted the race in a belittling manner. Many people also feared the society would eventually force deportation.

In Philadelphia in 1816, the earliest religious body that was distinctly African American, the African Methodist Episcopal Church, was formed as a protest against ACS. The organization of the African Methodist Episcopal Zion Church in New York City in 1821 was also in protest to ACS. These churches, along with many others, were crucial to the development of a cohesive African American culture and political movement. The churches gave the abolition movement its speakers and its audience and helped in the fight against bigotry; they served the social and cultural needs of the black community as well as its economic needs.

In fact, many Northern black abolitionists were pastors. In 1810, Reverend Daniel Cook wrote the protest pamphlet "Dialogue between a Virginian and an African Minister," which eloquently asserted the double standard of slavery by juxtaposing the moral loss of freedom with a mere financial loss:

> [E]mancipation would be unjust, because it would deprive men of their property but is there not injustice on both sides. . . . On one hand, we see a man deprived of all property; of all capacity to possess property; of his own free agency; of the means of instruction; of his wife and children; and of almost everything dear to him; on the other, a man deprived of eighty or one hundred pounds. (Cook 1969, 8)

A pastor of the first African Baptist Society in Albany, New York, Reverend Nathan Paul, pronounced out the hypocrisy of slavery within a democratic society in his address delivered in 1827 when New York abolished slavery:

> Strange, indeed, is the idea, that such a system, fraught with such consum-
> mate wickedness, should ever have found a place in this the otherwise hap-
> piest of all countries—a country, the very soil of which is said to be
> consecrated to liberty, and its fruits the equal rights of man. (Ploski 1971, 14)

Reverend H. Easton disputed the racial stereotyping in his 1837 treatise
entitled "A Treatise on the Intellectual Character and Civil and Political
Condition of the Colored People of the United States." Easton ironically
subverts the introduction of the Declaration of Independence's call to
abandon the British empire: "Good laws, and a good form of government,
are of but very little use to a wicked people" (Easton 1969, 27). He ration-
ally affirmed that "[c]omplexion has never been made the legal test of citizenship in any age of the world" (Easton 1969, 47). Easton discussed the
intellectual character and the political condition of blacks as he pointed
out the prejudice endured from the white populace as a result of unin-
formed generalizations. Printed into pamphlets, these men's ideas were
distributed to encourage more support to end slavery.

Newspapers were another social force within the black community that
tried to better the lives of blacks throughout the country. The first African
American newspaper was *Freedom's Journal* started March 16, 1827, by John
Russwurm and Samuel Cornish. The editors' intent was clear: "'In the spirit
of candor and humility we intend . . . to lay our case before the public with
a view to arrest the progress of prejudice, and to shield ourselves against its
consequent evils'" (Ploski 1971, 14). *Freedom's Journal* started four years
earlier than the more historically famous white abolitionist paper, *The Liberator*. Originally founded as part of the anti-colonization effort, *Freedom's
Journal*'s reach became much broader. With the journal, Russwurm and
Cornish provided a much needed voice for the black community:

> From the press and the pulpit we have suffered much by being incorrectly
> represented. Men whom we equally love and admire have not hesitated to
> represent us disadvantageously, without becoming personally acquainted
> with the true state of things, nor discerning between virtue and vice among
> us. (Cornish 2003, 4)

The journal, too, provided regional, national, and even international news
to its community. Its editorial topics covered slavery, lynching, and other
injustices. One of its goals was to bring equality to the black community.
The journal worked as a networking device for black leaders and their communities. The contributor list read like a who's who in the black Northern
communities of the 19th century. Though the journal lasted for only two
years, its existence was fundamental to the development of the emerging
African American community and set the precedence of the independent
press's importance in black activism. The newspaper changed both communication and organization within the African American community. By the
Civil War, at least 17 black papers were in existence, all of which were vital
in transforming the lives of African Americans.

Freedom's Journal in 1829 published David Walker's militantly antislavery tract, *An Appeal to the Coloured Citizens of the World*. Walker proclaims, "it

is no more harm for you to kill the man who is trying to kill you than it is for you to take a drink of water" (Walker 1969, 26). Because he knew it was not reaching the audience who really needed to hear it—the slaves—Walker printed up *Appeal* at his own expense as a pamphlet and distributed it down South. The scale at which Walker managed to infiltrate the South with the pamphlet was impressive and courageous, particularly given that it earned him a $3,000 bounty for his death and a $10,000 reward if he were captured alive. Walker called upon the slaves, asking, "Did our Creator make us to be slaves to dust and ashes like ourselves? Are they not dying worms as well as we?" (Walker 1969, 16). Because of this militant overtone, it was banned throughout much of the South. What really was revolutionary about Walker's tract, however, was the fact that he addressed the problem of consciousness that slavery created by indoctrinating the slave with ideas of "self" and "entitlement," two concepts the institution of slavery destroyed. The *Appeal* stressed empowerment of the slave and taught resistance to the oppression of slavery. Viewing a slave as a thinking, feeling human rather than as a beast or as an abstract cause was a radical perception and crucial in changing the lives of American blacks. Walker's *Appeal* embraced ideas that were later espoused by black nationalists of the 20th century: a unified struggle against oppression, racial pride, criticism of American capitalism, and the idea of self-government for African Americans.

The Negro Convention Movement influenced the black community of this time, and David Walker greatly influenced this movement with his involvement with the Massachusetts General Colored Association (MGCA) in 1828. Its organizational goals were unmistakable:

> The primary object of this Institution, is, to unite the colored population, so far, through the United States of America, as may be practicable and expedient; forming societies, opening, extending, and keeping up correspondences, and not withholding anything which may have the least tendency to meliorate our miserable condition. (Hinks 1997, 90)

The most political organization operating at the national level, the MGCA drastically changed the political consciousness of the African American community. The first National Negro Convention convened in 1830 in Philadelphia and decided on four main objectives for the black community: "Education, Temperance, Economy and Universal Liberty" (Hinks 1997, 90). With these four targets, the convention hoped to teach and support the African American community, from the wealthiest free black in the North to the lowliest slave down South. All of the conventions during this time further unified the community and raised its members above the societal factors that kept them down.

Slave Narratives and the Black Community

One of the most charismatic African American leaders of the 19th century was Frederick Douglass. Born a slave who escaped to freedom in

Henry Highland Garnet (1815–1882)

Born a slave in Maryland, Henry Highland Garnet's family escaped to New York where Garnet was fortunate enough to attend New York City's African Free School. Out of the city's nearly 16,000 children, he was one of only 300 who received any formal education. In 1835, he and three friends traveled 400 miles to continue their education at Noyes Academy in Canaan, New Hampshire. Because they were black, they were denied any sort of hospitality along the hard journey. They were at the school barely a month before an angry mob yoked the school building to ox and dragged it into a swamp half a mile away. Luckily, Oneida Institute in New York opened its doors to African Americans, and Garnet was able to become a Presbyterian minister; he dedicated his life to improving his community.

Garnet was, in many ways, a radical and he played a key role moving the abolition movement from the stance of moral suasion to one of political action. He reissued David Walker's *Appeal* in 1848 with his own "Address to the Slaves of the United State of America." Garnet proclaimed that it was sinful for the slaves to allow themselves to remain slaves: "Unless the image of God is obliterated from the soul, all men cherish the love of Liberty" (Garnet 1997). He called for the slaves to rise up and claim their freedom, "You had better all die—*die immediately* than live as slaves and entail your wretchedness upon your posterity" (Wiltse 1969). Three years later, Garnet's political views had evolved to supporting economic boycotts to

end slavery. He toured the British Isles and Europe lecturing and writing for the Free Produce movement, a group which encouraged boycotting products of the slave economy. By the 1856 elections, Garnet had joined the Republican Party in his efforts to end slavery.

When Congress passed the Thirteenth Amendment, Lincoln asked Garnet to commemorate the end of slavery with a memorial sermon in the chambers of the House of Representatives. It was a historic event; his eloquence and intelligence combined with his dark complexion and good looks were strong arguments against the myths of black inferiority bred by the institution of slavery.

Garnet was especially active in trying to get full voting rights for all black men. Unfortunately, his petitions to the New York state legislature were ineffective, and it took the Fifteenth Amendment to bring about those civil liberties. He encouraged the development of black newspapers and labor unions to educate the community and protect the rights of its members.

A man of action as well as words, Garnet administered to the black community in America and to the community abroad. He helped fugitive slaves escape to freedom and was physically beaten when he tried to desegregate the Buffalo and Niagara train. He founded a school for free children in Geneva, and as a missionary in Jamaica, he created a day school for black men and a Female Industrial School. Garnet died in Monrovia two months after assuming his position as U.S. minister to Liberia.

the North, it was only reasonable for Douglass to take up the abolition cause. Massachusetts Antislavery Society hired him as a lecturer in 1841. Douglass believed, like his mentor, the white abolitionist William Lloyd Garrison, in moral suasion. As a philosophy, it stressed the obvious moral and ethical problems of slavery: "Slavery makes it necessary for the slaveholder to commit all conceivable outrages on the miserable slave. It is impossible to hold the slaves in bondage without this" (Douglass 1993, 65). Douglass, a powerful speaker, told and retold the story of his life as a slave to audience after audience until he finally published in 1845 *The Narrative of the Life of Frederick Douglass: Written by Himself*. It was, in some ways, more compelling than his early lectures, partially because the written format clearly illustrated how gifted and eloquent Douglass really was. After his nearly two-year tour of Britain, he soon found himself to be a leader of the abolition movement in his own right, independent of Garrison and his influence. By the end of 1847, Douglass started his own newspaper, *North Star*, which rivaled the *Liberator* and would remain in publication under three different names for sixteen years. The severe nature of the Fugitive Slave Act of 1850 made Douglass see that a more proactive approach was necessary and he began to understand that violence might be necessary to end slavery's reign in the South. However, he could also see that the Constitution was the key to ending slavery.

Many other former slaves added their stories to the outcry against slavery. These personal accounts showed the travesties of slavery by pulling from the audience both sympathy for the slave and outrage against slaveholders. Henry Bibb, a slave in the Deep South, achieved his freedom through the death of his owner in 1842. He published his autobiography, *Narrative of the Life and Adventures of Henry Bibb, An American Slave*, seven years later. He was active with the abolition movement in New England and in Michigan. After the Fugitive Slave Act in 1850, he moved to Ontario and started a bimonthly abolition paper, *Voice of the Fugitive*, which he used to help other African Americans to immigrate to Canada. By his death in 1854, Bibb had helped, by way of Refugees' Home Society, forty immigrants get forty acres of land.

Harriet Ann Jacobs was another slave with a famous autobiography, *Incidents in the Life of a Slave Girl*. She recounted the constant sexual attention she received from her master, thus revealing the sexual perversity inherent to the dynamic of master and slave. Her story showed the double standard of womanhood within Southern culture because only white women were protected from sexual predators.

Lewis G. Clarke, originally a slave in Kentucky, became a renowned antislavery spokesman. His speech given in 1842 in Brooklyn discussed bluntly the devastating effects not just of the depraved sexual desires of slave masters but of the slave patrols, or as he calls them, "patter rollers." These patrols were effectively slave police and given free reign to do as they pleased. They whipped slaves and had their way with the slave women, often in front of husbands, brothers, fathers, and sons. "Maybe you think, because they're slaves, they ain't got no feeling and no shame! A woman being a slave don't stop her genteel ideas; that is, according to their way, and as far as they *can*. They know they must submit" (Clarke 1997, 631). Clarke co-authored a slave narrative that reached a wide audience both in the United States and abroad.

Sojourner Truth, a former slave, spoke out for the abolition of slavery and for women's rights in America. (Library of Congress)

Sojourner Truth was probably the most well-known 19th-century black woman. A slave in New York, she had a total of five masters and was freed July 4, 1827, when the state abolished slavery. She became a wandering evangelist in June 1843. By 1850, with the help of Garrison, she published the story of her life in *Narrative of Sojourner Truth: A Northern Slave*. She spoke out against the institution until its demise with the Emancipation Proclamation.

The Underground Railroad and Overt Resistance to Slavery

Free blacks fought slavery in more subversive ways than lectures and publications. The Underground Railroad was a network of routes and safe houses that aided the escape of slaves. Northern free states were destinations, but so, too, were Canada, Mexico, and locations overseas. One of the most celebrated of the Underground Railroad's conductors was Harriett Tubman. She escaped from slavery in 1843 because she was afraid of being sold farther down South. Later Tubman freed her parents and four brothers. She returned thirteen times to the South, personally escorted about seventy slaves, and freed seventy more just by way of her instructions.

In Boston, one of the Underground Railroad stops was the home of Lewis and Harriet Hayden. The Haydens were born into slavery in Kentucky, but they escaped in 1844. Harriet ran a boarding house out of their home on 66 Phillips Street and Lewis owned a clothing store. Beneath this prosperous middle-class exterior, they housed an underground tunnel. There, they hid escaped slaves, and Lewis used his clothing store to outfit runaways in the appropriate clothing of a free black.

In addition to the Underground Railroad, free blacks resisted fugitive slave laws. This resistance became greatly publicized after 1850 with the passing of a more severe Fugitive Slave Act. In 1851, Virginian masters and black abolitionists fought in Christiana, Pennsylvania, a conflict that had a bloody end. Boston saw an attempt to rescue Anthony Burns in 1854. Lewis Hayden was active in this rescue and in the Fredric Wilkins (also known as Shadrach Minkins) rescue from a Boston courthouse in 1851 as well. In the Oberlin-Wellington rescue of 1858, Charles Henry Langston, the grandfather of poet Langston Hughes, led a group of both black and white abolitionists to liberate John Price. Price, a resident of Oberlin, was kidnapped and held as a fugitive slave. Langston and his group successfully freed Price. Langston was tried and convicted for his involvement in the rescue, but his sentence was reduced because the community viewed Langston as a hero, not as a criminal.

Moses Dickson, a free black from Cincinnati, had another idea for ending slavery—a national uprising. He formed a secret organization called the Knights of Liberty. In 1856, more than 47,240 members had joined the organization throughout the country, all ready to fight for the freedom of their brothers still bound in the shackles of slavery. With the onset of the war, the group disbanded and many joined the Union.

Dred Scott was one slave who sought freedom not through flight nor the podium but rather through the courts. Born "Sam" in Virginia, once Scott's first owner died, a second man, John Emerson, bought him and they moved to Illinois, a free state, and Wisconsin, a territory. Scott repeatedly sought to buy his freedom or to escape but to no avail. In 1843, Emerson died and left his estate to his widow; she also denied Scott his freedom. He attained the aid of two lawyers who helped him sue for his freedom in a county court. He lost the first suit, but in 1847 won his

A slave who had moved with his owner to territory where slavery was prohibited, Dred Scott sued for his freedom in 1846, starting an eleven-year court battle that resulted in the landmark Supreme Court decision in *Scott v. Sandford* (1857). (Bettmann/Corbis)

freedom in a second trial. The positive ruling was based on the concept that moving residence to a free state invalidated his slave status. The Supreme Court overturned this ruling in 1857, stating that slaves were not citizens of the United States and therefore had no claims in a court of law. Although his owner finally gave him his freedom, the court's ruling allowed for the expansion of slavery into the territories and is one of the many factors that brought on the Civil War.

African American Leaders during and after the Civil War

The war changed the focus of the leaders of the black community. Tubman worked as a spy for the Union Army. She led a raid at Combahee Ferry in 1863; she suggested both the location and the plan for the raid. The attack liberated more than 750 slaves.

Douglass recognized that the secession could bring about emancipation so he continually urged Lincoln to free the slaves. The first few years of the war, he wrote editorials and gave speeches in support of the war. He was active in recruiting African Americans into the army, but he quit because of discrimination against black recruits. Douglass spent the latter part of the war touring with a new speech, "The Mission of the War." He argued that the country must view the war as a new revolution so that the nation could regenerate itself from the years of prejudice against African Americans that slavery and its dogma created.

Sojourner Truth recruited for the Union troops, too. She worked for National Freedman's Relief Association in Washington, D.C. during 1864 to make conditions better for her fellow African Americans. Truth also worked to desegregate the streetcars in D.C.

Civil Rights and Political Activism after the War

Once the war was won and slavery ended, the community shifted its energy to achieving social equality. Inroads to this goal were built before the war and their effects were felt well into the 20th century. William C. Nell led a campaign to desegregate Boston's railroads in 1843 and its performance halls in 1853. He co-authored a petition to Massachusetts' legislature to desegregate Boston schools as well; this petition had 2,000 signatures from people in the black community. Benjamin Roberts filed a suit to integrate Boston schools in 1848. Both these men laid the groundwork for *Brown v. The Board of Education* of the 1950s.

The 1870s witnessed many African Americans active in politics on local and national levels. In 1870, the first black member of the House of Representatives, Joseph H. Rainy, and the first black senator, Hiriam Dewels, held office. Richard H. Cain was elected to an at-large seat in the House for South Carolina and he pushed a civil rights bill proposed in 1870. Alonzo J. Ransier, another South Carolinian member of Congress, fought for a Civil Rights bill in addition to supporting a six-year presidential term and opposing a salary increase for federal employees. In 1875,

Congress passed a civil rights bill that prohibited discrimination in public places like hotels and theaters and sought to "'[m]ete out equal and exact justice to all, of whatever nativity, race, color, or persuasions, religious or political'" (Ploski 1971, 243). Unfortunately, the Supreme Court ruled that the bill was unconstitutional in 1883. During his term George Henry White tried to make lynching a crime by introducing a bill to Congress in the last years of the century.

Before the Civil War, lynching was not typically a crime against black people in the South. However, after the war, lynching increasingly was used against the black community. In a ten-year period, from 1882 to 1892, the number of blacks lynched increased by 200 percent. Journalist Ida B. Well began her anti-lynching campaign shortly after three of her friends were lynched because their business was doing better than a competing white business:

> Nobody in this section believes the old threadbare lie that Negro men assault white women. If Southern whites are not careful, they will overreach themselves and public sentiment will have a reaction, a conclusion will be reached which will be very damaging to the moral reputation of their women.
> (Royster 1997, 1)

These words led to her exile from the South and started her crusade. She wanted to debunk the lynching myth—that lynching was a response only to the rape of a white woman. She wanted to reveal the truth about lynching; it was a system of terrorism used by whites to keep the black community in check. She deconstructed the lynching myths with her own statistics and those provided by the *Chicago Tribune*, a reputable white newspaper. She wrote three pamphlets, "Southern Horrors: Lynch Law in All Its Phases," "A Red Record," and "Mob Rule in New Orleans." Wells went on speaking tours in England and wrote numerous articles and editorials for various sources about lynching. She brought lynching out as the hate crime that it really was. As a result of her campaign, Memphis newspapers actually denounced lynching as a practice and no lynchings occurred in Memphis for more than twenty years. Douglass was helpful in getting her campaign started. He wrote an introduction for her first pamphlet and introduced her to the women who sponsored her speaking tour of England; one of his speeches, "Why the Negro Is Lynched," inspired her second pamphlet.

After the war, Douglass continued his quest to better conditions for his fellow blacks. He continued with lectures and printed new editions of his autobiography. He took a post as the Haitian ambassador and his last speech denounced lynching, "The Lessons of an Hour." By Douglass's death February 20, 1895, Booker T. Washington had taken over as the new spokesperson of the African American community.

Washington was born a slave in 1856 in Virginia and was freed at age nine by the war. At the age of twenty-five, Washington became the principal of a new normal school for blacks in Alabama. This school became the Tuskegee University, an institution that provided many opportunities for the African American community. Though it provided academic education

Ida B. Wells (1862–1931)

Ida B. Wells was born July 16, 1862, in Holly Springs, Mississippi, to two slaves, James and Elizabeth Warrenton Wells. After the war, her parents were politically active, an inclination their daughter would inherent. At the age of sixteen, after her parents' death from yellow fever, Wells found herself in charge of her five siblings. She left school to pass her county's teaching examination and took a position 6 miles away. During the week, a friend of her mother looked after the children, and on the weekends, Wells came home to take care of the house and her family. Her aunt invited her to move to Memphis after a year of this grueling routine. Wells arranged for her two brothers to apprentice with a tradesman in Holly Springs and for relatives to take care of her physically handicapped sister. She and her two remaining sisters moved to Memphis. As a result of her teaching experience, she became the editor of *Evening Star*.

In 1884, Wells was forced from a seat on the ladies' coach on a train. Though she sued the railroad company and won the suit, the Tennessee Supreme Court overturned the ruling. *Living Way*, a weekly religious paper, asked her to write a weekly column. This column was in the form of letters to the reader, which she signed under the name "Iola," the name she signed for her infamous editorial that led to her exile from the South eight years later. Wells became co-owner of the *Free Speech and Headlight* in 1889. When she and J. L. Fleming bought out the other owner, the name was shortened to *Free Speech*. An editorial she wrote against the school board resulted in her being fired from her teaching position. By the age of twenty-six, Wells had become a businesswoman, a syndicated journalist, and an outspoken commentator on her community. Her political activism and outspoken nature was unusual not only for a woman so young but was extraordinary for any woman during this time period.

On March 9, 1892, Wells' future took a drastic shift. Three of her friends were lynched as a result of their store doing better financially than a store owned by a white man. She realized that lynching was not a matter of defending the honor of white women, as was the commonly held perception; she realized it was an act of terrorism designed to keep the black race subservient to whites. When she wrote her infamous editorial on May 21, she was on her way to a conference in New York. There she learned that the paper's offices had been broken into, the equipment was destroyed, and her partner barely escaped with his life. She also heard that some Memphis whites promised she would be tortured and killed should she ever come to Tennessee again. It would be thirty years before she would go south again. "Having lost my paper, had a price put on my life and been made an exile from home for hinting at the truth, I felt that I owed it to myself and to my race to the whole truth now that I was where I could do freely" (Wells 1997).

for teachers, its main focus was vocational skills for blacks. In fact this was the main focus of Washington's approach to civil rights:

> The education that the American Negroes most need for the next fifty to one hundred years should be mostly, but not exclusively, along scientific and industrial lines. When I say scientific, I mean science so applied that it will enable the black boy who comes from a plantation where ten bushels of corn

were being raised, to return to the farm and raise fifty bushels on the same acre. (Washington 1898, BR558)

He believed that thrift, patience, and industry would lead the way to equality for blacks. Because of his focus on work, ethics, and education, Washington befriended many white philanthropists such as Henry H. Rogers, Julius Rosenwald, and Anna T. Jeanes. In 1896, Washington asked George Washington Carver to teach agriculture at the school and to head the Tuskegee experiment station. Carver would later bring fame to himself, to the institute, and to the lowly peanut in the 1920s. Tuskegee made Washington the most powerful black man in America. He could buy black newspapers to control their coverage and could sway schools through his influence over philanthropists. He even had the president's ear. Washington secretly funded court cases that would further civil rights for African Americans.

In addition to promising the white audience that blacks would focus on the basic industries of life, Washington stated in his famous 1895 Atlanta Compromise Speech, "In all things that are purely social we can be as separate as the fingers, yet one as the hand in all things essential to mutual progress" (Washington 1974, 585). Many applauded his statements in this address; even his most adamant critic, W. E. B. Du Bois, supported Washington at first, but by the turn of the century, Du Bois disagreed with much of Washington's ideology. He felt that segregation only encouraged further misunderstandings between the races. He believed that only focusing on vocational education would sell short what he called "The Talented Tenth" of the black populace. Du Bois did not believe in the "Tuskegee Machine" because it was hypocritical of Washington to say that blacks should not get involved in politics then be heavily involved with politics.

Born a slave in 1856, Booker T. Washington became an activist for racial justice and one of the most influential educators in American history. (Library of Congress)

He distrusted the fact that all of Washington's money, and hence his power, came from white capitalists. Du Bois wrote, "The Negro intelligentsia was to be suppressed and hammered into conformity. The process involved some cruelty and disappointment but that was inevitable. This was the real force back of the Tuskegee Machine" (Du Bois 1962, 201). Du Bois held a doctorate from Harvard and received a fellowship to study Philadelphia's seventh ward slums; this was the first time anyone had applied the scientific approach to the social sciences. *The Philadelphia Negro* was an exhaustive work that showed the problems blacks faced were not rooted in their character but rather in their environment and circumstances, two things he felt that Washington's attitude encouraged. Ultimately, these two men foreshadowed the two paths future black leaders would take: the path of moderation and accommodation versus a more radical path that attacked prejudice head on.

One surprising Washington supporter was T. Thomas Fortune. A newspaper man responsible for *The Globe*, *The New York Age*, and *New York Freeman*, Fortune was known for his militancy, but he ghostwrote speeches for Washington. The term "Afro-American" was popularized by Fortune. He also created the Afro-American League, a predecessor of the National Association for the Advancement of Colored People (NAACP). With the League, he hoped to create a nonpartisan political and education agency for the black community to make protests against lynching, segregation, and discrimination more effective and more powerful. The League followed through with cases that had obvious legal violations of African American rights. Its first victory came when Fortune sued a white hotel where he was arrested for trespassing and disturbing the peace. He sued for false arrest and won, receiving $1,016.23. Another winning case was when Reverend William Heard sued a train company for being ejected from a car. He won a $300 settlement and a promise that Pullman would change their segregation policy. The League unfortunately did not have enough money to carry the case any further up the U.S. legal system and ended up being very short-lived; however, the Afro-American Council took the place of the League in 1899. The council was very liberal as its constitution stipulated that at least one woman must be included in the three executive positions. Just like the League, the council set the way for the NAACP of the 20th century. It is through these leaders of the 19th century that the African American community found its voice and its power for change.

References and Further Reading

Aptheker, Herbert. "The Event." In *Nat Turner: A Slave Rebellion in History and Memory*, ed. Kenneth S. Greenberg. Oxford: Oxford University Press, 2003.

Bacon, Jacqueline. *Freedom's Journal: The First African-American Newspaper*. Lanham, MD: Lexington Books, 2007.

Bell, Howard Holman. *A Survey of the Negro Convention Movement.* New York: Arno Press, 1969.

Bibb, Henry. *The Life and Adventures of Henry Bibb, an American Slave*, ed. Charles J. Heglar. Madison: University of Wisconsin Press, 2004.

Clarke, Lewis G. "The Testimony of a Former Slave." In *Sources of the African-American Past: Primary Sources in American History*, ed. Roy E. Finkenbine. New York: Longman, 1997.

Clinton, Catherine. *Harriet Tubman: The Road to Freedom.* New York: Little, Brown, 2004.

Cook, Daniel. "A Dialogue Between a Virginian and an African Minister." In *Negro Protest Pamphlets*, ed. William Loren Katz. New York: Arno Press, 1969.

Cornish, Samuel E., and John Russwurm. "The First Negro Newspaper's Opening Editorial, 1827." In *African American Political Thought*, vol. 5, *Integration vs. Separation: The Colonial Period to 1945*, ed. Marcus D. Pohlmann. New York: Routledge, 2003.

Crouch, Stanley, and Playthell Benjamin. *Reconsidering the Souls of Black Folk: Thoughts on the Groundbreaking Classic Work of W. E. B. Du Bois.* Philadelphia: Running Press, 2002.

Douglass, Frederick. *Narrative of the Life of Frederick Douglass, an American Slave, Written by Himself*, ed. David W. Blight. Boston: Bedford/St. Martin's, 1993.

Du Bois, W. E. B. "My Early Relations with Booker T. Washington." In *Booker T. Washington and His Critics: The Problem of Negro Leadership*, ed. Hugh Hawkins. Lexington, MA: D. C. Heath, 1962.

Du Bois, W. E. B. *The Philadelphia Negro.* Philadelphia: University of Pennsylvania Press, 1996.

Du Bois, W. E. B. *The Souls of Black Folk.* New York: Dover Publications, 1994.

Duff, John B., and Peter M. Mitchell, eds. *The Nat Turner Rebellion: The Historical Event and the Modern Controversy.* New York: Harper & Row, 1971.

Easton, Reverend H. "A Treatise on the Intellectual Character and Civil and Political Condition of the Colored People of the U. States; and the Prejudice Exercised Toward Them with a Sermon on the Duty of the Church to Them." In *Negro Protest Pamphlets*, ed. William Loren Katz. New York: Arno Press, 1969.

Egerton, Douglas R. *Gabriel's Rebellion: The Virginia Slave Conspiracies of 1800 and 1802.* Chapel Hill: University of North Carolina Press, 1993.

Egerton, Douglas R. *He Shall Go Out Free: The Lives of Denmark Vesey.* Madison, WI: Madison House Publishers, 1999.

Factor, Robert L. *The Black Response to America: Men, Ideals, and Organization, from Frederick Douglass to the NAACP.* Reading, MA: Addison-Wesley, 1970.

Finkenbine, Roy E., ed. *Sources of the African-American Past: Primary Sources in American History.* New York: Longman, 1997.

Finkleman, Paul. *Dred Scott v. Sanford: A Brief History with Documents.* New York: Bedford/St. Martin's, 1997.

Foster, Frances Smith. "Frances Ellen Watkins Harper." In *Black Women in America: An Historical Encyclopedia*, vol. 1, ed. Darlene Clark Hine. New York: Carlson, 1993.

Franklin, John Hope, and August Meier, eds. *Black Leaders in the Twentieth Century.* Champaign: University of Illinois Press, 1982.

Garnett, Henry Highland. "Let Your Motto Be Resistance." In *Sources of the African-American Past: Primary Sources in American History,* ed. Roy E. Finkenbine. New York: Longman, 1997.

Gross, Bella. "The First National Negro Convention." *Journal of Negro History* 31, no. 4 (October 1946): 435–443.

Harlan, Louis R. *Booker T. Washington: The Making of a Black Leader, 1856–1901.* London: Oxford University Press, 1975.

Harris Sheldon H. *Paul Cuffe: Black American and African Return.* New York: Simon and Schuster, 1972.

Harris, Thomas E. *Analysis of the Clash over the Issues between Booker T. Washington and W. E. B. Du Bois.* New York: Garland Publishing, 1993.

Harrold, Stanley. "Slave Rebels and Black Abolitionists." *A Companion to African American History,* ed. Alton Hornsby, Jr. Malden, MA: Blackwell Publishing, 2005.

Hinks, Peter P. *To Awaken My Afflicted Brethren: David Walker and the Problem of Antebellum Slave Resistance.* University Park: Pennsylvania State University Press, 1997.

Humez, Jean M. *Harriet Tubman: The Life and the Life Stories.* Madison: University of Wisconsin Press, 2003.

Jacobs, Harriet. *Incidents in the Life of a Slave Girl.* Clayton, DE: Prestwick House, 2006.

Justensen, Benjamin R. *George Henry White: An Even Chance in the Race of Life.* Baton Rouge: Louisiana State University Press, 2001.

Katz, Johnathan. *Resistance at Christiana: The Fugitive Slave Rebellion, Christiana, Pennsylvania, September 11, 1851—a Documentary Account.* New York: Crowell, 1974.

King, Martin Luther, Jr. "The Other America." Grosse Pointe High School, Grosse Pointe Farms, MI, March 14, 1968.

Mabee, Carleton, and Susan Mabee Newhouse. *Sojourner Truth: Slave, Prophet, Legend.* New York: New York University Press, 1993.

Muraskin, William A. *Middle-Class Blacks in a White Society: Prince Hall Freemasonry in America.* Berkeley: University of California Press, 1975.

Pasternak, Martin B. *Rise Now and Fly to Arms: The Life of Henry Highland Garnet.* New York: Garland Publishing, 1995.

Paul, Nathaniel. "An Address, Delivered on the Celebration of the Abolition of Slavery in the State of New York." In *Negro Protest Pamphlets*, ed. William Loren Katz. New York: Arno Press, 1969.

Pearson, Edward A., ed. *Designs against Charleston: The Trial Records of the Denmark Vesey Slave Conspiracy of 1822*. Chapel Hill: University of North Carolina Press, 1998.

Ploski, Harry A., ed. *Reference Library of Black America*. New York: Bellwether, 1971.

Pohlmann, Marcus D., ed. *Integration vs. Separation: The Colonial Period to 1945*. Vol. 5 of *African American Political Thought*. New York: Routledge, 2003.

Ragsdale, Bruce A., and Joel D. Tresse. *Black Americans in Congress, 1870–1989*. Washington, DC: U.S. Government Printing Office, 1990.

Robboy, Stanley J., and Anita W. Robboy. "Lewis Hayden: From Fugitive Slave to Statesman." *New England Quarterly* 46 (1973): 591–613.

Robertson, Dave. *Denmark Vesey*. New York: Alfred A. Knopf, 1999.

Sanchez-Eppler, Karen. *Touching Liberty: Abolition, Feminism, and the Politics of Body*. Berkeley: University of California Press, 1993.

Schor, Joel. *Henry Highland Garnet: A Voice of Black Radicalism in the Nineteenth Century*. Westport, CT: Greenwood Press, 1977.

Sheridan, Richard B. "Charles Henry Langston and the African American Struggle in Kansas." *Kansas History* 22 (Winter 1999/2000): 268–283.

Sidbury, James. *Ploughshares into Swords: Race, Rebellion, and Identity in Gabriel's Virginia, 1730–1810*. New York: Cambridge University Press, 1997.

Starobin, Robert S., ed. *Denmark Vesey: The Slave Conspiracy of 1822*. Englewood Cliffs, NJ: Prentice-Hall, 1970.

Thomas, Lamont D. *Rise to Be a People: A Biography of Paul Cuffe*. Urbana: University of Illinois Press, 1986.

Truth, Sojourner. *Narrative of Sojourner Truth*, ed. Margaret Washington. New York: Vintage Books, 1993.

Verney, Kevern. *The Art of the Possible: Booker T. Washington and Black Leadership in the United States, 1881–1925*. New York: Routledge, 2001.

Walker, David. *Appeal, in Four Articles Together with a Preamble to the Coloured Citizens of the World, but in Particular and Very Expressly to Those of the United States of America*, ed. Charles M. Wiltse. New York: Hill and Wang, 1969.

Washington, Booker T. "The Atlanta Exposition Address." In *Booker T. Washington and His Critics: The Problem of Negro Leadership*, ed. Hugh Hawkins. Lexington, MA: D. C. Heath, 1962.

Washington, Booker T. *Black-Belt Diamonds: Gems from the Speeches, Addresses, and Talks to Students*, ed. Victoria Earle Matthews. New York: Negro Universities Press, 1969.

Washington, Booker T. *The Booker T. Washington Papers,* vol. 3, ed. Louis R. Harlan. Chicago: University of Illinois Press, 1974.

Washington, Booker T. "Needs of the Negro: Passages from the Writing of Booker T. Washington." *New York Times.* August 20, 1898, BR558.

Wells, Ida B. *Southern Horrors and Other Writings,* ed. Jacqueline Jones Royster. Boston: Bedford/St. Martin's, 1997.

Primary Documents

Compiled by Shelby Callaway and Jennifer Hildebrand
Edited with comments by Dixie Ray Haggard

"An Oration on the Abolition of the Slave Trade," Reverend Peter Williams Jr., 1808

The United States banned the importation of slaves into the United States beginning on January 1, 1808. Although southerners managed to continue to bring in slaves illegally from Africa up to 1865, free African Americans and abolitionists in 1808 were hopeful that the United States was moving in the direction of abolishing the institution with the passage of this ban. Responding to the ban, Reverend Peter Williams Jr. gave this speech in to the New York African Church.

Fathers, Brethren, and Fellow Citizens: At this auspicious moment I felicitate you on the abolition of the Slave Trade. . . .

But to us, Africans and descendants of Africans, this period is deeply interesting. We have felt, sensibly felt, the sad effects of this abominable traffic. It has made, if not ourselves, our forefathers and kinsmen its unhappy victims; and pronounced on them, and their posterity, the sentence of perpetual slavery. But benevolent men have voluntarily stepped forward to obviate the consequences of this injustice and barbarity. They have striven assiduously, to restore our natural rights; to guaranty them from fresh innovations; to furnish us with necessary information; and to stop the source from whence our evils have flowed.

The fruits of these laudable endeavors have long been visible; each moment they appear more conspicuous; and this day has produced an event which shall ever be memorable and glorious in the annals of history. We are now assembled to celebrate this momentous era; to recognize the beneficial influences of humane exertions; and by suitable demonstrations of joy, thanksgiving, and gratitude, to return to our heavenly Father, and to our earthly benefactors, our sincere acknowledgments. . . .

. . . But let us no longer pursue a theme of boundless affliction. An enchanting sound now demands your attention. Hail, hail, glorious day, whose resplendent rising disperseth the clouds which have hovered with destruction over the land of Africa, and illumines it by the most brilliant rays of future prosperity. Rejoice, oh Africans! No longer shall tyranny, war, and injustice, with irresistible sway, desolate your native country; no longer shall torrents of human blood deluge its delightful plains; no longer shall it witness your countrymen wielding among each other the instruments of death; nor the insidious kidnapper, darting from his midnight haunt, on the feeble and unprotected; no longer shall its shores resound with the awful howlings of infatuated warriors, the deathlike groans of vanquished innocents, nor the clanking fetters of woe doomed captives. Rejoice, Oh, ye descendants of Africans! No longer shall the United States of America, nor the extensive colonies of Great Britain, admit the degrading commerce of the human species; no longer shall they swell the tide of African misery by the importation of slaves. Rejoice, my brethren, that the channels are obstructed through which slavery, and its direful concomitants, have been entailed on the African race. But let incessant strains of gratitude be mingled with your expressions of joy. Through the infinite mercy of the great Jehovah, this day announces the abolition of the Slave Trade. Let, therefore, the heart that is warmed by the smallest drop of African blood glow in grateful transports, and cause the lofty arches of the sky to reverberate eternal praise to his boundless goodness.

Oh, God! we thank Thee, that thou didst condescend to listen to the cries of Africa's wretched sons, and that Thou didst interfere in their behalf. At Thy call humanity sprang forth and espoused the cause of the oppressed; one hand she employed in drawing from their vitals the deadly arrows of injustice; and the other holding a shield, to defend them from fresh assaults; and at that illustrious moment, when the sons of '76 pronounced these United States free and independent; when the spirit of patriotism erected a temple sacred to liberty; when the inspired voice of Americans first uttered those noble sentiments, "We hold these truths to be self-evident, that all men are created equal; that they are endowed by their Creator with certain unalienable rights; among which are life, liberty, and the pursuit of happiness"; and when the bleeding African, lifting his fetters, exclaimed, "Am I not a man and a brother"; then, with redoubled efforts, the angel of humanity strove to restore to the African race the inherent rights of man. . . .

May the time speedily commence when Ethiopia shall stretch forth her hands; when the sun of liberty shall beam resplendent on the whole African race; and its genial influences promote the luxuriant growth of knowledge and virtue.

Source: Peter Williams, "An Oration on the Abolition of the Slave Trade," Delivered in the African Church, in the City of New York, January 1, 1808 (New York: Samuel Wood, 1808).

Freedom's Journal, *Initial Editorial on March 16, 1827*

The Editors of *Freedom's Journal* were John B. Russwurm and Samuel Cornish. In this editorial, they explain the purpose for publishing the first African American–owned and –operated newspaper.

TO OUR PATRONS

In presenting our first number . . . a moment's reflection upon the noble objects, which we have in view by the publication of this Journal; . . . For we believe, that a paper devoted to the dissemination of useful knowledge among our brethren, and to their moral and religious improvement, must meet with the cordial approbation of every friend to humanity.

The peculiarities of this Journal, renders it important that we should advertise to the world our motives by which we are actuated, and the objects which we contemplate.

We wish to plead our own cause. Too long have others spoken for us. Too long has the publick been deceived by misrepresentations, in things which concern us dearly, though in the estimation of some mere trifles; for though there are many in society who exercise towards us benevolent feelings; still (with sorrow we confess it) there are others who make it their business to enlarge upon the least trifle, which tends to the discredit of any person of colour; and pronounce anathemas and denounce our whole body for the misconduct of this guilty one. . . .

. . . The interesting fact that there are FIVE HUNDRED THOUSAND free persons of colour, one half of whom might peruse, and the whole be benefited by the publication of the Journal; that no publication, as yet, has been devoted exclusively to their improvement–that many selections from approved standard authors, which are within the reach of few, may occasionally be made–and more important still, that this large body of our citizens have no public channel—all serve to prove the real necessity, at present, for the appearance of the FREEDOM"S JOURNAL.

It shall ever be our desire so to conduct the editorial department of our paper as to give offence to none of our patrons; as nothing is farther from us that to make it the advocate of any partial views, either in politics or religion. What few days we can number, have been devoted to the improvement of our brethren; and it is our earnest wish that the remainder may be spent in the same delightful service.

In conclusion, whatever concerns us as a people, will ever find a ready admission into the FREEDOM'S JOURNAL, interwoven with all the principal news of the day.

And while every thing in our power shall be performed to support the character of our Journal, we would respectfully invite our numerous friends to assist by their communications, and our coloured brethren to strengthen our hands by their subscriptions, as our labour is one of common cause, and worthy of their consideration and support. And we most earnestly solicit the latter, that if at any time we should seem to be zealous, or too pointed in the inculcation of any important lesson, they will remember, that they are equally interested in the cause in which we are engaged, and attribute our zeal to the peculiarities of our situation; and our earnest engagedness in their well-being.

Source: Freedom's Journal, *March 16, 1827.*

Solomon Northup, a Freed Slave, Describes a Slave Auction, 1841

A free African American, Solomon was living in New York when he was captured by slave traders in 1841 and sold into slavery down in Louisiana. Eventually his wife with the aid of lawyers in New York was able to free him. He published his autobiography, *Twelve Years a Slave*, in 1853.

David and Caroline were purchased together by a Natchez planter. They left us, grinning broadly, and in the most happy state of mind, caused by the fact of their not being separated. Lethe was sold to a planter of Baton Rouge, her eyes flashing with anger as she was led away.

The same man also purchased Randall. The little fellow was made to jump, and run across the floor, and perform many other feats, exhibiting his activity and condition. All the time the trade was going on, Eliza was crying aloud, and wringing her hands. She besought the man not to buy him, unless he also bought her self and Emily. She promised, in that case, to be the most faithful slave that ever lived. The man answered that he could not afford it, and then Eliza burst into a paroxysm of grief, weeping plaintively. Freeman turned round to her, savagely, with his whip in his uplifted hand, ordering her to stop her noise, or he would flog her. He would not have such work—such snivelling; and unless she ceased that minute, he would take her to the yard and give her a hundred lashes. Yes, he would take the nonsense out of her pretty quick—if he didn't, might he be d—d. Eliza shrunk before him, and tried to wipe away her tears, but it was all in vain. She wanted to be with her children, she said, the little time she had to live. All the frowns and threats of Freeman, could not wholly silence the afflicted mother. She kept on begging and beseeching them, most piteously not to separate the three. Over and over again she told them how she loved her boy. A great many times she repeated her former promises—how very faithful and obedient she would be; how hard she would labor day and night, to the last moment of her life, if he would only buy them all together. But it was of no avail; the man could not afford it. The bargain was agreed upon, and Randall must go alone. Then Eliza ran to him; embraced him passionately; kissed him again and again; told him to remember her—all the while her tears falling in the boy's face like rain.

Freeman damned her, calling her a blubbering, bawling wench, and ordered her to go to her place, and behave herself, and be somebody. He swore he wouldn't stand such stuff but a little longer. He would soon give her something to cry about, if she was not mighty careful, and that she might depend upon.

The planter from Baton Rouge, with his new purchase, was ready to depart.

"Don't cry, mama. I will be a good boy. Don't cry," said Randall, looking back, as they passed out of the door.

What has become of the lad, God knows. It was a mournful scene indeed. I would have cried myself if I had dared.

Source: Solomon Northup, Twelve Years a Slave *(Auburn, MA: n.p., 1853).*

Frederick Douglass Writes His Former Master, September 3, 1848

To commemorate the tenth anniversary of his escape from slavery and use his experience as a method to attack the institution of slavery, Douglass wrote this open letter to his former master, Thomas Auld and printed it in his newspaper, *The Liberator.*

Sir— . . . I have selected this day on which to address you, because it is the anniversary of my emancipation; and knowing of no better way, I am led to this as the best mode of celebrating that truly important event. Just ten years ago this beautiful September morning, yon bright sun beheld me a slave—a poor, degraded chattel—trembling at the sound of your voice, lamenting that I was a man, and wishing myself a brute. The hopes which I had treasured up for weeks of a safe and successful escape from your grasp, were powerfully confronted at this last hour by dark clouds of doubt and fear, making my person shake and my bosom to heave with the heavy contest between hope and fear. I have no words to describe to you the deep agony of soul which I experienced on that never to be forgotten morning—(for I left by daylight). I was making a leap in the dark. . . .

. . . When yet but a child about six years old, I imbibed the determination to run away. The very first mental effort that I now remember on my part, was an attempt to solve the mystery, Why am I a slave? and with this question my youthful mind was troubled for many days, pressing upon me more heavily at times than others. When I saw the slave-driver whip a slave woman, cut the blood out of her neck, and heard her piteous cries, I went away into the corner of the fence, wept and pondered over the mystery. I had, through some medium, I know not what, got some idea of God, the Creator of all mankind, the black and the white, and that he had made the blacks to serve the whites as slaves. How he could do this and be good, I could not tell. I was not satisfied with this theory, which made God responsible for slavery, for it pained me greatly, and I have wept over it long and often. At one time, your first wife, Mrs. Lucretia, heard me singing and saw me shedding tears, and asked of me the matter, but I was afraid to tell her. I was puzzled with this question, till one night, while sitting in the kitchen, I heard some of the old slaves talking of their parents having been stolen from Africa by white men, and were sold here as slaves. The whole mystery was solved at once. Very soon after this my aunt Jinny and uncle Noah ran away, and the great noise made about it by your father-in-law, made me for the first time acquainted with the fact, that there were free States as well as slave States. From that time, I resolved that I would some day run away. . . .

. . . So far as my domestic affairs are concerned, I can boast of as comfortable a dwelling as your own. I have an industrious and neat companion, and four dear children—the oldest a girl of nine years, and three fine boys, the oldest eight, the next six, and the youngest four years old. The three oldest are now going regularly to school—two can read and write, and the other can spell with tolerable correctness words of two syllables: Dear fellows! they are all in comfortable beds, and are sound asleep, perfectly secure under my own roof. There are no slaveholders here to rend my heart by snatching them from my arms, or blast a mother's dearest hopes by tearing them from her bosom. These dear children are ours—not to work up into rice, sugar and tobacco, but to watch over, regard, and protect, and to rear them up in the nurture and admonition of the gospel—to train them up in the paths of wisdom and virtue, and, as far as we can to make them useful to the world and to themselves. Oh! sir, a slaveholder never appears to me so completely an agent of hell, as when I think of and look upon my dear children. It is then that my feelings rise above my control.

. . . The grim horrors of slavery rise in all their ghastly terror before me, the wails of millions pierce my heart, and chill my blood. I remember the chain, the gag, the bloody whip, the deathlike gloom overshadowing the broken spirit of the fettered bondman, the appalling liability of his being torn away from wife and children, and sold like a beast in the market. Say not that this is a picture of fancy. You well know that I wear stripes on my back inflicted by your direction; and that you, while we were brothers in the same church, caused this right hand, with which I am now penning this letter, to be closely tied to my left, and my person dragged at the pistol's mouth, fifteen miles, from the Bay side to Easton to be sold like a beast in the market, for the alleged crime of intending to escape from your possession. All this and more you remember, and know to be perfectly true, not only of yourself, but of nearly all of the slaveholders around you.

At this moment, you are probably the guilty holder of at least three of my own dear sisters, and my only brother in bondage. These you regard as your property. They are recorded on your ledger, or perhaps have been sold to human flesh mongers, with a view to filling your own ever-hungry purse. Sir, I desire to know how and where these dear sisters are. Have you sold them? or are they still in your possession? What has become of them? are they living or dead? And my dear old grandmother, whom you turned out like an old horse, to die in the woods—is she still alive? Write and let me know all about them. If my grandmother be still alive, she is of no service to you, for by this time she must be nearly eighty years old—too old to be cared for by one to whom she has ceased to be of service, send her to me at Rochester, or bring her to Philadelphia, and it shall be the crowning happiness of my life to take care of her in her old age. Oh! She was to me a mother, and a father, so far as hard toil for my comfort could make her such. Send me my grandmother! that I may watch over and take care of her in her old age. And my sisters, let me know all about them. I would write to them, and learn all I want to know of them, without disturbing you in any way, but that, through your unrighteous conduct, they have been entirely deprived of the power to read and write. You have kept them in utter ignorance, and have therefore robbed them of the sweet enjoyments of writing or receiving letters from absent friends and relatives. Your wickedness and cruelty committed in this respect on your fellow-creatures, are greater than all the stripes you have laid upon my back, or theirs. It is an outrage upon the soul—a war upon the immortal spirit, and one for which you must give account at the bar of our common Father and Creator.

. . . How, let me ask, would you look upon me, were I some dark night in company with a band of hardened villains, to enter the precincts of your elegant dwelling and seize the person of your own lovely daughter Amanda, and carry her off from your family, friends and all the loved ones of her youth—make her my slave—compel her to work, and I take her wages—place her name on my ledger as property—disregard her personal rights—fetter the powers of her immortal soul by denying her the right and privilege of learning to read and write—feed her coarsely—clothe her scantily, and whip her on the naked back occasionally; more and still more horrible, leave her unprotected—a degraded victim to the brutal lust of fiendish overseers, who would pollute, blight, and blast her fair soul—rob her of all dignity—destroy her virtue, and annihilate all in her person the graces that adorn the character of virtuous womanhood? I ask how would you regard me, if such were my conduct? Oh! the vocabulary of the damned would not afford a word sufficiently infernal, to express your idea of my God-provoking wickedness. Yet sir, your treatment of my beloved sisters is in all essential points, precisely like the case I have now supposed. Damning as would be such a deed on my part, it would be no more so than that which you have committed against me and my sisters.

. . . I intend to make use of you as a weapon with which to assail the system of slavery—as a means of concentrating public attention on the system, and deepening their horror of trafficking in the souls and bodies of men. I shall make use of you as a means of exposing the character of the American church and clergy—and as a means of bringing this guilty nation with yourself to repentance. In doing this I entertain no malice towards you personally. There is no roof under which you would be more safe than mine, and there is nothing in my house which you might need for your comfort, which I would not readily grant. Indeed, I should esteem it a privilege, to set you an example as to how mankind ought to treat each other.

I am your fellow man, but not your slave.

Frederick Douglass

Source: The Liberator, *September 22, 1848.*

An African American Response to the Fugitive Slave Act, 1850

Samuel R. Ward, the editor of the newspaper, *Impartial Citizen* wrote this response to the passage of the new Fugitive Slave Act as part of the Compromise of 1850. White abolitionists and free African Americans were outraged by its passage because it not only made northern states responsible for capturing runaway slaves, but it also made it easier for a free African American to be deliberately stolen or accidentally taken and forced into slavery.

Now, this bill strips us of all manner of protection, by the writ of habeas corpus, by jury trial, or by any other process known to the laws of civilized nations, that are thrown as safeguards around personal liberty. But while it does this, it throws us back upon the natural and inalienable right of self-defense—self-protection. It solemnly refers to each of us, individually, the question, whether we will submit to being enslaved by the hyenas which this law creates and encourages, or whether we will protect ourselves, even if, in so doing, we have to peril our lives, and more than peril the useless and devilish carcasses of Negro-catchers. It gives us the alternative of dying freemen, or living slaves. Let the men who would execute this bill beware. Let them know that the business of catching slaves, or kidnapping freemen, is an open warfare upon the fights and liberties of the black men of the North. Let them know that to enlist in that warfare is present, certain, inevitable death and damnation. Let us teach them, that none should engage in this business, but those who are ready to be offered up on the polluted altar of accursed slavery . . . and so let all the black men of America say, and we shall teach Southern slavecrats, and Northern doughfaces, that to perpetuate the Union, they must beware how they expose us to slavery, and themselves to death and destruction, present and future, temporal and eternal!

Source: The Impartial Citizen, *quoted in* The Liberator, *October 11, 1850.*

Protest of Jim Crow in Education, November 4, 1853

In his letter to the Philadelphia tax collector, Robert Purvis protested that his children had to go to an inferior school outside the city even though he had to pay taxes for the city's all-white public school system. This letter illustrates that Jim Crow–style segregation of the races existed in the North before the Civil War. This northern version of Jim Crow served as a template for the Jim Crow laws established in the South after Reconstruction.

You called yesterday for the tax upon my property in this Township, which I shall pay, excepting the "School Tax." I object to the payment of this tax, on the ground that my rights as a citizen, and my feelings as a man and a parent have been grossly outraged in depriving me, in violation of law and justice, of the benefits of the school system which this tax was designed to sustain. I am perfectly aware that all that makes up the character and worth of the citizens of this township look upon the proscription and expulsion of my children from the Public School as illegal, and an unjustifiable usurpation of my right. I have borne this outrage ever since the innovation upon the usual practice of admitting all the children of the Township into the

Public Schools, and at considerable expense, have been obliged to obtain the services of private teachers to instruct my children, while my school tax is greater, with a single exception, than that of any other citizen of the township. It is true (and the outrage is made but the more glaring and insulting) I was informed by a pious Quaker director, with a sanctifying grace, imparting, doubtless, an unctuous glow to his saintly prejudices, that a school in the village of Mechanicsville was appropriated for "thine." The miserable shanty, with all its appurtenances, on the very line of the township, to which this benighted follower of George Fox alluded, is, as you know, the most flimsy and ridiculous sham which any tool of a skin-hating aristocracy could have resorted to, to cover or protect his servility. To submit by voluntary payment of the demand is too great an outrage upon nature, and, with a spirit, thank God, unshackled by this, or any other wanton and cowardly act, I shall resist this tax, which, before the unjust exclusion, had always afforded me the highest gratification in paying. With no other than the best feeling towards yourself, I am forced to this unpleasant position, in vindication of my rights and personal dignity against an encroachment upon them as contemptibly mean as it is infamously despotic.

Source: Pennsylvania Freeman, *reprinted in* The Liberator, *December 16, 1853.*

Creation of the U.S. Colored Troops, 1863

The following order to allow African American troops to be enlisted into the Army had a significant impact on the war with more than 200,000 serving in the Union Army. Additionally, African American service in the war did much to dispel the myth of inferiority of African Americans in the North.

GENERAL ORDERS,
No. 143
WAR DEPARTMENT,
ADJUTANT GENERAL'S OFFICE,
Washington, May 22, 1863.

  I. A Bureau is established in the Adjutant General's Office for the record of all matters relating to the organization of Colored Troops, An officer will be assigned to the charge of the Bureau, with such number of clerks as may be designated by the Adjutant General.

 II. Three or more field officers will be detailed as Inspectors to supervise the organization of colored troops at such points as may be indicated by the War Department in the Northern and Western States.

III. Boards will be convened at such posts as may be decided upon by the War Department to examine applicants for commissions to command colored troops, who, on Application to the Adjutant General, may receive authority to present themselves to the board for examination.

IV. No persons shall be allowed to recruit for colored troops except specially authorized by the War Department; and no such authority will be given to persons who have not been examined and passed by a board; nor will such authority be given any one person to raise more than one regiment.

V. The reports of Boards will specify the grade of commission for which each candidate is fit, and authority to recruit will be given in accordance. Commissions will be issued from the Adjutant General's Office when the prescribed number of men is ready for muster into service.

VI. Colored troops maybe accepted by companies, to be afterward consolidated in battalions and regiments by the Adjutant General. The regiments will be numbered seriatim, in the order in which they are raised, the numbers to be determined by the Adjutant General. They will be designated: "—Regiment of U. S. Colored Troops."

VII. Recruiting stations and depots will be established by the Adjutant General as circumstances shall require, and officers will be detailed to muster and inspect the troops.

VIII. The non-commissioned officers of colored troops may be selected and appointed from the best men of their number in the usual mode of appointing non-commissioned officers. Meritorious commissioned officers will be entitled to promotion to higher rank if they prove themselves equal to it.

IX. All personal applications for appointments in colored regiments, or for information concerning them, must be made to the Chief of the Bureau; all written communications should be addressed to the Chief of the Bureau, to the care of the Adjutant General,

BY ORDER OF THE SECRETARY OF WAR:
E. D. TOWNSEND,
Assistant Adjutant General.

Source: General Order No. 143, May 22, 1863; Orders and Circulars, 1797–1910; Records of the Adjutant General's Office, 1780s–1917; Record Group 94; National Archives. Available at http://www.ourdocuments.gov/doc.php?flash=true&doc=35& page=transcript.

Letter from Lewis Douglass, to his betrothed from Morris Island, South Carolina, July 1863

The son of Frederick Douglass, Lewis Douglass wrote this letter after he and his regiment, the Fifty-fourth Massachusetts Infantry Regiment (Volunteers), participated in a gallant, but unsuccessful, attack on Ft. Wagner near Charleston, South Carolina. This battle was the first time African American troops actually fought in battle during the Civil War.

My Dear Amelia:

I have been in two fights, and am unhurt. I am about to go in another I believe to-night. Our men fought well on both occasion. . . . I escaped unhurt from amidst that perfect hail of shot and shell. It was terrible. I need not particularize, the papers will give a better [account] than I have time to give. My thoughts are with you often, you are as dear as ever, be good to remember it as I no doubt you will. As I said before we are on the eve of another fight and I am very busy and have just snatched a moment to write your. I must necessarily be brief. Should I fall in the next fight killed or wounded I hope I fall with my face to the foe . . .

This regiment has established its reputation as a fighting regiment, not a man flinched, thought it was a trying time. Men fell all around me. A shell would explode and clear a space of twenty feet, our men would close up again, but it was no use we had to retreat, which was a very hazardous undertaking. How I got out of that fight alive I cannot tell, but I am here. My dear girl I hope again to see you. I must bid you farewell should I be killed. Remember if I die I die in a good cause. I wish we had a hundred thousand colored troops we would put an end to this war.

Good Bye to all. Your own loving—Write soon—
Lewis

Source: Carter Godwin Woodson, The Mind of the Negro As Reflected in Letters Written During the Crisis, 1800–1860 *(Washington, DC: Association for the Study of Negro Life and History, 1926), 544.*

Minutes of an interview held at the Savannah headquarters of Major-General Sherman between General Sherman and twenty African American ministers and church officials, January 12, 1865

General Sherman and Secretary of War Stanton interviewed twenty African American ministers and church officials of Savannah. A former slave who bought his freedom in 1857, Garrison Frazier, served as their spokesman. The information gained in this interview helped lay the foundation for Sherman's January 16 orders to provide land and provisions to the freed slaves in the Low Country of Georgia and South Carolina.

First. State what your understanding is in regard to the acts of Congress and President Lincoln's proclamation touching the condition of the colored people in the rebel States.

Answer. So far as I understand President Lincoln's proclamation to the rebellious States, it is, that if they would lay down their arms and submit to the laws of the United States before the 1st of January, 1863, all should be well, but if they did not, then all the slaves in the rebel States should be free, henceforth and forever. That is what I understood.

Second. State what you understand by slavery, and the freedom that was to be given by the President's proclamation.

Answer. Slavery is receiving by irresistible power the work of another man, and not by his consent. The freedom, as I understand it, promised by the proclamation is taking us from under the yoke of bondage and placing us where we could reap the fruit of our own labor and take care of ourselves and assist the Government in maintaining our freedom.

Third. State in what manner you think you can take care of yourselves, and how can you best assist the Government in maintaining your freedom.

Answer. The way we can best take care of ourselves is to have land, and turn in and till it by our labor—that is, by the labor of the women, and children, and old men—and we can soon maintain ourselves and have something to spare; and to assist the Government the young men should enlist in the service of the Government, and serve in such manner as they may be wanted. (The rebels told us that they piled them up and made batteries of them, and sold them to Cuba, but we don't believe that.) We want to be placed on land until we are able to buy it and make it our own.

Fourth. State in what manner you would rather live, whether scattered among the whites or in colonies by yourselves?

Answer. I would prefer to live by ourselves, for there is a prejudice against us in the South that will take years to get over, but I do not know that I can answer for my brethren.

(Mr. Lynch says he thinks they should not be separated, but live together. All the other persons present being questioned, one by one, answer that they agree with "Brother Frazier.")

Fifth. Do you think that there is intelligence enough among the slaves of the South to maintain themselves under the Government of the United States, and the equal protection of its laws, and maintain good and peaceable relations among yourselves and with your neighbors?

Answer. I think there is sufficient intelligence among us to do so.

Sixth. State what is the feeling of the black population of the South toward the Government of the United States; what is the understanding in respect to the present war, its causes and object, and their disposition to aid either side. State fully your views.

Answer. I think you will find there is thousands that are willing to make any sacrifice to assist the Government of the United States, while there is also many that are not willing to take up arms. I do not suppose there is a dozen men that is opposed to the Government. I understand as to the war that the South is the aggressor. President Lincoln was elected President by a majority of the United States, which guaranteed him the right of holding the office and exercising that right over the whole United States. The South, without knowing what he would do, rebelled. The war was commenced by the rebels before he came into the office. The object of the war was not, at first, to give the slaves their freedom, but the sole object of the war was, at first, to bring the rebellious States back into the Union and their loyalty to the laws of the United States. Afterward, knowing the value that was set on the slaves by the rebels, the President thought that his proclamation would stimulate them to lay down their arms, reduce them to obedience, and help to bring back the rebel States, and their not doing so has now made the freedom of the slaves a part of the war. It is my opinion that there is not a man in this city that could be started to help, the rebels one inch, for that would be suicide. There was two black men left with the rebels, because they had taken an active part for the rebels, and thought something might befall them if they staid behind, but there is not another man. If the prayers that have gone up for the Union army could be read out you would not get through them these two weeks.

Seventh. State whether the sentiments you now express are those only of the colored people in the city, or do they extend to the colored population through the country, and what are your means of knowing the sentiments of those living in the country.

Answer. I think the sentiments are the same among the colored people of the State. My opinion is formed by personal communication in the course of my ministry, and also from the thousands that followed the Union army, leaving their homes and undergoing suffering. I did not think there would be so many; the number surpassed my expectation.

Eighth. If the rebel leaders were to arm the slaves what would be its effect!

Answer. I think they would fight as long as they were before the bayonet, and just as soon as they could get away they would desert, in my opinion.

Ninth. What, in your opinion, is the feeling of the colored people about enlisting and serving as soldiers of the United States, and what kind of military service do they prefer?

Answer. A large number have gone as soldiers to Port Royal to be drilled and put in the service, and I think there is thousands of the young men that will enlist; there is something about them that, perhaps, is wrong; they have suffered so long from the rebels that they want to meet and have a chance with them in the field. Some of them want to shoulder the musket, others want to go into the quartermaster or the commissary's service.

Tenth. Do you understand the mode of enlistment of colored persons in the rebel States, by State agents, under the act of Congress! If yea, state what your understanding is.

Answer. My understanding is that colored persons enlisted by State agents are enlisted as substitutes, and give credit to the States, and do not swell the army, because every black man enlisted by a State agent leaves a white man at home; and also, that larger bounties are given or promised by the State agents than are given by the States. The great object should be to push through this rebellion the shortest way, and there seems to be something wanting in the enlistment by State agents, for it don't strengthen the army, but takes one away for every colored man enlisted.

Eleventh. State what, in your opinion, is the best way to enlist colored men for soldiers.

Answer. I think, sir, that all compulsory operations should be put a stop to. The ministers would talk to them, and the young men would enlist. It is my opinion that it would be far better for the State agents to stay at home, and the enlistments to be made for the United States under the direction of General Sherman.

Source: Reported in The Liberator, *February 24, 1865.*

William Tecumseh Sherman's Special Field Orders, No. 15, January 16, 1865

This order lays the foundation for later efforts by African Americans to get the government to guarantee all freedmen "forty acres and a mule" to ensure their ability to survive economically as free citizens.

I. The islands from Charleston, south, the abandoned rice fields along the rivers for thirty miles back from the sea, and the country bordering the St. Johns River, Florida, are reserved and set apart for the settlement of the Negroes now made free by the acts of war and the proclamation of the President of the United States.

II. At Beaufort, Hilton Head, Savannah, Fernandina, St. Augustine and Jacksonville, the blacks may remain in their chosen or accustomed vocations—but on the islands, and in the settlements hereafter to be established, no white person whatever, unless military officers and soldiers detailed for duty, will be permitted to reside; and the sole and exclusive management of affairs will be left to the freed people themselves, subject only to the United States military authority and the acts of Congress. By the laws of war, and orders of the President of the United States, the negro is free and must be dealt with as such. He cannot be subjected to conscription or forced military service, save by the written orders of the highest military authority of the Department, under such regulations as the President or Congress may prescribe. Domestic servants, blacksmiths, carpenters and other mechanics, will be free to select their own work and residence, but the young and able-bodied negroes must be encouraged to enlist as soldiers in the service of the United States, to contribute their share towards maintaining their own freedom, and securing their rights as citizens of the United States.

III. Negroes so enlisted will be organized into companies, battalions and regiments, under the orders of the United States military authorities, and will be paid, fed and clothed according to law. The bounties paid on enlistment may, with the consent of the recruit, go to assist his family and settlement in procuring agricultural implements, seed, tools, boots, clothing, and other articles necessary for their livelihood.

IV. Whenever three respectable negroes, heads of families, shall desire to settle on land, and shall have selected for that purpose an island or a locality clearly defined, within the limits above designated, the Inspector of Settlements and Plantations will himself, or by such subordinate officer as he may appoint, give them a license to settle such island or district, and afford them such assistance as he can to enable them to establish a peaceable agricultural settlement. The three parties named will subdivide the land, under the supervision of the Inspector, among themselves and such others as may choose to settle near them, so that each family shall have a plot of not more than (40) forty acres of tillable ground, and when it borders on some water channel, with not more than 800 feet water front, in the possession of which land the military authorities will afford them protection, until such time as they can protect themselves, or until Congress shall regulate their title. The Quartermaster may, on the requisition of the Inspector of Settlements and Plantations, place at the disposal of the Inspector, one or more of the captured steamers, to ply between the settlements and one or more of the commercial points heretofore named in orders, to afford the settlers the opportunity to supply their necessary wants, and to sell the products of their land and labor.

V. Whenever a negro has enlisted in the military service of the United States, he may locate his family in any one of the settlements at pleasure, and acquire a homestead, and all other rights and privileges of a settler, as though present in person. In like manner, negroes may settle their families and engage on board the gunboats, or in fishing, or in the navigation of the inland waters, without losing any claim to land or other advantages derived from this system. But no one, unless an actual settler as above defined, or unless absent on Government service, will be entitled to claim any right to land or property in any settlement by virtue of these orders.

VI. In order to carry out this system of settlement, a general officer will be detailed as Inspector of Settlements and Plantations, whose duty it shall be to visit the settlements, to regulate their police and general management, and who will furnish personally to each head of a family, subject to the approval of the President of the United States, a possessory title in writing, giving as near as possible the description of boundaries; and who shall adjust all claims or conflicts that may arise under the same, subject to the like approval, treating such titles altogether as possessory. The same general officer will also be charged with the enlistment and organization of the negro recruits, and protecting their interests while absent from their settlements; and will be governed by the rules and regulations prescribed by the War Department for such purposes.

VII. Brigadier General R. SAXTON is hereby appointed Inspector of Settlements and Plantations, and will at once enter on the performance of his duties. No change is intended or desired in the settlement now on Beaufort [Port Royal] Island, nor will any rights to property heretofore acquired be affected thereby.

Source: Special Field Orders, No. 15, Headquarters Military Division of the Mississippi, January 16, 1865. Orders & Circulars, ser. 44, Adjutant General's Office, Record Group 94, National Archives. Available at http://teachingamericanhistory.org/library/index.asp?document=545.

The Thirteenth, Fourteenth, and Fifteenth Amendments

The Thirteenth, Fourteenth, and Fifteenth Amendments provided the foundation for African American civil rights in the nineteenth century.

AMENDMENT XIII, 1865

Neither slavery nor involuntary servitude, except as a punishment for crime where of the party shall have been duly convicted, shall exist within the United States, or any place subject to their jurisdiction.

AMENDMENT XIV, 1868

Section 1. All persons born or naturalized in the United States, and subject to the jurisdiction thereof, are citizens of the United States and of the State wherein they reside. No State shall make or enforce any law which shall abridge the privileges or immunities of citizens of the United States; nor shall any State deprive any person of life, liberty, or property, without due process of law; nor deny to any person within its jurisdiction the equal protection of the laws.

AMENDMENT XV, 1870

Section 1. The right of citizens of the United States to vote shall not be denied or abridged by the United States or by any State on account of race, color, or previous condition of servitude.

Source: Library of Congress, Virtual Services, Digital Reference Section, Primary Documents in American History, Civil War and Reconstruction, 1860–1877. Available at http://www.loc.gov/rr/program/bib/ourdocs/CivilWarRecon.html.

Atlanta Exposition Address, delivered at the Atlanta Cotton Exposition, 1895

In his address to the Atlanta Cotton Exposition, Booker T. Washington argued that segregation was acceptable to African Americans because their focus should be upon bettering their economic situation rather than trying to gain civil rights.

Mr. President and Gentlemen of the Board of Directors and Citizens:

. . . And in this connection it is well to bear in mind that whatever other sins the South may be called to bear, when it comes to business, pure and simple, it is in the South that the Negro is given a man's chance in the commercial world, and in nothing is this Exposition more eloquent than in emphasizing this chance. Our greatest danger is, that in the great leap from slavery to freedom we may overlook the fact that the masses of us are to live by the productions of our hands, and fail to keep in mind that we shall prosper in proportion as we learn to dignify and glorify common labor, and put brains and skill into the common occupations of life; shall prosper in proportion as we learn to draw the line between the superficial and the substantial, the ornamental gewgaws of life and the useful. No race can prosper till it learns that there is as much dignity in tilling a field as in writing a poem. It is at the bottom of life we must begin, and not at the top. Nor should we permit our grievances to overshadow our opportunities.

To those of the white race who look to the incoming of those of foreign birth and strange tongue and habits for the prosperity of the South, were I permitted, I would repeat what I say to my own race, . . . [Look to] the 8,000,000 Negroes whose habits you know, whose fidelity and love you have tested in days when to have proved treacherous meant the ruin of your firesides. . . . [Look] among these people who have, without strikes and labor wars, tilled your fields, cleared your forests, builded your railroads and cities, and brought forth treasures from the bowels of the earth, and helped make possible this magnificent representation of the progress of the South. . . . [Look] my people, helping and encouraging them as you are doing on these grounds, and, with education of head, hand and heart, you will find that they will buy your surplus land, make blossom the waste place in your fields, and run you factories. While doing this, you can be sure in the future, as in the past, that you and your families will be surrounded by the most patient, faithful, law-abiding, and unresentful people that the world has seen. As we have proved our loyalty to you in the past, in nursing your children, watching by the sick bed of your mothers and fathers, and often following them with tear-dimmed eyes to their graves, so in the future, in our humble way, we shall stand by you with a devotion that no foreigner can approach, ready to lay down our lives, if need be, in defense of yours, interlacing our industrial, commercial, civil, and religious life with yours in a way that shall make the interests of both races one. In all things that are purely social we can be as separate as the fingers, yet one as the hand in all things essential to mutual progress.

Source: Booker T. Washington, Up From Slavery! An Autobiography *(New York: Doubleday Page, 1901).*

Excerpt from Mob Rule in New Orleans, 1900

In her attack on lynching, Ida B. Wells clearly demonstrated that the reason for lynching had nothing to do with protecting southern, white women and everything to do with terrorizing African Americans and keeping them in a subservient position.

Of these thousands of men and women who have been put to death without judge or jury, less than one-third of them have been even accused of criminal assault. The world at large has accepted unquestionably the statement that Negroes are lynched only for assaults upon white women. . . .

. . . These figures . . . speak for themselves, and to the unprejudiced, fair-minded person it is only necessary to read and study them in orders to show that the charge that the Negro is a moral outlaw is a false one, made for the purpose of injuring the Negro's good name and to create public sentiment against him.

If public sentiment were alive, as it should be upon the subject, it would refuse to be longer hoodwinked, and the voice of conscience would refuse to be stilled by these false statements. If the laws of the country were obeyed and respected by the white men of the country who charge that the Negro has no respect for law, these things could not be, for every individual, no matter what the charge, would have a fair trial and an opportunity to prove his guilt or innocence before a fair tribunal of law.

That is all the Negro asks—that is all the friends of law and order need to ask, for once the law of the land is supreme, no individual who commits crime will escape punishment.

Individual Negroes commit crimes the same as do white men, but that the Negro race is peculiarly given to assault upon women, is a falsehood of the deepest dye. . . . [T]he Negro who is saucy to white men is lynched as well as the Negro who is charged with assault upon women. Less than one-sixth of the lynchings last year, 1899, were charged with rape.

The Negro points to his record during the war in rebuttal of this false slander. When the white women and children of the South had no protector save only these Negroes, not one instance is known where the trust was betrayed. It is remarkably strange that the Negro had more respect for womanhood with the white men of the South hundreds of miles away, than they have to-day, when surrounded by those that take their lives with impunity and burn and torture, even worse than the "unspeakable Turk."

Again, the white women of the North came South years ago, threaded the forests, visited the cabins, taught the schools and associated only with the Negroes whom they came to teach, and had no protectors near at hand. They had no charge or complaint to make of the danger to themselves after association with this class of human beings. Not once has the country been shocked by such recitals from them as come from the [southern] women who are surrounded by their husbands, brothers, lovers and friends. If the Negro's nature is bestial, it certainly should have proved itself in one of these two instances. The Negro asks only justice and an impartial consideration of these facts.

Source: Ida B. Wells, Mob Rule in New Orleans *(n.p., 1900).*

Reference

Dixie Ray Haggard

African An African is a native of Africa born in Africa.

African American An African American is a person with African ancestry born in America.

Black Codes After the Civil War, black codes were laws enacted by whites in the South in an effort to control freed slaves and put them in a condition similar to slavery. These black codes were based primarily on the **slave codes** in place before the Civil War.

Black Indians People with both Native American and **African** or **African American** ancestry or black people that lived primarily within a Native American community.

Black Seminoles Black Seminoles were runaway slaves, **free blacks**, and slaves of Miccosuki and Muscogee Seminoles that assisted these Native Seminoles in the first two Seminole wars against the United States. The U.S. Army later removed them with the Native Seminoles from Florida to Oklahoma. Some were married to Native Seminoles, others were descendants of Native Seminoles, and still another group had no Native Seminole ancestry.

Buffalo Soldiers **African American** soldiers who fought the Plains tribes in the late 19th century were called buffalo soldiers by these Natives because their dark skin and hair texture resembled that of the buffalo, which was revered by these people. Buffalo soldiers were feared as the most aggressive and determined of the American forces deployed against Natives on the Plains. The term may be anachronistic.

Chattel Slavery A particular form of slavery in which the slave has no rights and is the property of another individual, groups of individuals, or a business. This is the type of slavery developed in the southern United States from the 17th to the mid-19th centuries.

Civil Rights Civil Rights are the nonpolitical rights and personal liberties of a citizen.

Civil Rights Act of 1866   The Civil Rights Act of 1866 guaranteed that black citizens had the same rights in all states of the Union as white citizens. These rights included the ability to make and enforce contracts, to lawfully sue in state and federal courts, and inherit, and to purchase and sell property. These rights also included full protection and benefit of all federal and state laws.

Compromise of 1850   The Compromise of 1850 was the sectional crisis that arose over the question of allowing slavery to extend into the Mexican Cession acquired from Mexico in the Mexican-American War. The compromise allowed California to come into the Union as a free state, and organized the Utah (containing the present states of Colorado, Nevada, and Utah) and New Mexico (containing the present states of Arizona and New Mexico) territories, leaving these territories open to potentially becoming slave states. The compromise drew the present boundary between Texas and New Mexico as it is currently situated, created a new **Fugitive Slave Law**, and abolished the buying and selling of slaves in the District of Columbia.

Cotton   Tropical in their origination, cotton plants produce a white fibrous substance that consists of hairs of this fiber wrapped around the seed of the plant. Cotton fiber is used to make a host of textile products. Most of the southern plantation system in the 19th century was centered on the production of the short-fibered, green staple cotton. The production and processing of cotton became economically viable with the use of slave labor after the invention of the cotton gin by Eli Whitney. This situation prolonged the existence of slavery in the United States until slavery was made illegal after the end of the Civil War.

Cotton Gin   A cotton gin separates the cotton fiber from waste products like the seed and hull. Eli Whitney invented the cotton gin in 1796. At this point in time, it looked as if slavery in the United States was becoming economically unviable, but Whitney's invention made it easier to process green, short-staple cotton more efficiently. Because green cotton could be grown in upland areas, unlike Sea Island cotton, which needed an abundance of water to grow, its cultivation spread quickly throughout the South giving new life to the institution of slavery in the 19th century.

Creole   A Creole is a person of European or African descent born in the Americas during the colonial period.

De facto   De facto is a medieval Latin term meaning "from the fact." In the late 19th century, de facto **segregation** occurred as an established fact before it became law.

De jure   De jure is derived from a medieval Latin term, and its modern meaning refers to established law as passed by a legislature or decree issued from a court. *Plessy v. Ferguson* established legal **segregation** of the races based on the concept of separate but legal facilities for both whites and blacks. This decision by the Supreme Court made legal what was already an accomplished fact in many parts of the United States, not just the South.

Dred Scott Decision In the Dred Scott Decision of 1857, the United States ruled that blacks, whether free or slaves, could not be U.S. citizens. As a result of this, the court ruled that people of African descent could not sue in federal courts, and the federal government could not forbid slavery in the western territories before they became states.

Fifteenth Amendment The Fifteenth Amendment (1870) to the U.S. Constitution prohibited state governments and the federal government from using a citizen's race, color, or previous status as a slave as a voting qualification. It basically gave former slaves the right to vote.

Fifty-fourth Massachusetts The Fifty-fourth Massachusetts was the first all **African American** regular army unit raised to fight Union forces during the Civil War. Abolitionist and black communities in the Boston area reacted quickly to Abraham Lincoln's pronouncement of the Emancipation Proclamation, which not only freed slaves in the rebelling states but also made provisions for blacks to enlist in the Union Army. The regiment's first and most significant action during the war involved its participation in the assault on Confederate Fort Wagner, which helped guard the primary entrance to Charleston harbor in South Carolina. The Fifty-fourth Massachusetts suffered more than 200 hundred casualties including its commander, Colonel Robert Gould Shaw.

Fourteenth Amendment The Fourteenth Amendment (1868) to the U.S. Constitution overturned the *Dred Scott v. Sandford* (1857) decision by the U.S. Supreme Court by expanding the definition of what it meant to be a citizen of the United States. It allowed all people born or naturalized in the United States to be considered citizens, and this included people of African descent, but it excluded Native Americans and persons born to families of ambassadors or foreign ministers. Its due process clause undermined **black codes** being passed in the South to return **freedmen** to something like their former enslaved condition.

Fort Mose Founded in 1738 with the official name of Gracia de Real Santa Teresa de Mose and located just north of St. Augustine, Fort Mose was the first community of ex-slaves in North America. The Spanish established the community as an early warning station for St. Augustine against British invasions, and as an encouragement for slaves in the southern British colonies to run away to Spanish Florida.

Free Blacks Free blacks were people of some African descent that were not slaves. There were more free blacks in the North than in the South during the slave period of the 19th century. During the course of the first half of the 19th century, free blacks were gradually driven out of the South by law, threats of violence, and increasing restrictions on black social and economic opportunities.

Freedmen The term "freedmen" refers chiefly to former slaves emancipated during and after the Civil War. Although freedmen could be applied to those slaves set free before the Civil War by their owners or those residing in northern states when those states abolished slavery, the terms **free blacks** or free Negroes is usually applied instead of freedmen.

Freedmen's Bureau Known as the Freedmen's Bureau, Congress established the Bureau of Refugees, Freedmen, and Abandoned Lands on March 3, 1865. Intended to exist for only one year, Congress extended the duration of the bureau on July 16, 1866. Organized under the War Department, Major General Oliver O. Howard headed the bureau as its commissioner. The bureau chiefly focused on providing food, medical care, resettlement assistance, and legal assistance to former slaves. It managed abandoned and confiscated property, regulated labor issues, and established schools for **freedmen**. The Freedmen's Bureau built 1,000 schools, established teacher-training institutions, and founded several black colleges. Despite the bureau's success in education, it could not solve many of the problems that plagued former slaves, especially providing land to them. In trying to find employment for former slaves, the bureau encouraged them to work on plantations, but this later led to oppressive sharecropping and tenancy arrangements. Inadequately funded throughout its existence, Congress terminated the bureau in 1870.

Fugitive Slave Law Part of the **Compromise of 1850**, the Fugitive Slave Act of 1850 required the return of runaway slaves, regardless of where in the United States they were captured. Along with the passage of the rest of the Compromise of 1850, the Kansas-Nebraska Act, the ratification of Kansas' admission to the Union as a free state, and the election of 1860, this legislation was part of the chain of events that led to the secession of the South from the Union and the outbreak of the American Civil War.

The Fugitive Slave Act of 1793 was passed to enforce Article 4, Section 2 of the U.S. Constitution, which required runaway slaves to be returned to their owners. It forced authorities in non-slave-holding states to participate in the return of fugitive slaves. In response to this act, some northern states passed "personal liberty laws" in the early 19th century that mandated a jury trial before alleged fugitive slaves could be taken out of the state. These acts were passed to prevent **free blacks** from being kidnapped into slavery. Some states did not allow the use of local jails or the assistance of state officials in the arrest or return of accused fugitive slaves. Additionally, abolitionists organized resistance to the enforcement of the Fugitive Slave Law.

Because of limited enforcement of the original law, the Fugitive Slave Law of 1850 was strengthened to require federal marshals or other officials to arrest alleged runaway slaves or face a fine of $1,000. As a result, law enforcement officials throughout the United State had a duty to arrest anyone suspected of being a runaway. Suspected slaves could not testify on their own behalf or request a jury trial. Anyone caught aiding a runaway slave was imprisoned for six months and fined $1,000. Those who captured a fugitive slave received bonuses for their work. Because any suspected slave could not request a trial, many free blacks were forced into slavery under the Fugitive Slave Law of 1850.

Gang System The gang system refers to the harsher of two types of labor systems established on plantations during the era of slavery in the United States. Under the gang labor system, slaves worked in groups organized by their skills and abilities and forced to labor from sun up to sun down. Many historians believe the gang system is what made slavery profitable before the Civil War.

Grandfather Clause Between 1890 and 1915, southern states passed laws to disenfranchise **African Americans**. Some of these laws were called grandfather clauses, and these laws typically exempted citizens, or descendants of citizens, who had the right to vote before 1866 or 1867 from laws that required voters to meet state property and literacy requirements. Most former slaves were not allowed to vote before 1866 or 1867. Therefore, they and their descendants had to meet these strict, state property and literacy requirements to vote. Most had neither the financial means to meet the property requirements nor the education to meet the literacy requirements established by these southern states. This situation resulted in the majority of African Americans in the South not being able to vote in local, state, and national elections at the same time that it guaranteed the enfranchisement of most white males during this period.

Indentured Servant A person who paid for the voyage to the New World by signing a contract to serve a specific person or company for a set time period during the colonial era was known as an indentured servant. At the end of their servitude, the servant was to receive some type of compensation that would help them support themselves in the colonies. This compensation could include money, land, tools, clothing, and food. Because of the expense of compensating servants at the end of their servitude and the limitations of available land for these former servants to acquire, planters in Virginia and Maryland began using enslaved Africans as an alternative to indentured servants by the mid- to late 17th century. This led to the development of **chattel slavery** in the Chesapeake Bay region that eventually was imitated throughout the southern states after the United States of America became independent.

Indigo A plant typically grown by planters along the coast of South Carolina and Georgia. It was used to produce a blue dye used in the English manufacture of textiles. The height of its production was during the mid-18th century, but slaveholders using **chattel slavery** continued to grow indigo in the 19th century.

Jim Crow A white, minstrel show performer, Thomas "Daddy" Rice, created the Jim Crow character around 1830 when he blackened his face and danced at the same time he sang the lyrics to the song, "Jump Jim Crow."

After visiting the South, Rice created this character after meeting a crippled, elderly black man owned by a Mr. Crow. In Rice's presence, this slave danced and sang a song ending with these words: *"Weel about and turn about and do jis so, Eb'ry time I weel about I jump Jim Crow."* Rice later made this song and dance part of his minstrel act, and by the mid-19th century, the character of "Jim Crow" had become a standard in American minstrel shows.

Jim Crow Laws   Between 1818 and the early 1960s, most of the states in the United States passed **segregation** laws known as **Jim Crow** laws. However, these laws became mostly associated with the South. These laws forbid intermarriage between whites and blacks and required businesses and public institutions to separate their black and white clientele customers.

Ku Klux Klan (KKK)   Tennessee veterans of the Confederate Army founded the first Klan in 1865. The Klan hoped to restore white supremacy after the defeat of the South in the Civil War. The Klan tried to reestablish white control in the South by assaulting, murdering, and intimidating blacks and white Republicans. Southern leaders eventually tired of the Klan's methods because their violence became an excuse for the continuance of Reconstruction and the occupation of the South by federal troops. The U.S. government passed the Force Acts in 1870 and 1871 as a way to prosecute crimes by the KKK and other white supremacy groups. The enforcement of these acts initially led to diminished Klan activity, but other, new paramilitary groups such as the Knights of the White Camellia, the White Brotherhood, the Whitecaps, the White League, and the Red Shirts joined the Klan in a resurgence of race-based violence after 1874. This violence led to the end of the Republican Party in the South, the resurgence of the Democratic Party in the South, and the **segregation** of **African Americans** as second-class citizens.

Maroon Communities   The Spanish term "maroon" was applied to independent communities of escaped slaves. These communities did not exist for long because slaveholders continually sought to break up these communities and often used Native Americans as slave hunters to do so. However, maroon communities survived under Spanish rule at **Fort Mose** near St. Augustine during the early 18th century and at the **Negro Fort** in the panhandle during the early 18th century. After Florida came under U.S. control, a maroon community continued to exist in Florida under the protection of the Miccosukee and Muscogee Seminoles until 1842.

Middle Passage   The middle passage was the journey across the Atlantic made by slave ships leaving Africa. The fatality rate was high for slaves during this period due to malnutrition, poor sanitation, and exposure to epidemic diseases.

Miscegenation   Miscegenation refers to the mixing of the races. Specifically in the 19th century, it referred to the cohabitation, marriage, and/or sexual intercourse between a white person and a member of another race.

During the 19th century, a host of laws were past by states, especially those in the South, to prevent miscegenation. Most of these laws were aimed at preventing black men from having intercourse with white women. Although it was discouraged legally and socially, miscegenation regularly occurred because white male planters, overseers, and others often raped or coerced sexual intercourse with female slaves.

Negro Fort, the   In August 1814 as part of the War of 1812, a British force of more than 100 officers and men arrived in the Apalachicola River region of Spanish Florida. The British immediately began to recruit and train local Miccosukee Seminoles as allies. While there, the British built a fort 15 miles above the mouth of the Apalachicola and 60 miles below U.S. States territory. Originally called the British Post, the fort served as a base for British troops, and acted as a depot for the recruitment of ex-slaves and Miccosukee Seminoles to fight against the United States. After an evacuation in the spring of 1815 due to the end of the War of 1812, the British gave the fully functional fort to about 300 fugitive slaves and thirty Miccosukee Seminoles and Choctaws. News of the "Negro Fort" attracted another 800 black fugitives to settle in the surrounding area. An **African American** named Garson and an unnamed, Choctaw chief, led the forces at the Negro Fort in raids against the Georgia frontier. Seen as a military threat to the United States and a symbolic threat on southern slavery, the Negro Fort eventually came under attack by the armed forces of the United States. On July 27, 1816, American troops and their Muscogee Creek allies launched an attack on the Negro Fort. Both sides exchanged cannon fire, but the inexperienced African American gunners failed to hit their targets. A "hot shot" (a cannonball heated to a red glow) fired by the American side hit the fort's powder magazine, which ignited the gunpowder. The explosion destroyed the fort with only 30 of the 300 occupants surviving the blast. The Americans captured the surviving Garson and the Choctaw chief, and turned them over to the Muscogee Creeks. Both were executed by the Muscogee Creeks. Other surviving African Americans from the fort and others captured in the vicinity were re-enslaved.

Paternalism   As slavery developed in the 18th and 19th centuries, slaveholders attempted to soften their patriarchic relationship with their slaves and reinforce their control of their slaves by relating to the slaves' needs as individuals rather than relying simply on their status as slaveholders to exercise their authority. In implementing paternalism on their plantations, slaveholders, their sons, and their white overseers came into more intimate contact with slave women, which led to increased sexual exploitation of these women by white men.

Patriarchy   Slaveholders in the 18th and 19th centuries implemented a patriarchic system in which white males dominated women, children, and black slaves. This system promoted inheritance and family reckoning only through the male line. It also encouraged the domination of large slaveholders over smaller slaveholders in economic, political, and social arenas.

Plessy v. Ferguson   *Plessy v. Ferguson* was the landmark U.S. Supreme Court decision that upheld the constitutionality of racial **segregation** in public accommodations under the doctrine of "separate but equal." This decision remained law until it was nullified by the Supreme Court decision *Brown v. Board of Education* in 1954.

Poll Tax   The South used a poll or head tax during and after Reconstruction to circumvent the **Fourteenth Amendment** and deny **civil rights** to blacks by imposing a tax on voters that most blacks in the South could not pay.

Popular Sovereignty   During the mid-19th century, politicians in the Old Northwest (Ohio, Indiana, Illinois, Michigan, and Wisconsin) developed a doctrine under which the status of slavery in the territories was to be determined by the settlers themselves. Some believed the final decision should come at the time a territory petitioned Congress to become a state and others argued it should come much sooner. Lewis Cass made the concept popular when he ran for president in 1848. Popular sovereignty became part of the **Compromise of 1850**, and in 1854, Stephen A. Douglas incorporated it in the Kansas-Nebraska Act to garner southern support for the transcontinental railroad beginning in Chicago. This led to what was known as Bleeding Kansas, as proslavery and antislavery supporters began killing each other in what was a precursor to the Civil War.

Prejudice   During the 19th century, a majority of white Americans held hostile attitudes and feelings of superiority toward people of different races based on ignorance and the need to justify the existence of slavery in the United States and the treatment of Native Americans and other minorities during this period. In the case of **African Americans**, this prejudice developed into full-blown **racism**, which ultimately denied the humanity of African Americans.

Racism   During the 19th century, most white Americans, and especially southerners, developed a belief that **African Americans** were inherently inferior to whites, and this fact justified their enslavement in America. After emancipation, this belief manifested itself into fear and hatred of African Americans in the South, which led to the creation of **segregation** laws and organized terrorism of African Americans to keep blacks in their place.

Rice Cultivation   East Asians were the first to cultivate rice more than 4,000 years ago. Eventually the crop spread to other areas in the Old World where the climate was subtropical. By the end of the 17th century, West Africans grew the crop extensively. South Carolinians began deliberately importing West Africans as slaves to develop a rice industry during the 18th century. The Carolinians specifically sought Africans with expertise in rice cultivation, and thus the complex agricultural technology associated with rice production was transferred to America. Rice became a staple of the plantation economy along the coast of Georgia and South Carolina with rice planters typically employing the **task system** of labor with their slaves. Rice plantations usually were large, and many rice planters tended to be absentee owners, which led to the significant preservation of African cultural and social traditions in the areas where rice was grown.

Segregation   Racial segregation is the implementation of the physical separation of different racial groups in social and cultural settings. In the South, whites began to develop *de facto* segregation immediately after the end of the Civil War and the emancipation of the slaves as whites refused to interact with **freedmen** in social settings. After Reconstruction, white southerners began to gradually develop *de jure* segregation in which they used the legal system to enforce the physical separation of the races. White violence, intimidation, and terror tactics against **African Americans** accompanied *de facto* and *de jure* segregation as a means to guarantee the separation of the races in the South. The U.S. Supreme Court upheld legal segregation in the South with ***Plessy v. Ferguson*** in 1896.

Slave Codes   Most southerners considered slaves to be property rather than persons. Slaves had few legal rights, and in an effort to keep their slaves under control, southerners created slave codes to guarantee that they maintained control of their slaves. These codes included but were not limited to the prevention of slaves from striking a white person, even if attacked by one, from leaving their owner's premises without permission, from assembling unless a white person was present, from learning to read or write, and from marrying without their owner's permission. Punishment could include whipping, branding, imprisonment, and death for the violator.

Slave Narratives   During the antebellum period of the 19th century, a number of former slaves, mostly runaways, published accounts of their personal experiences as slaves and their escape or release from the institution. These narratives became significant elements in the abolition movement. Often these narratives drew on biblical allusion and imagery, abolitionist rhetoric, and the traditions of the captivity narrative to convince readers (mostly whites) of the harsh reality found within the institution of slavery and promote the abolition of the institution.

Task System   The task system of labor was the less harsh of the two primary types of labor systems used in American slavery. The task system allowed the slaves more autonomy than did the **gang system**. The rice culture in the Low Country of Georgia and South Carolina led to the development of the task system. In the task system, the overseer or driver assigned the slave to a specific area or task to be completed. In most cases, the slaves could work at their own pace, so that tasks could be completed relatively quickly or perhaps stretched out over the entire day.

Those slaves who finished early then had time to grow their own crops and raise farm animals in small areas near the slave quarters. This allowed slaves to improve their diets, and in some rare cases, acquire limited amounts of money.

Thirteenth Amendment   In 1865, Congress passed the Thirteenth Amendment to the Constitution. This Amendment abolished slavery by stating that neither slavery nor involuntary servitude could exist in the United States.

Three-fifths Clause   Also known as the three-fifths compromise, this clause in the U.S. Constitution counted a slave as three-fifths of a person for the purposes of representation in the Congress and taxation. The Thirteenth Amendment nullified this clause.

Tobacco Cultivation   Europeans picked up the habit of smoking tobacco from Native Americans, although Native Americans used it only for ceremonial purposes and not for recreation. During the colonial period, tobacco became popular as a trade item. In the Chesapeake Bay region, it fostered the colonial economy and guaranteed the survival of first Virginia and later Maryland as colonies. John Rolfe raised the first commercial crop of tobacco at Jamestown, Virginia, in 1612. Initially, the English used **indentured servants** primarily from England to cultivate the tobacco, but over time, the use of indentured servants became economically and politically impractical, because the servants eventually gained their freedom and the colony gradually ran out of land for them to acquire to begin their own plantations. Therefore, the colonies began to replace English indentured servants with **African** slaves by the end of the 17th century.

Underground Railroad   The Underground Railroad was a vast network of people who helped fugitive slaves escape to the North and to Canada. It consisted of many individuals who worked within small, localized networks to aid fugitives. These local networks were interconnected in such a way that no one person knew the details of the overall operation. This way if anyone was caught helping fugitive slaves only the local network that this one person knew was compromised. Yet despite the lack of centralization, this network assisted hundreds of runaway slaves in their flight northward. The Underground Railroad began at some point near the end of the 18th century. People began calling the system the Underground Railroad around 1831.

Bibliography

Annotated Bibliography

Abrahams, Roger D. *Singing the Master: The Emergence of African American Culture in the Plantation South*. New York: Pantheon, 1992.
> Abrahams explores the interaction of African American and white culture that occurred each year during corn shucking. The customs that developed around this activity demonstrate the mingling of European and African traditions. He argues the singing, the display of the crop, the joking, and the speech making were derived from English cultural celebrations, and the appearance of these celebration and the social way these celebrations were performed illustrated African cultural influence.

Anderson, James D. *The Education of Blacks in the South, 1860–1935*. Chapel Hill: University of North Carolina Press, 1988.
> Anderson interprets the African American education system within the framework of the larger American education system by focusing on slavery and free market capitalism.

Aptheker, Herbert. *American Negro Slave Revolts: On Nat Turner, Denmark Vesey, Gabriel, and Others*. 5th ed. New York: International Publishers, 1983.
> Aptheker's book provides a well-documented narrative that illustrates the scope and prevalence of slave resistance and rebellion. With this monograph, Aptheker discredits the belief that slaves accepted their situation and erases the concept as a plausible historical assessment of slaves' condition within the peculiar institution.

Berlin, Ira. *Many Thousands Gone: The First Two Centuries of Slavery in North America*. Cambridge, MA: Harvard University Press, 1998.
> Berlin's landmark book synthesizes the history of the institution of slavery and the history of the enslaved people themselves. He examines the differences between four distinct regions: the North, the Chesapeake, the Low Country, and the lower Mississippi Valley over three time periods stretched over the course of two centuries. Berlin stresses the autonomy of the enslaved throughout all four regions during all three time periods.

Berlin, Ira. *Slaves without Masters: The Free Negro in the Antebellum South.* New York: Pantheon, 1974.

> Berlin's groundbreaking monograph examines the cultural and organizational history of southern free African American communities up to 1875 with a specific focus on the system of laws, institutions, and racism established to maintain white dominance in the South. He argues that regional differences existed and conditions for these communities changed over time. Up to the publication of this book, scholars of the Old South focused on either free whites or enslaved African Americans and basically ignored the historical experience of free blacks.

Berlin, Ira, and Philip D. Morgan, eds. *Cultivation and Culture: Labor and the Shaping of Slave Life in the Americas.* Charlottesville: University Press of Virginia, 1993.

> Berlin and Morgan's collection of eleven essays discusses various elements of slavery with a focus on the ability of slaves to establish some element of control over their lives.

Blassingame, John W. *The Slave Community: Plantation Life in the Antebellum South.* 2nd ed., rev. and enl. New York: Oxford University Press, 1979.

> Blassingame uses an enormous amount of primary documents to develop this groundbreaking study of life in slave communities by providing new interpretations of the nature of slave life through the eyes of slaves, planters, and travelers.

Boles, John B., ed. *Masters and Slaves in the House of the Lord: Race and Religion in the American South, 1740–1870.* Lexington: University Press of Kentucky, 1988.

> This collection of essays examines the interconnection between Christianity and race in the antebellum and postbellum South, and the complications caused by biracial participation in southern churches.

Bracey, John H., August Meier, and Elliott M. Rudwick, eds. *American Slavery: The Question of Resistance.* Belmont, CA: Wadsworth, 1971.

> *American Slavery* is an intriguing collection of essays that explores a wide range of historical interpretations of slave resistance from day-to-day refusal to obeying overseers and masters to outright rebellion.

Burton, Orville Vernon. *In My Father's House Are Many Mansions: Family and Community in Edgefield, South Carolina.* Chapel Hill: University of North Carolina Press, 1992.

> Burton's case study discusses the social relationships in the 19th century between African Americans and whites over several generations in Edgefield County, South Carolina. Burton suggests that the predominance of black, female-headed households in towns caused the myth of African American matriarchy. He finds that this household structure does not hold up for African American homes in rural areas. On the whole, Burton delivers a plethora of knowledge concerning the relationships within African American and white families, slaveholder and slaves, and men and women.

Bynum, Victoria E. *Unruly Women: The Politics of Social and Sexual Control in the Old South*. Chapel Hill: University of North Carolina Press, 1992.

Bynum's focus is on those women who did not conform to southern social norms such as those who sought divorces, those who violated expected sexual conduct, and those who challenged the authority of the Confederate government. She argues that southern authorities sought to control the reproductive abilities of those women who did not perpetuate the southern system by producing either slaves or heirs. Therefore, the code of conduct for women in general sprang from the needs of their slave society and not from any moral or religious ideals.

Campbell, Randolph B. *An Empire for Slavery: The Peculiar Institution in Texas, 1821–1865*. Baton Rouge: Louisiana State University Press, 1989.

Campbell extensively uses census records, manuscript collections, newspapers, and tax rolls to describe slavery in Texas as not being significantly different from slavery in other areas of the Old South. He also argues that slavery was a cornerstone of early Texas history and growth economically.

Cashin, Joan E. *A Family Venture: Men and Women on the Southern Frontier*. New York: Oxford University Press, 1991.

Cashin's narrative traces the movement of planter-class men and women from the Atlantic seaboard to the Old Southwest, and she argues along the way that men abandoned paternalism with regards to how they treated their slaves. She argues that these planter men had sexual relations with their female slaves more often than their counterparts in the older slave states.

Cornelius, Jane Duitsman. *"When I can read my title clear": Literacy, Slavery, and Religion in the Antebellum South*. Columbia: University of South Carolina Press, 1991.

Cornelius argues that religion promoted literacy among slaves by encouraging slaves to read the Bible for themselves, and it encouraged whites to teach slaves to read in an effort to spread Christianity among the slave community.

Creel, Margaret Washington. *A Peculiar People: Slave Religion and Community-Culture among the Gullahs*. New York: New York University Press, 1988.

Creel's influential work questions the assumption of planter paternalism and the slaves' acceptance of their station as the norm for slave communities. This book studies the Sea Island culture off the coast of Georgia and South Carolina and reveals how communal spirit, African heritage, and resistance sustained these communities despite the trauma of slavery. Specifically, African beliefs helped form the religion practiced by these communities and established a foundation for resistance to white domination.

Curry, Leonard P. *The Free Black in Urban America, 1800–1850: The Shadow of the Dream*. Chicago: University of Chicago Press, 1981.

Curry provides an original narrative that compares free African American communities in large cities and demonstrates how communal pressures and internal relations allowed African Americans in these communities to pursue the American dream.

Dillon, Merton L. *Slavery Attacked: Southern Slaves and Their Allies, 1619–1865*. Baton Rouge: Louisiana State University, 1990.
   Dillon uses synthesis and original research to discuss the end of the institution of slavery. The Old South's participation in the Atlantic World gave southern planters their economic success, but at the same time, exposed their system of chattel slavery to the renunciation by the rest of the Atlantic World in the 19th century. Dillon claims the institution of slavery was assailed on five fronts: (1) slavery produced an ever-increasing number of its fiercest opponents, African Americans; (2) slavery was threatened during times of warfare as an exploitable weakness of the United States; (3) slaveholders needed the support of some non-slaveholders to perpetuate the institution; (4) slaveholders had to resist the leveling and egalitarian elements of the Enlightenment and evangelical Christianity; and (5) free blacks and white northerners increased their attacks over time on the legitimacy of the institution.

Egerton, Douglas R. *He Shall Go Out Free: The Lives of Denmark Vesey*. Madison, WI: Madison House Publishers, 1999.
   Instead of writing a history of Denmark Vesey's revolt, Egerton provides us with a biography that provides more insight into the man that led the revolt. Therefore, we can better explain the revolt itself by knowing more about the man. This book is well researched and well written, but it is rather speculative in the material covering Vesey's life early on.

Elkins, Stanley M. *Slavery: A Problem in American Institutional and Intellectual Life* [1959]. 3rd ed. Chicago: University of Chicago Press, 1976.
   Drawing heavily on the discipline of social psychology to develop his argument, Elkins stated that slaves were truly childlike "Sambos" and not merely presenting the veneer of an infantile personality to the owners and overseers. He argues they developed childlike modes of behavior because of the intensity of the brutality found within the institution of slavery. Elkins argued that the capitalist economy set up the condition that caused the equation of slaves as property, which thus allowed the cruelty that created the Sambo personality.

Engs, Robert Francis. *Freedom's First Generation: Black Hampton, Virginia, 1861–1890*. Philadelphia: University of Pennsylvania Press, 1979.
   Engs case study examines how whites and blacks had two different views of what African American life should have been after the Civil War. African Americans expected equality as whites imposed paternalism, which limited black social, political, and economic development.

Equiano, Olaudah. *The Life of Olaudah Equiano, or, Gustavus Vassa, the African* [1837 ed.], ed. Paul Edwards. New York: Negro University Press, 1969.
   Equiano's book is an autobiography of an enslaved African that traveled throughout North America for the better part of forty years in the late 18th century.

Escott, Paul D. *Many Excellent People: Power and Privilege in North Carolina, 1850–1900*. Chapel Hill: University of North Carolina Press, 1985.

Escott demonstrates that a small, elite class of businessmen and planters repeatedly ignored and violated the rights and economic opportunities of blacks, workers, and yeoman farmers in their efforts to control the state by exploring adjustment and consistencies in social attitudes and social structure.

Escott, Paul D. *Slavery Remembered: A Record of Twentieth-Century Slave Narratives*. Chapel Hill: University of North Carolina Press, 1979.

Escott's thesis claims that North Carolina was run by a small group of elites that consistently ignored the basic rights of African Americans, yeoman farmers, and workers throughout the second half of the 19th century, and these elites' primary focus was capitalistic. This work is groundbreaking in that it challenges previous interpretations of social and economic structures and relationships within the state.

Fox-Genovese, Elizabeth. *Within the Plantation Household: Black and White Women of the Old South*. Chapel Hill: University of North Carolina, 1988.

Fox-Genovese's thesis is insightful and pathbreaking in its originality. This monograph centers solely on the relationship between elite white women and their slaves in the household. Fox-Genovese uses a blend of social, political, and gender methodologies to argue that class and race were of primary importance in developing female identities and behavior in these households. She argues that the racism of white women often eclipsed that of white men in the same household.

Franklin, John Hope. *The Free Negro in North Carolina, 1790–1860*. New York: W. W. Norton, 1971.

According to Franklin's detailed study, free blacks in North Carolina tended to live in rural areas as opposed to their counterparts in other states and were more numerous than in other states with the exception of Virginia and Maryland. The separation from whites that rural life afforded free blacks protected them from attacks by whites that fell more often on free blacks in urban areas. However, rural living left free blacks with fewer economic opportunities and a stunted social life when compared with free blacks in other states.

Frederickson, George M. *The Arrogance of Race: Historical Perspectives on Slavery, Racism, and Social Inequality*. Middletown, CT: Wesleyan University Press, 1988.

Frederickson's book is a collection of his writings spanning two decades. The central theme of these essays attacks the neo-Marxist interpretations of race issues in U.S. history and argues that irrational cultural and psychological concepts affected economic decision making rather than logical assessments.

Gatewood, Willard B., Jr. *Black Americans and the White Man's Burden, 1898–1903*. Urbana: University of Illinois Press, 1975.

> Gatewood's book demonstrates that African Americans had mixed feelings about American imperialism at the turn of the 20th century, but as it became apparent that their situation was becoming progressively worse, they became less and less supportive of American imperialism.

Genovese, Eugene D. *Roll, Jordan Roll: The World the Slaves Made*. New York: Pantheon Books, 1972.

> Genovese's cornerstone work argues that planter paternalism and slave acceptance of planter control through accommodation permitted the persistence of the slave institution in the United States that otherwise might have faded.

Gerber, David A. *Black Ohio and the Color Line, 1860–1915*. Urbana: University of Illinois Press, 1976.

> Gerber examines racial interactions over time and the evolution of African American communities, and how these elements were different from place to place.

Gomez, Michael A. *Exchanging Our Country Marks: The Transformation of African Identities in the Colonial and Antebellum South*. Chapel Hill: University of North Carolina Press, 1998.

> Gomez explains how African slaves and their children became Americans at the same time they preserved elements of their African heritage within their evolving societies and cultures. Importantly, Gomez, as an African trained scholar, demonstrates how the points of origin in Africa laid the foundations for the regional differences in African American cultures across the South.

Gutman, Herbert. *The Black Family in Slavery and Freedom, 1750–1925*. New York: Vintage, 1976.

> Gutman illustrates how slaves maintained kinship and family connections despite the difficulties created by slavery and emancipation. He specifically attacks the thesis that slavery and emancipation lay the seeds for disorganization among African American families.

Harlan, Louis R. *Booker T. Washington: The Making of a Black Leader, 1856–1901*. London: Oxford University Press, 1975.

> Harlan breaks free of the traditional dichotomy that portrays Washington as either a pragmatic, black leader or the philosophic opponent of W. E. B. Du Bois during the Jim Crow era and develops a more balanced and realistic biography.

Hinks, Peter P. *To Awaken My Afflicted Brethren: David Walker and the Problem of Antebellum Slave Resistance*. University Park: Pennsylvania State University Press, 1997.

> In his well-researched book, Hinks describes David Walker as a capable political philosopher that saw a future of freedom and independence for

African Americans. Born free in the Cape Fear region of North Carolina where blacks outnumbered whites, Walker eventually moved to Boston where he wrote and published *Appeal to the Colored Citizens of the World*. In *Appeal*, Walker argued that white people needed to recognized the potentialities and capabilities of Africans and called for blacks to not accept the status of inferiority placed on them by a racist society.

Hodges, Willis Augustus. *Free Man of Color: The Autobiography of Willis Augustus Hodges*, ed. Willard B. Gatewood, Jr. Knoxville: University of Tennessee Press, 1982.

> Co-founder of *Ram's Horn* and descended from an African American family free since the 18th century, Hodges wrote his autobiography as a testament for all free African Americans in the South.

Jacobs, Harriet. *Incidents in the Life of a Slave Girl* [1861]. New York: W. W. Norton, 2001.

> Harriet's female slave narrative examines the unique circumstances and problems faced by slave women, including motherhood, rape, and resistance, and provides a personal tale that recounts her escape from slavery and participation in the abolition movement.

Johnston, James Hugo. *Race Relations in Virginia and Miscegenation in the South, 1776–1860*. Amherst: University of Massachusetts Press, 1970.

> Johnston's book is problematic in its structure because it is an unrevised dissertation, but its coverage in the nature of miscegenation, its impact on southern society, and its judicial systems was groundbreaking for the time it was published.

Jones, Jacqueline. *Labor of Love, Labor of Sorrow: Black Women, Work, and the Family from Slavery to the Present*. New York: Basic, 1985.

> Jones discusses African American working women in the United States, and she argues that African American women's experience in history differed from that of African American men as well as that of white women.

Joyner, Charles. *Down by the Riverside: A South Carolina Slave Community*. Urbana: University of Illinois Press, 1984.

> Joyner uses an interdisciplinary approach to develop a paternalistic interpretation of the history of African Americans in All Saints' Parish in South Carolina.

Katzman, David M. *Before the Ghetto: Black Detroit in the Nineteenth Century*. Urbana: University of Illinois Press, 1973.

> Katzman's case study examines urban life for African Americans in the 19th century before the creation of the ghettos in the 20th century.

Kemble, Frances Anne. *Journal of a Residence on a Georgia Plantation in 1838–1839*. Athens: University of Georgia Press, 1984.

> Kemble's early-19th-century, firsthand account provides a provoking insight into the problems caused by absenteeism and the problems faced by female slaves.

Koger, Larry. *Black Slave Owners: Free Black Slave Masters in South Carolina, 1790–1860*. Jefferson, NC: McFarland & Company, 1985.

Using a host of genealogical sources and state and federal records, Koger's case study demonstrates that the numbers of black masters grew quickly in the years from 1820 to 1840 and then fell afterward because of economic and legal conditions. These black masters were generally of mixed heritage and could be found in the planter, small farmer, and artisan classes primarily in the Charleston area. These masters tended to try to buy and free enslaved relatives, but they still tended to identify with their white relatives and accepted the slave system as it existed.

Kusmer, Kenneth L. *A Ghetto Takes Shape: Black Cleveland, 1870–1930*. Urbana: University of Illinois Press, 1976.

Kusmer examines the cultural, economic, political, and social aspects of urban life for African Americans in Cleveland, Ohio, and argues that racially segregated neighborhoods occurred in a much later period than they did in other northern cities.

Lane, Ann J., ed. *The Debate over Slavery: Stanley Elkins and his Critics*. Urbana: University of Illinois Press, 1971.

Lane collected a wide range of critics of Stanley Elkins's book, *Slavery: A Problem in American Institutional and Intellectual Life*. These critics either attacked his misrepresentation of the slave personality or his portrayal of the slave system in the Americas, or conversely, they praised his work as groundbreaking.

Malone, Ann Patton. *Sweet Chariot: Slave Family and Household Structure in Nineteenth Century Louisiana*. Chapel Hill: University of North Carolina Press, 1992.

Malone's book is well research, and it examines slave family life in Louisiana, which centered on communal unity.

Nash, Gary B. *Forging Freedom: The Formation of Philadelphia's Black Community, 1720–1840*. Cambridge, MA: Harvard University Press, 1991.

Nash's case study of the black community in Philadelphia provides a close look at black society in the Early Republic. It is especially relevant because it examines the development of this community in the face of growing racism in the city. Nash uses a wide array of sources, including church records, coroner's reports, and ships' crew lists. This work's strength comes from its coverage of the evolution of the city's African American community, which expanded quickly with the arrival of freed slaves from Pennsylvania's countryside.

Oakes, James. *Slavery and Freedom: An Interpretation of the Old South*. New York: Knopf, 1990.

Oakes argues that American slavery developed within a liberal capitalist environment and remained under its influence throughout its existence. In making his argument, Oakes examines the position of slavery within American economics and politics as well as the structure of the institution and master-slave relations.

Owens, Lelsie Howard. *This Species of Property: Slave Life and Culture in the Old South*. New York: Oxford University Press, 1976.
>   Owens's well-research monograph uses autobiography, slave narratives, and plantation records to examine and illustrate the inner workings of slave life.

Painter, Nell Irvin. *Exodusters: Black Migration to Kansas after Reconstruction: The First Major Migration to the North of Ex-slaves*, with a new introduction by the author. New York: Alfred A. Knopf, 1977. Reprint, New York: W. W. Norton, 1992.
>   Painter sees the move of freedmen to Kansas as a working class answer to the white supremacy movement that developed in the South after the Civil War.

Porter, Kenneth W. *The Black Seminoles: History of a Freedom Seeking People*. Revised and edited by Alcione M. Amos and Thomas P. Senter. Gainesville: University Press of Florida, 1996.
>   Porter's work is divided into two parts. The first section focusing on the Seminole Wars in the East before Removal, and the second section explores Black Seminole life in Oklahoma, Texas, and Mexico after Removal. After Removal in Oklahoma, Black Seminoles found themselves hunted down, kidnapped, and reenslaved by Creeks. This forced many to leave for Texas and Mexico before 1850. In Mexico and Texas, Black Seminoles made their living fighting hostile Natives in both places for the Mexican and U.S. governments.

Rabinowitz, Howard N. *Race Relations in the Urban South, 1865–1890*. Urbana: University of Illinois Press, 1980.
>   Rabinowitz explores the late-19th-century history of the five cities of Atlanta, Montgomery, Nashville, Raleigh, and Richmond to better understand Reconstruction, explain the origins and evolution of segregation, and examine the lives of urban African Americans. Interestingly, he argues that race relations were fluid in these cities throughout this period and segregation did not begin until it became a legal viability. The strength of this book centers on the author's ability to recreate the daily experience of African Americans in these five cities.

Rawick, George P. *From Sundown to Sunup: The Making of the Black Community*. Volume 1, *The American Slave: A Composite Autobiography*. Westport, CT: Greenwood Press, 1972.
>   Rawick's monograph uses previously unexplored slave narratives generated by the Works Progress Administration to proved an innovative interpretation of slave social structure, the role of African heritage, and resistance as sustaining slave communities.

Smith, Julia Floyd. *Slavery and Plantation Growth in Antebellum Florida, 1821–1860*. Gainesville: University Presses of Florida, 1973.
>   Smith's narrative discusses the lives of Florida cotton planters (an area not well known to most historians) and their plantations, but it does

little to further understanding of the institution of slavery and its social impact on the slaves.

Stampp, Kenneth M. *The Peculiar Institution: Slavery in the Ante-Bellum South*. New York: Alfred A. Knopf, 1956. Reprint, New York: Vintage Books, 1964.
   Stampp argues that slaves remained socially and culturally isolated at the same time that they resisted the slave system. He discusses how planters profited from the oppressive system they established.

Starobin, Robert S., ed. *Denmark Vesey: The Slave Conspiracy of 1822*. Englewood Cliffs, NJ: Prentice-Hall, 1970.
   Starobin's work claims that a conspiracy existed and that slave rebellion was more likely to occur in urban settings.

Wade, Richard C. *Slavery in the Cities: The South, 1820–1860*. New York: Oxford University Press, 1964.
   Wade's book compares urban slave communities in ten cities, and it argues that the nature of the urban environment, free African Americans living in urban areas, and the constant intermingling of the races led to the end of urban slavery.

Webber, Thomas L. *Deep Like the Rivers: Education in the Slave Quarter Community*. New York: W. W. Norton, 1978.
   Webber used oral history to demonstrate slave autonomy in the socialization of the young into the established slave communal life.

Weinstein, Allen, Frank O. Gatell, and David Sarasohn, eds. *American Negro Slavery: A Modern Reader*. 3rd ed. New York: Oxford University Press, 1979.
   Weinstein, Gatell, and Sarasohn compile a good collection of essays discussing the history of slavery and its importance to the United States. Specifically, its discussion of slavery includes the institution's impact on slave society and culture, the economics of the institution, and the political impact of the institution on the United States. Unfortunately, this collection does not contain an essay by Eugene Genovese, which leaves it lacking in comprehensiveness.

White, Deborah Gray. *Ar'n't I a Woman? Female Slaves in the Plantation South Carolina*. Columbia: University of South Carolina Press, 1973.
   White was the first to write a full monograph on female slaves. She found that the female slave experience was vastly different from that of male slaves due to motherhood and she claims that sexual equality existed in slave communities.

White, Shane. *Somewhat More Independent: The End of Slavery in New York City, 1770–1810*. Athens: University of Georgia Press, 1991.
   White uses advertisements about runaways, almanacs, census records, city directories, criminal court records, and popular magazines to explore the reasons slavery ended in New York City, and he tries to explain what it meant to live in New York and be an African American. The shifting economic climate eventually caused slavery to

become unprofitable by 1810 and thus caused the institution to be abandoned.

Wilson, Theodore Branter. *The Black Codes of the South*. Tuscaloosa: University of Alabama Press, 1965.
> Wilson argues that the black codes were not attempts to reestablish slavery but rather evolved out of a "gray institution" that shaped race relations before the Civil War and that included free and enslaved African Americans.

Additional Bibliography

Alexander, Roberta Sue. *North Carolina Faces the Freedmen: Race Relations during the Presidential Reconstruction, 1865–1867*. Durham: Duke University Press, 1985.

Andrews, Thomas F. "Freedmen in Indian Territory: A Post-Civil War Dilemma." *Journal of the West* 4 (1965): 367–376.

Andrews, William L. *To Tell a Free Story: The First Century of Afro-American Autobiography, 1760–1865*. Urban: University of Illinois Press, 1986.

Ayers, Edward L. *The Promise of the New South: Life after Reconstruction*. New York: Oxford Univ. Press, 1992.

Bacon, Jacqueline. *Freedom's Journal: The First African-American Newspaper*. Lanham, MD: Lexington Books, 2007.

Bell, Howard Holman. *A Survey of the Negro Convention Movement*. New York: Arno Press, 1969.

Berlin, Ira. "The Slave Trade and the Development of Afro-American Society in English Mainland North America, 1619–1775." *Southern Studies* 20 (1981): 122–136.

Berlin, Ira. "The Slaves Were the Primary Force behind Their Emancipation." In *The Civil War: Opposing Viewpoints*, ed. William Dudley. San Diego: Greenhaven Press, 1995.

Berlin, Ira, Marc Favreau, and Steven F. Miller, eds. *Remembering Slavery: African Americans Talk About Their Personal Experiences of Slavery and Freedom*. New York: The New Press, 1998.

Berlin, Ira, Barbara J. Fields, Steven F. Miller, Joseph P. Reidy, and Leslie S. Rowland, eds. *Free At Last: A Documentary History of Slavery, Freedom, and the Civil War*. New York: The New Press, 1992.

Berwanger, Eugene H. *The West and Reconstruction*. Urbana: University of Illinois Press, 1981.

Bibb, Henry. *The Life and Adventures of Henry Bibb An American Slave*, ed. Charles J. Heglar. Madison: University of Wisconsin Press, 2004.

Bigham, Darrel E. *We Ask Only for a Fair Trial: A History of the Black Community of Evansville, Indiana*. Bloomington: Indian University Press, 1987.

Bishir, Catherine W. "Black Builders in Antebellum North Carolina." *North Carolina Historical Review* 61 (1984): 423–461.

Blight, David W. *Frederick Douglass' Civil War: Keeping Faith in Jubilee*. Baton Rouge: Louisiana State University Press, 1989.

Boles, John B. *Black Southerners, 1619–1869*. Lexington: University Press of Kentucky, 1983.

Bonner, T. D. *The Life and Adventures of James P. Beckwourth: Mountaineer, Scout, Pioneer and Chief of the Crow Nation* [1856]. Minneapolis: Ross and Haines, 1965.

Botkin, Benjamin A., ed. *Lay My Burden Down: A Folk History of Slavery*. Chicago: University of Chicago Press, 1945. Reprint, Athens: University of Georgia Press, 1989.

Brewer, James H. *The Confederate Negro: Virginia's Craftsmen and Military Laborers, 1861–1865*. Durham, NC: Duke University Press, 1969.

Brown, James Seay. *Up before Daylight: Life Histories from the Alabama Writers' Project, 1938–1939*. Tuscaloosa: University of Alabama Press, 1982.

Brown, Letitia W. *Free Negroes in the District of Columbia, 1790–1846*. New York: Oxford University Press, 1972.

Burton, Arthur T. *Black, Red, and Deadly: Black and Indian Gunfighters of the Indian Territory, 1870–1907*. Austin, TX: Eakin Press, 1991.

Campbell, Edward D. C., Jr., and Kym S. Rice, eds. *Before Freedom Came: African American Life in the Antebellum South*. Charlottesville: University Press of Virginia, 1991.

Campbell, Thomas M. *The Moveable School Goes to the Negro Farmer*. Tuskegee, AL: Tuskegee Institute Press, 1936.

Carroll, John M., ed. *The Black Military Experience in the American West*. New York: Liveright Publishing, 1971.

Cheek, William F., and Aimee Lee Cheek. *John Mercer Langston and the Fight for Black Freedom, 1829–1865*. Urbana: University of Illinois Press, 1989.

Clarke, Lewis G. "The Testimony of a Former Slave." *Sources of the African-American Past: Primary Sources in American History*, ed. Roy E. Finkenbine. New York: Longman, 1997.

Clinton, Catherine. *Harriet Tubman: The Road to Freedom*. New York: Little, Brown and Company, 2004.

Cook, Daniel. "A Dialogue between a Virginian and an African Minister." *Negro Protest Pamphlets*, ed. William Loren Katz. New York: Arno Press & The New Yorker, 1969.

Crouch, Stanley, and Playthell Benjamin. *Reconsidering the Souls of Black Folk: Thoughts on the Groundbreaking Classic Work of W. E. B. Du Bois*. Philadelphia: Running Press, 2002.

Daniel, Pete. *Breaking the Land: The Transformation of Cotton, Tobacco, and Rice Cultures since 1880*. Chicago: University of Illinois Press, 1985.

Davis, Adwon Adams. *Plantation Life in the Florida Parishes of Louisiana, 1836–1846, as Reflected in the Diary of Bennett H. Barrow*. New York: Columbia University Press, 1943.

Davis, Angela. "Reflections on the Black Woman's Role in the Community of Slaves." *The Black Scholar* 3–4 (1971): 2–15.

Davis, David Brion. *The Problem of Slavery in the Age of Revolution, 1770–1823*. Ithaca, NY: Cornell University Press, 1975.

Douglass, Frederick. *Narrative of the Life of an American Slave in Autobiographies* [1845]. New York: The Library of America, 1996.

Du Bois, W. E. B. "My Early Relations with Booker T. Washington." *Booker T. Washington and His Critics: The Problem of Negro Leadership*, ed. Hugh Hawkins. Lexington, MA: D. C. Heath, 1962.

Du Bois, W. E. B. *The Souls of Black Folk,* edited with an introduction by David W. Blight and Robert Gooding-Williams. New York: Bedford Books, 1997.

Du Bois, W. E. B. *The Suppression of the African Slave Trade to the United States, 1683–1870*. New York: Russell and Russell, 1898.

Duff, John B., and Peter M. Mitchell, eds. *The Nat Turner Rebellion: The Historical Event and the Modern Controversy*. New York: Harper & Row, 1971.

Dunn, Richard S. "The Tale of Two Plantations: Slave Life at Mesopotamia in Jamaica and Mount Airy in Virginia, 1799 to 1828." *William and Mary Quarterly* 3rd ser., 34 (1977): 32–65.

Durham, Philip, and Everett L. Jones. *The Negro Cowboys*. New York: Dodd, Mead, 1965.

Easton, Reverend H. "A Treatise on the Intellectual Character and Civil and Political Condition of the Colored People of the United States; and the Prejudice Exercised toward Them with a Sermon on the Duty of the Church to Them." *Negro Protest Pamphlets*, ed. William Loren Katz. New York: Arno Press & The New Yorker, 1969.

Egerton, Douglas R. *Gabriel's Rebellion: The Virginia Slave Conspiracies of 1800 and 1802*. Chapel Hill: University of North Carolina Press, 1993.

Factor, Robert L. *The Black Response to America; Men, Ideals, and Organization, from Frederick Douglass to the NAACP*. Reading, MA: Addison-Wesley Publishing Company, 1970.

Farley, Reynolds. "The Demographic Rates and Social Institutions of the Nineteenth-Century Negro Population: A Stable Population Analysis." *Demography* 2 (1965): 386–398.

Faust, Drew Gilpin. "Culture, Conflict, and Community: The Meaning of Power on an Antebellum Plantation." *Journal of Social History* 14 (1980): 83–97.

Fields, Barbara J. *Slavery and Freedom on the Middle Ground: Maryland during the Nineteenth Century*. New Haven, CT: Yale University Press, 1985.

Feldstein, Stanley. *Once a Slave: The Slaves' View of Slavery*. New York: W. Morrow, 1971.

Finkenbine, Roy E., ed. *Sources of the African-American Past: Primary Sources in American History*. New York: Longman, 1997.

Finkleman, Paul. *Dred Scott v. Sanford: A Brief History with Documents*. New York: Bedford/St. Martin's, 1997.

Fireside, Harvey. *Separate and Unequal: Homer Plessy and the Supreme Court Decision That Legalized Racism*. New York: Carroll & Graf Publishers, 2004.

Fite, Gilbert C. *Cotton Fields No More: Southern Agriculture, 1865–1980.* Lexington: University Press of Kentucky, 1984.

Foner, Eric. *Reconstruction: America's Unfinished Revolution, 1863–1877.* New York: Harper and Row, 1988.

Foster, Frances Smith. "Frances Ellen Watkins Harper." *Black Women in America: An Historical Encyclopedia*, Vol. I., ed. Darlene Clark Hine. New York: Carlson, 1993.

Foster, Lawrence. *Negro-Indian Relationships in the Southeast.* Philadelphia: 1935.

Frey, Silvia R. *Water from the Rock: Black Resistance in a Revolutionary Age.* Princeton, NJ: Princeton University Press, 1991.

Gallman, Matthew. *The North Fights the Civil War: The Home Front.* Chicago: Ivan Dee, 1994.

Garrett, Henry Highland. "Let Your Motto Be Resistance." *Sources of the African-American Past: Primary Sources in American History*, ed. Roy E. Finkenbine. New York: Longman, 1997.

Graaf, Lawrence B. De, Kevin Mulroy, and Quintard Taylor, eds. *Seeking El Dorado: African Americans in California.* Los Angeles: Autry Museum of Western Heritage; Seattle: University of Washington Press, 2001.

Glatthaar, Joseph T. *Forged in Battle: The Civil War Alliance of Black Soldiers and White Officers.* New York: Free Press, 1990.

Glave, Dianne D. "'A Garden So Brilliant with Colors, So Original in Its Design': Rural African American Women, Gardening, Progressive Reform, and the Foundation of an African American Environmental Perspective." *Environmental History* 8 (July 2003): 395–411.

Gooding, James Henry. *On the Altar of Freedom: A Black Soldier's Civil War Letters from the Front,* ed. Virginia Matzke Adams. Amherst: University of Massachusetts Press, 1991.

Grace, John. *Domestic Slavery in West Africa.* New York: Barnes & Noble Books, 1975.

Grim, Valerie. "African American Landlords in the Rural South, 1870–1950: A Profile." *Agricultural History* 72 (Spring 1998): 399–416.

Gross, Bella. "The First National Negro Convention." *The Journal of Negro History* 31, no. 4 (October 1946): 435–443.

Hahn, Steven. *A Nation under Our Feet: Black Political Struggles in the Rural South from Slavery to the Great Migration.* Cambridge, MA: Harvard University Press, 2003.

Hair, William Ivy. *Carnival of Fury: Robert Charles and the New Orleans Race Riot of 1900.* Baton Rouge: Louisiana State University Press, 1976.

Hale, Grace Elizabeth. "'For Colored' and 'For White': Segregated Consumption in the South." In *Jumpin' Jim Crow: Southern Politics from Civil War to Civil Rights,* ed. Jane Daily, Glenda Elizabeth Gilmore, and Bryant Simon. Princeton, NJ: Princeton University Press, 2000.

Haliburton, Rudi, Jr. "Black Slave Control in the Cherokee Nation." *Journal of Ethnic Studies* 3 (1975): 23–36.

Haliburton, Rudi, Jr. "Origins of Black Slavery Among the Cherokees." *Chronicles of Oklahoma* 52 (1974–1975): 483–496.

Haliburton, Rudi, Jr. *Red over Black: Slavery Among the Cherokee Indians.* Westport, CT: Greenwood Press, 1977.

Hall, Gwendolyn Midlo. *Africans in Colonial Louisiana: The Development of Afro-Creole Culture in the Eighteenth Century.* Baton Rouge: Louisiana State University Press, 1992.

Hallowell, A. Irving. "American Indians, White and Black: The Phenomenon of Transculturation." *Current Anthropology* 4 (1963): 519–531.

Hammond, Peter B. "Afro-American Indians and Afro-Asians: Cultural Contacts Between Africa and the Peoples of Asia and Aboriginal America." *Expanding Horizons in African Studies,* ed. Gwendolan M. Carter and Ann Paden. Evanston, IL: 1969.

Harding, Vincent. *There Is a River: The Black Struggle for Freedom in America.* New York: Vintage, 1983.

Harris, Sheldon H. *Paul Cuffe: Black American and African Return.* New York: Simon and Schuster, 1972.

Harris, Thomas E. *Analysis of the Clash over the Issues between Booker T. Washington and W. E. B. Du Bois.* New York: Garland Publishing, 1993.

Harrold, Stanley. "Slave Rebels and Black Abolitionists." *A Companion to African American History,* ed. Alton Hornsby, Jr. Malden, MA: Blackwell Publishing, 2005.

Hawkins, Hugh, ed. *Booker T. Washington and His Critics: The Problem of Negro Leadership.* Lexington, MA: D. C. Heath, 1962.

Hersey, Mark D. "Hints and Suggestions to Farmers: George Washington Carver and Rural Conservation in the South." *Environmental History* 11 (April 2006), 239–268.

Hofstader, Richard. "U. B. Phillips and the Plantation Legend." *Journal of Negro History* 29 (1944): 109–124.

Horton, James Oliver, and Lois E. Horton. *In Hope of Liberty: Culture, Community, and Protest Among Northern Free Blacks, 1700–1860.* New York: Oxford University Press, 1997.

Huggins, Nathan Irvin. *Black Odyssey: The Afro-American Ordeal in Slavery.* New York: Vintage, 1979.

Humez, Jean M. *Harriet Tubman: The Life and the Life Stories.* Madison: University of Wisconsin Press, 2003.

Jones, Allen W. "Improving Rural Life for Blacks: The Tuskegee Negro Farmers' Conference, 1892–1915." *Agricultural History* 65 (Spring 1991): 105–114.

Jones, Jacqueline. "My Mother Was Much of a Woman: Black Women, Work, and the Family under Slavery." *Feminist Studies* 8 (1982): 235–269.

Jones, Norrece T. *Born a Child of Freedom, Yet a Slave: Mechanisms of Control and Strategies of Resistance in Antebellum South Carolina*. Middletown, CT: Wesleyan University Press, 1990.

Johnson, Charles S. *Shadow of the Plantation*, with a new introduction by Joseph S. Himes. New Brunswick, CT: Transaction Publishers, 1996.

Johnson, Michael P., and James L. Roark. *Black Masters: A Free Family of Color in the Old South*. New York: W. W. Norton, 1984.

Jordan, Winthrop D. *White over Black: American Attitudes toward the Negro, 1550–1812*. Chapel Hill: University of North Carolina Press, 1968.

Justensen, Benjamin R. *George Henry White: An Even Chance in the Race of Life*. Baton Rouge: Louisiana State University, 2001.

Katz, Jonathan. "Resistance at Christiana: The Fugitive Slave Rebellion, Christiana, Pennsylvania, September 11, 1851, a Documentary Account." *The History Teacher* 9, no. 3 (May 1976): 515–516.

Katz, William Loren. *Black Indians: A Hidden Heritage*. New York: Ethrac Publications, 1986.

Kenner, Charles L. *Buffalo Soldiers and Officers of the Ninth Cavalry, 1867–1898: Black and White Together*. Norman: University of Oklahoma Press, 1999.

Kolchin, Peter. *American Slavery, 1619–1877*. Rev. ed. New York: Hill and Wang, 2003.

Kulikoff, Allan. *Tobacco and Slaves: The Development of Southern Cultures in the Chesapeake, 1680–1800*. Chapel Hill: University of North Carolina Press, 1986.

Leckie, William H. *The Buffalo Soldiers: A Narrative of the Negro Cavalry in the West*. Norman: University of Oklahoma Press, 1967.

Leiker, James N. *Racial Borders: Black Soldiers along the Rio Grande*. College Station: Texas A&M University Press, 2002.

Levine, Lawrence W. *Black Culture and Black Consciousness: Afro-American Folk Thought from Slavery to Freedom*. New York: Oxford University Press, 1977.

Littlefield, Daniel F., Jr., and Lonnie E. Underhill. "Slave 'Revolt' in the Cherokee Nation." *American Indian Quarterly* 3 (1977): 121–131.

Litwack, Leon. *Trouble in Mind: Black Southerners in the Age of Jim Crow*. New York: Alfred A. Knopf, 1998.

Lofgren, Charles A. *The Plessy Case: A Legal-Historical Interpretation*. New York: Oxford University Press, 1987.

Lofton, John. *Denmark Vesey's Revolt: The Slave Plot That Lit a Fuse to Fort Sumter*. Rev. ed. Kent, OH: Kent State University Press, 1983.

Lofton, John M., Jr. "White, Indian, and Negro Contacts in Colonial South Carolina." *Southern Indian Studies* 1 (1949): 3–12.

Lynd, Staughton. *Class Conflict, Slavery, and the United States Constitution: Ten Essays*. New York: Bobbs Merrill, 1967.

Mabee, Carleton, and Susan Mabee Newhouse. *Sojourner Truth: Slave, Prophet, Legend*. New York: New York University Press, 1993.

McFeely, William S. *Frederick Douglass.* New York: W. W. Norton, 1991.

McLaurin, Melton A. *Celia, a Slave.* Athens: University of Georgia Press, 1991.

McLoughlin, William G. "Red Indians, Black Slavery and White Racism: America's Slaveholding Indians." *American Quarterly* 26 (1974): 367–385.

McPherson, James. *The Negro's Civil War.* Urbana: University of Illinois Press, 1982.

Meier, August. *Negro Thought in America, 1880–1915: Racial Ideologies in the Age of Booker T. Washington.* Ann Arbor: University of Michigan Press, 1988.

Mills, Gary B. *The Forgotten People: Cane River's Creoles of Color.* Baton Rouge: Louisiana State University Press, 1977.

Morgan, Edmund S. *American Slavery, American Freedom: The Ordeal of Colonial Virginia.* New York: W. W. Norton, 1975.

Morgan, Philip D. *Slave Counterpoint: Black Culture in the Eighteenth-Century Chesapeake and Lowcountry.* Chapel Hill: University of North Carolina Press, 1998.

Morton, Patricia, ed. *Discovering the Women in Slavery: Emancipating Perspectives on the American Past.* Athens: University of Georgia Press, 1996.

Muraskin, William A. *Middle-Class Blacks in a White Society: Prince Hall Freemasonry in America.* Berkeley and Los Angeles: University of California Press, 1975.

Nash, Gary B. *Red, White, and Black: The Peoples of Early America,* 4th ed. Englewood Cliffs, NJ: Prentice-Hall, 1999.

Oates, Stephen B. *The Fires of Jubilee: Nat Turner's Fierce Rebellion.* New York: Harper & Row, 1990.

Omori, Kazuteru. "Race-neutral Individualism and Resurgence of the Color Line: Massachusetts Civil Rights Legislation, 1855–1895." *Journal of American Ethnic History* 22, no. 1 (Fall 2002): 32–58.

Orville, Vernon Burton, and Robert C. McMath, Jr., eds. *Class, Conflict, and Consensus: Antebellum Southern Community Studies.* Westport, CT: Greenwood Press, 1982.

Otto, John Soloman. "A New Look at Slave Life." *Natural History* 88 (January 1979): 8–30.

Otto, John Soloman. *Cannon's Point Plantation, 1794–1860: Living Conditions and Status Patterns in the Old South.* Orlando, FL: Academic Press, 1984.

Oubre, Claude F. *Forty Acres and a Mule: The Freedmen's Bureau and Black Landownership.* Baton Rouge: Louisiana State University Press, 1978.

Pasternak, Martin B. *Rise Now and Fly to Arms: The Life of Henry Highland Garnet.* New York: Garland Publishing, 1995.

Paul, Nathaniel. "An Address, Delivered on the Celebration of the Abolition of Slavery in the State of New York." *Negro Protest Pamphlets,* ed. William Loren Katz. New York: Arno Press & The New Yorker, 1969.

Pearson, Edward A., ed. *Designs against Charleston: The Trial Records of the Denmark Vesey Slave Conspiracy of 1822.* Chapel Hill: University of North Carolina Press, 1998.

Peningroth, Dylan C. "Slavery, Freedom and Social Claims to Property Among African Americans in Liberty County, Georgia, 1850–1880." *Journal of American History* 84 (1997): 405–435.

Perdue, Theda. *Slavery and the Evolution of Cherokee Society, 1540–1866.* Knoxville: University of Tennessee Press, 1979.

Philips, Ulrich B. *Life and Labor in the Old South.* Boston: Little, Brown, 1929.

Ploski, Harry A., ed. *Reference Library of Black America.* New York: Bellwether, 1971.

Porter, Kenneth W. "Negroes on the Southern Frontier, 1670–1763." *Journal of Negro History* 33 (1948): 53–78.

Porter, Kenneth W. "Relations between Negroes and Indians within the Present Limits of the United States." *Journal of Negro History* 17 (1932): 287–367.

Price, Edward T. "A Geographic Analysis of White-Negro-Indian Racial Mixtures in Eastern United States." *Annals of the Association of American Geographers* 43 (1953): 138–156.

Quarles, Benjamin. *The Negro in the American Revolution.* 1961.

Quarles, Benjamin. *The Negro in the Civil War* [1953], with an introduction by William S. McFeely. Reprint, New York: Da Capo, 1989.

Raboteau, Albert J. *Slave Religion: The "Invisible Institution" in the Antebellum South.* New York: Oxford University Press, 1978.

Rael, Patrick. *Black Identity and Black Protest in the Antebellum North.* Chapel Hill: University of North Carolina Press, 2002.

Ragsdale, Bruce A., and Joel D. Tresse. *Black Americans in Congress, 1870–1989.* Washington, DC: U.S. Government Printing Office, 1990.

Rampp, Lary. "Negro Troop Activity in Indian Territory, 1863–1865." *Chronicles of Oklahoma* 47 (1969): 531–559.

Redkey, Edwin S. *Black Exodus: Black Nationalist and Back-to-Africa Movements, 1890–1910.* New Haven, CT: Yale University Press, 1969.

Reiss, Oscar. *Blacks in Colonial America.* Jefferson, NC: McFarland & Company, 1997.

Ripley, C. Peter. *Slaves and Freedmen in Civil War Louisiana.* Baton Rouge: Louisiana State University Press, 1976.

Robboy, Stanley J., and Anita W. "Lewis Hayden: From Fugitive Slave to Statesman." *New England Quarterly* 46 (1973): 591–613.

Robertson, Dave. *Denmark Vesey.* New York: Alfred A Knopf, 1999.

Rosengarten, Theodore. *All God's Dangers: The Life of Nate Shaw.* Chicago: University of Chicago Press, 1974.

Rucker, Mary U. "The Story of Slave Uprising in Oklahoma." *Daily Oklahoman*, October 30, 1932.

Sanchez-Eppler, Karen. *Touching Liberty: Abolition, Feminism and the Politics of Body*. Berkeley: University of California Press, 1993.

Savitt, Tod L. *Medicine and Slavery: The Diseases and Health Care of Blacks in Antebellum Virginia*. Urbana: University of Illinois Press, 1978.

Schor, Joel. *Henry Highland Garnet: A Voice of Black Radicalism in the Nineteenth Century*. Westport, CT: Greenwood Press, 1977.

Schubert, Frank N. *Black Valor: Buffalo Soldiers and the Medal of Honor, 1870–1898*. Wilmington, DE: Scholarly Press, 1995.

Schubert, Frank N. *Buffalo Soldiers, Braves, and the Brass: The Story of Ft. Robinson, Nebraska*. Shippensburg, PA: White Mane Publishing, 1993.

Schwalm, Leslie Ann. *A Hard Fight for We: Women's Transition from Slavery to Freedom in South Carolina*. Champagne: University of Illinois Press, 1997.

Schwarz, Philip J. *Twice Condemned: Slaves and the Criminal Laws of Virginia, 1705–1865*. Baton Rouge: Louisiana State University Press, 1988.

Schweninger, Loren. "John Carruthers Stanly and the Anomaly of Black Slaveholding." *North Carolina Historical Review* 67 (April 1990): 159–192.

Sensbach, Jon F. *A Separate Canaan: The Making of an Afro-Moravian World in North Carolina, 1763–1840*. Chapel Hill: University of North Carolina Press, 1998.

Sibury, James. *Ploughshares into Swords: Race, Rebellion and Identity in Gabriel's Virginia, 1730–1810*. New York: Cambridge University Press, 1997.

Simonsen, Thurdis, ed. *You May Plow Here: The Narrative of Sara Brooks*. New York: W. W. Norton, 1986.

Smith, Eugene Allen. *Geological Survey of Alabama: Report for the Years 1881 and 1882, Embracing an Account of the Agricultural Features of the State*. Montgomery, AL: W. D. Brown and Co., 1883.

Smith, Mark M. *Mastered by the Clock: Time, Slavery, and Freedom in the American South*. Chapel Hill: University of North Carolina Press, 1997.

Sobel, Mechal. *Trabelin' On: The Slave Journey to an Afro-Baptist Faith*. Princeton, NJ: Princeton University Press, 1988.

Spear, Allan H. *Black Chicago: The Making of a Negro Ghetto, 1890–1920*. Chicago: University of Chicago Press, 1967.

Spivey, Donald. *Schooling for the New Slavery: Black Industrial Education, 1868–1915*. Westport, CT: Greenwood Press, 1978.

Sterkx, H. E. *The Free Negro in Ante-Bellum Louisiana*. Rutherford, NJ: Fairleigh Dickinson University Press, 1972.

Stevenson, Brenda. *Life in Black and White: Family and Community in the Slave South*. New York: Oxford University Press, 1996.

Stowe, Steven M. *Intimacy and Power in the Old South: Ritual in the Lives of Planters*. Baltimore: Johns Hopkins University Press, 1987.

Stuckey, Sterling. *Going through the Storm: The Influence of African American Art in History*. New York: Oxford University Press, 1994.

Stuckey, Sterling. *Slave Culture: Nationalist Theory and the Foundations of Black America*. New York: Oxford University Press, 1987.

Sweet, John Wood. *Bodies Politic: Negotiating Race in the American North, 1730–1830*. Baltimore: Johns Hopkins University Press, 2003.

Tadman, Michael. *Speculators and Slave: Masters, Traders, and Slaves in the Old South*. Madison: University of Wisconsin Press, 1989.

Taylor, Joe Gray. *Negro Slavery in Louisiana*. Baton Rouge: Louisiana Historical Association, 1963.

Taylor, Orville Walters. *Negro Slavery in Arkansas*. Durham: Duke University Press, 1958.

Taylor, Quintard. "The Emergence of Black Communities in the Pacific Northwest, 1865–1910." *Journal of Negro History* 64 (1979): 342–345.

Thomas, Lamont D. *Rise to Be a People: A Biography of Paul Cuffe*. Chicago: University of Illinois Press, 1986.

Truth, Sojourner. *Narrative of Sojourner Truth*. New York: Oxford University Press, 1991.

Tyler-McGraw, Marie, and Gregg D. Kimball. *In Bondage and Freedom: Antebellum Black Life in Richmond, Virginia*. Richmond: Valentine Museum, 1988.

Ulman, Victor. *Martin R. Delany: The Beginnings of Black Nationalism*. Boston: Beacon, 1971.

Usner, Daniel H. *Indians, Settlers and Slaves in a Frontier Exchange Economy: The Lower Mississippi Valley before 1783*. Chapel Hill: University of North Carolina Press, 1992.

Verney, Kevern. *The Art of the Possible: Booker T. Washington and Black Leadership in the United States, 1881–1925*. New York: Routledge, 2001.

Washington, Booker T. *Black-Belt Diamonds: Gems from the Speeches, Addresses and Talks to Students*, ed. Victoria Earle Matthews. New York: Negro Universities Press, 1969.

Washington, Booker T. *Up From Slavery by Booker T. Washington, with Related Documents*, edited with an introduction by W. Fitzhugh Brundage. New York: Bedford/St. Martin's, 2003.

Whitten, David O. *Andrew Durnford: A Black Sugar Planter in Antebellum Louisiana*. Natchitoches, LA: Northwestern State University Press, 1981.

Wikramanayake, Marina. *A World in Shadow: The Free Black in Antebellum South Carolina*. Columbia: University of South Carolina Press, 1973.

Wiley, Bell I. *Southern Negroes, 1861–1865*. New Haven, CT: Yale University Press, 1938. Reprint, Baton Rouge: Louisiana State University Press, 1974.

Williams, David. *A People's History of the Civil War: Struggles for the Meaning of Freedom*. New York: The New Press, 2005.

Williams, David, Teresa Crisp Williams, and David Carlson. *Plain Folk in a Rich Man's War: Class and Dissent in Confederate Georgia*. Gainesville: University Press of Florida, 2002.

Williamson, Joel. *New People: Miscegenation and Mulattoes in the United States.* New York: Free Press, 1980. Reprint, New York: New York University Press, 1984.

Willis, William S., Jr. "Divide and Rule: Red, White, and Black in the Old South." *Red, White, and Black: Symposium on Indians in the Old South*, ed. Charles M. Hudson. Athens: University of Georgia Press, 1971.

Wilson, Elinor. *Jim Beckwourth: Black Mountain Man, War Chief of the Crows, Trader, Trapper, Explorer, Frontiersman, Guide, Scout, Interpreter, Adventurer, and Gaudy Liar.* Norman: University of Oklahoma Press, 1972.

Wilson, Keith P. *Campfires of Freedom: The Camp Life of Black Soldiers during the Civil War.* Kent, OH: Kent State University Press, 2002.

Wilson, Walt. "Freedmen in the Indian Territory During Reconstruction." *Chronicles of Oklahoma* 49 (1971): 230–244.

Winston, Sanford. "Indian Slavery in the Carolina Region." *Journal of Negro History* 19 (1934): 431–440.

Wood, Betty. *Slavery in Colonial Georgia, 1730–1775.* Athens: University of Georgia Press, 1984.

Wood, Peter H. *Black Majority: Negroes in Colonial South Carolina from 1670 through the Stono Rebellion.* New York: 1974.

Wood, Peter H. "'It Was a Negro Taught Them': A New Look At Labor in Early South Carolina." *Journal of Asian and African Studies* 9 (1974) 160–179.

Wormser, Richard. *The Rise and Fall of Jim Crow.* New York: St. Martin's Griffin, 2003.

Wright, Gavin. *The Political Economy of the Cotton South: Household, Markets, and Wealth in the Nineteenth Century.* New York: W. W. Norton, 1978.

Wright, George C. *Life Behind a Veil: Blacks in Louisville, Kentucky, 1865–1930.* Baton Rouge: Louisiana State University Press, 1985.

Yentsche, Anne E. *A Chesapeake Family and Their Slaves.* New York: Cambridge University Press, 1994.

Zelnick, Melvin. "Fertility of the American Negro in 1830–1850." *Population Studies* 20 (1966): 77–83.

Index